Art Work

THE ARTS AND INTELLECTUAL LIFE IN
MODERN AMERICA

Casey Nelson Blake, Series Editor

Volumes in the series explore questions at the intersection of the history of
expressive culture and the history of ideas in modern America. The series
is meant as a bold intervention in two fields of cultural inquiry. It
challenges scholars in American studies and cultural studies to move
beyond sociological categories of analysis to consider the ideas that have
informed and given form to artistic expression—whether architecture and
the visual arts or music, dance, theater, and literature. The series also
expands the domain of intellectual history by examining how artistic works,
and aesthetic experience more generally, participate in the discussion of
truth and value, civic purpose, and personal meaning that have engaged
scholars since the late nineteenth century.

Advisory Board: Steven Conn, Lynn Garafola, Charles McGovern,
Angela L. Miller, Penny M. Von Eschen, David M. Scobey, and
Richard Cándida Smith.

Art Work

Women Artists and Democracy in Mid-Nineteenth-Century New York

April F. Masten

PENN

University of Pennsylvania Press
Philadelphia

Published by
University of Pennsylvania Press
Philadelphia, Pennsylvania 19104-4112

Printed in the United States of America on acid-free paper

10 9 8 7 6 5 4 3 2 1

Library of Congress Cataloging-in-Publication Data
ISBN-3: 978-0-8122-4071-9

For my mother, Billie Barbara Masten, actress, poet, and artist, who drove me to town and waited in the car endless days and nights, so that I could study history and the arts.

Contents

Introduction
"American Louvre"

Probably on a morning in 1856, a little wisp of a girl holding a pasteboard folder walked up Broadway's brick-paved sidewalk beside a bespectacled gentleman with a fringe of beard. The wide avenue was already bustling with vendors pulling handcarts, wagons toting barrels, and horse-drawn streetcars loading passengers. Brushing past the pair, men and women walked intently or strolled along in and out of the many-storied buildings where shopkeepers and artisans marketed their wares. On the corner a group of boys tussled with one another, vying for a good place to hawk the daily news and illustrated weeklies. The child and man turned in at 436 Broadway, ascended a dark stairway, and entered a large bright studio filled with women and girls. Seated on benches at tables pushed up against windows, each of them was absorbed in the work of her hands. Pencils scratched paper, while pens inked and gravers scored the surfaces of small blocks of wood.

The purpose of the pair's expedition was to meet the school's director, Henry Herrick, a formidable looking man with long hair who strode forward to greet his visitors. Standing respectfully still, the child looked up at the face of her companion, Horace Greeley, as he shook the director's hand and began to make her case. At ten she was very young, Greeley granted, and he realized the age of acceptance was set at fourteen. Mr. Herrick nodded, his lips pressed into a straight line. But hadn't she already begun her training with her father, an engraver and inventor, and hadn't boys apprenticed at just this age not long ago? The poor girl's mother was deceased. Why wait until she was a woman and destitute to offer her an art education? "Mr. Greeley had a winning smile and real coaxing, compelling eyes when he chose to exert an influence." He did not believe the school's lady managers would find her age a problem once they saw her drawings and noticed the wee girl's fierce determination. Glancing down over the top of his spectacles, Greeley smiled at the child, who opened her folder and held up a picture. Herrick looked, and then turned without a word to find her a place at the bench. And so Alice Donlevy was admitted under age to the New York School of Design for Women.

Fifty years later, in an article commemorating Herrick's teaching, Donlevy recalled the day the editor of the *New-York Tribune* launched her professional life as an artist.[1] Her beginning was singular, yet her journey was neither solitary nor unique. Every year after the founding of the School of Design in 1852, scores of young women headed for New York City and careers as artists. Like Alice, many of these aspirants came from the city itself or crossed the Hudson River by ferry from Long Island, Staten Island, and New Jersey. The majority, however, were like twenty-eight-year-old Annie Delano of Penn Yan, plucky young women who traveled from upstate and western New York, towns like Minetto, Norwich, Oswego, Utica, Oneida, and Syracuse, or from farther afield, places like Ansonia, Connecticut; South Framingham, Massachusetts; Belfast, Maine; Glenwood, Pennsylvania; Salisbury, Illinois; Grand Rapids, Michigan; and Montreal, Canada, areas situated near the canals, rivers, and railroads that carried out into the nation the remarkable news that New York City had a free art school. The chapters that follow tell the story of this large and successful, though now forgotten, group of women artists.

This book recaptures an incredibly egalitarian moment in America history when aesthetics, economics, politics, and ethics came together to create an ideology called "the Unity of Art." Set down in the writings of British art critic John Ruskin, the Unity of Art ideal did not distinguish between fine and applied art, between imagination and execution, or between male and female artists. American artists and artisans, eager to create a democratic culture, embraced this ideology and put it into action. They elevated the printed arts to the level of painting, critiqued the work of designers and engravers with equal vigor, and tried to mitigate the damaging effects of industrialization on their trades by educating and employing women artists.

If asked today, few people could name more than a single American woman artist from the nineteenth century. In fact most people think that historically women artists were rare. And yet, if we follow Donlevy and her cohort into New York City, and take a look around, we find women artists everywhere, studying and working at every kind of art. The aspirations and experience of these women paint a new picture of the capitalist transformation of American society in the middle decades of the nineteenth century. The influence of democratic politics on aesthetic practice, the fluid class structure of a free-market economy, and the flowering of the illustrated press after the Civil War gave women artists an unprecedented opportunity to gain professional status and to occupy a central role in the American art world.

Propelled into self-support by the ravages of economic depressions, industrialization, and war, several thousand American women headed to New York City between 1850 and 1880 to study art and pursue careers as painters, designers, illustrators, engravers, colorists, and art teachers. Egalitarian ideals and financial imperatives, not middle-class privilege, led these women to become artists and shaped their understanding of art and work. As a group they attended the School of Design for Women, an institution established by reformers who linked the poverty of women to the degradation of workers in industrial society. There, they were taught to draw, paint, and engrave by master artists who based their curriculum on the Unity of Art ideal. Armed with practical skills and egalitarian aesthetics, women artists emerged from art school with high expectations and launched careers in a number of art fields. They worked independently for exhibition, on commission for publishers, and as wage earners for manufacturers. They joined art movements, formed professional networks, and founded artist associations for mutual support. Many of the most acclaimed owed their success to the rise of the illustrated press and a cohort of editors who commissioned, published, and praised their work in print. Like other Americans, women artists presumed no tension between artistic values and the values of the marketplace. Some of them, like illustrator Mary Hallock, achieved fame and good prices for their art, others, like illuminator Alice Donlevy, found steady work and made competent livings, while the rest, like oil painter Annie Delano, had to produce art in a number of fields to make ends meet. But whether successful or struggling, oil painter or engraver, they all came to recognize one crucial reality: that the value of a woman's art was closely tied to the value of her labor.

Women artists' accomplishments and disappointments expose tensions within American art practice that are often hidden in histories of male artists. While allowing that some artworks are clearly more aesthetically important than others, this book questions the assumption that "Art" is discrete from the labor that produced it and the false distinction between art produced for money and art created for art's sake. Like men, most women became artists because they had the desire and ability to make art. Their inspiration and gifts were individual, but their choices were shaped by circumstances. Women artists thrived at mid-century because a particular combination of markets, ideas, and institutions provided them with places to train, venues for exhibition and sales, and audiences for their art. This convergence also influenced the form and content of their work. In the 1860s and 1870s, many of America's most outstanding artists expressed themselves as illustrators and engravers because aesthetic hierarchies (such as the primacy of oil painting over engraved illustration) had been relaxed. This complex material and ideological situation sustained the rise of illustration as a fine art. When those circumstances changed art practices changed, aesthetic ideals changed, and the standing of illustrators changed.

I was drawn to this topic by my own experience as a songwriter. I thought the history of women artists might explain why it had been so difficult for me, a young 1980s woman, to make music my work. Art historians explaining the scarcity of women artists in Europe argue that the "total situation of art making" was "mediated and determined by specific and definable social institutions," such as art academies, systems of patronage, and mythologies about the artist, which excluded women.[2] I set out to look for similar barriers in nineteenth-century America and to find the few women who were able to overcome them to see how they did it. Imagine my surprise, then, when instead of finding closed institutions and a few "heroic" individuals, I found hundreds of women pursuing art careers. My preconceptions were dashed! Now, my goal was to find out why there were so many.

Answering that question has entailed tapping nontraditional sources and crossing conceptual boundaries. Rather than relying on the art reviews and prescriptive literature typically used to explain the absence of women artists, I looked for documents written by women artists and their advocates, who as it turned out were not your typical art patrons. My sources include letters and memoirs, public records, political pamphlets, institutional reports, exhibition registers, business documents, popular and trade newspapers, and illustrated magazines. I also rely on works of fiction and art. Thanks to Alice Donlevy who saved many of the letters women artists sent to the Ladies' Art Association, an organization of professional artists begun in 1867, I began with women artists' own words. What struck me most was the common description of women artists as workers.

If we think of art as work, and in many cases middle-class women's work, we are confronted with an unfamiliar cultural landscape in nineteenth-century America. Women artists are usually regarded as either amateurs or anomalies in histories of art and art is rarely studied as an occupational category in labor histories. Yet, between 1850 and 1880, American women artists insisted that in their lives, art and work were inseparable. This claim places women artists at the center of broad political and commercial developments, for the unity of art and labor was also a rallying cry of artisanal workers and social reformers combating industrial degradation.

For a small group of reformers who began as journeymen mechanics,

men such as Greeley and inventor-philanthropist Peter Cooper, the aesthetic education of a girl like Donlevy represented the reunion of "Art and
Industry," which they believed was essential to the progress of republican
society. During the 1850s, Greeley's *Tribune* and other newspapers and journals began publicizing increased opportunities and success for women in
the arts alongside editorials about the social problems caused by capitalist
industry. During those same years, Cooper and philanthropists in other
cities founded educational institutions to support the professional aspirations of American workers and women artists. Everyone was trying to find
a strategy to combat a disturbing consequence of capitalist development—
the devaluation of skilled manual labor.

Nineteenth-century Americans referred to any process whereby a
manufacturer created more units for less money as "capitalist industry."
This increased output was often accomplished by specializing in one product, splitting the process of making it into a series of steps, and hiring more
workers to produce it. There was nothing wrong with that process per se,
they agreed, so long as the dignity of labor was kept intact. But between
1840 and 1880, many artisanal trades, from carpentry to shoemaking to
chromolithography, were industrialized and "degraded." Industrial degradation was the term they used to describe the divorce of moral, intellectual,
and aesthetic value from labor, which often occurred when the arts and
crafts were subdivided into low-paid semi- or unskilled tasks or piecework.
Lithographers in the 1840s, for example, were generalists, master artisans
who knew every step of the production process and passed that "secret"
knowledge on to their journeymen apprentices. But over the next fifty
years, as lithography became a popular means of reproducing art, the process was broken down and distributed to more workers, so that by 1894 it
was possible to identify sixteen broad divisions of semiskilled labor within
a single lithographic firm.[3] This subdivision was good for art workers as it
provided more jobs, but it often degraded the former artists/artisans by
lowering their status and salaries. It also caused animosity among workers
who feared that newcomers, especially women and boys, would displace
them or further depress their wages.

What the experiences of women artists show, however, is that art was
democratized as well as proletarianized by early industrialization. While
certainly divided and multiplied by capitalist industries such as publishing,
art work was not immediately deskilled or degraded. Its value was maintained by the aesthetic knowledge attached to art and to the institutions
developed to train artists and educate the public about art. Most nine-

teenth-century Americans considered the women who produced and de-signed art in industrial settings "Artists" because their work required training and skill in both mental and manual artistic techniques. Industrial or commercial art was, therefore, a way for women to enter the marketplace as autonomous laborers and still have socially meaningful, well-paid work. Through their art, midcentury women artists seized in the economic realm what had been denied them politically—their independence.

The years of my study are not pivotal in the first social history of nine-teenth-century American art. In his pioneering work, *The Artist in American Society*, Neil Harris argued that, "The enjoyment, production and consump-tion of art was tinged with guilt for Americans, not because it was wasteful, but because it was dangerous and irrelevant . . . its consumption an outlet for superfluous wealth, its expression an opening for undisciplined energies, its enjoyment a relief for unsatisfied cravings." Harris sees the gradual legiti-mization of art in America as the result of European art practices being brought home by expatriate artists after the Civil War. Not until American artists became professionalized, he believes, were Americans able to embrace art.[4] However, a very different picture emerges if one pays more attention to the democratic art movement that Harris identifies during the antebellum period *and* adds women artists to the picture. These Americans thought the arts would profit the nation, commercially and politically.

Art appreciation did not begin in America in the final decades of the nineteenth century; rather, those were the years in which it lost its pecu-liarly egalitarian nature. Lawrence Levine and other cultural historians argue that what we think of as high art today was considered popular enter-tainment in antebellum America. Prior to the 1870s, high culture ("a strongly classified, consensually defined body of art distinct from 'popular' fare") failed to develop.[5] High art forms such as Shakespeare, opera, paint-ing, and sculpture were simultaneously popular and elite, and such condi-tions offered greater degrees of choice and freedom of action to audiences. Consistent with this line of reasoning, I have found that a lack of cultural hierarchy, when coupled with widespread consumption, offered greater freedom to art producers as well. Women artists took advantage of this rich, popular, relatively unstratified culture and produced a wide array of art forms that were snatched up by customers who believed the variety of art and artists in America was a testament to just how well the democratic ex-periment was working.

Legal and economic rights were essential to women's success as artists. A dramatic increase in the number of women who pursued art careers came after the revision of women's property rights (to benefit male debtors) in the 1840s and 1850s, and again after the passage of women's "earnings" laws between 1860 and 1880.[6] These laws offered women more than financial independence. For a woman artist, the ability to sell was always as essential to her professional identity as her ability to create. No matter how beautiful or sublime her art was, a woman was not considered an artist unless she worked for money.

The purpose of my study is not to identify lost artist geniuses, although there certainly were women who had a genius for the visual arts. Choosing individual artists and their work to represent American cultural production only perpetuates the centrality of certain life stories. In general, these lives belong to those artists who seemed to work independently of the market. This characteristic limits the number of people to whom the identity "artist" can be given and excludes most women, minorities, and working-class people. Biographies and monographs tend to make gender the primary characteristic of the artist's identity, with women artists circumscribed by their sex and male artists liberated by theirs. But if we assume that men were innately more privileged than women, we fail to notice other factors that contribute to an artist's success.

Nor does this book try to identify a separate women's culture, for to do so would misrepresent American cultural practice. Most nineteenth-century girls discovered their love of art and its significance to their society in the same places as boys—through discussions at home, in the popular press, at church, and in educational institutions. Men and women also shared a familiarity with and enjoyment of high and popular art forms. Women artists worked within established art circles, studied and produced alongside men, and were accepted by them. Segregation into single-sex classes did not mean women were denied access to the aesthetic techniques or ideas of men. On the contrary, men were often their mentors, and inevitably male and female students discussed art outside of class.

Being female may have been the most powerful social attribution limiting the lives of mid-nineteenth-century women, but gender was only one of a number of resources by which women artists configured themselves in the world. Their numbers alone show that women who became artists were acting on common ideas and compelled by similar events. Women artists reveal how ordinary people draw on political ideas to interpret the world and their relationship to it, and to influence the form and organization of their work.[7]

Rather than rely on social meanings that are more available and recognizable, I have attempted to present the "meanings and values" of art as it was actually "lived and felt" by nineteenth-century women and men. One of the letters Alice Donlevy saved while at the Ladies' Art Association came from a member touring the British Isles in 1877. Accompanying the missive were some pages from the artist's sketchbook, "a very hastily scratched volume, but possibly capable of communicating ideas, especially to imaginative minds." Along the edge of the first page she added: "I think I need not sign my name, and yet when I think of 'future generations' and that this sheet may be placed in some American Louvre inscribed with the legend— 'Attributed to Miss Coggswell'—I hasten to put down my initials L. A. B."

These sketches never made it to the American Louvre, if the Metropolitan Museum of Art is that institution. And it is strange to think that anyone would have worried about an unsigned work of art being attributed to the engraver Charlotte Cogswell, a name that is as obscure today as the initials L.A.B. Long before Louise Bradbury's letter was deposited in the archives of the New York Public Library, people had forgotten why women's designs for engraved illustration were significant. During the 1880s, the proletarianization of labor, the consolidation of the middle class, an influx of female amateurs, and a new form of professionalism among male artists undermined the Unity of Art ideal. As a result woman artists, painters and engravers alike, suffered the same fate as male artists who relied solely on industrial art markets—their work was devalued and they were forgotten.

Yet, Bradbury's words are still significant, for they express a "structure of feeling" common to her generation.[8] In 1877 women artists knew that something incredible had happened. All around them they saw women artists taking part in the creation of a truly American art, the product of their nation's democratic institutions and economic prowess, an art worthy of its own Louvre. What their letters, documents, and artwork reveal is that for one brief thrilling generation ideology and practice, Art and Industry, worked together to produce a field in which women could realize their potential as artists alongside men. This book recovers that moment. It is a tale of individual aspiration and shared responsibility, aesthetic dreams and manual labor, human ability and institutional assistance, friendship and betrayal. It is also the story of how art is used to create, alter, and justify a nation's political economy. In the end, *Art Work* is women artists' chronicle of both the liberating and the destructive effects of capitalist production in a democratic society.

Chapter 1
Democratic Proclivities

During the 1820s, Anna and Sarah Peale traveled between Baltimore and Washington, D.C., painting oil portraits of eminent congressmen
and still lifes of watermelons. Ruth W. Shute and her husband Samuel
moved through the New England countryside capturing the likenesses of
small-town Americans in a mixture of media. Emily and Maria Ann Maverick worked in New York City alongside their father as associates in an engraving and lithography business. Hannah Lucinda Forbes created
memorial paintings on velvet for bereaved neighbors and other customers,
and Mrs. B. F. Ladd taught "Poonah," or theorem painting, on fabric and
paper, as well as embroidery, bead, wax, and shell work in Charleston,
South Carolina. These women artists were not anomalies in the early republic; they were the product of a particular intellectual and cultural milieu.
American women worked as professional artists because they lived in a society that linked political rights to the economic freedom offered by a market economy. A combination of democratic and liberal ideas inspired
Americans, male and female, to produce and consume an indigenous art.

After the War of 1812, many Americans began to believe they could
create a political economy that would encourage both moral and material
progress. To them the burgeoning system of capitalist exchange seemed free
from political manipulation and therefore a powerful site in which to promote an egalitarian society of independent producers. Historians have
named the ideas and activities of Americans who linked prosperity to democracy in this way "liberal republicanism."[1] This generation hoped the
equality initiated by republican government would eventually characterize
all the nation's institutions—economic, social, and cultural. They assumed
that both political independence and cultural greatness stemmed from the
individual's freedom in the growing market. But the only way to forge an
egalitarian social order through capitalism (which generates and gives
power to capitalists) was for virtuous individuals to willingly subordinate
their private interests to the good of the community. The ultimate goal of

this group was not personal gain (although no one eschewed it). The pursuit of profit did not, in itself, benefit the nation or make it more egalitarian. Rather, they felt it was the duty of each individual to use his or her freedom and resources to serve the common good and promote democracy.[2]

Since the 1790s, American artists and artisans had attempted to democratize their society through the dissemination of art training and appreciation. These early nationalists were interested in spreading equality from the political realm to the cultural world because they saw art fulfilling two important political functions: it would show the greatness of the new republic and prove that the leveling tendencies of their democratic experiment were compatible with the development of the highest culture.

The artists, engravers, architects, and sculptors who established America's first art institution in Philadelphia did not believe that art should be the province of a wealthy few. They wanted their organization to be a public institution, unlimited in membership and supported by government funds, that emphasized the education and discipline of young artists. Rather than looking to cultivate private patronage for art, they praised the development of popular markets as opportunities for artists.[3]

While America's first art institution did not live up to its democratic educational goals, the art ideals on which it was founded pervaded the country, owing to the expansion in markets, transportation, and print that stimulated and facilitated the circulation of ideas, goods, and people during the first half of the nineteenth century. After the opening of the Erie Canal in 1825, America's art center settled in New York City. Artists and entrepreneurs took advantage of New York's particular combination of democratic ideas and markets to create an eclectic art world of studios, shops, institutions, and industries that welcomed women artists into the fold of American genius.

Liberal Republican Artists

The daughters and nieces of revolutionary generation artists and artisans were the first women to benefit from liberal republican ideas. Two of the most exuberant and well-known proponents of liberal republican ideology were Philadelphia's Charles Willson Peale and his brother James. Although he visited London in 1766 to study portrait and history painting at the Royal Academy, Charles never accepted the idea that art was a mystery meant only for gifted geniuses. He believed that anyone of reasonable intelligence could learn to draw and paint. In his *Autobiography*, Peale contested the suggestion that women were incapable of making art because of female anatomy or nature: "What a variety of mechanick arts may be executed by the fair sex, nay their slender fingers fit them in some things to excell the other sex, and when they possess a reflecting mind and genius? What excellency of work may they perform in the watch-making or engraving line? In Painting, that does not require labour, but as an essential a lively imagination, what excellencies might their fancy produce?"[4] Other republican artists agreed. Both Peales advocated women's education and trained female pupils, including their own daughters, and passed along this tradition to their sons.[5]

Historically, women artists have tended to be the daughters of artists. But with the growth of the market economy in the 1820s and 1830s, the number of female artists trained by artist/artisan fathers increased. Ironically, the dependent status of unmarried daughters made them more reliable partners than sons or apprentices. In the eighteenth century, the passing on of the father's skills and commissions to sons and other boys through apprenticeship was common in many family enterprises, as was the passing on of the mother's skills to daughters and other girls. Apprenticeship was an extension of the dependent status of all children. Often even married sons did not gain economic autonomy from their families until their late twenties or thirties, and many unwed daughters never did become independent.[6] Dependent children ensured that family firms would survive into the next generation. But after the Revolution, as ordinary people began to challenge the customs of deference that tied them to their betters and as opportunities shifted with emerging markets, many young men began to feel that the "dull tyranny of apprenticeship" was an imposition on their liberty. Ties between master and apprentice deteriorated. More sons left home at an earlier age, and family businesses began to fall apart. So artist fathers began to put more emphasis on training daughters.[7]

One patriarch who took his daughters into his business when male apprentices exasperated him was Peter Maverick. In 1812, while his children were small, Maverick, who had learned to engrave in his own father's workshop, took Asher B. Durand as his apprentice. He also began to teach the trade to his two eldest daughters, Emily and Maria Ann. In 1817 Maverick established an engraving firm with Durand in New York City, but ended the partnership three years later when Durand accepted a commission for himself (without notifying Maverick) to engrave John Trumbull's 1822 painting *Signing of the Declaration of Independence*.[8] Instead of taking on a new apprentice, Maverick turned to his daughters for support.

The critical role Maverick's daughters played in the operations and success of the family shop is captured in the art they produced. Emily and Maria Ann Maverick had worked in their father's shop as pupils and assistants in drawing and engraving since they were children, but in 1824 they became his active associates in a new artistic venture in the field of lithography. The status that Maverick's daughters held as partners, and not merely assistants, is revealed in their signatures, which represent a break from the patriarchal organization of the trade.[9] Ordinarily, only the initials of the father-owner were added to commissioned engravings, and many firms followed the artisanal practice of not signing work at all.[10]

Maverick's decision to make his daughters associates in the family firm was indicative of the way democratic ideas and new markets were permeating the art world in the 1820s, as was the circumstance that led to his reconciliation with Durand. When the younger artist independently accepted Trumbull's engraving proposal, he was declaring artistic autonomy from Maverick; and although this break hurt him, Maverick understood Durand's desire for self-determination. In 1826 the two men joined together again to help found the National Academy of Design in New York City, an artist-run organization based on the egalitarian principle that "every profession in society knows best what measures are necessary for its own improvement."[11] Maverick's new partners, Emily and Maria Ann, must have agreed with this sentiment, as they became "Artists of the Academy" in 1827 and elected "Associate Members" in 1828.

Republican Art Institutions

Conceived of by artist/inventor Samuel F. B. Morse, the National Academy was organized by a group of thirty disgruntled young male artists convinced that the directors of New York's first art institution, the American Academy of the Fine Arts, were insensitive to their needs. This generation did not agree with the American Academy's founders that good taste was the product of an appreciation of old paintings. Rather, they asserted, it was developed through the study of contemporary American philosophy and works of art like their own. "The encouragement of national genius is more directly promoted by giving *practice* to our own artists in the highest department of painting, than by any efforts to place before them the best *models*," proclaimed Morse.[12]

The aim of National Academy artists was to provide a school and gallery where anyone whose work had been approved by a committee of member-artists and who was of "good moral character" could study and exhibit free of charge. Their most egalitarian policy was the exhibition rule that only new works by living artists would be received. Until at least 1860, Academy judges accepted paintings by almost every artist who submitted work to its annual exhibitions. This policy meant that artists of every caliber were given the same opportunity to have their work judged and to judge their own work in relation to others, regardless of their educational background, region of origin, choice of subject, or sex. Annual exhibitions also showed a range of graphic art genres, including paintings of every size produced in a variety of media, engravings, and medallion designs. Such egalitarianism proved to be a savvy decision, as the National Academy's first annual exhibitions were so popular that admission receipts paid for the school and exhibition expenses.[13]

In a review of the 35th annual exhibition, *The Crayon*, an idealist art journal that aimed to promote "high art" in America, highlighted the democratic nature of the National Academy's selection policy: "The hanging committee have rejected over 150 works, always retaining, however, one work by every contributor when more than one was sent; there are but very few exceptions to this rule. . . . no exhibition in the world—certainly not in Europe—is hung with the same consideration for the rights of all." One of the artists who defied the one-work rule was painter Elma Mary Gove who exhibited "five heads of marked excellence, which are superior to any previous work; we would indicate 'Apples, Sir,' as the best one."[14] Works by female artists featured in all the National Academy's annual exhibitions, and Academy members actively supported women artists' professional activities. In 1859 three drawings by "Pupils of the New York School of Design for Women, Cooper Institute" were exhibited and in 1867 the Academy opened its galleries for shows by the Ladies' Art Association.[15]

Genre painter Lilly Martin Spencer exhibited her first paintings at the National Academy in 1848, while living in Cincinnati, and continued to show her work at annual exhibitions for the next ten years[16] (Figure 1). Lilly Martin received her first art lessons at the National Academy as a little girl, after her family emigrated from France to New York. But in 1832 her formal training ended when her parents moved to Marietta, Ohio, to escape New York City's cholera epidemic. In Marietta, Martin continued to study paint-

Figure 1. "Mrs. Lilly M. Spencer," engraving by Gihon from an original drawing,
Sartain's Union Magazine of Literature and Art 9, 2 (August 1851): 157. Personal copy.

ing with the help of drawing manuals and itinerant artists. In 1841 she took her first step toward an art career by moving to Cincinnati, where she kept a studio in the Western Art-Union building, painting portraits on commission and fancy pieces for sale on speculation. She also sent her paintings back to New York, Philadelphia, and Boston, where they were exhibited and sold at art unions, galleries, and the National Academy.

Recognizing that residence in a major eastern city was a necessity for a professional artist, Spencer moved her family (she had married Benjamin Spencer and had two children by then) to New York in the fall of 1848. At first Spencer felt overwhelmed by the quality of the competition. "When we came to New York," she wrote her parents in 1850, "I found myself so inferior to most of the artists here that I found that if I did not want to be entirely lost among them I would have to make the closest study of almost every part of my art and also paint some as well as I could to sell . . . I felt so provoked to find myself so far behind even painters that had no reputation whatever. . . . but I determined to try all I could to improve myself."[17] Spencer worked to amend her deficiencies by attending the National Academy's free night classes twice a week. Apparently, she was successful. In 1851, the National Academy elected her "Honorary Member, Professional."

Spencer's National Academy membership, like those of engraver/lithographers Emily and Maria Ann Maverick and portrait-sculptor Emma Stebbins, reflected the popular and critical recognition women working in almost every art field had gained in New York by the 1850s. The National Academy invited and accepted a wide range of artists as members, but reflecting the contradictory objectives of republican institutions (to be both democratic and exclusive) restricted full membership to about thirty men. The "Honorary" and "Associate" form of memberships allotted to women may seem like a kind of discrimination—Honorary and Associate members were not regular voting members—but honorary membership was a distinction reserved for professional artists alone, and shared by most of the male members as well.

Although the number of female National Academy members was small, exhibition records suggest that the number of women who became artists increased as art institutions were democratized. The American Academy's exhibitions held between 1802 and 1839 involved a miniscule number of women artists. Twelve were patrons and approximately twenty-five exhibited, but only one was admitted as an Associate member. On the other hand, the National Academy elected its first female member during its second year and at least 118 women, including 14 elected members, exhibited between 1826 and 1860.[18] "The exhibitions of the Academy of Design have, year by year, shown not only an increase in numbers, but have also given evidence of steady application and consequent growth of ability on the part of our women artists," the *New York Times* reported in 1866. "Brought into direct competition with men," they have won a high place "both in popular favor and critical appreciation," which "is itself proof of their powers."[19]

The National Academy of Design also welcomed women as students. In 1831 female pupils were enrolled in the "Antique School," where they studied the human form by copying plaster casts of classical sculpture. National Academy council members took turns instructing the "class of ladies," charging them no fees, even though male students paid five dollars annually. In 1846 Academy president Asher B. Durand predicted that the "Female Department" would "doubtless eventuate in no small advantage to the cause of Art."[20] But while Durand envisioned women trained in drawing influencing the profession through their husbands and sons, most of the women who took the class intended to become professionals. Enrollment of women varied according to the Academy's financial situation, which tended to fluctuate with that of the national economy. But after the Civil War female students became a permanent part of the Academy schools.[21]

Conventional art historical sources, such as institutional records and critical reviews, do not always lead us to the women artists who took advantage of this increasingly democratized art world. Art reviews, while an important sign of recognition, do not necessarily reflect an artist's stature, popular taste, or the number of artists showing and selling their work at galleries and exhibitions. Only a few of the women artists whose work was hung at National Academy annual exhibitions regularly featured in critical reviews of the shows. One of those was Lilly Martin Spencer. Reviews of Spencer's paintings were always mixed, but in a *New-York Tribune* review of the Academy's 1854 annual exhibition, *Portrait of an Infant* by L. M. Spencer received a scathing notice: "There is one picture which is such an utter deformity in itself, and seems so much to involve the sense of moral evil that it is our duty to condemn it strongly, and to condemn the Committee of Arrangements for giving it a place on the walls."[22] One would never surmise from this review that Spencer was a well-known and respected artist by 1854, or that women artists were a common feature at Academy exhibitions. But the "vulgar" wit that characterized Spencer's paintings, and appalled this critic, had made them extremely popular by the 1850s. It also ensured they would be singled out for review in large exhibitions. Women who painted and sold appropriate subjects were not so noteworthy. The *Tribune* reviewer makes no mention, for example, of the landscapes and street scenes of Miss Caroline L. Ransom or Mrs. A. T. Oakes, Mrs. T. Heller's three figure paintings, the five portraits by Miss Elma Mary Gove, Miss Anna Mary Freeman's two miniatures, the composition by Miss S. N. Foreman, or the four portraits and one fancy piece by Mrs. Hermina Dassell, another Honorary Member of the Academy, all of which are listed in National Academy records for the 1854 exhibition.

The Democratization of Art

Many of the women artists who studied and exhibited their work at the National Academy did not have the good fortune to grow up in an artisan family, attend a female seminary or academy, or live near a town or city where artists offered classes. So where did their art educations begin? Inspired by an impulse to democratize art and art appreciation, dozens of professional artists published books, manuals, and instructional cards designed to educate the untrained populace in the secrets of the art trade.[23] These drawing manuals swept through the country between 1820 and 1860, reflecting a more general "Every Man His Own _____" trend that had ordinary citizens training themselves in almost every profession from lawyer to carpenter to limner. On the sketchbook pages of countless aspiring artists and even the whitewashed walls of May Alcott's bedroom in Concord, Massachusetts, one can still see exercise drawings in pencil and pen copied from examples in *The American Drawing Book* and other drawing manuals.

While aimed at the general public, very few drawing manuals were produced with the leisured dabbler in mind. Rather, they were written by male and female working artists, educators and printers, who essentially agreed on the meaning of art and the methods for making it. The best known of the art crusaders—New York painter of historical scenes John Gadsby Chapman, Brooklyn painter of urban vistas John Rubens Smith, and figure painter/portraitist Rembrandt Peale—all considered it their democratic mission to be teachers. They believed that popular art education required an ordered, rational system of drawing instruction, that drawing for any purpose was a practical, learnable skill, and that "democratic art" did not have to look any different from "aristocratic art."[24]

Most manuals were based on a combination of ideas and models borrowed from *Discourses on Art* by British artist/academician Sir Joshua Reynolds, exercises developed by Swiss education theorist Johann Heinrich Pestalozzi, and illustrated examples of contemporary and historical art work. American artists used Reynolds to establish their basic premise that art could be learned by anyone because it consisted of teachable knowledge ("general truths" or principles established by the great masters) and skill ("labour is the only price of solid fame").[25] The techniques promoted by drawing manuals, and the templates offered in them, were appropriate for any American, regardless of age or sex. Most followed a highly structured system of drawing based on the theory that lines are the essence of form, but they differed from European models in choice of subject matter. These alterations had the purpose of attracting men by dispelling the association of the fine arts with immorality, effeminacy, and triviality, but the "Puritan" ethic reflected in their content also made art more accessible to American women.

In Europe the ideal nude was considered the chief link between the aesthetic standards of the first half of the nineteenth century and the classical works of ancient Greece. Yet, in England the idea that it was improper to expose women to nude models was used by the Royal Academy to exclude even professional women artists from life classes.[26] In most early American manuals, sketching from live models was attacked as a waste of time, and the idea that women needed to sketch nude figures was simply not considered.[27] In fact, until after the Civil War, disquiet about naked bodies kept the nude figure in a minor position in American art.[28] Most artists agreed with Charles Willson Peale that subjects unsuitable for women to look at could not be the defining point of art in America.[29] By breaking this link with classicism the leaders of the democratic art movement developed a style and art ideology that women artists could easily and openly follow.

Instead of emphasizing ideal naked bodies, the majority of American art manuals demonstrated the "practical" side of drawing and encouraged an association of the arts with industry. Fashionable European techniques, asserted drawing manual authors, could not lead to a new and democratic art. They countered the association of art education with frivolity by offering histories of European mechanics and farmers who found drawing indispensable, and practice plates of mechanical and classical subjects to copy. John Gadsby Chapman's *The American Drawing Book*, the most widely circulated drawing manual of the middle decades, contained explicit step-by-step instructions on how to draw, paint, etch, or engrave a sequence of images from simple lines, to geometrical figures, household objects, land-scapes, and finally, the human form.[30] Despite or possibly because of their practical bent, drawing manuals appealed to both sexes. A few manuals criticized the use of art education for the refinement of elite young ladies. But these authors were protesting the idea that only rich people should develop taste and not the practice of teaching women to draw.

Many drawing manuals directed their campaign to American women in particular, and women artists came to symbolize the meaning of the art crusade. The first page of *The American Drawing Book* is an engraving of a "Seated Woman with pencil and drawing pad" (Figure 2). Dressed in a republican toga, this woman was more than a personification of art. She embodied the idea that women artists represented democratic progress. Under her feet is the crusader's motto: "ANY ONE WHO CAN LEARN TO WRITE, CAN LEARN TO DRAW." In his text, Chapman asks: "What village school-girl is there, whose ambition does not reach to the imitation of natural objects in needle work? and, although it may often puzzle the most acute to discover a rose from a tulip . . . in her worsted-picture, yet the taste, the inclination—to try—is there. . . . could she have the means and opportunity afforded her, by proper instruction, of perpetuating, by her pencil or brush, the flower she has reared, the home she has been happy in, the resemblance of friends she has loved, what a new source of intellectual enjoyment would be opened to her. And not to her alone."[31] Speaking through the language of domesticity, Chapman offered women artists as proof that in America equality would be reached "by lifting up the many" rather than pulling down the few, and worth would be judged "by talent and virtue alone and not by fortune or descent."[32] For art crusaders, a society in which even schoolgirls had a knowledge and appreciation of art was a better society.

But Chapman also speaks as a labor republican in his manual, linking the destiny of women artists to that of male workers. For him both represented a promising and untapped American aesthetic resource, in need of education. Mechanics, as a class, are "the most original and deserving among the people," he declares, and the devaluation of their work is the result of aesthetic ignorance, theirs and that of their society.[33] Similarly, a woman, if taught to draw and design, might be saved from the unhappy fate of "thousands of dependent females who are compelled to toil, night as well as day, to the destruction of health and life, and who are often tempted into paths of vice and misery by absolute necessity. Give them strength, by proper education, to feel what they can accomplish, and we

Figure 2. John Gadsby Chapman, "Seated Woman with Pencil and Drawing Pad," *The American Drawing Book*, 1847. Courtesy of American Antiquarian Society.

shall soon see the broken-hearted victims of incessant toil worth the wages of men, in departments of industry and usefulness for which they are by nature so well adapted."[34] Chapman was only one of a number of antebellum Americans to note the connection between industrialization and female dependence and to cite a "proper education" in art as a way to uncouple the two.

Armed with these books and sharing the egalitarian sentiment that stimulated their production, young men and women throughout the country began training themselves to draw and paint. If their efforts showed talent, those who could headed for metropolitan areas that held out the promise of higher education, exhibition, and sales. Like men, women artists clustered in centers where large numbers of artists could be found, especially New York and Brooklyn, Philadelphia, Boston, Charleston, Baltimore, New Orleans, and Cincinnati.[35] But the majority moved to New York City, which by the 1840s boasted an interlocking cultural milieu of art markets, institutions, journals, societies, salons, studios, and schools.

New York City's Art Emporium

During the second quarter of the nineteenth century, New York City became the nation's cultural capital, outstripping Philadelphia and Boston in its inventory of American art. The city's port, Hudson River, and Erie Canal created a bustling marketplace for domestic and foreign goods that assisted the development of numerous commercial industries, and they in turn expanded its art market. Among New York's art consumers were a new breed of patrons, men and women who had benefited from the city's open market for their talents and were eager to support native talent themselves. Besides buying and commissioning works of art these nationalist patrons built institutions and schools for artists, furnished them with connections to a broader cultural world, offered them various types of work, entertained them at their clubs and homes, and provided goods and services that enabled artists to maintain professional careers.[36]

New York City offered artists a host of professional attractions including several art centers, schools and academies, and art journals. Before the 1850s, artists arriving in Manhattan looked for rooms in most any building on or near Broadway. Male artists, just starting out, often resorted to "small, ill-lighted dormitories, approached by filthy stairs, and situated in buildings appropriated to different and uncongenial purposes."[37] Female artists could hardly have hoped to flourish in such an environment, but they too looked for cheap rooms. For the most part single studios and those attached to living accommodations were situated in the upper regions of older business buildings, tucked away "upstairs in an out-building" or in a "loft over a frame-maker's," on Broadway from Houston Street up. Lilly Martin Spencer's first New York studio was a room in the living accommodation of her family, "oddly perched" above a coffin store on Broadway. Mary Freeman [Goldbeck], a miniature and crayon portraitist, kept a second-story studio at the corner of Broadway and Thirteenth Street, over Clark's restaurant.[38]

Most studio accommodations were clustered along lower Broadway, in what became known as the graphic arts district. Located within a few blocks of each other were the National Academy and all the major art galleries, auction houses, art dealers, art supply stores, and studio buildings, with publishing houses to the south. When Spencer separated her professional and family life in 1851, she took a studio at 72 Crosby Street, moved it to 435 Broome Street in 1852, and after the Panic of 1853 relocated to 193 Bleeker Street in the artists' boarding house district. Artists also collected farther uptown, where they worked from studios on Broadway's 1200 block and at residences on a number of cross streets. By 1857 there were three hundred spaces where independent artists opened for business each day in lower Manhattan. To accommodate the burgeoning population, the Appleton Building at 346 Broadway (owned by the publishing firm) was remodeled with rooms specifically designed for artists on its upper floors. Other large businesses and public buildings followed suit.[39]

Studio buildings concentrated professional and social life in a congenial setting and gave artists a respectable situation in which to conduct their business. There, artists could work in a professional atmosphere, receive newspapermen, customers and friends, teach classes, and exhibit their art. Knowledgeable collectors, gallery owners, and critics often previewed, reserved, and purchased works destined for National Academy annual exhibitions at the studio buildings. Artists displayed works sold at their studio at academy exhibitions with the buyer listed as lender, or the purchaser might become the exhibitor. In 1857, Frederick E. Church sold his painting *Niagara* to the art dealers Williams, Stevens and Williams, who followed its progress at Church's studio in the Tenth Street building. On its completion in May the owners exhibited the painting at the artist's studio, and then in June at their gallery on Broadway.

As art dealers, Williams, Stevens and Williams did not commission the

picture but rather negotiated its purchase early on, as they knew other collectors and dealers would see it in progress during studio visits. They also
purchased the right to make and sell a chromolithograph copy of the painting. *Niagara* was displayed several times in New York and London, where
sales of the print copy yielded more profits than exhibition admission tickets.[40] Art dealers used large works by women artists in similar ways. Also in
1857, Goupil and Knoedler put together a New York exhibition of French
art including works by Rosa Bonheur. However, they saved Bonheur's
painting *The Horse Fair* [1853–55], which was twice the size of *Niagara*, for
a single-picture exhibit. By the time of the showing in December 1857 (also
at Williams, Stevens and Williams's gallery), Bonheur's painting had been
purchased by an American connoisseur, Mr. J. M. Wright of New York, and
was subsequently chromolithographed by Nicholas Sarony.[41]

Besides open house exhibitions, studio buildings held receptions for
artist residents as a group. Dodworth's Studio Building was the home of
several studios and a dance school, and the studio building most hospitable
to women artists.[42] There, the first in a series of "Art Conversazioni" was
held by the Artists' Reception Association, formed in 1858. This novelty was
a combination exhibition, concert, and soirée that united artistic, financial,
and social ambitions. Resident artists produced pieces especially for these
receptions and issued tickets as personal invitations to distinguished guests.
"We do not know how Art can be better amalgamated with our social system," commented *The Crayon*, which advertised the Artists' Reception Association's first series. In 1859 the Studio Building at West Tenth Street
followed Dodworth's lead, offering its own reception. The egalitarian-
minded *Cosmopolitan Art Journal* was none too pleased. It worried that
New Yorkers were taking on European airs and warned young artists
against "Reception reputation." Bohemian artists who gave receptions
"purposely to hear themselves praised by pretty women and long-bearded
men" would never compare to true artists, it remonstrated, who "are not
in want of such nurseries of conceit."[43] Artists' receptions were here to stay,
however, as they immeasurably increased the morale of American artists
and expanded the society around them.

Beyond the distinguished guests who frequented studio open houses
and receptions was a wide and growing market for American art and artists
created by New York's rising middle class population. Interested in displaying their educations and taste, these consumers purchased artwork directly
from artists and through art dealers; at exhibitions of art unions, artists'
fund societies, and art associations; at shows in galleries, churches, bazaars,

auction houses, industrial and sanitary fairs, art schools, historical societies, and private homes; through raffles and lotteries; by responding to artists' newspaper and journal advertisements; and from displays in shop windows.[44]

Lilly Martin Spencer captured the spirit of this newly affluent class in many of her paintings. In *Kiss Me and You'll Kiss the 'Lasses* [1856] the artist depicts a slender young woman, dressed in silk and an apron, standing sideways (to best reveal an ideal figure enhanced by fashion) in a luxuriously carpeted room before a dessert table laden with fruit (Figure 3). The woman looks directly at the viewer, who is apparently male, with a sly, mischievous smile on her caricatured face. In her hand is a spoonful of molasses. This young woman is not simply a lovely object to be admired; she too participates in the looking and in this case also threatens to act, albeit playfully. Although Spencer's characters are often set in the lush comfort of urban households, their demeanor reminds us that they are the *new* middle classes. The direct address and exaggerated features and gesture of this young woman contrast with her sumptuous surroundings, informing the viewer of the fluid nature of American society. Underneath the surface, the picture seems to say, we are *all* still just plain folk whose true identities might emerge at any moment. The market revolution was giving more people access to the material refinement depicted by the artist and democratic ideals gave them the confidence to display it. In fact the painting was created for the walls of that very class.

These new art consumers developed and satisfied their taste for art through another liberal republican institution, the American Art-Union. Begun in New York City in 1838, the Art-Union's mission was to foster American art through the financial and moral encouragement of artists and the aesthetic education of the public. Following New York's lead, art unions and buildings were established throughout the country in Philadelphia, Cincinnati, Washington, and other large cities, and local branches organized in their environs. Every subscriber to an art union who paid an annual fee of five dollars was entitled to an engraving of an artwork by an American artist and a chance to win an original oil painting in a lottery drawing. Subscription fees were used to commission and distribute the engravings, to purchase or commission works of American art for the lottery, and to publish and distribute an art journal and record of the organization's transactions. The success of New York's American Art-Union was phenomenal. Its membership grew from 800 in 1839 to almost 19,000 in 1849. Works of art distributed by lot grew from a few dozen to over a thousand per

Figure 3. Lilly Martin Spencer, *Kiss Me and You'll Kiss the 'Lasses*, 1856. Oil on canvas. The Brooklyn Museum, New York. A. Augustus Healy Fund.

year.[45] Through its journal and lotteries, the American Art-Union and its many local branches created the first mass audience for studio artists in the United States.

The development of the American Art-Union between the economic depressions of 1837 and 1839 signaled a consensus among the growing population of art enthusiasts that older patterns of patronage could not support artists in a boom-and-bust economy. National Academy artists painted on speculation and exhibited to gain sales or commissions from private art collectors or patrons. Art unions, on the other hand, bought paintings directly from the artists in their studios, exhibited and sold them at their galleries, and distributed them by lottery.[46] Self-consciously eclectic, art union officials attempted to "secure the public favor" and subsidize the greatest number of artists by purchasing as many low-priced pictures as funds would allow and only occasionally spent the bulk of subscription fees on large and expensive paintings by famous artists.[47] The highest sum often went to the engravers of the prints distributed to members. These inclusive purchasing policies declared that nationalistic sentiment would support contemporary art so long as it was made affordable and public culture was kept distinct from commercial entertainment.[48]

Among the artists patronized by the art unions was Spencer, whose genre scenes answered the American Art-Union's call for paintings that would appeal "most strongly to the national feeling." Art union officials and American buyers in general preferred American subjects, particularly still life, landscape, and genre scenes.[49] These pictures challenged the aristocratic tradition of painting ideal and historical subjects for the wellborn and promoted a native art that was intellectually and economically accessible to everyone. During their annual meetings and in their publications, Art-Union organizers advised artists and the public that to establish an American school of painting and sculpture, we must "release ourselves from that strange infatuation about foreign arts and artists . . . and dare and love to be ourselves."[50]

The Art-Union's sentiments matched Ralph Waldo Emerson's 1837 description of the "revolution in the leading idea" of American art: "the same movement which effected the elevation of what was called the lowest class in the state, assumed in literature a very marked and as benign an aspect. Instead of the sublime and beautiful, the near, the low, the common, was explored and poetised. . . . The literature of the poor, the feelings of the child, the philosophy of the street, the meaning of household life, are the topics of the time. . . . This perception of the worth of the vulgar, is fruitful in discoveries."[51] Familiar scenes of everyday life in the house, on the street, or in the countryside, imbued with a light moral message and immaculately rendered by a highly skilled artist, that was American genius. To art union officials, Spencer's paintings epitomized this American aesthetic. While residing in Cincinnati in 1847, the artist entered eight paintings in a special exhibition held for the opening of the Western Art-Union. Four of her works were subsequently bought by that art union for its lottery distribution, and in 1849 the organization paid New York artist Alfred Jones $1,200 to engrave Spencer's painting *Life's Happy Hour* as the first premium awarded its members.[52]

Art unions seem to have paid men and women comparable prices for their work and encouraged the public to do the same.[53] The paintings Spencer sold to the American and Western Art-Unions fetched sums ranging from $100 to $327. Overall these prices were above average and placed her among both art unions' highest paid artists. At one exhibition, only paintings by Frederick Church and Richard C. Woodville sold for more than Spencer's works, which consistently drew sums equal to or exceeding those received by George Caleb Bingham, John James Audubon, Eastman Johnson, William S. Mount, and Asher B. Durand.[54] Often the payments Spencer received were below her asking price, but so too were the amounts offered to most of the artists. In one case Spencer was disappointed to hear that the executive committee of the Western Art-Union had agreed to buy a painting for $250, despite having been shown a letter by her "fixing the price at $350."[55] The Art-Union's constitution provided that artists should receive the amount they had fixed on their paintings, but Union officials often offered as little as fifty percent of set prices.

Some artists were indignant when the organization's buyers offered them less than their asking price, but Spencer recognized that the distribution of money "by purchases, among the Artists at their studios" was an egalitarian policy, meant to benefit artists struggling to survive in a city with a cash-scarce economy where "Artists are as thick as grass."[56] She wrote to her parents in 1851 that "to be able to get work, one must work cheap, and . . . do better work than the rest." Particularly troublesome was the "complete stagnation in the way of picture buying." Artists were obliged to hawk their wares to store owners, who took a percentage of the price, or sell at auctions, where auctioneers did the same. Under such circumstances the regular purchases of the Art-Union were welcome, even if the amounts paid were low. Spencer sold most of her "pictures" through the Art-Union, but it too had more inventory than it could move. Prices paid to artists were therefore low. Spencer also complained of the Union's practice of buying on six months credit and then paying with checks, "which to be used must be discounted."[57]

Sadly, the art unions' attempt at creating a democratic art market was put to an end by competitive envy. Their demise stemmed largely from inadequate financial resources, exacerbated by a decline in the nation's general economy and a stagnation of consumer demand. Licensed lotteries had long been used in America to raise funds needed for community projects. Art unions attempted to augment patronage for artists by using lotteries to bring critical money into their coffers. Lotteries were particularly appealing to art unions because, as with their uses in funding specific canal projects and other internal improvements, they could focus attention and money-raising efforts on one spectacular event or art show (Figure 4). But during the 1840s lotteries came under attack by reformers who associated recreational gambling with urban poverty and immorality. Furthermore, the democratic rhetoric used to justify its purchasing policies opened the Art-Union to attack from all sides, including the genteel press that saw the Art-Union challenging the National Academy's claim to professional expertise, the penny press that cast itself as the incorruptible critic of privilege, and artists who had been passed over by Art-Union buyers.[58] In 1851, the sponsorship of artists by the American Art-Union collapsed when its lotteries were pronounced "illegal and unconstitutional." The organization was forced to sell its art works at auction, pay off its debts, and close up shop.

Spencer assessed the impact of the American Art-Union's demise in a letter to her parents. The Art-Union had badly needed organizational improvement and alteration, she agreed, but it was "better than nothing." Alas, "they have completely smashed it, and the pictures (which were to have been distributed all over the United States) have been disposed of at publick auction in the City, filling houses of picture buyers, without one cent's worth of benefit to the Artists." Still, as an artist, Spencer was pleased to see that at the auctions her pictures "brought pretty good prices being (excepting in the case of one picture) once and a half more than what they gave me." So she took advantage of the situation and varnished some old pictures never bought by the union to sneak into the sales.[59]

Commercial Cellar Door

The popular interest in art on which the art unions and artists like Spencer depended was not so much the product of the art crusaders' drawing manuals as of the rapidly expanding commercial print industry that manufactured them. Between 1825 and 1861, printers and engravers swept up in New York's entrepreneurial surge increased the quality, variety, and number of their prints and added lithography to their production lists. With ready ac-

Figure 4. Francis D'Avignon, *Distribution of the American Art-Union Prizes at the Tabernacle, Broadway, New York, December 24, 1846*. Lithograph by Sarony & Major, 1847, Graphic Arts Collection, National Museum of American History. Smithsonian Institution, SI-96-297.

cess to the supplies necessary to elevate standards and increase mass production (especially the limestone suited to lithography and the iron needed
to make new presses), printers updated their equipment regularly and incorporated the latest technologies from abroad. In the process they created
a popular market for a spectrum of prints ranging from political cartoons
to music, maps, and bank notes, to illustrations in books, newspapers and
magazines, to trade cards, billheads and advertising materials, to wallpaper
and calico. They also stocked a market for quality prints aimed at an elite
group of New York art connoisseurs and cheaper versions intended for
everyone else.[60]

Between 1835 and 1885, art appreciation and consumption was democratized in America through the "commercial cellar door." The lithograph
when supplemented by a few fine painters, claimed Homer Saint-Gaudens,
satisfied "a fundamental desire in our land." Anyone could join the ranks
of art buyers because the "retailed price of these prints ran somewhere
about two for a quarter. As time went by you found them everywhere from
livery stable doors to Grandpa's front parlor."[61] Chromolithography and
colored prints made the possession of art "an easy sequence of desire,"
noted the *Aldine*, an elegant journal devoted to typographic art, as they go
"where pure Art cannot go."[62] In the 1850s, prints followed the paths forged
by the art crusaders, finding venues for distribution in "premium systems,
traveling salesmen, art galleries, museums, commission agents, furniture
dealers, religious and fraternal organizations . . . promotional giveaways . . .
direct mail order, . . . lyceum lecturers and traveling bible salesmen."[63] Publishers of lithographs and colored engravings catering to this "fundamental
desire" were the first industrialists to employ large numbers of female artists as workers. They also were steady patrons of a small number of women
painters.

During the 1850s, Lilly Martin Spencer sold dozens of genre paintings
to print dealers, publishers, their agents, and directly to chromolithographers. William Schaus purchased Spencer's paintings as the American representative of Goupil, Vibert and Company, which lithographed and hand-
colored prints of them in France and then shipped them back to sell
through their representative in America, Michel Knoedler. Schaus and
Knoedler, and also Louis Prang, Herman Bencke, and Currier & Ives, represented a new kind of art agent, who served as a conduit between artists,
chromolithographers, and the public. Publishing agents bought paintings
from contemporary artists, negotiated purchases for print publishers, produced prints themselves, distributed the finished products to art stores

throughout the country, and often resold the original paintings for a profit.[64] They became dealers in works of art, with their print shops serving as eclectic galleries.

Women artists took advantage of the opportunity to sell paintings for reproduction and did not mind at first that print publishers paid no royalties. Cheap prints could stimulate an interest in art that increased the number of Americans who wanted to buy paintings. But at the same time, they encouraged a taste for art that did not discriminate between originals and reproductions.[65] Spencer felt confident that fame based on the publication and sale of prints of her art would bring in orders for paintings. In 1852 the artist enthusiastically wrote her mother: "The engraving of a picture of mine . . . is expected daily from Paris, by the Goupills—print publishers. This will be of no pecuniary benefit to me, but it helps to spread my name." She was right on both accounts. Dozens of Spencer's paintings were engraved and lithographed by publishers, and close to one million prints of her work circulated in America and Europe. But because copyright law at the time regarded the producer of a copy in the same light as the artist who invented the original design, proceeds from the sales of those prints went to the publisher. To top it off, the recognition Spencer received from print sales did not translate into commissions. "I had expected that after having so many of my pictures engraved that I should have had plenty to do, but it is not so," she admitted four years later. "When once publishers have got what they want, there is no one to buy."[66]

During the financial crisis of 1857, private patrons virtually stopped buying Spencer's genre paintings. And while prints of her paintings became a familiar sight in middle-class parlors, she did not fare well. "You may think dear Mother because you read so many puffs about me that my fame does me a great deal of good, but it does not—fame is as hollow and brilliant as a soap bubble; it is all colors outside, and nothing worth kicking at inside."[67] To help make ends meet, Spencer turned to art publishers again, taking in work coloring prints, ironically often of her own paintings. She also accepted an offer from the author/historian Elizabeth F. Ellet, who included Spencer in her 1859 survey of American women artists, to illustrate a series of articles for *Godey's Lady's Book* and design drawings for bookplate engravings.[68]

Writing, illustrating, and engraving grew as primary fields for women artists along with the expansion of the illustrated press in the 1840s and 1850s. Illustrated women's magazines like *Godey's Lady's Book* (1830) and general periodicals such as *Graham's* (1841) began circulating in America as early as 1828. These groundbreakers were followed by weeklies and monthlies aimed at adults, such as the *Union Magazine* (1847), which became *Sartain's Union Magazine* (1849), *Gleason's* (1851), *Leslie's Illustrated* (1855), the *Atlantic Monthly* (1857), and *Harper's Weekly* (1857); and juvenile periodicals such as *Merry's Museum for Boys and Girls* (1841). Most general magazines regularly included steel or copperplate engravings and woodcuts, and occasionally lithographic or mezzotint prints. Some periodicals also offered hand water-colored fashion plates with every issue, while others occasionally included engraved or chromolithographed supplements. American subscribers considered graphic art the greatest feature of these new periodicals.

Up until the 1850s, pictures engraved on metal dominated the content of general magazines. In fact the editor of *Godey's*, prized for its engravings and fashion plates, often did not even call the pictures in his magazine illustrations. Instead, he referred to some story or sketch as "the illustration of the plate." This understanding of illustration, turned on its head to mean the written accompaniment to a picture, was no wonder at the time. With no easy alternative available, people were aware of the skill and time it took to cut (in reverse on steel or copper with an etching needle) the thousands of lines that made up one inch of an engraving. "When you see in the shop windows a line engraving like this" today, a defender of the art asserted in 1872, "you never say 'how wonderful' *that* is, nor consider how you would like to have to live, by producing anything of the same kind yourselves."[69]

American engraving on wood was by comparison fairly "crude but forceful" and used mainly to illustrate juvenile periodicals. However, during the 1840s the emigration of English master engravers to the United States and the publication of magazines, tracts, and books illustrated by literally thousands of pictures precipitated a marked progress in woodcuts. By the Civil War wood engraving was the principal reproductive medium through which any graphic art was brought to the greater public.[70]

Intricate metal plate engravings were expensive, costing somewhere between $300 and $1,500. Publishers sometimes paid more for one new plate than for all the literary contents of a publication, so many monthlies resorted to publishing impressions from steel and copper plates that already had been used. Despite the expense, prosperous magazines printed many plates. *Graham's Magazine* made illustration one of its leading features by abandoning the second-hand policy at the beginning. Its publisher had new plates made expressly for each number and saved money by engaging a few engravers to work exclusively for that magazine.[71] *Godey's* claimed to pay seven thousand dollars for "Embellishments" in its first eighteen months, even though the majority of its seventy pictures were woodcuts, which were far cheaper.[72] For the illustrated magazine, "the plate was the thing"— always newly designed, engraved, and in the case of *Godey's* fashion plates, hand-colored, all of which meant work for women artists.[73]

Competing Ideologies

Designing her illustrations for *Godey's* at home in the evenings, Spencer painted portraits for private customers at her studio during the days. She also worked on genre paintings for the Cosmopolitan Art Association, an organization begun in 1854 that combined the democratic ideals of the art unions with the capitalist motives of the publishing industry. The Cosmopolitan Art Association purchased, exhibited, and sold American paintings and sculptures and published a popular magazine, the *Cosmopolitan Art Journal*, which provided subscribers with articles on art, biography, and general literature, and as premiums provided free engravings and a chance to win works of art.[74] The prizes awarded to subscribers included copies and original works of art by Europeans and Americans.[75] Unlike the art unions, the Cosmopolitan Art Association was an overtly commercial operation whose major beneficiaries were art consumers, not producers. Nevertheless, it considered its publication *the* national art journal. "In all things it is *American*," sang an 1860 editorial, "in paper, in illustrations, in matter, in printing; and the Association sends it forth with the assurance that the public has a right to expect and demand just such a production."[76]

To women artists like Spencer, the Cosmopolitan Art Association represented a new marketing outlet, but to the Association she was much more than a producer. Spencer was its idea of a truly American artist, a feminine embodiment of republican virtue, national genius, and liberal enterprise. Of her the *Cosmopolitan Art Journal* wrote in 1856: "Such success against obstacles everywhere thrown in woman's way, is a double triumph, and commands not only the respect we bestow upon true genius and cultivated taste, but also the admiration we must bestow upon those moral heroes who conquer the obstacles which time and circumstance and a false system of social etiquette throw before the lowest, independent, honest heart."[77] According to the *Cosmopolitan*, Spencer was a hero because she was a painter *and* a woman. Not only had she succeeded within Old World conceptions of genius and taste, by doing so she had undermined the hierarchical system on which those ideals were based. To democratic enthusiasts, she proved that in America, where art belonged to the "lowest, independent, honest heart," a woman could triumph over tradition and gain for herself (and her country) the artistic recognition she deserved.

In a nation struggling to create a democratic cultural identity, it was prudent to allow that women artists had genius. Like other female artists of her day, Spencer was called a genius and her work was said to contain genius. Until the eighteenth century, genius referred to a person's abilities and judgment. It was a quality people possessed or something they could attain. This early modern version of genius was easily granted to a woman since it referred to a measure of talent and did not connote greatness or originality. Indeed, one could improve genius through imitation, following artistic rules, or copying previous masters. But during the late 1700s, an early-Romantic concept of genius began to gradually replace the neoclassical view. Romantics spoke of a person as *being* a genius. Genius was an innate identity, a gift one was born with, and by the end of the nineteenth century genius also was almost universally male. The twentieth-century concept of the great artist as a man of individuality and originality, who creates art with universal appeal, is derived from that definition.[78]

For a time in nineteenth-century America these two concepts of genius overlapped. The neoclassical version continued to have cultural relevance because Americans resisted the Romantic's definition of artistic genius as a person born with natural advantages, someone already privileged. In a republican society, anyone could be "inspired by the Divine Soul which also inspires all men" if only they were given the opportunity to develop their talents.[79] References to Lilly Martin Spencer's genius capture this transitional moment in American thought. In a letter to Spencer, friend and artist Frank Carnes referred to her style of painting as having "ever so much genius in it, and ever so much sublimity and skill." Because the term genius could refer to either the artist's masterly abilities or sublime state (where the passions and imagination could be freely expressed), Carnes felt the need to specify that he meant she possessed both.[80]

In 1857 the *Cosmopolitan Art Journal* offered Spencer's genius as a symbol of "the genius of the people." It claimed: "No person is doing more than Mrs. Spencer to 'popularize' art, and for that the people owe her a debt of gratitude." They also thought "no picture in this county" was better fitted for popular appreciation than Spencer's painting *Shake Hands?*.[81] In *Shake Hands?* the artist depicts a woman in a kitchen as if she were an arti-

Figure 5. Lilly Martin Spencer, *Shake Hands?*, 1854. Oil on canvas. Ohio Historical Society, Columbus, Ohio.

san surrounded by the tools and materials of her trade—pans, knives, produce, a furnace burning in the background, kettles heating on the stove.
Cheeks red with the heat of labor, skirts tucked under an apron, sleeves
rolled up exposing arms thick with muscles—the worker offers a hand
soiled with the stuff of her craft, bread dough (Figure 5). In that detail lays

the humor and the democratic sensibility of the painting that the *Cosmopolitan* celebrated. Seemingly ensconced in the domestic realm, the woman in the painting asserts her own sense of equality through her gesture.

Beyond praising Spencer in its journal and premiums catalogue, the Association commissioned a number of paintings, including *Kiss Me, and You'll Kiss the 'Lasses,* and in 1857 distributed to subscribers a free engraving of *Shake Hands?*. Two years later the *Cosmopolitan* credited Spencer with helping "convince our people . . . that the genius of this country is as strong in the field of art as in the more strictly commercial and scientific walks," and listed her among the American painters and sculptors recognized by European art critics as having developed a "successful native art-expression" and contributed to "the formation and establishment of a national school of art" in America.[82]

While Spencer benefited from the Cosmopolitan Art Association's attention individually, the Association also advocated for women artists as a group. Throughout the 1850s, the journal's "Art Gossip" columns followed the progress of several women, including Spencer, sculptors Harriet Hosmer, Emma Stebbins, and Louisa Lander, French artist Rosa Bonheur, and actress Charlotte Cushman, a patron of women artists. It ran portrait plates and biographical sketches of several up-and-coming women artists (and some budding male artists as well) and printed an extensive obituary of portraitist Hermina Dassell. The journal also encouraged women artists' aspirations by addressing advice to "the artist (male or female)" and printing reviews of histories of female artists to "show woman what her sex has accomplished, and to stimulate her to still greater achievements in the world of art."[83] And in practice the Association supported female artists by commissioning the New York School of Design for Women to illustrate and engrave plates for its journal and catalogues.

The "sole object" of the Cosmopolitan Art Association, according to the *Cosmopolitan Art Journal,* was to create "the *means* of reaching, effectually, cheaply, all classes" so as to continue "the encouragement of art-workers, and the dissemination among us of a love for their labors."[84] It praised painters with a "democratic proclivity" and called genre "pictures of New-York Street life, of newsboys, etc." an advance in American art. It both touted and critiqued the radical aesthetic theories of the influential English art critic John Ruskin, and demonstrated its egalitarian objective by discussing a variety of individuals and groups producing, marketing, and buying art in midcentury America, including oil painters and marble sculptors, illustrators, engravers, lithographers, and art publishers, photographers, and the "useful arts" or manufacturers.[85]

The *Cosmopolitan Art Journal*'s pluralism and self-proclaimed role as herald of America's national "school" of art threatened some professional painters feeling the pinch of increased competition and a stagnating market for studio art during the financial depression of the midfifties. These artists reacted to the situation by reexamining their interests and dropping their democratic rhetoric. In 1855 landscape painters William Stillman and John Durand (son of Asher B.) began publishing *The Crayon*. To challenge the *Cosmopolitan*'s eclectic definition of American art, *The Crayon* called upon Ruskin's aesthetic theory as well, announcing in its pages that nature was the model of perfection for "the artist, the individual, the nation, and the world."[86]

These two art journals represented the extremes of the discourse on art in 1850s New York City. *The Crayon* tended to discuss art on a high intellectual level, to dissociate it from market or democratic ideology, and to accept European aesthetics. The *Cosmopolitan* maintained a more chatty, popular style intended to engage "the people," particularly women, compared art to other commercial endeavors, and promoted a separate American aesthetic.[87] The *Cosmopolitan* openly discussed the trade in art and proclaimed that the free-market economy could benefit the hard-working artist; *The Crayon* generally ignored the economics of art and focused on aesthetic issues.[88] But while the idealist framework of *The Crayon* left no space for monetary concerns, it could not keep the exigencies of the marketplace from invading its pages. Economic conditions were precarious in 1855 and disastrous in 1857. Editors of *The Crayon* expressed their financial distress in pleas for subscribers and moralistic admonishments against the insidious materialism of commerce.[89] These different postures reflected an emerging divide among artists and members of the art-buying public along class and gender lines.

During the financial panic of 1857, *The Crayon* attacked the Cosmopolitan Art Association for fashioning itself an "association" when "it is a scheme for private gain only, based upon popular ignorance of Art." To *Crayon* editors, the *Cosmopolitan*'s offer to compensate "ladies throughout the country" willing to secure subscribers and organize clubs was particularly galling evidence that "The Cosmopolitan Art-Association is one of those fungus inspirations that are entirely supported by the corruptions of commercial life" and whose democratic rhetoric is "a gross humbug." "[We] *know* that the association is of no benefit to Art nor artists; its 'prizes,' with very few exceptions, are of the most commonplace description, . . . called Art by commercial courtesy—but in reality nothing more than Art trash, made to sell."[90]

The Cosmopolitan countered such criticism in an 1861 overview of *"Its History, Plan, and Objectives"*: "We educate in *everything* which conduces to our *material* prosperity, but we leave the soul of the people to educate itself. And hence it is that we have won the name of money-worshippers, and are regarded as wanting in *true* refinement and the highest cultivation." Yet, it was "to meet and answer this great want—this absence of art influences and aesthetic culture—that the Cosmopolitan Art Association was called into existence." "The *people* took a lively interest in the institution," it declared. Hence, when *The Crayon* criticizes us, it criticizes our *"one hundred and seventeen thousand six hundred and seventeen subscribers."*[91]

To the Cosmopolitan Art Association, these subscription numbers were evidence that along with an interest in art that was cheap enough for "the people" to buy, a distinctly American aesthetic was developing, expansive enough to appreciate both the luminous qualities of a landscape painting and the worth and character of a good steel engraving.[92] But its unwillingness to clearly distinguish between public art and commercial art (or between producers and marketers) distressed the very "art workers" it claimed to be supporting, especially female artists dependent on popular and industrial art markets for their livelihoods. Painter Annie Delano, working in the small town of Penn Yan in upstate New York, bemoaned the "woolen monstrosities, oriental tinsel, & Grecian Art humbug" that her *Cosmopolitan*-reading neighbors took for art, while illuminator Alice Donlevy, working in New York City, resisted the joining of her work with "commonplace" art "made to sell" by the *Crayon*-reading public. What was needed, both knew, was for "culture and education" to "establish a great appreciation of true art in every country hamlet [and urban setting] in America," so that *true artists* would be recognized no matter where they worked.[93] This culture and education was exactly what New York City's aesthetic philosophers, education reformers, and institution builders hoped to achieve by promoting the Unity of Art ideal.

Chapter 2
"The Unity of Art"

In her manual *Practical Hints on the Art of Illumination*, which came out in 1867 to good notices, Alice Donlevy emphasized the relationship between aesthetics and remunerative labor in industrial fields. Learning mechanical copying by hand, she informed her readers, is only the elementary step in the art of book decorating and is insufficient to secure employment. "Progress in the various processes of art reproduction will render the works of imitators useless, but will bring out thought, and create a demand for original design." Studying the art of design could lead to other employment as well, because "the principles which govern the art [of book illumination] are identical with the laws of the polychromatic decoration of any flat surface" (Figure 6). To prove that the arts overlapped, Donlevy drew attention to women artists in England who were employed designing elaborate ornamental labels for manufacturers, and pointed out that "Owen Jones, distinguished alike as architect and illuminator, draws a type border or designs a calico pattern with equal facility."[1] Donlevy's admonition that women artists who intended to work for industrial markets should study the principles of art was a "practical" rendering of an aesthetic philosophy she had imbibed at the New York School of Design: the Unity of Art ideal.

The personal and professional lives of women artists like Donlevy exemplified the intermingling of fine, industrial, and decorative art, which dominated American aesthetic practice during much of the nineteenth century. Derived from the writings of British art critic John Ruskin, the Unity of Art principle held no "decided [or] wide separation between the applied and the fine arts" or between artisan and artist. It erased the line between design and execution, and emphasized the idea that any art-related work involving invention, regardless of where the work was performed, was art, and therefore intrinsically valuable. This ideal was both progressive and democratic. "It means that the educated sense of the beautiful is not the especial property of one class, but that it may be possessed and enjoyed by all."[2]

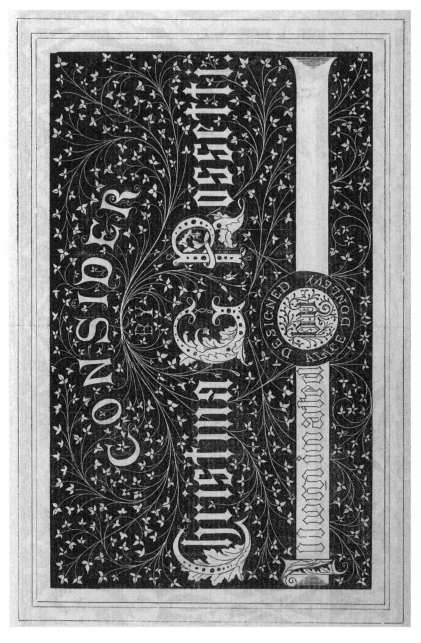

Figure 6. Alice Donlevy, "Consider," *Practical Hints in the Art of Illumination*, 1867, plate 1. Illumination design. Courtesy of American Antiquarian Society.

Art education based on the Unity of Art ideal started from the position that aesthetic and mechanical instruction should be applied to all the common trades and occupations, as well as to the fine arts, explained journalist George Ward Nichols in 1877. "The broad meaning of the term 'art education' has not always been understood. It is most often used in its relation to the fine arts of painting, sculpture, and architecture, as if these higher arts and the industries were not mutually dependent, or as if the boundary which is supposed to separate them were not, in all three of the arts, constantly invaded, so that often the product of the industry may be called a work of art."[3]

The impact of the Unity of Art ideal in the United States lay in its resonance with the labor republicanism of leading artists and artisans and the progressive opinions of education reformers. By the 1850s attitudes about art, labor, industrial progress, education, and women's position as wage earners overlapped in many American minds. This convergence occurred because the critique of industrial society lodged by reformers and mechanics (skilled workers), the aesthetic theories of artists and art critics, and the economic and social activities of the founders of industrial schools stemmed from the same moral philosophy. Whether trying to identify a national art ideal or solve the problems associated with industrialization, many people shared the belief that social progress in America would be determined by the extent to which its citizens recognized the transcendent connection between the moral/political and material/economic worlds. The activities inspired by this merging of ideals and purpose formed a Unity of Art movement.

In New York City, the Unity of Art ideal had an inherently democratic and expansive character that incorporated women within a broad-ranging faith in the linkage of art and industry. That faith was the inspiration for the founding of the New York School of Design for Women and its incorporation into the Cooper Union in the 1850s. But the extent of the Unity of Art ideal's influence on antebellum culture was far greater. This multifaceted movement created a progressive and egalitarian world of artists, advocates, and educators in New York that broadened the aesthetic and economic prospects of women artists.

The Reunion of Art and Industry

Many of antebellum America's leading thinkers claimed to have been influenced by the teachings of Emanuel Swedenborg (1688–1772), a Swedish seer, whose doctrine of correspondences posed the theory that there was a spiritual antitype for every natural object, which made the mind/spirit and body/matter equivalent. Transformed into Transcendentalism by New England writers in the 1830s, the theory of correspondence passed into general circulation in the 1840s and 1850s through the rhetoric of labor republicans and associationists, who stressed the ennobling, spiritual, and aesthetic qualities of work and critiqued the severing of those qualities from industrial labor, and through the writing of English art critic John Ruskin. Popular in America for over a decade, Ruskin's art criticism assessed with equal fervor painting, architecture, and illustration, dispelling the suggestion that the "highest order of Art" could only include painting and sculpture. In doing so, he and others provided aesthetic rationale for equating the entire body of artists.[4]

With the publication of the first two volumes of *Modern Painters* (1843 and 1846), Ruskin became the most influential and controversial art critic in the English-speaking world. His dominance lingered well into the 1870s. During the 1850s and 1860s Ruskin's ideas and teaching practices permeated the United States through American editions of his books, emigration of his students, and after 1855 in excerpts, letters, and articles published in *The Crayon*, which followed his precepts on truth to nature. In his chapter "The Nature of Gothic" from *Stones of Venice* (1851–53), Ruskin defined art as "the expression of [man's] rational and disciplined delight in the forms and laws of the creation of which he forms a part." An artist's meticulous fidelity to specific natural forms could be both a kind of individual spiritual act and national expression. Aesthetic matters were never separate from material or social matters. "I could show you, in all time, that every nation's vice, or virtue, was written in its art," he would say.[5] Ruskin broadened the definition of art and removed the rigid boundaries between the fine and applied arts by taking into account the intent of their creators. "There is not a definite separation between the two kinds," he said, "a blacksmith may put soul into the making of a horseshoe, and an architect may put none into the building of a church. Only exactly in proportion as the Soul is thrown into it, the art becomes Fine."[6]

Antebellum artists and their contemporaries were aware of the discourse that distinguished between artist and artisan, but their democratic convictions and commercial markets discouraged such rigid categories. Most Americans agreed with Ruskin that the "only essential distinction between Decorative and other art is the being fitted for a fixed place . . . all the greatest art which the world has produced is thus fitted for a place, and subordinated to a purpose. There is no existing highest order of art but is decorative. The best sculpture yet produced has been the decoration of a temple front—the best painting, the decoration of a room. . . . Get rid, then, at once of any idea of Decorative art being a degraded or a separate kind of art."[7]

In 1859 Ruskin delivered a lecture entitled "The Unity of Art," which clarified his position on the differences between Manufacture, Art, and Fine Art. He acknowledged that each had its own principles and "each must be followed separately," but he stressed that "the one must influence the other." Manufacture was anything "proceeding from the hand of man," he said; "but it must have proceeded from his hand only, acting mechanically, and uninfluenced at the moment by direct intelligence." Art was the "operation of the hand and the intelligence of man together: there is an art of making machinery; there is an art of building ships; an art of making carriages; and so on." Fine Art was "that in which the hand, the head, and the *heart* of man go together."[8] The curse of modern industry was that it crushed the heart out of man and the art out of work. The one way to reverse the situation was to establish as quickly as possible a condition of things wherein each worker could realize according to his ability, and according to the nature of his work, that sense of life which comes in fullest measure to the creative artist.

Ruskin's aesthetic theories were part of an indictment of modern society being put forward by social reformers and labor radicals in Britain and America interested in correcting the adverse effects of capitalist manufacture, in particular its failure to make possible the necessary social conditions for creative labor. This critique, which was given voice in the United States by the *New-York Tribune*, was indebted to another British theorist, Thomas Carlyle (1795–1881).[9] Carlyle was morally outraged by the capitalist ethic, which wiped out the "chivalry of work" by insisting that the worth of a thing is only its cash value.[10] Ruskin agreed with Carlyle's condemnation of the cultural standards that accompanied capitalism, values which encouraged people to live in terms of their own self-interest and the narrowest utilitarian morality. They argued for the pursuit of beauty in all endeavors so that remunerative labor would be reconciled with larger social and ethical ends.[11]

The social-economic philosophy and reform activities of *New-York Tribune* editor Horace Greeley amplified the significance of the Unity of Art ideal in America. In a pamphlet published sometime before the Civil War, he proclaimed: "No man can have observed the tendencies of the age in which we live without perceiving that there is everywhere a restless uneasiness under the present circumstances of society, and an earnest desire for Advancement and Progress."[12] Greeley pathologized the "restless uneasiness" of his age, calling it a symptom of the "disease . . . deep-seated and chronic . . . under which Society labours." To cure the disease, he argued, society must fulfill this "earnest desire" for advancement by reuniting "Art & Industry" and, thereby, providing every person with meaningful, productive, well-remunerated work.[13] His particular prescription for women, whose symptoms were poverty and earnest restless desire, was training and jobs in the arts.

Greeley's interests were so varied that biographers easily overlook his promotion of women artists.[14] "Uncle Horace" was the most widely known and generally revered American newspaper editor of the nineteenth century (Figure 7). A difficult figure to pigeon-hole, Greeley was a professed Whig (the party opposed to Jacksonian popular rule), who worked all his life to bring a greater share of material and political benefits to the common man. The secret to Greeley's popularity was his sincerity and his faith that the masses could be attracted by reason as well as emotionalism. "A leader of the group standing for a continuance of the *status quo*, he was one of the most 'radical' men of his age. At a time when the democratic process was under great stress, Greeley put his faith in the unshackled mind.'"[15]

In 1841 he founded and became editor of the *New-York Daily Tribune* and the nationally circulated *Weekly Tribune*, operating both papers during the heyday of personal journalism in the United States, until his death in 1872 after a devastating presidential campaign. He created a successful penny paper that relied on culture and stimulating ideas rather than sensationalism to attract readers, and never wrote "down" to the common man. Greeley also openly lived his consciousness of responsibility and advocated for a fairer distribution of wealth by giving away to his employees all but a few shares of the fortune made by the *Tribune*.[16] Antebellum Americans grew up reading and listening to the ideas offered in Greeley's daily and weekly papers, ideas that had perhaps the greatest effect on females of the working middle class.

Besides having a kindly, winning smile, Greeley attracted followers with his optimistic contention that the United States was ripe with the promise of prosperity for anyone willing to exert the effort, *if only simple justice could be made to prevail.* He encouraged all people to believe they had the power to work out their own deliverance and, if they worked together, the power to reform American society. Benevolent agencies could

Figure 7. Portrait of Horace Greeley, J. Rogers, sc. Engraving of a photo by Brady, from Horace Greeley, *Recollections of a Busy Life* (New York, 1868), frontispiece. Personal copy.

never eradicate the poverty and suffering of the masses, he contended, because these ills are not caused by "the voluntary imprudence or vices of the individuals" but by the "organization of industry."[17]

In its present form, Greeley complained, American society was characterized by a "universal and utter DIVERGENCY OF INTERESTS" between all the branches of work—from domestic service to agriculture, manufacture, commerce, education, science, to the fine arts—and between labor and capital, laborer and laborer, and men and women. But his remedy for the defects of society—poverty, exploitation, and degradation—never included the abolition of capitalism. He recognized no inevitable antagonism between capital and labor, although he did see that capitalists were exploiting laborers and that competition undermined cooperation between workers. What was needed, he argued, was the "adoption of some method by which we can produce CONVERGENCY OF INTERESTS." His solution called for a reunion of "Art & Industry" and reeducation of the public in the intellectual content of all skilled or productive labor.[18]

The organization of society and industry, especially the general separation between agriculture, manufacture, science, art, and popular education, had rendered all manual labor "repugnant, monotonous, dishonorable, and degrading, so that it becomes desirable for all men who are able, to escape from work."[19] Everyone knew that some jobs were simply low-paying drudgery, but in America anyone was supposed to be able to work him- or herself up. If all manual labor was lowered to the same level this could not happen. Furthermore, when people found no meaning in manual work apart from its instrumental value, acquisitive values ("a mere selfish scramble for gain") gained ascendancy over more republican principles (equality, morality, and law).

Greeley believed that an industrial economy, if it was organized properly, could offer everyone the "opportunity to Labor and to secure the fair recompense of such Labor." Furthermore, if men and women were educated in the branches of art and knowledge practically applicable to their daily occupations, they would experience emancipation and attain social mobility. Industrial employment was good because it provided jobs for skilled workers without the restrictions of guild rules. This advantage, he insisted, held true for male and female mechanics alike.

Greeley's answer to the degradation of labor and poverty of women represents a personal reformation of the ideas of two antebellum movements—associationism and labor republicanism. Associationism was a form of collective living promoted in the columns of the *New-York Tribune* by Albert Brisbane, American prophet of the French philosopher Charles Fourier. Fourierism was a scheme for curing the ills of modern society through the creation of harmonious associations of mutual help and protection.[20] In an industrial society, Fourier believed, man lost his natural rights and freedom because he was forced to do work that caused him nothing but torment. Fourierist phalanxes were to be communities of volunteers, carefully selected for skills, who would engage in a variety of economic activities with profits to be distributed according to a fixed ratio between labor, capital, and skill. By living in a single large building or "phalanstery," the participants would be able to pool childcare and homemaking, freeing both men and women for tasks outside their families. The objective was to match every person's tastes and abilities with an appropriate job, or in Fourier's terms, to create "attractive industry." Fourier's ideas inspired scores of socialist "utopian" communities in the 1840s. Most lasted for a year or less but some endured for a generation or more. By the 1860s over one hundred Fourierist phalanxes had been established across the United States.[21]

The association movement was not limited to utopian reformers. Between the panics of 1837 and 1857, the disruptions caused by industrial capitalism encouraged horizontal alliances of every kind. By midcentury, most artisans were earning roughly half the wages necessary to maintain their families at a comfortable level. Workers also lamented the decline of personal relationships in shops and factories; the days when every worker knew his employer were gone. Labor reformers inspired by the political successes of Jacksonian Democrats and the rhetoric of utopian socialists called for workers to form their own associations or cooperatives, become their own employers, and own and enjoy the fruits of their labor.

During these years, women's productive work left the home, women's domestic labor lost its social and economic status, and women's waged labor declined in value.[22] The numerical ratio between women and men changed as well. While there were more men in the country at large, by 1860 Connecticut, Maryland, Massachusetts, New Hampshire, New Jersey, New York, North Carolina, and Rhode Island counted 74,360 more women than men. In New York State alone women of marriageable age exceeded men by 38,783.[23] Especially in large cities, an increasing number of single women signaled an increased number of potentially exploitable workers. The high proportion of unmarried women incited enthusiastic advocacy for women's freedom to labor and vocational educations. But industrialization placed middle-class women in a precarious position. On the one hand, it allowed for the rise of a gendered and classed domestic ideology, which warned women that accepting manual labor jeopardized their class status; on the other hand, it forced more and more middle-class women into waged labor. This dilemma was widely recognized, and some reformers made acrobatic attempts to reconcile domestic ideology with women's need to earn.[24] Others revived the republican code of virtuous independence, creating a language that working women eagerly adopted.[25]

Greeley regarded the problems of labor degradation and women's economic dependence in the same light, and his goal for workers was the same as his goal for women: "Emancipation of Labor . . . from ignorance, vice, servitude, insecurity, [and] poverty," and "Emancipation of Women from their past and present condition of inferiority, to an independence of Men . . . [and their] freest access to all stations, professions, employments, which are open to any." The theory of "equality for Women" could "be enforced only by ignoring the habitual discrimination of men and women, as forming separate *classes*, and regarding all alike as simply *persons*,—as human beings."[26] He insisted that factory work, in places where it was organized in a Waltham-type system, had already "emancipated" many females by releasing them from poverty or economic dependence on marriage or family.

To someone like Greeley, one of the obvious places to begin to reunite art and industry was in publishing and the illustrated press. The rise and mass circulation of the penny press and popular magazines in the 1830s encouraged the breakdown of print manufacture, originally the responsibility of a single artisan printer and a small workshop, into a series of semiskilled tasks. Published art, both reproductions of paintings and the illustration or embellishment of books and periodicals, vastly increased employment opportunities for female artists with technical skills and design abilities. Mass production of colored plates and engraved illustrations found in magazines like *Godey's* required a score of workers. Some of the tasks called for autonomous labor and others assembly line production. A single fashion plate entailed designing, drawing, engraving, printing, and coloring, and publishers began hiring different artists to accomplish each of these jobs. In 1845, the *Broadway Journal* ribbed publisher Louis Godey for keeping "almost as many ladies in his pay as the Grand Turk," and in 1852 *Godey's Lady's Book* announced with pride "our corps of one hundred and fifty female colorers."[27] Printers and publishers hired female workers for every stage of production, but before the Civil War most women worked as colorists.

Even in its most humble form, art work enjoyed relatively high status and pay. At first all the artists involved in the production of lithographs were skilled workers; even colorists carrying out what seems like unskilled task work had art educations. The partners Nathaniel Currier and James Ives were artists who worked closely with their firm's designers, lithographers, and colorists. Currier & Ives hired British-born artist Fanny Palmer to design lithographic prints and a staff of about twelve young women, all trained artists, to color them. For stock prints, colorists "worked at long tables from a model set up in the middle of the table, where it was visible to all." The models were colored by one of the staff artists, Louis Maurer for instance or Fanny Palmer, and approved by the one of the partners. "Each colorist applied only one color and, when she had finished, passed the print on to the next worker, and so on until it was fully colored. The print would then go to the woman in charge, known as the 'finisher,' who would touch it up where necessary." Other female (and some male) artists were hired to color at home. "Large folios were sent out in lots with models to regular colorists who worked outside the shop. . . . These artists were often indigent young artists who earned a modest living at this kind of work while awaiting recognition of their own work." Currier & Ives paid one cent a piece to colorists for the small prints, and one dollar for coloring twelve large folios.[28]

Although print colorists, finishers, and embellishers were among the first American artists to experience factory production, their proletarianization did not necessarily mean their degradation. In an 1847 series of articles on the circumstances of labor in industrializing New York, the *New-York Daily Tribune* cited the printing trades as a field that offered the best conditions and most rewards for male and female workers. An article on "The Map-Colorers" claimed that new technologies had considerably improved the conditions and rewards of art work for women. Print colorers used to be "toil-worn" and "heart-smothered" pieceworkers, humble tracers and markers who dream the dreams of the poor "after their long day and evening work—over which they often fall asleep as the hours grow big with midnight" (Figure 8). But in today's most extensive establishments, claimed the *Tribune*, map-colorers and stainers "do not work, on the average, more than eight or nine hours a day, and their wages range from three to five dollars per week."[29]

Women working in this profession needed art training. Most colorers still work by the "piece," warned the author, which allows poorer establishments to pay them less for more work. But because picture coloring often required a good deal of care and skill, "the majority of girls engaged in the business are tolerably and some very well educated," and the better-paid

LIVE PORTRAITS.—No, 3.
THE MAP-COLORER.

I NNOCENT PINKFINGERS grows dainty and picturesque under the influence of her occupation; and nothing is easier than to distinguish her and her companions by the bright and strongly-contrasted colors of their F r e n c h calico dresses and the wavy, map like outline of their shawls and bonnets as they glide through the crowd homeward, after their long day and evening work—over which they often fall asleep as the hours grow big with midnight, and drooping the weary head upon a hand whose fingers look as if stained with the blood of ripe berries, the dreary present is transmuted to some pleasant and sunny scene, worthy so dear and well-deserved a dream. Yes —the dreams of the poor, the toil-worn, the heart-smothered, whose destiny is to live without a destiny, are indeed their most precious rewards. Here, during the little hour of sleep, the heart of the poor forgets that it is a desolate, uncared-for thing—that it is a crime to have ambition or aspirations—and that, in aught so lowly, vanity and self-love go to make up, with independence of spirit or refinement of taste, the unpardonable sin against society. But the waking reality comes soon enough. So let the tallow candle flare in the heavy night air that leaks in through the damaged casement, and let the map of a l l Yankeedoodledom (we can't tell whether it includes Santa Fe and California) catch fire and burn up, if it will. The young empire grows so fast that it must have a new suit of maps throughout every year—so the loss will not be great. Therefore, dream on, humble tracer-out of rivers and boundaries—marker of the routes of railroads and excavations for new canals! Dream that you are a princess, if you will, and that the whole fairy troop of Viennoise dancers are your obedient slaves. They would be pretty little people enough to live in one of your carmine-colored paper kingdoms that stretches through ten parallels of latitude and thrice as many degrees of longitude on a single sheet of India post. True map-population they!—Lilliputians slept out from types—genii performing on most ungenial boards! But now to Picture-coloring:

The number of girls engaged in coloring maps in this city is perhaps two hundred. They work by the piece generally, and are paid from three to ten cents a sheet, according to the quality of the work done. Ordinary maps containing four sheets, pay a shilling each for coloring. A common industrious hand will color five maps in a day.

Some of the work is very fine, and requires a good deal of care and skill. Much of this is performed by girls who have partially studied Painting and Drawing, and frequently by those who have taught those branches, and find themselves out of employment.

The coloring of Lithographic Prints is an employment that comes under the same head as Map-coloring, and employs an equal if not a greater number of hands. The number of coarse, common Lithographs—such as the Black-Feet Indians draw with elder-juice on the dried hides of buffalos—is almost incredible. Barbers'-shops, groggery-walls, country taverns, pedlers' packs, the parlors and bedrooms of sailors' boarding-houses, &c. &c., furnish ornamental use for hundreds of thousands of these pictures—to describe any one of which accurately would set one's teeth on edge.

The colorers and stainers of these inimitable and inappreciable works of art are usually employed by the week, and receive, in the most extensive establishments, from $2,50 to $3,50 per week. Free competition, however, has over-supplied the demand, even for these precious pictures. Prices of coloring, consequently, have been pushed down, until in some concerns we find that wages are on a par with those of classes generally far less favored.

The harvest of the Colorists comes about mid-winter, when all the shops, high and low, are preparing for St. Valentine's Day. Then delicate pinkfingers are in huge demand, and their lucky proprietors can have as much work as they choose. Better prices, too, are given at this time for all kinds of coloring, and the profession of Paper-Colorer rises to an equal importance with that of the Paper-Discolorers who scribble for the Journals and the book-makers.

The majority of girls engaged in the business are tolerably, and some very well educated, and they are generally of good character.— Most of them reside with their relatives or friends, and nearly all have a great fondness for showy dresses—a taste which, whether acquired by their high-colored labors, or derived from the instinctive inspirations of the sex, many of them strain every nerve to gratify. In common with many other classes of working women, they give themselves much needless anxiety in trying to reproduce in muslin and calico the gaudy vulgarisms which the unrefined wealthy flaunt along Broadway in silk and velvet. But while many of them thus waste their earnings in hopeless attempts to imitate what is in itself only contemptible, others learn prudence and forethought from their observations and experiences, and lay aside all they can spare from the fruits of their labor. Many of them thus accumulate snug little sums of money, which at the proper time serve to establish them in life, and to embellish for them comfortable and happy homes.

OUR GALLANT NAVY.

President POLK, as well as YANKEE DOODLE, pays a deserved tribute, *en passant*, to our gallant Navy. He says that although its achievements have not perhaps been "so brilliant" as they might have been, yet this has been only on account of the enemy having no force to meet it. This is evidently a mere clerical error—being clearly intended to read "reach" it. It is certain that the Mexicans tried hard enough to get at our brave fellows at Alvarado—but owing to the extraordinary skill and admirable sailing qualities of our fleet, they were thwarted in their bloody purpose, and our force retired with only a severe splashing.

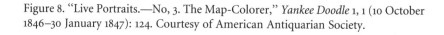

fine work was "performed by girls who have partially studied Painting and Drawing, and frequently by those who have taught those branches, and find themselves out of employment." These educated women exerted a positive influence on their coworkers, who were inclined to fritter away their earnings on clothes and such: "But, while many of them thus waste their earnings in hopeless attempts to imitate what is in itself only contemptible, others learn prudence and forethought from their observations and experiences, and lay aside all they can spare from the fruits of their labor. Many of them thus accumulate snug little sums of money, which at the proper time serve to establish them in life."[30] Art labor could both enhance a woman's virtue and make her economically independent!

As Greeley saw it, women's rights was a labor issue, not a suffrage issue. "Political franchises are not intrinsically valuable," he insisted; they "are but means to ends." He supported the "Rights of Woman—the right to vote, to be elected to office, to serve on juries, fight battles, &c., &c., [but only] if these are calculated to aid her industrial and social emancipation." For women, as for men, political freedom meant, "enlarged opportunities, more ample and varied employment, a more liberal and just recompense for industry, and . . . a position of real and heartfelt independence."[31] His advice was the same for both male and female workers: get trained in a valuable skill, do not waste money on drink or dress, and go into business for yourself. If given these rights, contended Greeley, a prudent, skilled woman worker, like her brother laborer, could use waged work as the first step toward political equality.[32]

Like the progressive educators of his era, Greeley considered the reunion of "the Ideal and the Actual" in higher education key to American progress. As he put it: "Attractive Industry, the dream of the past age, the aspiration of the present, shall be the fruition and joy of the next. The reunion of Desire and Duty . . . is a Moral renovation . . . but false is the deduction that it is wrought or endures regardless of Physical conditions."[33] Labor and capital had to be taught the meaning (or Desire) behind work that was performed out of need (or Duty) if productive industry was to be given its full value. The "moral renovation" of society would not take place, however, until capital awarded the mental content of manual labor both material (Physical) and what Greeley called "Poetic" recognition. The most important examples of the reunion of art and industry would serve both to reeducate the public in the virtues and creative content of productive labor and retrain the laborer in the arts and knowledge of his or her trade. During the 1850s this education and training was taking place in two arenas: at the

Crystal Palace Exhibitions of the Products of Art and Industry of All Nations in London (1851) and New York City (1853) and in newly established manual labor schools, people's colleges, and schools of design.

Reformed Education

The idea of offering "art educations" or "artistic and scientific instruction" to everyone, no matter what trade or occupation they were headed for, was central to education reform in antebellum America.[34] The extension of the franchise to propertyless men during the first decades of the nineteenth century was accompanied by an impulse to democratize education. Newly enfranchised citizens believed free schooling of good quality, with no stigma of pauperism attached, was the most important avenue for improving one's lot and rising in the social and economic world.[35] Formal education provided by schools steadily gained in importance during the Jacksonian period, under the leadership of Henry Barnard and Horace Mann, while training in families, churches, and through apprenticeship declined. Nevertheless, public schools remained an inadequate conduit for knowledge in an aggressive democratic society demanding equality of opportunity.[36]

Girls were at a particular disadvantage when it came to public education. Although an increasing number of women were being prepared for higher education, they were barred from attending men's colleges. Male academies focused on professions not open to women, such as the law, medicine, and the ministry. Girls also were barred from attending public high schools, which served as training schools for students learning to be printers, architects, clerks, or even politicians. Few city fathers were willing to finance high school education for girls because, as they saw it, only the daughters of the elite would have the leisure to attend. They also rarely entertained the idea of preparing poor girls to earn a living, as they did not expect women to enter the competitive economic world. Yet as early as 1826, a popular demand for some kind of public high schools for girls arose, especially among lower-middle-class families who recognized the value of educating daughters for self-support.

The art crusade and manual labor school movement were two attempts to remedy the problems of public education, followed by the coeducational American College movement of the 1840s and 1850s, of which schools of design for women were a part. Creative manual labor articulated by Ruskin and promoted in Chapman's 1847 *American Drawing Book* powered all of these movements. Initially manual labor schools were established to help male seminary and academy students meet their immediate expenses through agricultural and handicraft work. But the theory behind these schools was that mental labor should *not* be separated from physical labor. This philosophy had deliberate republican and anti-elitist implications; for while the early manual labor school movement was concerned with the undeveloped physical faculties of theological seminarians, reformers and labor radicals used the same principle of symbiotic faculties to promote higher education for workers of both sexes, and to confront class and gender discrimination.

Spokesmen for the American College movement, including Horace Greeley, claimed that the remedy for the poverty and dependence attached to industrial society was education that reunited intellectual work with farm work, manufacture, and domestic labor. Chapman and other labor republicans argued further that the correlation of socially necessary servile labor with the poor, the uneducated, and the working classes in general would disappear if every individual were obliged to perform mental *and* manual labor. American colleges would reverse the divorce of learning from labor that helped make physical work disreputable and create bonds of sympathy and understanding between the learned and the laboring classes, bonds necessary to the well-being of a republican society.

Women were included in this scheme, as one of the primary impulses behind the American College movement was the abolition of "domestic servitude." American colleges "should afford equal facilities and opportunities to young women as to young men," Greeley announced in 1858 at an address in honor of the laying of the cornerstone of the People's College in Havana, New York, "allowing each student, under the guidance of his or her parents, with the counsel of the faculty, to decide for him or herself what studies to pursue and . . . [in the case of the female student] what acquirements would most conduce her own preparation for and efficiency in the duties of active life."[37] Greeley justified co-education through the concept of symbiosis (not the coexistence of differences, but their mutual influence). Educating men and women together, he claimed, had the advantage of "imparting strength, earnestness, and dignity to woman, and grace, sweetness, and purity to man." Proponents of coeducational manual labor schools hoped that by educating male and female, elite and working-class students together and alike "for productive industry," menial and domestic labor might be rendered more honorable and the laboring classes more respected.[38] They believed that the commingling of the sexes, like the commingling of the classes, represented an egalitarian assault on the "barriers of caste."[39]

One of the first schools to provide women with educations and employment in creative manual labor was the New York School of Design for Women. "This institution is steadily developing the purposes for which it was organized," reported *The Crayon* in 1856. "During the past winter fifty pupils have attended its rooms; some learning to draw, some learning to engrave, and others practicing the art of wood-engraving as a profession. The fact of the latter being graduates of the school, supporting themselves by their Art, is proof of the advantages of such an institution for women [as well as] the advantages of a profession for females *combining labor and feeling,* work and Art, together, so as to make both compensating to the individual."[40]

According to this report, the School of Design, organized to teach women skills and to help them find work, was creating a "profession" for women by combining art and labor. This institution was a prime example of Greeley's "moral renovation" of society because it gave women the potential to change their social and physical conditions through an employment that united "labor and feeling." In this context, feeling did not refer to the "natural" sentiment or love of beauty attached to femininity; it alluded to the "ideal"—or moral and intellectual—work needed to reunite "Art & Industry" in a capitalist economy. Women's work had to be thought of as skilled labor *and* as involving these higher faculties if it was to be well compensated.

Horace Greeley personally and publicly supported the New York School of Design for Women, which clearly had both an aesthetic and a bread-winning side, referring and recommending young aspiring artists to its directors and following their progress in his paper. In fact, the idea for the school may have been gestated in his home.

Cultural Networks

In addition to publicizing their radical ideas about art, education, and manual labor in books and newspapers, men like Chapman and Greeley shared their ideas with their peers at the "decidedly male affairs" at men's clubs, like the Century Club where artists, literary men, and "men of affairs" met to socialize and do business, and at the decidedly mixed gatherings at New York City's literary salons, where women added their ideas. "Friday evenings" at the various residences of Horace Greeley and his wife Mary Cheney were always well attended, recalled Greeley's sister Esther Cleveland. "Nearly all the men and women of note at that time" were to be found in their parlors.[41] Among the guests at these gatherings were editors of popular newspapers and magazines, Universalist pastors and their intellectual wives, and numerous literary contributors to the *Tribune*, including Elizabeth F. Ellet ("in 1836 a handsome bride, who had come up from the South and was contributing translations from the French and German" to the *New Yorker*), and Madame Botta (the poet Anne Charlotte Lynch), who held her own Saturday night soirées for writers, artists, musicians, actors and actresses, where the portraitist Hermina Dassell "was often seen."[42] At the Greeleys' "Friday evenings," men and women laced their discussion of arts and letters with talk of reform and community service, including the benefits of arts education for working men and women.

In the early 1850s an industrial design school movement, instigated by reformers impressed by the South Kensington Museum and its schools in London, emerged in American cities.[43] Interested in the opportunities and commercial value higher education in the arts might offer Americans, philanthropists in Philadelphia, Boston, and New York City founded similar institutes and schools of design for workers and women.[44] Like Greeley and many others among his guests, Mary Morris Hamilton (granddaughter of Alexander Hamilton) and her cousin and brother-in-law George L. Schuyler (grandson of Revolutionary General Philip Schuyler) were greatly impressed by the productions of European schools of design displayed at the 1851 World's Fair in London.[45] Assisted by "other enthusiasts of New York City," Hamilton and Schuyler began their school with the pecuniary purpose of providing "the more cultivated class of women" with the means "to earn a living by the practice of some of the branches [of art] taught in it, or to become teachers in other schools."[46] These reformers and professionals regarded art training as a solution to the deteriorating economic position of middle-class women *and* as a resource for American industrialists.

The New York School of Design for Women opened in a private residence in 1852 and moved shortly thereafter to 436 Broadway (at the corner of Broome Street), where it could accommodate larger classes. Many of the first students to attend were brought to the school by Hamilton's circle of friends and relatives, who also served as the first board of managers.[47] Alice Donlevy described the school's students as old and young—"mature women who acted as protectors to the few pretty young ladies who were learning to draw or engrave on wood, or were preparing to teach." Donlevy "sat on her bench" with three others students and learned to engrave under the tutelage of Miss Gulielma Field.[48]

Curricula at the New York School of Design reflected a radical shift away from the type of art education women learned at female seminaries. Rather than preparing ladies to perform domestic chores with taste and skill, the goal of the school was to educate them for art-related employment, much of which was industrially based. Pupils were taught "elementary drawing with reference to furnishing original designs for manufactures and other purposes where ornamental designs are required." Lessons also were given in "Wood and Steel Engraving, Lithography, or in whatever branches are found to be most advantageous and profitable."[49] This industrial curricula set the New York School of Design apart from other design schools open to women in the city, none of which listed engraving, printmaking, or designing for manufacture as course options. For example, "Miss Dwight's School of Design, No. 569 Broadway," advertised on the same page of the *Tribune* as Hamilton's school, offered "the best instruction . . . in the arts of Drawing and Painting, at $5 for a term of twenty lessons. Payments advanced." This limited offering suggests that the "ladies" who trained at the New York School of Design probably had more in common with Miss Dwight the art teacher than with her students.[50]

Managers of the New York School of Design believed that a basic foundation in drawing and other mechanical skills would make women with "a feeling for beauty" employable artists, but some allies insisted this kind of art education was not enough. In an article published in the *New-York Daily Tribune* a few months after the School of Design opened, Elizabeth Palmer Peabody—writer, education reformer, aesthetic theorist, transcendentalist, and associationist—commended the founders for recognizing that New York City, a city rich in manufactories, was a perfect place to raise a subscription for an industrial art school. But she warned that the philanthropic aims of the school could undermine its ultimate goal to serve as an occupational aid. Women being trained in industrial arts, she claimed, needed to know the "intellectual philosophy" that supported the creation of fine art. "The most ignorant and unscientific are susceptible of delight in perfect beauty," wrote Peabody. "But they cannot analyze their delight, and often attribute to one cause what comes from another." Women must be educated by artists who have a conscious knowledge of the theory and principles of art, "even in a metaphysical form," if they are to transform their taste and skill into designs that are "more beautiful" than those imported from Europe. They must understand that the laws of design and fine arts are the same.[51]

The great manufacturers of New York City will not "subscribe money *to give poor women employment,* but to make for themselves a resource for their manufactures," she explained. "There is doubtless a larger development, at present, of the sentiment of benevolence than of love of art . . . more purse-strings will loosen at the call of Benevolence than of Beauty. But it is no less true that beauty will not '*stoop* to conquer.'" What the New York School of Design needed was a director who could explain to pupils the aesthetic principles that lay behind the industrial skills they were expected to master. "Designing is not imitation of the artistic creations of others," she advised the *Tribune*'s readers. "In designing, much more must the mind go before the hand. To learn the laws of beauty, which is the same thing as to learn the laws of the highest delight, a certain portion of intellectual philosophy is involved, and the teacher who is to guide the minds that are to guide the pencils of young designers, must have this intellectual philosophy, and be able to impart it."[52]

Peabody was particularly critical of the directors' decision to hire as principal Miss L. Cordelia Chase, a "Teacher of Drawing and Design," and to have her guide the students through "the Pestalozzian system," a quick and easy course of study, in which students were taught to draw spatial form through the rendering of simplified, familiar objects. Heinrich Pestalozzi (1746–1827) was a Swiss education theorist who developed a system and method for teaching children from Jean Jacques Rousseau's ideas of stage-related learning. The Pestalozzian system included "object lessons," using familiar objects to teach the child simplified concepts of number and language, and what Pestalozzi called "the ABC's of spatial form." "[T]he Pestalozzian system is at best only good for infant learners," Peabody admonished, "whose highest appreciation of the art of drawing is to be of machinery, furniture, and other mechanical forms. Its manipulation is a positive drawback upon the power to create beauty."[53]

Peabody disapproved of the New York School of Design's pedagogical plan on both theoretical and political grounds. In her 1849 *Aesthetic Papers,* she had argued that aesthetics, or the theory of the beautiful, had to be enlarged into "a component and indivisible part in all human creations which are not mere works of necessity; in other words, which are based on idea, as distinguished from appetite."[54] All human labor could rise to the degree of creative genius, she contended a few years later. "Fine Art, that is, architecture, sculpture, painting and music, are now the forms of this creative activity; but not all, for every form of human activity, even individual formation of character, will become Fine Art when principles of eternal order and beauty, for the use and pleasure of men, shall be embodied in them."

In her brief introduction to a lecture by Cardinal Wiseman, Peabody replaced the term "workingmen" with "working-people" and noted that "Those who are interested in the establishment of Schools of Design in our country could not ask a better presentation of the importance of their cause."[55]

The problem with the Pestalozzian system was that it did not give students "a conscious knowledge of the theory and principles of art," and, therefore, perpetuated a distinction between the fine and applied or decorative arts. In the academic discourse of art, those objects used to adorn people and homes were termed "applied," "decorative," or "secondary" arts. Ruskin countered that the inferiority of decorative art was not inherent but arose from the "general law" that if the usage of a thing should cause it to be injured, worn out, or torn, then it is better to apply to it a more consistent ornament, for instance a zigzag, than a more natural ornament, such as a landscape. But in European academic discourse, aesthetic hierarchy was maintained "by attributing to the decorative arts a lesser degree of intellectual effort or appeal and a greater concern with manual skill and utility" and manipulated to exclude women and artisans, whose art work was more likely to take a "decorative" or "useful" form.[56]

We must "give what may be called the rudiments of Art to every one, if possible," Peabody proclaimed, in a pamphlet entitled *The Identification of the Artisan and Artist*: "we must not satisfy ourselves with the idea that we can educate a great number of artisans to a middling degree of artistic feeling, in the hope that thereby we may influence the character of our manufactures; but we must endeavor to combine the two, to bring down the high Art to mingle with the lower, in the feeling that it is the common interest and duty of artists to improve the productive arts, *and to carry into actual work—not merely into design*—the powers which they possess."[57] "The economical ends which the School of Design is to serve," Peabody advised in the *Tribune*, "can only be effectively attained by the production of designs which are as beautiful if not more beautiful than those which our manufacturers import from other countries."[58] And in those countries, artisans and artists, female and male, were given the same educations.

A Teacher for the Head and Hand

The directors of the New York School of Design heeded Peabody's advice. A few months after her letter appeared in the *Tribune*, Chase invited artist/

engraver Henry Herrick to teach classes at the school, and in 1856 he replaced her as the school's director. Herrick offered his students in practice
what Peabody and Ruskin advocated in theory. "Henry W. Herrick was a
master in white line engraving, and knew every expression a line could
give," recalled Donlevy.[59] He encouraged his pupils to invent their own designs, even though at that time engraving was an art form most frequently
used to copy other works. "If you intend the fullest expression of humanity
that art can give," he advised them, "draw from Life." Looking back at the
art training she received under him, Donlevy realized that Herrick was a
desirable teacher and highly successful artist in the 1850s for the same reasons he was almost forgotten in 1910: "His manner and habits were conservative. His aims for women were radical. His influence was ideal."[60] In
Herrick the artisan and artist were unified.

Like other artists of his generation, Herrick was drawn to New York
City's thriving cultural milieu while still a young artist. Moving from Manchester, New Hampshire, in 1844, he immediately began studying in the antique class at the National Academy of Design, where he met Benjamin J.
Lossing, an engraver and historian who later recommend him for the job at
the New York School of Design. Lossing was interested in women's higher
education and, jointly with Samuel F. B. Morse, in the 1860s experimented
with the idea of incorporating studio art classes and a gallery into Vassar
College. Six months later Herrick got his first art job engraving Felix O. C.
Darley's illustrations for Appleton & Company's publications. By 1849 he
was designing and engraving for a list of publishers, including Harper &
Brothers, the American Tract Society, Carter and Brothers, and the American Bank Note Company.[61] Among the works Herrick helped design and
engrave during these years was Chapman's *American Drawing Book*.

By the time Herrick joined the New York School of Design in 1853 he
was a well-known and successful wood-block engraver. This job was his
first teaching position and the experience made him a passionate advocate
of women's right to art educations and employment, despite the dire situation facing male artists and engravers at the time. Herrick took a studio at
Broadway and Broome across the street from the school, and came to teach
classes three times a week for two hours. Alice Donlevy recalled with admiration the way Herrick set up shop and initiated professional relationships
between female artists and New York publishers: "It was Mr. Herrick's plan
to appoint Miss Field and Miss Tooker as all-day teachers, ready to teach
those who needed instruction and to receive orders for engraving on wood,
to collect the money, to pay each engraver, deducting a commission to add

to the funds of the school and to help pay expenses. Besides this, Mr. Herrick asked Mrs. Corinne B. Nye, a native Canadian lady, who came from a highly cultured family and was an art collector with a fine library and an income, to represent the school whenever necessary. She went with Miss Field to publishers and business firms."[62]

Herrick's decision to run his classes like a business was innovative and necessary in the 1850s, as female engravers represented competition to male artists struggling under difficult economic conditions. Wood engraving was "a business hitherto monopolized by men," acknowledged Donlevy, and those men entering the trade objected when Herrick and later the Cooper Union opened engraving classes exclusively for women. "'Keep them out, else they will interfere with our bread and butter.' This was the cry then against woman's higher art education." Herrick's plan worked, Donlevy recalled, because "there were some exceptions among painters and publishers, and some celebrities of that time."[63] Still, in 1853, artists who taught women how to compete with men went against the grain.

At the School of Design, Herrick's job was to turn art into "an honourable profession for women of talent and culture"; but his pupils remembered him for doing far more. Donlevy admired his ability to imbue art with the dignity of artisanal skill, the aesthetics of the ideal, and the virtues of republicanism. "He felt, and made all under his jurisdiction feel, that the School of Design was an experiment, and that it could only achieve success by the most earnest and ideal endeavor of all." In defending the higher education in art for women, he "courageously confronted the prejudices of the large majority of a nation." He was "a good man, a refined American, a public-spirited citizen, and a Defender of the Faith in Human Progress," who "knew how to cultivate a sense of public spirit among women."[64]

Between 1852 and 1856, the New York School of Design thrived as Herrick brought to the school both his expertise and connections to the academic and publishing worlds. Interest in the school and the students' success in finding jobs generated positive attention in daily newspapers, popular weeklies, art journals, and books about female employment. In particular, "there were many descriptions of the school and its aim and results published in the *New York Tribune*," recalled Donlevy. Greeley had great respect for Herrick and showed it by sending "the best educated of the *Tribune* staff to visit the school."[65] Press coverage helped fill the classes to overflowing and interest other reformers in the venture.

During the panic of 1857, the New York School of Design struggled to keep afloat financially. Costs of running the school were mostly paid for by voluntary subscriptions collected from friends of the directors and tuition did not bring in much revenue, as instruction was offered either free or at low rates. Other art schools suffering from the panic raised their price of tuition and altered their curricula. Henry Tuckerman, for instance, upped the cost of his School of Design from five to ten dollars in 1857 and discontinued teaching designing for manufacturers, claiming: "There is no lack either of pupils or talent, but American manufacturers find it much cheaper to appropriate French and English designs to their own uses than to pay our artists for doing them."[66] Unwilling to give up on the objective of offering poor women superior art educations, Herrick and the school's managers devised several schemes for raising money, including a series of public lectures by "six silver-tongued orators from New England and New York."[67] But while these lectures received an enthusiastic response, they did not solve the school's financial problems. So, Herrick and a few of the school's managers and students got together and worked out a plan for interesting the father of Amelia Cooper Hewitt (one of the managers) in taking over the school.

Peter Cooper was an inventor, manufacturer, philanthropist, and Jacksonian Democrat, who called himself a "mechanic of New York City." With almost no formal education, Cooper prospered as a young man by working as a grocer, founding the Trenton Iron Works in New Jersey in 1828, and inventing and manufacturing things like equipment to cut cloth, glue, and steel and telegraph wire. His success was linked to his public-spirited aims. He always used the best methods and ingredients for his products and treated his workers fairly. He was active in civic politics, including the Common Council, Civic Reform Party, Citizens' Association, Mechanics Society, and Public School Society. As a New York City civic reformer, he worked to free firemen and policemen from political interference, to ensure an adequate water supply and better sanitation, to improve prison conditions, and to furnish public education for the poor. In 1876, Cooper also unsuccessfully sought the presidency as a Greenback Party candidate.[68]

A strong adherent of liberal republicanism, Cooper was among the first nineteenth-century Americans to proclaim that wealth was a trust. Property is sacred only "so long as the rights of others are not infringed," he told Cooper Union students in 1871: "the production of wealth is not the work of any one man and the acquisition of great fortunes is not possible without the cooperation of multitudes of men; . . . therefore the individuals to whose lot these fortunes fall . . . should never lose sight of the fact that as they hold them by the will of society expressed in statute law, [they] should administer them as trustees for the benefit of society as inculcated by the moral law." Cooper lived these ideals. His willingness to donate his fortune to the public good while he was alive was singular, and his commitment to free education for workers and woman was groundbreaking.[69]

Americans like Cooper were driven by a concept of social duty that relied on what one historian has termed "egalitarian moralism," a system of beliefs derived from traditional republicanism, Christian ethics, and liberalism.[70] Advocates of free labor and industrial reform, Whigs like Greeley and Democrats like Cooper operated under a nonpartisan optimistic faith in democratic equality and economic freedom and a humanitarian belief in the integrity and perfectibility of mankind.[71] They heartily embraced the doctrine of individual rights, but not a self-serving individualism. For them individual liberty was inextricably connected to the freedom, equality, and sovereignty of the people. This generation recognized that capitalist economic activity was often guided more by "extreme individual selfishness" than democratic liberalism, but did not believe that such possessive individualism was an inevitable consequence of capitalism.[72]

This Enlightenment-derived concept of individualism was complemented by Protestant Evangelical social teachings (and also Jewish thought) that connected liberty to duty. Unitarians and Quakers, in particular, believed that individual freedom was connected to divine natural law and that all the rights human beings possessed derived from, depended on, and were constrained by a framework of objective duty. Because the universe was fundamentally good, they argued, man's original nature was animated through love, home, and the desire to do good. This same reconciling of morality and reason led many Americans to praise and sanction the free-market economy as a wellspring for virtue rather than for the unregulated pursuit of self-interest.[73]

Like many other artisans reared in the early republic, Cooper felt that his own lack of higher education had placed him at a disadvantage. It also obliged him to remedy that deficiency in others. In the 1830s he became intrigued by the General Society of Mechanics' efforts to educate boys and girls together and to help apprentices help themselves. He also was fascinated to hear about European lyceums and mechanic institutes that featured lectures on science "applied to the common purposes of life." "I then determined to do what I could to secure to the youth of my native city and country the benefits of such an institution," he recalled, "and throw its doors open at night so that the boys and girls of this city, who had no better opportunity than I had to enjoy means of information, would be enabled to improve and better their condition, fitting them for all the various and useful purposes of life."[74]

Cooper envisioned his school replacing the lopsided training of the master/apprentice system with a higher form of education suited to a new age. "Machinery has, in a great measure, driven out the old trades, and the discipline of the old apprentice system has passed away. Our youth in the industrial classes begin life under very different auspices." Common schools did not solve the problem because too many children "must go to some work at the age of ten or twelve . . . before they have acquired even the rudiments of a good education."[75]

This situation was particularly troublesome for girls who rarely had the advantage of apprenticeship and were easily exploited by their employers, and also for "young women of refinement and general culture" thrown upon their own resources by "the peculiar conditions and characteristics of American life."[76] "All I want," Cooper was remembered often saying, "is that these poor women shall earn decent and respectable livings, and especially that they shall be kept from marrying bad husbands."[77] Female contemporaries realized that Cooper's concern for middle-class women was paternalistic. "That women were often imposed upon, were ill-used and broken down, he had a lively conviction," recalled Susan Carter, who headed the School of Design in 1872, "and all his chivalry and sense of fatherly protection were enlisted to save them, so far as he could, from these ordinary misfortunes." But they also recognized the radical thinking that backed his actions. "Mr. Cooper was perhaps as true a democrat as ever lived. I never could perceive that social distinctions made the least impression on him. . . . [M]en and women were alike interesting as they were his fellow-creatures, to whom he could be a brother man."[78]

In Cooper's mind, the unhappy marriages of middle-class women were a symptom of industrial society: "While the world is now occupied with the question of what women can be taught, their 'higher education,' and many kindred subjects, Mr. Cooper's acute genius discovered, as by intuition, many years ago, the relation of women of the middle class to society, to industries, and the family. He saw that many of them could not marry, and he realized what must be the forlorn position of a number of elderly daughters of a poor man." Cooper's chivalry lay in his desire to free women from their dependence, "to help women to be happy, independent, and virtuous."[79] But his genius lay in his ability to see that middle-class women, like mechanics, could either be saved or destroyed by industrialization and therefore belonged in his school.

The cornerstone for the edifice that would house Cooper's mechanics institute was laid in 1852, on some lots just a few blocks north of the New York School of Design for Women.[80] The nearby location was just one of the many ties existing between the two schools in 1857, when Herrick, with the help of Cooper's daughter Amelia and neighbor Henrietta Desportes Field, "planned an evening reception, for the purpose of interesting Peter Cooper in the school." Female mechanics had always been included in Cooper's night school plans, and he intended to set aside special rooms at the Institute for "ladies" wishing to study the practical and natural sciences.[81] At the reception, Cooper was "as astonished as he was pleased" with specimens of drawing and engraving by the School of Design's students "arranged on the walls and in portfolios." "[B]efore he left the house he promised an entire floor of the Cooper Institute for the higher education of women in art."[82]

The next episode of the story took place at another of New York City's cultural salons held near Cooper's Gramercy Park home. In 1853, three years after emigrating from France to New York, a painter named Henriette Deluzy-Desportes married Presbyterian minister, abolitionist, and writer Henry M. Field. In 1854, Field left his Connecticut church to become editor of the New York *Evangelist*, and the artist-writer couple began hosting an informal soirée of "inquiring minds" in their narrow brownstone at no. 102 East Eighteenth Street. Every Sunday the Fields' home became "the accepted gathering place of a variety of friends and visitors to New York," men of letters, artists, philanthropists, foreign visitors, and inventors.

Among the Fields' regular guests were Cooper, Henry's brother engineer-entrepreneur Cyrus Field, and National Academy artist and inventor Samuel Morse, who together devised the plan to lay a telegraph cable across the Atlantic at one of these gatherings. Also present were the poet William Cullen Bryant, the "brilliant preacher" Henry Ward Beecher and his famous sister Harriet, *Scribner's* author-editors Josiah Gilbert Holland and Richard Watson Gilder, and painter Eastman Johnson.[83] It was after one of these Sunday gatherings that Cooper, intrigued by a watercolor study she was drawing of "an immigrant girl with her few possessions, waiting for entrance to America," asked Mrs. Field if she would help plan the Cooper Union art school and possibly teach painting to the girls.[84] As the circumstances surrounding Cooper's decision show, New York's cultural world was close knit in the 1850s. Everyone at the School of Design, the National Academy, the Century Club, and in publishing was at the least acquainted with everyone else.[85] This network proved quite beneficial to women artists trained at the School of Design.

The New York School of Design for Women moved to the fourth floor of the Cooper Union for the Advancement of Science and Art in 1858, a year before the building was finished, and was legally incorporated when the institute officially opened in January 1859. With that move women's higher art education was merged with the reeducation of mechanics and the philosophies and goals of the antebellum generation—the Unity of Art ideal—took a material form. As news of Cooper's offer of free education spread, letters seeking admission poured in from across the country, written mostly by poor girls and women who saw in the School of Design the possibility of satisfying at last their "earnest desire" to become artists.

Chapter 3
"*Art Fever*"

In 1868, Louisa May Alcott began a story about the experiences of Psyche, a young woman trying to reconcile familial duties with artistic desires, with these words: "Once upon a time there raged in a certain city one of those fashionable epidemics which occasionally attack our youthful population. . . . it was a new disease called the Art fever, and it attacked the young women of the community with great violence."[1] Alcott's younger sister May was an aspiring artist, and Louisa drew upon May's experiences for the story.[2] "Mistaking enthusiasm for inspiration," Alcott wrote, the young artist attempted "every branch of art with youthful audacity." May later attended drawing and sculpture classes in Boston and traveled to France and England to study oil and watercolor painting. But May was not the sole inspiration for her sister's tale. Although fictional, "Psyche's Art" documents an actual phenomenon. Between 1850 and 1880, thousands of American women studied art and pursued art careers with unbending determination and high expectations (Figure 9).

Among these women was Adaline M. Knowles, the younger daughter of a struggling farmer in Cambridgeport, Massachusetts. In 1861, her sister wrote to the Cooper Union's School of Design for Women in New York City describing, diagnosing, and prescribing a cure for Knowles's suffering: "I have a young sister, age sixteen years, and for the last two years she has been so completely under the influence, or desire, to learn the art of Drawing, or Sculpture, that she has not been able to apply herself to anything, and she has not even had the slightest taste for school. She seems restless and uneasy, and is continually trying to draw, or to fashion some figures or other. She thinks that she has the elements for the one, or both. But the diciplin[e] and direction & study is what she needs, and from what I have seen of her feeble attempts, I think it may be as I have described."[3]

Knowles was accepted into the Cooper Union's program the following year, along with about 150 other women and 50 men. By 1868, the year "Psyche's Art" was published, three thousand women had passed through the

THE GIRL WHO WANTED TO BE AN ARTIST.

Figure 9. Mary E. Edwards, "The Girl Who Wanted To Be An Artist," *One Hundred & One Stories for Boys & Girls* (New York, ca. 1886). Courtesy of American Antiquarian Society.

School of Design, many of them, reported the *Revolution*, a woman's rights newspaper, having "struggled through poverty, sickness, and uncomplaining misery to obtain an artistic knowledge which would afford them remunerative employment." With that knowledge Cooper graduates gained a living "by engraving, designing for manufacturers, illustrations of books, coloring photographs, and as artists, where they have the requisite talent."[4] Clearly, artistic aspiration was a common affliction among girls of May Alcott and Adaline Knowles's generation.

Who were these aspiring artists? Why were they so susceptible to "Art fever"? What did they think art study would do for them? And, why did their families, social observers, and institution builders take their aspirations seriously? Knowles's sister believed Adaline deserved an art education because eventually she would "be dependent upon her own exertions for a livelihood" *and* because she longed for it. These two rationales—need and desire—appear in almost every letter of application or reference to the School of Design. They motivated women to leave the home and enter art careers.

The joining of economic and emotional life in letters of application to the Cooper Union School of Design ties women's artistic aspirations to the aspirations of degraded artisans, poor wage laborers, and starving seamstresses experiencing the destructive effects of industrial expansion. The reunion of "labor and feeling" was not just a prevalent motif in the stories of novelists, but also in the polemical writing and oration of newspaper editors, labor and women's rights activists, aesthetic philosophers, and education reformers. Alcott and Knowles were members of a generation trying to find its way in a rapidly changing society, a workforce looking for security in a precarious market economy where panics and depressions threatened their families with poverty and misery at every turn. For them art study was not a frivolous activity; it was education and training that promised women "honorable and comfortable livelihoods" at the end. Art was a calling with the possibility of fulfilling very personal needs, ideals, and passions. It had intellectual and emotional content lacking in most female employments. Art was also a virtuous occupation that met the economic necessities of family *and* the aesthetic requirements of American industry. Moreover, art work satisfied the democratic principles of the nation by making individual accomplishment equal public service.

The young women who applied to the Cooper Union School of Design belonged to what Louisa May Alcott called "that large class of women who, moderately endowed with talents, earnest and true-hearted, are driven by necessity, temperament, or principle out into the world to find support, happiness, and homes for themselves."[5] While some women may have felt circumscribed by their sex, those who became artists acted on alternative ideas and conventions. They discovered their abilities and love of art, and internalized the political and philosophical knowledge of their era, in many of the same arenas as boys: at home, in books and newspapers, at church, and in educational institutions. By listening carefully to what women artists say about themselves and their art, therefore, we can hear the most common ideas of their day.

Necessity

Of the three agents that drove women to art school—"necessity, temperament, and principle"—necessity was the most compelling. Mid-nineteenth-century women artists came from a wide variety of backgrounds and circumstances, but most were children of the middling classes who took up the profession when forced to earn a living. They were the daughters and wives, orphans and widows of degraded artisans, struggling farmers, poor ministers, and distressed merchants who fell victim to the economic upheavals of the 1840s and 1850s, and to the Civil War. They grew up in both urban and rural areas across the country. They were native born and immigrants, occasionally black or American Indian, downward and upwardly mobile. Most came from Christian backgrounds, quite a few were Quaker, some were Jewish. The median age of those entering the School of Design was about eighteen, although some were girls as young as ten and others young women pushing spinsterhood at twenty-six and older. The majority was single: some were unmarried, some widowed. Many of them worked outside of school part-time to pay for room and board, a few lived with relatives and studied full-time. In the 1850s and 1860s, such women filled New York City's schools of design, outnumbering by the thousands the female "amateurs" who studied art for pleasure or as an "accomplishment." Financial distress, not middle-class privilege, gave these women the justification and opportunity to become artists.

The Panic of 1857 drove representatives from every class of woman to take up the pen or brush when their families had financial problems, or had suffered the death, sickness, or aging of providers. Parents and guardians who could not support unmarried daughters encouraged their artistic endeavors, realizing that in a market economy girls, like boys, needed to acquire skills. Many women supported not only themselves but also invalid or aged parents, siblings, and children. The daughters of artisans made up one segment of the young women applying to the Cooper Union. In his letter of introduction, H. S. Vrooman identified himself as a working man from Hoboken endeavoring to help his daughter Ada learn a trade: "Being to[o] busy at work to come with my daughter myself. Send this note to say that her name . . . was entered the first of this month for a place in the school of design for women. . . . She is desirous of qualifying herself for teaching, and drawing as [a profession]. By admitting her to the benefits of your institution you will confer a favor on a worthy daughter of poverty and oblige her father." Annie Delano, the daughter of a cabinetmaker, "an industrious man and good mechanic," was encouraged by her relative General Swift to attend the School of Design when her parents fell into "narrow circumstances." Adaline Knowles's sister, Mrs. L. A. Gillan, supported Knowles's desire to study art so that she might escape the conditions faced by her rural farming family.[6]

Immigrant women and widows were encouraged to take up art as well. During the 1830s and 1840s, immigration primarily from Ireland and Germany dramatically changed the composition of the American workforce and contributed to the rapidly growing population in American cities. The newcomers supported themselves mainly through physically demanding unskilled manual labor, including domestic service, but those with skills found work in manufactories. Rev. Carrigan from the Office of the Irish Emigrant Society may have had such work in mind when he wrote that if Helen A. Daley were admitted as a pupil to the School of Design a "worthy person" would be able to "earn an honest and honourable support." Mary Morris Hamilton appealed to the Cooper Union in behalf of a member of "the industrious poor," a woman "in poor health" with "a mother and invalid sister very much dependent upon her earnings," who already taught art at public school. She "requires besides, private pupils for her support," wrote Hamilton, who requested the "lady teacher" be granted permission to hold classes at the rooms in the Cooper Union building on Saturdays.[7] A "well educated, pious, and refined" widow hoped to obtain "employment to support her family of small children," wrote her referee Virginia Penny. "She draws and paints very well," and wants to "turn her talents to account."[8]

The low pay attached to most women's work encouraged even those who were already employed to seek art educations so as to improve their prospects and earn more money. Lucie A. Hale, the daughter of a Congregational minister "(you know they are not often troubled with much money)," had been working for three years as an assistant art teacher at Southold Academy on Long Island when she applied to the Cooper Union in 1860.[9] Burdened with his deceased parents' debt and the support of younger siblings, J. B. Graham sought assistance for his sister despite the fact that she already worked part-time at a country school. Our sister "displays more than ordinary talent for drawing and Painting," he wrote from Schenectady, but "can receive no further instruction in those branches she desires to pursue at any of the academies about and wishes to avail herself of instruction at a higher acdy. She has been teaching all of the past year in order to save funds for that purpose but the wages around [here] are so small that she has not been able to save much. Another sister who earns her means by the same laborious means offers to help her some and I will endeavor to contribute my mite."[10] The Graham siblings were willing to contribute their own wages because they believed by enhancing her art education they would make their sister independent.

Lucie Hale and Miss Graham probably received their first art lessons at seminary. Between 1749 and 1871 private single-sex seminaries, academies, and colleges were the prevailing type of institution for girls' secondary education. A few cities maintained girls' public high schools but education beyond the common school usually took place at private institutions that charged tuition and board.[11] Most of the girls who attended were from financially secure families. At northern seminaries suitable instruction for females was moral and religious, literary, domestic, and ornamental. Girls learned spelling, reading, writing, English-grammar, arithmetic, geography, rhetoric, and composition.[12] They also were trained in the fine arts of music, needlework pictures, drawing, and watercolors.[13] Young women mastered these "accomplishments" to sharpen their "natural" female character traits and enhance their desirability as wives.[14]

Despite the emphasis on amateur practice, art skills learned at seminary could be turned to financial benefit when economic pressures made it necessary to work. Some women employed these skills to help their families through hard times, while for others they became the individual's or family's sole means of survival, especially after the death of a father or husband. The work of seminary-trained artists, both in production and teaching, generally took place in the home (or another female institution), it was often part-time or temporary, and the money received, usually less than a living wage, was rarely recorded. This "shadow economy" is discernible in the letters of Cooper applicants and also in notices of exhibitions, biographies of artists, and pages of journals and books published in the early nine-teenth century.[15] Art production allowed many middle-class women to stay home when economic problems might have sent them out to find jobs and therefore did not disturb the belief that capitalism created a vast society of middle-class families in which husbands worked and wives did not. Semi-nary-trained artists sold their work privately and through local and regional exhibitions. Fellow townsfolk often thought of a seminary-trained neighbor as the community artist, commissioning her to capture local scenes, per-haps a countryseat or old courthouse before its demolition, in watercolors or oils. Some seminary-trained artists supported their families designing fancy needlework patterns; a few sold drawings or paintings to publishers for reproduction in newspapers, journals, or books; and many became pri-vate tutors or seminary teachers.[16]

In the 1850s, public schools, private students, and industrialists alike had begun to demand art teachers who had mastered modern techniques of drawing and design.[17] Women applied to the School of Design to obtain that higher education. Even teaching art to other women, a job that seemed a reasonable extension of a middle-class lady's role and education, required more than talent and taste. Helen Burt, who had taught classes at the semi-nary from which she graduated, considered herself well prepared to teach anywhere in her first letter to the Cooper Union: "I wish to fit myself for a Teacher of Painting or professional Artist and thought perhaps I could get a situation as an assistant teacher in the School of Design and get sufficient compensation to pay for my board and tuition." But by the time she wrote her second letter, Burt had recognized her deficiencies: "I am now exceed-ingly desirous to go to N.Y. and enter the industrial class . . . to fit myself to teach painting. I have had considerable experience in Pastel Painting and have painted in Oil but have had no instruction."[18] By 1860, accomplish-ments learned at seminary or acquired through independent study no longer counted as art training.

The number of women with some higher educations applying to schools of design increased in the 1850s, when two severe depressions, one in 1853 and one following the panic of 1857, added the daughters of once-successful merchants and professionals to the pool of women in need of employment and independence. In 1860 Frances Bunce cited her father's "pecuniary embarrassment" as justification for her application to design school and impatient desire to study painting.[19] Bianca Bondi's father, a banker, "lost his fortune" in 1857. This desperate financial situation drove the Bondi family into totally new circumstances. "When he came here" from Dresden, she recalled, "he was associated with all the leading writers and thinkers, and was for years the editor of the Hebrew Leader." But because of the "'financial panic,' . . . I, at the age of fourteen, entered Cooper Union, then the only recognized art school in the city."[20] The economic situation of this class of aspiring artists validated their decision to pursue art as a profession rather than an "amateur" avocation.

Trying to turn talent or taste into a career when a father or husband was financially ruined was a widespread phenomenon among women in the Northeast. It was also a popular theme in midcentury fiction. In Nathaniel Hawthorne's 1859 romance, *The Marble Faun*, the leading female character, Miriam, attracts considerable notice as a painter. Miriam is, however, unwilling to disclose her origins. Among the many possible explanations her fellow artists conjure up for Miriam's career choice are "romantic fables" of escape from undesired betrothals and inheritance. But those with a more "probable air," the narrator notes, were the "surmises . . . that Miriam was the daughter of a [Jewish] merchant or financier, who had been ruined in a great commercial crisis: and, possessing a taste for art, she had attempted to support herself by the pencil, in preference to the alternative of going out as governess."[21] Hawthorne modeled the character of Miriam on the successful American sculptor Harriet Hosmer, with whom he became acquainted while living in Italy. Having "determined to rely entirely upon her art for a support" after her father suffered financial reverses in the 1850 panics, Hosmer permanently established herself as a professional sculptor in Rome.[22]

Letters of application to art school abound with allusions to financial ruin. "My niece," explained S. G. Hitchcock, is "left both fatherless and motherless." "Her father, Simon O. Oley, died in Utica in 1857 leaving an estate of $28,000. By some mismanagement, the children are likely to become dependent upon their own exertions." Friends and relatives of children and spouses assumed that art study would enable women eventually to support themselves. Miss Margaret Thompson's relations allowed her to claim "great refinement, cultivation and character." She applied to the School of Design "to qualify herself as a teacher" and thereby cope with "a great change of circumstances."[23]

Temperament

Despite the financial advantages and job opportunities attached to the idea of art education, art work was not for everyone. It required a certain natural ability and temperament. "It is folly for any one to devote herself to art as a career, unless she has some genius and a fondness for it," warned Virginia Penny, an advisor on women's employments.[24] But what exactly was an artistic temperament? Evidence of aptitude, a "feeling for beauty," and a spirited yet serious demeanor were the main characteristics. Every Cooper Union applicant who claimed she *needed* to depend upon her own exertions for support also believed she possessed one or more of those traits.

Necessity forced women out of the home and into employment, but earnest desire directed them to art. Ann A. Saw hoped her financial situation would allow her to satisfy a craving at the Cooper Union: "My father's means are limited, and I know of no other way that I can acquire that knowledge which I long to possess." Mary E. Terry, forced to make a living, felt justified at last to fulfill a lifelong aspiration: "It has been from early childhood my earnest desire to become an artist but my circumstances have been such as to prevent me from doing anything more than to spend now and then an hour in copying with pencils, crayons, or in pastel." Lizzie S. Dickey characterized herself as "A Lover of Art who has already paid some attention to the subject." Lucie Hale was "very anxious" to study at the School of Design for two reasons: "the first and most important is I wish to make a teacher of it. the second is I love it *very much*: but I am not able to meet the expenses."[25]

Girls with a precocious ability in drawing, young women with a lively or deeply sensitive nature, and women with an innate understanding of artistic principles all applied to art school. Annie Delano's referee pronounced her a "young lady with much spirit" who attracted attention "to her uncommon natural facility with the pencil." Ada E. Vrooman's father highlighted her "artistic genius and mental maturity." And Knowles's eclectic, undisciplined attention to "Animal drawing & also to females & children," as well as her "taste for copying & design" recommended her for admission.[26]

Beginning in the early modern period precocity in drawing became a traditional signifier of artistic temperament. Common to biographies of famous artists is the discovery of genius in the untrained child by family, friends, or teachers. Such anecdotes signified that the artist in question belonged to the community of geniuses; and, in the nineteenth century, they proved the Romantic notion that aesthetic ability was innate. In a biographical sketch of Lilly Martin Spencer written in 1859, art historian Elizabeth Ellet begins by transforming her subject into the child prodigy. "When between eight and nine, she was taken to the old Academy of Design. There she selected the 'Ecce Homo' as a special subject for imitation. The girl-pupils laughed at her taste, and Lily, abashed, burst into tears. Mr. Dunlap, [the teacher], . . . reproved the girls, and predicted that the young stranger would be remembered when they were all forgotten."[27] Knowles had "never been shown anything at all about drawing," yet her sister had "faith that she may yet become an artist if she could only receive the proper kind of instruction." Precocity was a sign of her genius.

Innate genius was not a necessary signifier of artistic temperament, however. In fact the idea was controversial in midcentury America, where genre painter George Caleb Bingham identified a convergence of the "various and conflicting opinions as to what constitutes the ideal in Art."[28] For Louise A. Bradbury, one of Herrick's former students at the New York School of Design, the true artist was a person who recognized her natural talents ("spontaneous growths") in art and nurtured them. "I don't deprecate work, I am not one of those who look with admiring eyes on those erratic geniuses who are quite at the mercy of 'moods' and 'fits of inspiration,' and I have no patience with those who are so bigoted as not to be willing to learn any style of art . . . I have not time during my short and infrequent round in my art-garden to spend much labor on very unpromising soil."[29]

Bradbury's theory encapsulated an idea of genius that fluctuated between divine inspiration and the imitation of nature. American artists such as history and literature painter Washington Allston, who brought Romanticism to America, stressed the transforming power of the artist, his almost godlike ability to create works in which "objects perceived by the senses are transformed and transcended by the moral imagination or the Soul [of the artist] in tune with the Infinite Harmony of Creation"; while artists such as Bingham, who shared the convictions of antebellum "realists," insisted that "the ideal in Art is but the impressions made upon the mind of the artist by the beautiful or Art subjects in external nature." "Art power," Bingham maintained, "is the ability to receive and retain these impressions so clearly and distinctly as to be able to duplicate them upon our canvas."[30]

These "conflicting opinions" caused the internal tension in the definition of artistic temperament expressed by women applying to the Cooper Union. Bingham's artist genius was a master of perception and skill, who perceived the "soul" in his subjects rather than possessing a superior soul himself. This kind of "Art power" was more teachable. Therefore, Bingham's more democratic ideal was more accessible to women. Yet, the metaphysical idea of artistic genius, as expressed by Allston, excited the longing that drove young artists to the studio or school of design. Its possibility made art more than necessity. Hale, who applied to the Cooper Union because she loved art so very much, also considered it a prerequisite that she had "practiced drawing more or less from a child." Each aesthetic philosophy described an aspect of the artistic temperament Hale thought she would need to succeed as a professional artist.

The two concepts of genius also suggested particular artist types to the mid-nineteenth-century popular imagination. In *The Marble Faun*, Hawthorne describes two kinds of woman artist and the main characteristics of her artistic temperament. Miriam, a painter of original scenes, is the inspired artist whose remarkable "imaginative sympathies" cause her to suffer for her art. She begins each sketch "with a passionate and fiery conception of the subject" and ends "in utter scorn, as it were, of the feeling which at first took such powerful possession of her hand." Hilda, the copyist, is the skilled artist whose power lies in her "depth of appreciation." "Assisted by the delicate skill and accuracy of her slender hand," she is able to execute the ideal a great Master had conceived in his imagination, "but had not so perfectly succeeded in putting upon canvas."[31] Each woman's genius for art lay in her sensibility and choice of genre; each represented an art ideal. But the antebellum American ideal combined the two.

Many young women had imbibed these conflicting ideals before they applied to the Cooper Union. Reminiscing about her introduction to the School of Design, Mary Hallock combined romantic and artisanal terms. As a child, she mused, "I began to be called the artist of the family," and at sixteen "was sent away to learn the trade. . . . Sarah took my artless efforts over to Mrs. Cudahy, who was principal of the school that year, and showed her the desire of the moth for the star (I think one of them was my Lady of Shallot). What ever they did show, Mrs. Cudahy made the most of. . . . I was hailed as a budding genius and squeezed into the school . . . my apprenticeship had begun."[32] By juxtaposing the words "artist" and "trade," "genius" and "apprenticeship," Hallock evoked the Unity of Art. Furthermore, her sample work, "the Lady of Shallot," suggests that she was familiar with the English Pre-Raphaelite Brotherhood, a group of painters championed by John Ruskin who sought to revive the traditions of medieval artisanship.[33]

British artists and American girls shared a love for the poems of Alfred Lord Tennyson, who retold medieval history and legend for a nineteenth-century audience. American poets retold colonial history for the same audience. John Greenleaf Whittier's poem *Mabel Martin, A Harvest Idyl* (1860) reveals its debt to Tennyson by turning into legend the story of the daughter of a woman hung as a witch in Salem, and the illustrations to the 1875 edition drawn by Hallock show the influence of the Pre-Raphaelites. Mabel Martin, a shunned girl living out her days in rural isolation, is championed by and in the end weds the town's most important citizen. Hallock's frontispiece depicts Mabel as a spinster at her wheel: the spindle of thread and the woman's slumped body expressing the unending trials she must endure (Figure 10). This picture echoes the illustration to the 1857 edition of Tennyson's *Lady of Shallot*, based on a design originally sketched in 1850 by William Holman Hunt, a member of the English Pre-Raphaelite Brotherhood. Hunt's "Lady of Shallot" is like Hallock's "Mabel Martin" in figure, form, and content. The posture and arms of Hallock's seated woman mirror those of Hunt's standing lady, and the spinning wheel against which she leans echoes the circular loom inside of which Hunt's figure is trapped. The attention to detail also is alike. Both artists use white line hatching to create interiors with depth and objects with surface texture, and to enhance the beauty of their compositions through obvious workmanship. In her picture, Hallock placed "Mabel Martin" at her spinning, like the "Lady of Shallot" at her weaving, two moths reaching for the star, like herself on the threshold of the Cooper Union.

Artistic temperament was conveyed if a woman's art seemed to be as much the product of inspiration, love, or desire as of need. Helen Daley, who earned a living working in Mr. Loeffler's art shop after graduating from the School of Design, found that her art education filled emotional needs as well. On the days she was "a little bit sick," Daley admitted to a colleague from her art school days, she enjoyed the "real luxury" of "painting at home."[34] Daley's feelings stemmed from metaphysical philosophy. The true artist in search of the ideal let go of the material world, and her ability to do so seemed intuitive. Even Hawthorne's copyist worked "absorbed, unconscious of everything around her, seeming to live only in what she sought to do." This transcendence was the state in which "genius burned."[35] It transformed working into a pleasurable escape from the mundane world.

Midcentury Americans did not separate the business of art from the transcendence of art; each supported the other. The object of art, whether produced by a starving artist or a businessman, always went beyond the pursuit of money. Women wanted to become artists because they believed with Hawthorne that artists "were not wholly confined within the sordid compass of practical life; they had a pursuit which, if followed faithfully

Figure 10. Mary A. Hallock, "Mabel Martin," from John Greenleaf Whittier, *Mabel Martin* (Boston, 1875), frontispiece. Personal copy.

out, would lead them to the Beautiful, and always had a tendency thitherward, even if they lingered to gather up golden dross by the wayside."[36] Annie Delano revered people who tried to make an artistic calling into a business, whether or not they were successful. She refused to accept that financial need, which propelled her into remunerative fields, was antithetical to chasing "after the will O' the-Wisp—Art." Only the artist who gave up "palleto, pens, [and] colors" to grasp the "almighty dollar," she claimed, joined the "man in the world."[37] Hawthorne claimed, "We love the artists, in every kind." "Sculptors, painters, crayon-sketchers, or whatever branch of aesthetics they adopted, were certainly pleasanter people" than those met in everyday society. That they talked about art "very much as other men talk of cotton, politics, flour-barrels, and sugar" did not exclude them from Hawthorne's "Ideal."[38] Any person who believed in the importance of art enough to try to make a living by it, no matter what branch of art or how meager a living, was an artist.

Early signs of talent, a spirited disposition, a deep sensibility, and a burning need to create were all signs of an artistic temperament. But so too were meticulous work habits and a serious demeanor. Alice Donlevy described the tone set at the New York School of Design as "very high, very earnest, very aspiring. . . . There was no daubing of paint on clothes or wall as a testimony of genius. Quickness and exquisite cleanliness in using the brush were a requisite to success in drawing on wood for engraving."[39] The renovation of the female self into a professional artist was not the same as the creation of a Bohemian artist; a woman who needed to make a living did not have the luxury to indulge her feelings, even if they were what had initially attracted her to the studio.

Donlevy's description revealed what she believed to be the woman artist's most significant quality: genius shown through earnest, aspiring work. "There was no flippant conversation. There was no attempt at Bohemian manners. True, two pretty girls did talk about their beaux at lunch time, but only then." Louisa May Alcott distinguished the female with "Art fever" from the Bohemian male in her description of the studio building where Psyche worked. As the women artists glided through the sacred halls, "bearing portfolios in hands delicately begrimed with crayon, chalk, and clay," the male artists offered them "studies from life" of "picturesque gentlemen posed before easels, brooding over master-pieces in 'a divine despair,' or attitudinizing upon couches as if exhausted by the soarings of genius."[40] Gillan expected art training to cure Knowles's brooding, not encourage it, and she worried that her sister would languish if exposed to "attitudinizing" artist types. But the requirements laid out for Cooper Union students appeased her fears. Assured that "*strict* order is, or will be, expected of *every* pupil," she enrolled her sister in "the Industrial, or Professional, class."[41]

Temperament alone would never have made a woman a candidate for the Cooper Union, as "a feeling for beauty" was not only a characteristic of the artist but had long been one of the defining traits of middle-class femininity and gentility. Many women found it necessary to downplay their "natural" sympathy for art when trying to give their artistic achievements economic value. They were not attending design school to learn the social and cultural graces needed to attract a husband; they sought to transform their accomplishments into moneymaking assets. Before the School of Design, explained Alice Donlevy, "girls were taught painting as an accomplishment." But during the financial panics and the Civil War, women in need of livelihoods forcefully criticized this practice. Donlevy recalled one young Southern lady lodging a powerful indictment when she complained: "'My father paid thousands of dollars for my education in fashionable schools in the North, but to-day I cannot earn one cent with all my accomplishments.'"[42]

The Cooper Union replaced fashionable educations that prepared women for the marriage market with training in technical skills geared toward self-support. This educational shift was backed by domestic ideology, which drew on the market economy to repudiate the patriarchal system of southern society, based on the exchange of women. Like any ideology in the making, domesticity was ambivalent and invited oppositional formulations. It relegated women to the home, but also endowed women with "internal qualities" that fitted them to act on their own volition. It therefore could just as easily encourage a woman's aspirations as stifle them. Midcentury suffragists used the social authority invested in domesticity to condemn the patriarchal system; women artists used it to defend their professional ambitions.[43]

Ironically, the economic distress of middle-class families and not their cultural pretensions gave women as a group the means and liberty to indulge their artistic temperaments. "Until the late commercial [failure] my Father has always promised to send me to a School of Design," wrote Frances M. Bunce to Abram Hewitt in 1860. "But owing to pecuniary embarrassment he has been unable to do so and cannot for two or three years to come. I do not want to wait so long."[44] Not until she had to fend for herself did Bunce gain the advantage to pursue her talents. Her need also permitted her to compare her own temperament, if not her talent, to the most famous living woman artist of her era, Rosa Bonheur. A French oil painter whose spectacular picture *The Horse Fair* (1853) was touring America at the time Bunce wrote her letter, Bonheur was a critical and financial success.[45] By choosing Bonheur, a single yet independent woman, as her "example," Bunce hinted at what many an American girl hoped a solid training in the arts would do for her. She might not become as famous as Bonheur, but she would at least gain the financial and psychological freedom that the artist represented. Nathaniel Hawthorne underscored this sentiment when he wrote: "The customs of artist-life bestow such liberty upon the [female] sex, which is elsewhere restricted within so much narrower limits." For a midcentury women like Bunce, becoming a professional artist was a way to "remove the shackles" of convention and bring her identity in line with her temperament and, oddly enough, her democratic principles.[46]

Principle

Discontented middle-class women often looked to art as a cure for ennui, and this aspect of their interest was emphasized when detractors labeled female artists "dabblers."[47] But the desire for meaningful work was not confined to the comfortable. In her 1873 semi-autobiographical novel *Work: A Story of Experience*, Louisa May Alcott explored the theme of women with lively temperaments who sought work out of a desire to lead meaningful and principled lives. "You say I am discontented, proud and ambitious, that's true, and I'm glad of it," says Christie, the protagonist. Christie's discontent stemmed from her choice between a dependent life and "this dull one made up of everlasting work, with no object but money."[48] For Christie being a "useful, happy woman" meant finding a job that would fulfill her impulse to support herself, if need be, with work that had personal and social significance. Art work offered women the possibility of finding satisfaction on both levels.

For American women living in the middle decades of the nineteenth century, leading a principled life meant becoming independent *and* contributing to their society. But how did American girls learn that they should support themselves? And how did they come to think that studying art and making a career of it was patriotic work? The answer seems to be that they read it in the popular press and heard it from the church pulpit. Carrie

Mayhew from South Framingham, Massachusetts, saw a newspaper notice of the "Cooper Institute" and decided it met her wish to find "the means of gaining a living." Pauline Backus of Grand Rapids, Michigan, said she had "several times seen descriptions and pictures of the 'Cooper Institute' [in the papers] . . . and in the 'Harpers Weekly,'" which "excited" in her "a desire to become a pupil of the Institution." After the Civil War had commenced, Emma Brace wrote from Utica, New York: "Some time ago I saw a notice in the Evangelist of the Schools of Design for Women . . . Will you please tell me about the schools? whether in the present state of the country I can make it profitable or not?"[49]

In her *Reminiscences*, Cooper Union graduate Mary Hallock [Foote] recalled how she came to her understanding of principle. As a girl, Hallock learned to think about the world in three places: at Quaker meeting where "instead of silence or mild personal testimonies . . . there was reading aloud from the Bible and printed discourses by men of note who filled the Unitarian pulpits of the day," by observing aunts and sisters who worked for pay, and from the popular press. "Children of my generation (I was born in 1847) came to their consciousness of public events at a very forcing period. It was our father's custom in the evening to read aloud to the family assembled the Congressional debates and the editorials in the *New-York Tribune*. A child of eight or nine would have been lacking in ordinary intelligence if she had not gathered some notion of what they were talking about."[50]

As they read newspapers and listened to religious and political debates, girls like Hallock learned a concept of social duty that was as compelling as economic need and artistic temperament in women's decisions to leave home in search of art educations and careers. Middle-class parents—farmers, artisans, and merchants—taught their sons and daughters that they had a moral obligation to find a means by which they could provide for themselves. Parents did not expect to support unwed children after they reached maturity. In mid-nineteenth-century America, the middle classes did not immediately separate themselves from the culture of work in an attempt to distinguish themselves from the working classes. Alcott offhandedly described this American perception of "class" in an 1867 newspaper short story, when the heroine observed: "The city was deserted by all but the wretched poor and the busy middle class, who live by daily labor."[51] For Americans, being middle class meant having work to do.

A tradition of middle-class working women arose from this sense of duty in the early nineteenth century, and was promptly *made invisible* by etiquette manuals and romances that portrayed and idealized a nonproductive role for women. Such writings, known by historians as the "cult of true womanhood," were derived and sometimes copied from British publications that served as guides for a rising upper-middle class wishing to distinguish itself from the masses.[52] In them the middle class is differentiated from the working class through the wife and daughters' freedom from work. This sentimental ideal rose in popularity in America as capitalist manufacture undermined the domestic production of women and the status of skilled manual labor. But the popular fiction written by American women at mid-nineteenth century is chock full of middle-class girls and women finding employment.[53] Even the spokeswomen for domestic ideology encouraged women to be prepared to become self-sufficient. Just after the Civil War, for instance, Catharine E. Beecher announced in an "Appeal" at the end of her *American Woman's Home* that a large portion of her next book "will be devoted to instruction, in the various ways in which women may *earn an independent livelihood*, especially in employments that can be pursued in sunlight and the open air."[54]

Many girls were raised to believe they had the same obligation as boys to make their own way. Marrying was the ideal, and families taught girls to perform domestic chores with this possibility in mind. But marriage was not the only option. Lucy Larcom, who at age eleven began working as an operative in the Lowell mills, and later supported herself as an editor, teacher, and poet, recognized that attitudes about women working outside the home shifted in the 1830s and 1840s: "In the olden times it was seldom said to little girls, as it always has been said to boys, that they ought to have some definite plan, while they were children, what to be and do when they were grown up. There was usually but one path open before them, to become good wives and housekeepers. . . . But girls, as well as boys, must have desired to cultivate and make use of their individual powers. When I was growing up, they had already begun to be encouraged to do so. We were often told that it was our duty to develop any talent we might possess."[55]

Parents who taught daughters to prepare to work often derived their belief from Judeo-Christian teaching, which connected natural rights to social duties. Larcom recalled that "the religion of our fathers overhung us children like the shadow of a mighty tree . . . we were taught to work almost like a religion."[56] Sometimes, the work ethic took on political significance. In Alcott's stories, girls are taught to work by parents whose lessons rely on the republican idea of virtue. " 'Work is wholesome,' " said Mrs. March to her daughters in *Little Women*, " 'and there is plenty for every one; it keeps us from *ennui* and mischief, is good for health and spirits, and gives us a sense of power and independence better than money or fashion.' "[57]

Daughters learned from parents, relatives and friends that economic responsibility was a part of their national heritage. In America, they were told, women were valued for their ability to work. In Alcott's novels, even a well-made marriage was the result of the health, spirits, power, and independence that accompanied wholesome work. Meeting a young woman from England for the first time, Meg, the eldest sister in *Little Women*, is embarrassed when she realizes her work as a governess represents a difference between herself and the British girl. She has been told that in England middle-class daughters do not work, because to do so would imply that their fathers were not good providers. Meg's father is certainly deficient in that department, but Mr. Brooke, Meg's suitor, is quick to deny that Meg works only out of need: "'Young ladies in America love independence as much as their ancestors did,'" he says, "'and are admired and respected for supporting themselves.'" America was better than England because it allowed women to work without losing status. "'There's no place like America for us workers, Miss Margaret,'" Brooke, who is a young teacher, reminds Meg: "and [he] looked so contented and cheerful, that Meg was shamed to lament her hard lot. 'I'm glad I live in it then. I don't like my work, but I get a good deal of satisfaction out of it after all, so I won't complain; I only wish I liked teaching as you do.'"[58] Through Mr. Brooke, Alcott informed her readers that remunerated work, not financial inheritance, gave Americans their deep sense of independence.

Alcott's combination of political and domestic ideology infused more than fiction. In an 1848 article entitled "The Sphere of Woman," published in *Union Magazine*, a journal devoted mainly to American art, Horace Greeley mocked the kind of "gallantry" which prompted men to give up to women their omnibus seats and nothing else: "Why should it stop at the coach-door? Why not step into the fancy store, the engraver's shop, and wherever else man usurps employments which women might aptly fill, and say, 'Room *here* for ladies!'"[59] According to Greeley, domestic ideology demanded that American men honor women by exhibiting a truly "chivalric remorse"—he must decline to take the advantage.[60] Let him be the first to do more than simply acknowledge "ages of gross injustice"; let him free "Woman" from her "degrading bondage"—or, "the frequent necessity of choosing between a union at which her soul revolts, and a life of galling dependence on remote relatives, or of precarious struggle for daily bread."

To persuade his readers of the rightness of women's working for pay,

Greeley appealed to the ideal of womanhood. To be a "true woman," he told his readers, "implies qualities which render her useful, respected, and happy, though it should be her destiny to lead an independent life. . . . It is the dictate of wisdom, therefore, no less than of female dignity and delicacy, that every woman should be educated for independent usefulness and happiness, as well as to discharge wisely and nobly the duties of wife and mother." Not only should American principle dictate the concept of appropriate labor for women, it should redefine femininity. If "Woman" is to fulfill her social role, he explained, women "must be assured a wider field for exertions in productive industry and the useful arts."[61]

Unwed women trying to make art their careers shared Greeley's understanding of true womanhood. By becoming independent through useful, satisfying work, Josephine Dewey believed she would fulfill the duties of a daughter. Dewey wanted to prepare "herself for giving instruction in the art of design, as a means of obtaining a livelihood and of relieving her parents, who are in reduced circumstances, from the necessity of supplying her with the means of existence."[62] The same union of domestic and democratic principles that underlay Greeley's concept of "woman's sphere" bolstered Dewey's definition of a virtuous daughter as self-sufficient. Annie Delano decided to study art at the Cooper Union to help her father, who was recently burdened with the support of his widowed sister and niece.[63] Faced with economic necessity, American women went to work. For them, the natural love and duty to family required by domestic ideology was identical to the love and duty to society required by their nation.

Midcentury American girls also agreed with Greeley that even if there were different roles for men and women in American society, anyone could change her circumstances if she applied her natural abilities and took advantage of the liberal economy. The younger generation felt more confident in this advantage. Older sisters, like *Little Women*'s Meg, often felt trapped by their options: teaching or marriage. Now-a-days, " 'men have to work, and women to marry for money. It's a dreadfully unjust world,' said Meg bitterly." But her younger sister saw the arts as an escape from that dilemma: " 'Jo and I are going to make fortunes for you all; just wait ten years, and see if we don't,' said Amy, who sat in a corner, making mud pies, as Hannah called her little clay models of birds, fruit, and faces."[64] Knowles's older sister, who described herself as a "poor, and at present invalid widow," considered art training Adaline's ticket to the happy life and satisfying work she would never have: "I can from experience sympathize with her yearnings for assistance as I have always been during my whole life

longing, and striving to break through the circumstances that have surrounded me & try my fortune as an Artist, still I see no wrong to do so. but
I most sincerely hope for better success to attend my Sister. she being young
with life before her."[65] Like "Amy" and Adaline, many American women
envisioned art training as a way to expand their choices beyond typical
women's employment. "When I thought what I should best like to do, my
first dream—almost a baby's dream—about it was that it would be a fine
thing to be a school-teacher, like Aunt Hannah," recalled Larcom. "Afterward, when I heard that there were artists, I wished I could some time be
one."[66]

A young woman's determination to pursue an artistic life might inten-
sify as she witnessed an older female relative struggling to fulfill her duty
within restricted options. Hallock chose art as her particular line after her
father, a Quaker farmer, gave the family savings to his eldest and most un-
reliable son. All the younger Hallock children, male and female, were expected to find the means to support themselves. "I can speak as one who
had no share herself in the sacrifices that were called for," Hallock recalled,
"as long as I lived at home my work was protected and my profits, after
paying my board as a son would, if he could, were my own. With John and
Bessie and with Phil, my next oldest sister, it was quite another matter.
Seeing what was before her if she never married, Phil asked only the means
to fit herself for teaching, and teaching became her life and all her life except
its generosity and its courage and its love."[67]

The benefits of having prepared herself for art work at an early age
were clear to Hallock. In fact, choice itself gave her a sense of self-respect.
Hallock considered Phil's request for "only the means to fit herself for
teaching" a sacrifice because it was more a reaction to her situation than a
choice, while her own early decision to study art enabled her to pay her
own way, through work that she loved. She experienced "the joy of relative
independence" and "sense of choice," recurrent in the literature of Larcom's generation of mill workers, which she felt her siblings did not share.[68]
"I was in high spirits all through my unwise teens, considerably puffed up,
after my drawings began to sell, with that pride of independence which was
a new thing to daughters of that period. I did not of course launch out in
dress and travel, but I made more friendships outside the family than the
other sisters, and my work was a constant refreshment and striving and excitement while theirs was just work, the same from day to day."[69]

The "pride of independence" that Hallock derived from the sale of her
drawings was not separate from the duty and devotion to family she was

taught as an American Quaker. Yet like Larcom years before her, Hallock was aware that art carried a different social value than other women's work. Unlike much of the labor performed by daughters, Hallock's work as an artist made her a public person, and that gave the pride she felt in it political meaning. Application letters show that many women decided to pursue an art career when they saw the Cooper Union advertised in newspapers and periodicals; but those ads were not all they must have read. Women's artistic aspirations were encouraged and exonerated by the editorial opinions expressed in the columns of newspapers such as Greeley's *New-York Tribune*, from which Hallock said the children of her generation gained their "ordinary intelligence." When art became her work, Hallock was not only liberated from her dependence on family (and thereby helping them out), she connected to a larger, more exciting world of activity and meaning.

The public value of her drawings made Hallock's work more than "just work," and so too did the constant striving that art production entailed. Art filled different emotional needs than other work. Hallock took pride in her housework, as well, admitting: "There was a certain joy in that work too, the satisfaction of perfect success: there is such a thing as a perfect spongecake—I have done pretty well in that line myself—but I never made a perfect drawing." Domestic labor never gave Hallock the sense of exhilaration she got from art labor because for her the mystery that made a drawing perfect made art profound.

Young American men shared in the desire for meaningful work, but their economic options made their art fever less acute. On 15 August 1860, William James wrote to his friend Thomas Sergeant Perry, "I have come to the conclusion that 'Art' is my vocation." James's enthusiasm was tempered by uncertainty about his talent. "At any rate I am going to give it a fair trial, and if I find I have not the *soufflé* give it up."[70] Having the "soufflé" for art was not the same thing for James as making the "perfect drawing" was for Hallock, whose only alternative was "spongecake." For most young men, art represented only one socially significant vocation among many, while for young women like Hallock it often represented the only possibility for paid work and "pride of independence."

Still, gender expectations and familial duty could make it just as difficult for boys with art fever to avoid prescribed roles as for girls. Three young siblings named Foster, Emma, and Henry Cross studied art under Henry Herrick, their neighbor in Manchester, New Hampshire. All three eventually became artists, but that was not what their father intended. Despite his appreciation for their skills, Joseph Cross expected the boys to remain farmers. "There should be some planting done and if you work on your [wood] blocks [in Manchester] you can see to it," he wrote to Foster from the battlefront in Mississippi in 1863. Relieved of that familial responsibility after his father returned from the Civil War in 1867, Foster left farming to pursue the wood-engraving business exclusively. Mr. Cross supported Foster's decision but consequently expected Henry to remain on the farm. Eventually, Henry too left the farm to pursue painting. Emma remained at home and helped support the family as a teacher. Finally, in 1876, after setting her parents up on their new farm, she followed her brothers to Boston and began art work as a photo retoucher.[71]

Another daughter of the period, Libbie, invoked her duty to find paid work as justification for her willful intention to continue studying art away from home: "I had quite a serious time, showing cousin John and Lou that it was *right* for me to stay in N.Y. this winter, and continue my engraving at the Institute. They wanted Father to promise, that if I was not strong and well, he'd send me to spend the winter with them, but father looked at me, and I shook my head, telling them, if I ever expected to earn my living [at] it, I must work *now*, and let my own pleasure go, also that of my friends. (they said). but I could not help it if they *did* think me headstrong and obstinate! perhaps it is the 'nature of the beast,' who knows!"[72] Libbie knew that if her art study were treated as a mere accomplishment or pleasure, she would have no right to assert her will. Her opinion would only be taken seriously because art was to become her work. She felt proud in her resolution to "work *now*, and let my own pleasure go." Louisa May Alcott gave voice to the principles behind Libbie's words in both her diary and story after story: "My democratic ideas of honesty and honor won't let me be idle or dependent," she wrote, and "I want to realize my dream of supporting the family and being perfectly independent."[73] For middle-class daughters like Hallock and Libbie, earning a living through art *was* pleasure because it was a democratic assertion of independence and individuality. Stirred up by the promise of economic opportunity, they set out to perform their duty to self, family, and society by learning to make art.

The Cure

American women with "Art Fever" applied to art school out of need, desire, and principle. Through art study and work they hoped to escape poverty and dependence, perform their duty to family, and assert their republican values. They chose art work over other forms of employment because it was more than "just work"; it had a social worth. The difference between a woman who made art her living and another working woman was the meaning her society gave to the labor that her temperament and principle demanded of her. But what made art the right choice in America in the 1850s and 1860s? The antebellum generation may have inherited the liberal republicanism of their forebears who connected art to independence, but they also benefited from the largesse of Americans born a generation earlier whose political beliefs drove their financial and cultural activities.

The women who attended New York City's first schools of design, and the men and women who built those institutions, envisioned art education meeting more than economic ends. Both artists and their advocates believed in the doctrine of individual rights, both aspired toward a self and a society that stood for something good, and both hoped their actions might even enhance human existence.[74] When Alcott had Christie declare her repugnance for work with no object but money and Delano praised the starving artist for his principles, they were sharing a concern held by Ruskin, Greeley, Cooper, and other social reformers. The methods and ethics of capitalists, they believed, had drained away the intrinsic value of work. Art would put it back. Art fever was not a young women's disease, it was a possible remedy for the ills of industrial society.

At the Cooper Union women artists' aspirations were taken seriously. Back home in Penn Yan during the first year of the Civil War, Annie Delano wrote in a letter to her classmates at the School of Design: "So you are all assembled together in the same old way as though the arts were of some importance in the world, and not a sheer waste of time, an idle frittering away of the precious moments that might more gratifyably be devoted to— worsted work—for instance! As a neighbor said to me. 'Now if it was something useful, something that would make a show, but this daubing away with a paint brush, peer to me rather small business!' Ah well! . . . 'the good time is coming' let us believe, . . . when culture and education shall establish a great appreciation of true art in every country hamlet in America."[75] The opportunity to study at the School of Design did not cure Delano's "Art fever"; it intensified her hopeful expectations that through art she might become independent and perform a service to society. For most women artists, it would take the experience of poverty and unemployment to suppress that yearning.

Women applying to art school understood that they had to connect their needs and desires if they were to attain their goal of perfect independence. The question was when to emphasize art and when to emphasize work in trying to give value to two things that, if they were accomplished by women, could be seen as having no financial value. When Libbie, Mary Hallock, and Josephine Dewey told family and friends that art was their work, they emphasized training and manual skill in order to give an extrinsic meaning, or social and economic worth, to their art. But when Hallock, Lucie Hale, and Annie Delano claimed that art was more than work, they emphasized the intrinsic value, or intellectual and moral content of art, in an effort to raise the status of their work. Art was work; work was art, and tied together each was more. Outside New York City and the Cooper Union School of Design this equation might have seemed obscure, but inside it dominated the discourse of art.

Chapter 4

"Harrahed for the Union"

Worried about the state of the country during the construction of his school in the 1850s, Peter Cooper decided to put the single word "Union" on the most conspicuous front of the building looking south and dedicate it to a "union of effort" in the nation. Against his wishes, the New York legislature added his name to the title. This addition was apt, for Cooper's values, influence, and presence pervaded every part of Cooper Union for the Advancement of Science and Art.[1] "On the evening of the yearly reception," recalled School of Design Principal Susan Carter in 1883, "Mr. Cooper stood or sat at the south corner of the east corridor to receive the thousands of people who attended. . . . Surrounded by his family, the venerable founder of the Cooper Union was always present,—the chief attraction of the evening."[2]

Shortly after leaving the School of Design, Annie Delano answered a letter from Alice Donlevy describing the yearly reception of 1861. Afire with patriotic zeal, Delano's reply articulates the experiences of many of the women who studied at the Cooper Union during the Civil War decade. "Your description of the reception was so graphic and spirited, that it spirited me right there," she declared. "Heard the music, saw all the dear girls again: dodged the crowd; brushed by all those little flags, and had the red, white & blew fervor as usual, at the fluttering of those colors; grew patriotic and harrahed for the Union.—Cooper, and—'tother; grew artistic, and harrahed for the School of Design, especially and particularly became sofficated with a smothered home-sick feeling to be back with you and all again!" Romantic devotion and fervent loyalty to the Cooper Union and the nation ('tother union) are confounded in Annie's letter. She is proud that the women's "life class corner" was honored with a "bust of Washington, draped in the glorious colors of our country," because drawing from live models represented the fullest expression of artistic freedom for women, and she mockingly compares the ugly set of plaster casts usually relegated to women artists studying human anatomy to "Jef Davis" in the act of "embracing the Goddess of Cotton."[3] She longs for the life that occupies the Cooper Union, the art and all the "dear girls," and fears for the young men, especially that "splendid little fellow" who had just returned with the crack Seventh New York Regiment. "I devoutly hope his little mother, will take that 'new uniform' and throw it out of the window, and set 'her boy' quietly at his easel again." She feels indignant at New York City for "coldly" receiving the "immortal Seventh" back from Washington, just "because they did not leave half their number to water the soil of the rebels with their blood," and yet homesick to be back again, in a place where artists of every kind mingled on an equal footing. Annie "grew patriotic and harrahed" for the Cooper Union because it was there that she first experienced everything "'tother" Union stood for.[4]

Goings on at the Cooper Union School of Design for Women make a fascinating case study of the way the Unity of Art ideal transformed higher art education into a skirmish against the devaluation of industrial artists during the Civil War decade.[5] In its daily routines and structure, enrollment policy, curricula, and choice of teachers and directors, and in the methods of its educators, the School of Design practiced the Unity of Art ideal. "Mr. Cooper cared little for art *per se*," explained Carter. "And so he looked with some suspicion and incredulity on the headless Torso of 'Victory,' in the Elgin Marbles, and could see no beauty in the 'Fates'; but he was well content to trust such matters to more experienced judges."[6] By allowing aesthetic experts to decide what to teach to women artists, Cooper transformed the School of Design into an ideological battlefield for the contest over cultural power in America.

Between 1859 and 1872 six different principals headed the School of Design. These frequent changes in leadership evinced an attempt by Cooper Union Trustees to move the school in a direction more perfectly in line with the Unity of Art ideal. Everyone agreed that male and female design students should be offered a balance between training in technical skills and education in aesthetic principles, but when it came to teaching women, the specific nature of that balance was unclear.[7] The Ladies Advisory Council maintained that female students benefited more from manual training than aesthetic education and worried that if women focused on fine art principles their aspirations would exceed abilities and cause women to squander precious time on unnecessary knowledge. The male artists who taught the classes countered that women could not compete in markets for design and art labor unless they understood the principles behind their work. The students appealed to the deeply egalitarian convictions of their benefactor and objected to rules and actions taken by the school's administration that they deemed restrictive or conservative. Also weighing in on the debate were art critics and parents swept up in new currents of aesthetic and social thought. Wrangling came to a head in 1868 around the directorship of William Rimmer, whose pedagogy seemed too idealist for a school dedicated to helping women artists gain financial independence.

Changes in staff, admission policy, and curricula at the School of Design demonstrate just how daunting a task it was to find the balance between aesthetic education and manual training that would serve women artists. The task was especially challenging in a complex society being rapidly altered by war and industrialization. Yet by shouldering that burden the Cooper Union set a new standard for art education in America during the second half of the nineteenth century, saved hundreds of women from unskilled jobs, and won the hearts of artists like Annie.

The Cooper Union

Broadway was heavily populated by "the lady element," reported the *Crayon* in 1858. A "small sprinkling of lady-like women" and a "great number of . . . ladies unattached" crowded the sidewalks. Many of those ladies were art students traipsing from home or boarding house to class and studio.[8] From 1864 to 1867, Mary Hallock walked the two miles from the ferry docks up Broadway to the Cooper Union every day during term, and after graduating fearlessly ventured into the offices of magazine and book publishers on her own.[9] Finding accommodations, negotiating one's way through New York's busy streets, and doing business with men were all part of the experience of art study at the Cooper Union (Figure 11).

The Cooper Union building at Seventh Street (Astor Place) between Third and Fourth Avenues was a locus for workers and reformers. Rooms on the first two floors were rented as stores and offices. On the third floor was a large well-stocked reading room, free of charge and open to all from 8:00 A.M. to 10:00 P.M. The basement housed a great lecture hall, where popular orators and politicians, including Abraham Lincoln and Stephen Douglas, addressed the public and debated controversial issues of the day. During the war years, the building also accommodated the activities of New York City's Sanitary Commission and the Workingwomen's Protective Union. The School of Design spread over three floors. Painting studios were on the sixth floor, the art library and architectural studios on the fifth floor,

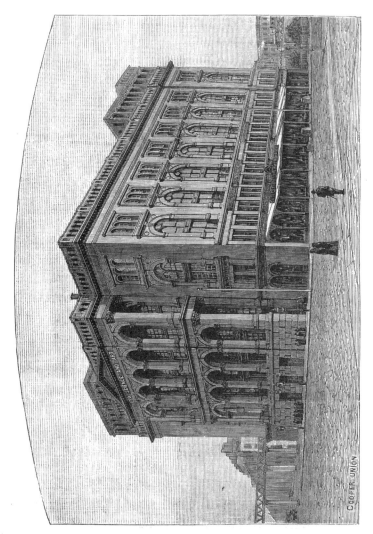

Figure 11. The Cooper Union Building. "New York City.—The Monument of a Philanthropist: The Cooper Union and Its Schools of Art," *Frank Leslie's Illustrated Newspaper* (14 April 1883): 126. Courtesy of Newark Public Library.

and the exhibition gallery and engraving classroom on the fourth floor. Encircling the gallery were long corridors that connected rooms and alcoves lit by wall windows and used as workshops and practice studios by female students (Figure 12). Two partial floors at the top of the building held lecture rooms and drafting rooms with skylights.

About two thousand women and men enrolled at the Cooper Union in 1859, the year it officially opened. Art school enrollment, approximately 200–250 students, was a small portion of the total school attendance. Female students dominated, at times comprising over three-quarters of art enrollees.[10] Cooper Union was an experiment in democratic education that fulfilled the dreams of education reformers. No one was excluded because of sex, color, creed, or political opinion.[11] Coeducation was school policy: "Woman is admitted to all the privileges of the institution on an equal footing with man."[12] And while the course of instruction at night was designed mainly "for men engaged in mechanical pursuits," 50 women "availed of its privileges" each year and were "among the best scholars who have attended the night classes."[13] Indeed, women were among the award winners every year.

Because the night classes better served the needs of men, Cooper provided for "'the instruction of women in the arts of Design,' and in 'such other art or trade as will tend to furnish them with suitable employment'" during the day.[14] Separate day and evening schools did not mean that men and women were trained differently. The same teachers taught all the School of Design students in the same manner. The day school was designed to address the disadvantages women faced on account of their sex, in particular their exclusion from the workshop training male artists and artisans received.

Male and female pupils, teachers, and administrators frequently mingled in the Cooper Union building at lectures, exhibitions, receptions, and in the corridors and stairwells. "[I] met young Mr. Van Der Weyde in the hall and hardly knew him in his new uniform," Donlevy wrote to Delano in 1861, to which Delano replied: "Swing that 'allarming bloomer' of yours, and hope he will stay there, for he is too handsome a young man . . . to be disfigured by a sudden gash of sharp steel across his breast . . . 'Well really! All this about a young man, and he, a stranger!' Bah! I hate conventionality, and shall write what I please about the young men!"[15]

The policy of educating women and men at the same institution, if not always in the same classes, was meant to give them a chance to encounter and judge one another as peers. This mixed-sex environment caused some

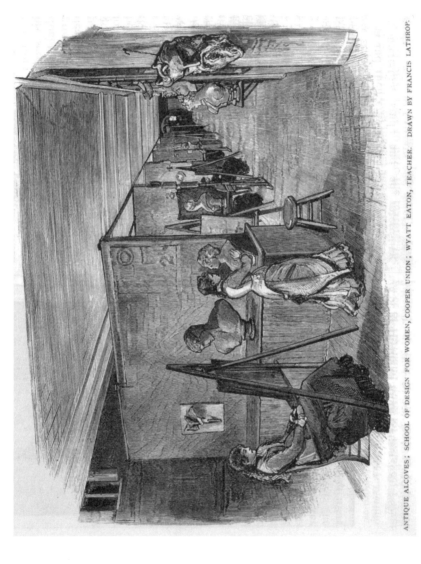

Figure 12. "Antique Alcoves; School of Design for Women, Cooper Union; Wyatt Eaton, Teacher. Drawn by Francis Lathrop." *Scribner's Monthly* 16, 6 (October 1878): 772. Courtesy of American Antiquarian Society.

concern among social observers. A few parents worried that their daughters might be lured into the sort of "alarming" behavior suggested by Delano's "unconventional" letter. Others worried about a different sort of female misconduct. Among that vast population of "ladies" spotted on Broadway was a "great number of undomesticated ladies, not necessarily of a doubtful character, but ladies unattached."[16] Coeducation would only increase the number of single women who were ill prepared to lead lives as wives. "We believe that both sexes are gainers by learning together," Cooper's son-in-law Abram Hewitt, who administrated the School of Design, assured them all. "In six years we have not had a single case of scandal in Cooper Union and we should as soon think of excluding the young men as the young women."[17]

Staffing the School of Design

In making his gift, Peter Cooper asked the "cultivated and intelligent ladies" who founded the New York School of Design to oversee its move to his building, add to their numbers, and remain associated with the school as an advisory council, headed by his daughter Amelia Cooper Hewitt. Duties of the voluntary Ladies' Advisory Council included regularly visiting the school and soliciting progress reports from its Principal, fund-raising, overseeing admissions, and advising the trustees on educational policy, such as expanding course offerings into fields that promised viable employment to women artists.[18]

The Advisory Council worked together with the family and friends Cooper named as trustees to build a diverse staff of distinguished and newly acclaimed artists to teach the classes, direct the departments, and head the art school. The Principal of the School of Design was an artist/educator who had charge of the day-to-day affairs, record keeping, faculty hiring, and decisions regarding teaching methods. Henry Herrick did not move with the School of Design to the Cooper Union. The first Principal was Thomas Addison Richards, a painter, engraver, and illustrator, and the Corresponding Secretary of the National Academy of Design. Richards took over the "entire professional direction of the School of Design" in 1859, the year it became "an organic part of the Institute." His directorship established a permanent connection between the Cooper Union and the National Academy, which subsequently admitted any Cooper Union pupil who passed a required examination into its school[19] (Figure 13).

Richards was replaced as Principal in 1861 by Advisory Council Member Henrietta Desporte Field, an artist and friend of Peter Cooper who taught painting at the School of Design. During her two years as Principal, Field expanded course offerings, added reputable European- and American-trained artists to the faculty, and supported, if sometimes critically, the newer graphic techniques these artists brought with them. Nevertheless, some students criticized her directorship. At issue seems to have been Field's inability to have a collegial relationship with male artists, which evidenced a conservative attitude that proved detrimental to the school and the women artists who trained there. "Madam Field tolerates only two classes of men, vis. those whom she manages, and those who manage her," one student complained. And since our teachers "would as utterly scorn to attempt to the one as to submit to the other," she will cause them to leave.[20]

Field's background made her an odd choice for director to begin with. While a governess to the children of the Duc de Praslin in Paris in 1847, Henreitte Deluzy-Desporte was accused of instigating her employer to murder his wife. Kept under armed guard during the trial, Field pleaded her own case before the chancellor of France and eventually won her freedom. She then took refuge in America, where she turned to art as a profession.[21] Field was replaced as Principal in 1862 by Mrs. Lucy A. Cuddehy [Cudahy], about whom Mary Hallock wrote: "The school at that time needed an enthusiast and she was one."[22]

New York's art community was curious about Cooper's experiment. Encouraged by an administration that sought close ties, affirmation, publicity, employers for students, and new faculty, artists frequently came to the School of Design to observe and evaluate the students' work. "Several artists have visited the school this month," Field reported in March 1862. "They have entered into the details of the system and inspecting the drawings of the pupils, speaking here and there a word of encouragement to those introduced to them. Such visits of our principal artists have a very happy effect in exciting the enthusiasm of the pupils in their studies, and it is to be wished that they might often be repeated."[23] Asked by Abram Hewitt to teach figure drawing at the School of Design, genre painter John Ehninger consulted with some of his "brother-artists upon the subject" and became "deeply interested in the concepts of this undertaking." He accepted the job, offering to work for "materially less than I can earn by my regular profession."[24]

Teaching at the School of Design turned many artists who sympathized with Cooper's motives into advocates for women artists. In 1861 Rob-

Figure 13. "Sketch Class, National Academy of Design; Prof. L. E. Wilmarth, Teacher. Drawn by Miss Jennie Brownscombe," *Scribner's Monthly* 16, 6 (October 1878): 763. Courtesy of American Antiquarian Society.

ert O'Brien, who replaced Herrick as director of the women's engraving department when the School of Design moved to the Cooper Union, informed the Trustees that the experience of "two years at the school has convinced me, that females acquire a knowledge and practice of the art of engraving as readily as the other sex. Indeed I should say if there is any difference it is in favor of females."[25] His successor, William J. Linton, "undertook the task with considerable misgivings, and in a spirit of pecuniary self sacrifice," yet was entirely satisfied after one year "that women can not only become good engravers, but admirable designers." Proof of this assessment was to be found in the steady demand for their work and the substantial compensation they received.[26]

New York painters also were convinced by their experience at the School of Design to support women's art education. Landscape painter Worthington Whittredge observed "a deep interest among the pupils, a great willingness to learn in a proper way, and in many instances very much talent. And what would be irksome in a less studious school, becomes a pleasure in an institution which supplies a want and is so ready to impart a proper knowledge of art."[27] His experience as a temporary replacement so impressed Whittredge that he offered to return at any time for little payment, and did so two years later. Through their contact with School of Design students there developed over time a recognizable community of male artists who championed women artists.[28]

Enrollment and Curricula

Enrollment policy at the School of Design reflected Cooper's republican objective to teach workers "what they could apply to use," and "to raise the standard of [their] character" so as to instill an interest in "public affairs."[29] With those aims in mind both "Industrial and Amateur pupils" were received into the art school so long as they were "not under twelve years of age." Industrial pupils, "the class for whose advantage the School is more particularly designed," were those women and girls who desired "to cultivate their art talents for practical and professional employment, as Designers for Art-manufactures, and book illustrations, as Engravers on Wood, as Teachers of Drawing and Painting, as Workers in various branches of Industrial Art, or as artists in higher walks." To be admitted to the Industrial Class, applicants had to produce "satisfactory evidence of good character and fitness in other respects," and those willing to "devote the greatest amount of time and assiduity to study" were given preference. Industrial students were charged no tuition, but were asked to "aid in the instruction of younger pupils." The school also allowed in a small number of paying "Amateurs" with no object beyond "the acquisition of a knowledge of Art as an elegant accomplishment," so long as their admission did not lead to the exclusion of Industrial Scholars.[30]

Courses fell within two general areas. Everyone took freehand drawing in the mornings until twelve and then split into engraving and painting classes in the afternoons. Curricula covered a broad range of genre and media, including pencil and crayon drawing; drawing from casts and life; perspective and sketching from natural objects; painting landscapes, heads, figures and flowers in oil, water color, and pastel; designing and drawing on wood; lithography; etching on stone; painting on china; and wood engraving. Most classes also included pedagogy. Amateurs were not required to follow any particular course of study nor were they barred from any class, but their admission was "necessarily limited" to available space.[31]

The Ladies' Advisory Council insisted on admitting Amateur pupils because they believed "the superior class of women, both as to position and education," would have a good influence on students from poor families and might provide professional contacts.[32] However, almost immediately the dividing line between the Industrial and Amateur class began to blur. Approximately 600,000 fathers, brothers, and husbands died during the Civil War, an event that had both short- and long-term effects on the School of Design. In 1861 and 1862, Field reported to the Trustees that enrollment had remained steady despite "the disasters which have fallen so heavily upon the country." What had changed was the ratio of women from "good families" seeking admittance to the Industrial rather than the Amateur class. As the "Amateurs" switched into the Industrial class, the attendance of pupils from poorer families declined. Field believed this change occurred because the "hard times" that accompanied war affected the classes differently. During a crisis the middle classes felt the need of some resource for their daughters but could not afford to pay even the "dollar a week" expected of "Amateur" pupils, while the very poor needed to work for immediate support and could not afford to give up the time it took to learn a profession.[33]

Principal Field was pleased with the new ratio, believing the increase of Amateurs or potential Amateurs who enrolled as regular students "had not a little to do in checking any tendencies to rudeness and noisy vulgarity." In a school such as the Cooper, "open to all classes," she deemed "a strict discipline is absolutely necessary to maintain the dignity and moral tone."[34] Unable to see beyond the class prejudice that tied loose morality to poor workingwomen, Field failed to notice how Civil War exigencies were undermining the class structure on which that prejudice was based. By admitting poor women from "good families" as industrial pupils preparing for remunerative work, the School of Design was reconfiguring the middle class to include workingwomen.

Objections to the presence of amateurs at the School of Design arose alongside issues of class that surfaced with the labor situation during the Civil War. Since women typically outnumbered men, there was always a surplus of women seeking jobs in cities, and by the war's end that surplus had increased by 20,000 in New York City alone. In such a world, women workers were incredibly exploitable. "Desperate women were sometimes hired to work without pay until they learned the trade and then were fired when they thought they were qualified."[35] In response to these appalling conditions, social observers and newspapers like the *New York Times* urged men in employments that could be filled by female workers to vacate their jobs and look for other work.

The unfair treatment of women in almost every industry was so bad by 1864 that a mass meeting was held at Cooper Union to launch the Workingwomen's Protective Union, an organization intended to raise wages, procure legal protection from fraud, and shorten the hours of labor for women. By September, thousands of women had signed a petition urging Secretary of War Edwin Stanton to set women's wages at a level commensurate with the cost of living. The Workingwomen's Protective Union also opened an employment office in the Cooper Union building, to help women find better pay and persuade employers that female workers could be profitably hired as wood engravers, typesetters, cigar makers, and telegraphers. In 1865 that office claimed to have found jobs for more than 6,000 women. The Cooper Union aided in this endeavor by providing all classes of women with higher art educations and training.[36]

The shift of female artists from amateur to industrial status at the School of Design during those same years prompted later changes in admission policy.[37] In the spring of 1866, Cooper Union Trustees chose Boston-based artist William Rimmer (b. 1816) as the school's Principal, and Rimmer's first move was to discontinue the "Amateur" class entirely. This policy reversal created a learning environment where women artists knew they were judged "by talent and virtue alone and not by fortune or descent." It also nurtured a body of students who attributed their middle-class status to their work as artists.

William Rimmer was a self-taught painter and sculptor whose critical acclaim rested on his skill as a draftsman, his incredibly thorough knowledge of anatomy (he was also a medical doctor and phrenologist), his dynamic teaching style, and his high profile as a teacher of women in Boston.[38] From personal experience and his engagement with some of the most popular and controversial theories of the era, Rimmer had arrived at the conclusion that great artists generally came from the lower classes and "that art intellectually is as independent of sex as thought itself." Between 1863 and 1866 he operated a school of drawing and modeling "for artists and amateurs of both sexes" at the Lowell Institute. He accepted the job at the Cooper Institute because he believed that art ability was "the same in women as men" and hence "saw no reason why the same knowledge should not be conferred upon the one as well as the other."[39] In fact, he thought women had a superior capacity for art, an observation he supported through the science of phrenology.[40]

Under Rimmer the School of Design required every student to attend a course of lectures on art principles and to master drawing techniques before selecting a specialization. He expected students to attend his lecture courses on art anatomy, composition and expression, systematic and structural botany, primitive forms (i.e., action, motion, proportion, size, color, light and shade), and manners, customs, and implements.[41] To demonstrate composition and art anatomy, one School of Design student recalled, "He would begin with the toe at the top of the board, and run down through a number of figures as fast as he could handle the chalk,—so fast that one could scarcely tell when one figure was done and another begun." While many of his students found Rimmer's program and methods useful and exhilarating, others found it "impracticable and queer."[42]

Like most of his contemporaries, Rimmer emphasized drawing. "Learn to draw" had been the cry of art crusaders and their manuals since the 1820s, and the same advice was given to women who wanted to make art their careers during the Civil War. In 1863, Philadelphia artist and mezzotint engraver John Sartain advised women interested in joining the field: "The mere mechanical skill required in *any* kind of engraving is easily attained; but the art of *drawing* is a key that admits to a wider range of arts than I can readily enumerate, and successful and profitable employment in any engraving depends on *that*. . . . For whatever branch of the fine arts is to be followed, the first requisite is *drawing*, and the next is *drawing*, and the third and last is *drawing*."[43]

Administrators and teachers at the School of Design agreed with Sartain's assessment, even if a few students and their parents protested. Mrs. B. F. Stevenson complained to Abram Hewitt that her daughter, who had traveled from Illinois to the Cooper Union "to pursue *oil painting*, in which she had made some progress . . . now writes us that they are sketching only, from casts and she cannot ascertain from her teacher how long they are to continue this. Now we feel, Sir with all due regard to the teacher, that it is *a waste of time* and we are unwilling to be to the expense of keeping her from home to do what we think she is already mistress of . . . If the rules of your Institute forbid the entrance of pupils to the painting department without preparatory lessons we would like to know what that preparation is . . . There are other places where [she] can secure the advantages we wish."[44]

In answer to this impatient parent and student, Hewitt confirmed the Cooper Union's commitment to the requirement that all students master drawing and underscored the Unity of Art precept that the same skills and principles were at the root of every art form. He quietly ridiculed the inference that drawing lessons were inferior to painting lessons. Our "school aims only to be an industrial school of art, & does not profess to educate mere artists," he explained, "there are other schools in which this kind of instruction is given, and if your daughter desires merely to paint, she does not properly belong in this institution."[45] By using the phrases "mere artists" and "merely to paint," Hewitt insinuated that painting on its own was not a skill sufficient to build a professional career.

Experience and Employment

After a semester of study, School of Design directors encouraged any student who showed no artistic promise to consider another profession, and dismissed those with a less than serious attitude. They also tried to find alternative employment for students "who did not display the requisite capacity for learning." T. Addison Richards quickly identified those students who showed potential as artists. In 1860 he informed the Board of Trustees that he had "just engaged one of our pupils to fill the place of 'Teacher of Drawing and Painting' in the Female Academy at Cherry Valley, N.Y." He also identified those with none: "two of our pupils who seemed to be working without much hope of success have, upon advice, withdrawn."[46]

School of Design students left the school for their own reasons as well. Of the original forty-six students who registered for the Fall and Spring terms of 1871–72, engraving department director Charlotte Cogswell reported in May, only thirty-three remained. "Three are absent from the city . . . One entered in November and died in March. One is married. Four left on account of home duties, one for ill health. One found politics more profitable than art; and two were not suited to the business."[47] The course of study usually took four years, but many students left when a good job came along. "Two are teaching in Mr. Brace's school," reported the School of Design Principal in 1873, "one has become a clerk to one of our first artists and in a number of other cases, persons applying to me for intelligent assistance have been able to procure it among the scholars."[48]

The Cooper Union's engraving department continued to function like a workshop or business office, with the director acting as master artisan, taking orders and assigning work to his staff of engravers, the more advanced students acting as journeymen filling those orders, and newcomers studying like apprentices in training. Publishers and other prospective clients were invited to "assist the School, with commissions for drawings and engravings on wood, and art-manufacturers with orders for designs, drawings of patents, etc., which work will always be well executed and at very reasonable prices." New Yorkers interested in commissioning the students often frequented the classrooms. "Two master Engravers have been at the School," reported Mrs. Cuddehy in 1863, "and expressed themselves both pleased and surprised at the style of work done in the Engraving class. They have promised some orders."[49]

As Principal, Henrietta Field followed the engraving department's lead offering studio-like space to painting students ready for commissions. "Several of the pupils of the Life Class are now able to take portraits for money and they have requested the permission to have their sitters come to the School," she informed the Advisory Council in 1862. "Finding that it gave a fresh stimulus to their work, and was one of the best means of improvement, I have set apart one alcove where the pupils might receive their sitters, making it however a strict condition that the name and position of the person sitting, whether male or female, be made known to me, before being allowed to come." Several of our pupils have a few students of their own, she continued, and "at the end of the term, if the times are a little more favorable I have no doubt that we shall show the great benefits of the school."[50]

The School of Design's annual exhibitions attended by thousands of

interested New Yorkers served as a kind of job fair for the students. Jervis
McEntee's landscape painting class was particularly successful at these
events. "Three young ladies have already left it to occupy places as teachers," Field informed the Advisory Council after the 1861 reception. Other
genres did equally well that year. "A number of the pupils of the School
have received orders for portraits," she reported. "One executed by a pupil
of two years has already been paid fifty dollars." Women artists also met
prospective students at receptions, added Field. "One of the pupils of the
Life Class has opened a school of drawing in this city, and is succeeding
very well. Miss Barthold teaches at the Rutgers Institute."[51]

Interest in the engraving department at the School of Design swelled
so rapidly that by November of 1860, O'Brien found it "necessary to give
out some work to former pupils in consequence of there not being a sufficient number of experienced engravers to execute the orders in the time
required."[52] During that one term, reported *Harper's Weekly* in March 1861,
School of Design "scholars earned over eleven hundred dollars for themselves in engraving alone."[53] Proceeds from work accomplished in the engraving class were paid to the pupil by whom it was done, with a deduction
of 5 percent for the expense of collecting.[54] "Of the orders executed in the
school probably about one half were received unsolicited," O'Brien told the
Trustees, "the balance were obtained by the personal exertions of the pupils." In general, the school's faculty encouraged students "to exert themselves in soliciting orders, rather than to depend upon such as may be
brought to the school, as in this way only can [women artists] become truly
independent."[55]

Practicing artists teaching at the School of Design recognized that to
compete in their field female students needed the means to establish professional identities: paid work, a good work environment, and a knowledge of
art principles that set them above untrained or semiskilled art workers.
O'Brien was sensitive to the obstacles women artists faced at home and out
in the world and tried to find ways to remove them. "Quite a number of
the pupils have expressed a wish to attend during the vacation for practice,"
he told the Trustees, and this "is very desirable, as . . . experience has shown
that when the pupils attempt to keep up their practice at their homes they
are liable to so many interruptions that they accomplish very little."[56] Yet
to keep business contacts alive, women artists needed to be able to work
year round.

O'Brien requested that the more advanced students be allowed to remain in the engraving class longer than the four years specified in the "rules

for the government of the school." This change in policy would benefit both the School of Design, which expected its students to take orders from book publishers, and the artist. There always "should be two or three skilled engravers in the class . . . able to execute orders which would be beyond the ability of the less experienced to execute so as to give satisfaction." Allowing the advanced students to stay on would also place them on a more equal footing with male engravers. Few of the women at the School of Design attained sufficient proficiency to compete with men in four school terms, he argued, and "at present it is impracticable for female [engravers] to obtain employment in offices where they might receive instruction as payment in part for their services, not to speak of the objection which most young women would have to working in offices where only men are employed."[57]

The objection that the men working in those shops might have to the presence of female engravers concerned O'Brien as well. "Labor unionism was unknown," recalled former student Bianca Bondi, "but I remember well what a storm of protest was raised by the young men then employed as wood-cut artists when they heard that there was to be a class for women in Cooper Union."[58] To allay that protest, School of Design students needed to become more than competent engravers. They had to prove their competitive worth in a market that used female labor to undercut the wages of men.[59]

Male engravers' complaint against women's entry into the field stemmed from their fear that the proletarianization they witnessed in other trades would infiltrate their protected occupation. To increase profits, capitalists divided the manufacturing process into tasks and diluted the skill level by hiring lower-paid semi- or unskilled workers, usually women, children, or immigrants, whom they trained on the job to carry out those tasks at home as piecework or in a factory setting.[60] This process did not take place at the same time or rate for all industries nor even within a single industry. The extent to which a craft could be subdivided was limited by the amount of skill and training needed to carry out the work. Special abilities and knowledge could "protect" workers or at least give them a bargaining edge. Crafts that involved irreplaceable knowledge and technical skill, such as shipbuilding, job printing, and wood engraving, were not easily sweated. Some industrial employers who had once been artisans themselves respected craft tradition by hiring trained workers and paying them wages that were relatively high.[61]

In the "arts" where traditional knowledge or new graphic techniques ruled production, artisans and artists maintained their jobs and guarded their wages far longer than in other trades. Printing was a craft that retained its status despite mechanization, although the division of labor did lower the journeyman's wages and make it more difficult for him to open his own shop. On average, even the poorest-paid male printers earned more than sweated tailors or shoemakers. This status was extended to women trained as compositors, engravers, and in other areas of print production. Even after mechanization, master printers and publishers welcomed skilled female journeymen into their shops and paid them fair wages.[62] An 1855 engraving crosscut of a publishing house shows women working in almost every level of operation.[63] Female printers who had been apprenticed to master printers did not pose the same threat to other workers as untrained boys or women, so long as they were as competent as their male colleagues.[64] In fact, the status and good wages of many women artists had much to do with their connection to the printing trade.

Crises that increased competition between male workers inevitably amplified the outcry against women entering the trades. Word on the street had it that industrialists hired women to reduce labor costs, and that many women employed for their skills were paid according to their sex. During the Civil War women's engraving commanded "as high a price as men's labor, when brought into the market," one observer noted, "but when women are employed in engraving establishments, the grossest injustice is shown them in the inequality of the payments made. A woman will receive, in the same place, for the same amount of labor, a sum not exceeding half of that paid to the men in the same employment."[65] This injustice helps explain why at a time when most male engravers began their careers working as members of large business firms or newspaper staffs where they experienced specialization, most female engravers began working as members of small female-dominated shops, like the School of Design, where they were responsible for designing and/or cutting the entire engraving block.[66]

The lower pay offered to most female mechanics did pose a real threat to the livelihoods of male workers, but women's presence in a trade did not necessarily indicate deskilling or a decline in wages. School of Design teachers responded to the practice of paying women less for their work by offering artists destined for industrial jobs superior education and training. It was untrained labor not female labor that degraded industrial work. Art industries that hired semiskilled workers to copy or color bits and pieces, rather than trained artists to work on original designs, eroded the value of the trade and the status of the artist/artisan. Women were the most threatening art workers because they represented the cheapest labor to industrialists. But well-trained women artists who thought of themselves as equals were more likely to fight to maintain the value of their labor, and thereby buttress the status of men in their field.

O'Brien's second request was granted and the policy of allowing former students to use the engraving classroom as a workshop for as long as they needed was maintained under subsequent directors.[67] Throughout the 1860s, engravers and designers working at the School of Design had parity with their male competitors. "The earnings of the pupils in the classes of drawing and engraving are as varied as their skill and experience," reported Virginia Penny in 1863, "but are about the same as those of men who have been at those branches of art the same length of time."[68] After the war, the *Revolution* announced that women in the engraving class at the Cooper Union earned "about $20 a week at this employment, which would be very good pay if it was continuous, but in most cases it only lasts a portion of the year, when the publishers are getting out illustrated books."[69] In fact, seasonal work was common for men and women in many industries and twenty dollars a week was excellent pay. Most women employed in manufacturing during the 1860s toiled for less than three dollars a week, while skilled men earned twelve dollars or more.[70] What the Cooper Union offered its female engravers was a leg up that other women workers lacked.

Among the graduates who took advantage of the Cooper Union "apprenticeship" and open workshop were Alice Donlevy, Amelia Van Horne, Sarah B. Denroche, and Mary A. Jacot, who all stayed at the School of Design for close to ten years (Figure 14). "I think the class was never in as promising condition during the seven years that I have been connected with the school as it is at the present time," O'Brien optimistically proclaimed in 1866. "Although there is still some prejudice existing against female engravers I believe that it is gradually giving way" as "the young ladies of the class . . . demonstrate that they are as worthy of the confidence of publishers as any of the other sex."[71]

Drawing and Painting Class

Outside the engraving shop in their drawing and painting classes, School of Design students were introduced to the "various and conflicting opinions as to what constitutes the ideal in Art."[72] These opinions lay behind the methods teachers used in the classroom to teach drawing and design. Academic or Romantic artists like Whittredge and Henry Peters Gray, who also

Figure 14. Peter Cooper (seated) pays his respects to Robert O'Brien's wood engraving class at the Cooper Union, ca. 1865, *Magazine of Art* (October 1947): 243.

taught at the National Academy, celebrated the sublime in nature as revealed in the artist's creation. European academic convention allowed the artist working in the studio to invent what he did not see. Art was never confined to mere factual matter; artists conceived and represented their subjects poetically, "as apprehended through strong, complicated, and personal feelings." These painters expected their students to begin by drawing from models produced by other artists, such as lithographs or plaster casts, but their compositions were to reflect "choice and invention." For technique, Gray introduced a "quick sketch" method, whereby students worked rapidly in charcoal to acquire a "light, free touch."

Realist artist Thomas Charles Farrer (b. 1839), who taught drawing and painting at the School of Design throughout the Civil War (except for a brief stint in the Union Army), challenged that tradition. Farrer had studied draftsmanship and painting with John Ruskin at the London Working Men's College and embraced the aesthetic in all things and all men. Art was "truth to nature"; artists allowed "people and objects to strike the beholder as beautiful, or to inspire emotion, to exactly the degree that they would in real life." Farrer expected his students to begin by copying natural objects brought into the studio (or sketched on outdoor excursions) exactly as they appeared, "selecting nothing and rejecting nothing" (Figure 15). Their work should indicate "observed" nature rather than "composed" nature. For technique, Farrer introduced meticulous renderings from close observation in clean and tight pencil sketching.[73] Academics urged the artist to avoid the particular; Pre-Raphaelites believed the particular was everything.[74]

Farrer's methods and ideals were derived from the distinctive course of study he received at the Working Men's College. In her 1861 letter to the Trustees, Principal Field acknowledged "the wisdom of that rigid *adherence to Nature* which is the main principle of [Farrer's] teaching." But she modified her appraisal after hearing from artists invited to comment on the school's system. Several of these judges objected to the Pre-Raphaelite technique initiated by Farrer, while Clarence Cook, who taught architectural drawing at the School of Design, favored it. That system is "a very excellent one as far as it goes," reported Field. "Mr. Farrer's method is to teach pupils to copy with the most literal fidelity small objects from Nature, such as mosses, flowers and shells. This is very pleasant work, but . . . *very easy.* . . . These studies are . . . the mere alphabet of the science."[75]

Field understood the merit of having "unaccustomed hands" copy natural objects "with all the accuracy possible." But she and others at the School of Design worried the realist aesthetic and methodology was too simplistic and limited for students headed for design work. In response, Farrer suggested that "a man of thorough knowledge and true feeling should be engaged during the winter months to *Lecture on Art*" to both the day and evening pupils. "In a Lecture not only my class but the whole School could learn in a few hours the great principles and far reaching effect on the human mind involved in their work." Cooper Union pupils were the medium through which art would be carried "into almost every section of our country," Farrer explained. "Especially in a new country where *real* knowledge of art is so small and exclusive, is it vitally necessary that they should be well grounded in the knowledge of the *right* and *wrong* in art."[76]

Farrer found most of his female students "earnest and industrious"

Figure 15. Fidelia Bridges, *Calla Lily*, 1875. Watercolor on paper. The Brooklyn Museum, New York.

and a few "decidedly clever" and "gifted," and those of his students who had been drawn to art by their own reading of Ruskin excelled in his classes. In January 1863, Farrer called a number of artists sympathetic to realist or Pre-Raphaelite (named after the English painters championed by Ruskin) precepts to his studio at 32 Waverly Place to form the Association for the Advancement of Truth in Art.[77] The purpose of the Association, according to their journal the *New Path* (named after Ruskin's lecture series "The Two Paths"), was to influence the "visual arts, manufacture and design, and architecture" by developing "latent artistic ability, especially among the class of mechanics." True to their egalitarian pledge, *New Path* artists promoted inexpensive media, such as watercolor, that fell within the means of poorer artists and counted women among their number.[78]

Male and female *New Path* artists intermingled professionally and personally. They joined one another on art excursions, made studies of similar subjects, and exhibited at the same receptions. In 1862, Farrer asked Thomas Lee Bulson in Albany to make "some drawings of leaves" for Miss Cook to engrave. Bulson replied that he met "a young lady who seemed pleased with your Ideal of Art. She is a subscriber for the New Path and says she endorses a great many of the sentiments expressed in that paper."[79] In 1867, John W. Hill asked Clarence Cook to thank Margaret J. McDonald for the drawing she had sent: "It is rather hard in its execution but still there is so much truth and correctness. It pleases me very much." McDonald subsequently accepted Hill's invitation "to spend a week or two with us this season" at his home in West Nyack, New York, "when we will try and do something out of doors."[80]

The most successful female adherents to *New Path* precepts included Fidelia Bridges, Elizabeth C. Field, Annie McLane, Maria Nims, Mary L. Booth, Louisa W. Cook, Sarah Barney, Miss S. M. Hitchcock, Sarah S. Tuthill, Margaret J. McDonald, and Nina Moore, a number of whom were School of Design students[81] (Figure 16). Cooper student Fidelia Bridges and teacher Thomas Farrer exhibited their first watercolor studies of ferns at the same Brooklyn Art Association exhibition in March 1863, not long after their friend William Trost Richards exhibited his in Troy, New York, in 1862. Bridges showed her work alongside other *New Path* artists at Philadelphia in 1864 "to support the United States Sanitary Commission," at the Artists' Fund Society of New York in 1866, and the Pennsylvania Academy in 1868. She exhibited in Brooklyn in 1866, *Study of Moss and Ferns*, which applied *New Path* theory to oil on panel work.[82] Two watercolors by Bridges were exhibited and sold at the Centennial Exhibition in Philadelphia in

Figure 16. Fidelia Bridges, ca. 1864. Courtesy of the Oliver Ingraham Lay, Charles Downing Lay, and Lay family papers, 1789–2000. Archives of American Art, Smithsonian Institution.

1876, and in 1878 the *Brooklyn Monthly* featured Bridges's art on its cover in conjunction with an article on her career.[83]

After Farrer left the School of Design in 1865, another former teacher and *New Path* artist Clarence Cook published an article in *Round Table* condemning the school's opposition to Pre-Raphaelite methodology and noting the lack of vitality in classes taught by Academy artists McEntee, Gray, and Whittridge.[84] Although Cook later turned against the American realists as well, his criticism drew attention to a deepening bifurcation in the School's system.[85] To bridge that gap, and reorganize the school under one pedagogical style, the Trustees hired William Rimmer, whom they considered "eminently fitted to lay the foundation of a good artistic education, so far as drawing is concerned."[86]

Rimmer and "Ideal Work"

Rimmer's concept of art combined the tenets of academics and realists in a peculiarly American way. "He did not rightly appreciate study from nature," one contemporary recalled, "prizing unduly what he called 'ideal work.'"[87] Rimmer expected each student to produce compositions that were both sublime and scientific arising from observation and knowledge. "Art can have no existence in any community in which the imaginative in Art is not recognized," he explained in his 1868 Annual Report. "To describe mere forms, or imitate mere color, requires no other than mechanical skill, and gratifies no other than a visual want."[88] For technique he stressed "memory sketching," advising his students to "'Take a good look at something that you see in the street, in the house, anywhere,—a rag-picker stooping over an ash-barrel; a woman lifting a child in her arms; any thing, anybody: try and photograph it, so to speak, on the mind, and then draw it from memory. In this way you will learn to seize only the salient points of every thing, discarding all that is superfluous.'" As one student put it: "Uninteresting and vulgar detail, he made us despise."[89] This approach, which relied on neither models nor natural objects, made him a controversial teacher.

For Rimmer imagination and invention served as a moral bridge between art and labor. Like the Pre-Raphaelites, "He had great faith in the integrity of the working-classes," and often said, "'I believe in the genius of work and in the diversity of art talent.'"[90] At the School of Design, "His constant cry as he passed a pupil was, 'Work, work, work!'" "He gave himself to his pupils without stint," one pupil recalled, "especially to those who were earnest." But "to amateurs, and those whose money was their only recommendation, he was utterly unhelpful and indifferent; and they consequently gave untrue reports of his method and instruction."[91]

Rimmer agreed that drawing was the most fundamental element of art, but his focus on "ideal work" tended to shift the focus of his teaching away from that skill. That shift worried the Ladies' Advisory Council. It also generated a scathing review of the 1868 Annual Reception in the *New-York Tribune*. The critic, most likely Clarence Cook, contended that asking design students to rely on their imaginations was a ridiculous disservice. "It may seem unkind to speak so bluntly about the work of a hundred or more girls, if it did not seem unkind to keep silent," he wrote. But the "evident fact" was that "after a winter of apparently hard work, some hundreds of young people of both sexes appear to have been wasting time and money in a deplorable fashion." Those few male students who had studied under Constantine Herzberg, and stuck to "mechanical drawing," showed some ability, he admitted, "but when we come to the Women's Department hardly any sign of talent or ability is to be seen."

The problem was that the students had chosen "subjects of the most ambitious kind, historical subjects, portraits from life, scenes illustrating plays, poems, and romances, to say nothing of elaborate compositions of fruit, and flowers, and game. Now, it would seem as if any man of sense . . . ought to know that . . . subjects of this nature . . . cannot be taught in any school but that of experience. It is the duty of a teacher—so it seems to me—to dissuade a pupil from attempting subjects that are . . . unsuited to her or his abilities, and indeed to more than dissuade, to forbid it positively."[92]

Such intense criticism stung badly, yet some Cooper Union students took it as a good sign. "How that Tribune critic demolishes us," Mary Hallock wrote to a School of Design friend: "unfortunately, there is enough truth in his onslaught to make it impossible not to feel it. But sincerity, however disagreeable, I think is better than being judged by a lower standard of criticism as we women too often are."[93] Considering the source, the criticism was not surprising. Of the American realists, Cook was the most extreme, emphasizing exactitude in representation of simple natural subjects and denouncing any idealization as old-fashioned. He was notorious for his audacious criticism of America's most distinguished artists in the *New Path* and as art critic for the *Tribune* since 1864. In fact, idiosyncratic Cook had already strayed from the "path" by 1867, writing in a *Tribune* review that "for all the Realist's labor," their painting lacked "the effect of nature" and needed to take a turn toward imaginative suggestion.[94]

Rather than disparaging women's abilities, Cook's critique voiced the concerns of the Ladies' Advisory Council, which held that women in need of employment should not aspire to produce the complicated compositions of history painting, which took time and commanded only a small market. Rimmer responded to Cook in the *New York Sun* and defended his students in his 1869 Annual Report. "The attempt to instruct women in Art, with a view to securing a livelihood, may be pronounced a success," he wrote, as "the only failures which occur, aside from the want of natural capacity, are due solely to the lack of industry and perseverance on the part of the pupil. Such failures occur quite as often with men as with women, and hence the Trustees see no cause for discouragement."[95]

To remedy what they considered a deficiency in Rimmer's directorship and teaching, the trustees followed the advice of the Ladies' Advisory Council and hired Ellen E. Childe, a graduate of London's South Kensington School of Design, to take over "all the mere business of the school" in 1870 and to give "exclusive instruction [in elementary drawing] to all the new pupils."[96] Feeling that his authority had been undermined, Rimmer threatened to resign and the Trustees accepted this threat as a resignation despite his subsequent backpedaling.

Students protested the dismissal by refusing to return to classes and presenting a petition to Hewitt, signed "respectfully" by 88 students, demanding Rimmer's reinstatement.[97] Mary McLain felt strongly enough to write her own letter to the Trustees. Dr. Rimmer's "removal from the directorship is a loss that is irremediable, and the nobleness of our generous patron Mr Cooper in founding such a school, is milked of half its benefits to us women, by depriving those of us who wish to enter the foremost ranks of Art, of the free instruction that will enable us to do so."[98] According to McLain, Rimmer's pedagogy offered exactly what Cooper had envisioned for women. But wishing "to enter the foremost ranks of Art" before you mastered the skills was exactly the problem, according to Cook and the Ladies' Advisory Council. Rimmer's indulgence of the imagination (figuratively and literally) was no better a method of teaching women artists destined for self support than Farrer's suppression of it had been.

Engraving Class: Man of Genius or Practical Teacher

Some Ladies' Advisory Council members saw William J. Linton, who took over for O'Brien as head of the engraving department in 1868, as a counterbalance to William Rimmer, with Linton's skill complementing Rimmer's imagination. At one of her Saturday night receptions, Mrs. Botta asked Linton whether he thought it was better for a School of Design to be taught "by a thoroughly accomplished teacher and man of genius" or what (he supposed) she would call "a more practical teacher." Reiterating the Unity of Art ideal, Linton replied that "the man of genius is also really the more practical," as he teaches principles and taste, and the other teaches only by application and routine.[99]

Botta, who apparently considered Linton the more practical teacher, did not recognize the insult implicit in her question. Linton was recognized as a man of genius, an embodiment of the midcentury American notion of the "fine artisan." In 1867 the *New York Times* singled out Linton's engravings at the National Academy Exhibition as paradigmatic of the art. His work stood out and endured because it reproduced with meticulous imitation *and* indulged the imagination. "Students of wood engraving, who desire to see what magnificent effects can be produced in this material by a master of the art, should study the specimens of Mr. Linton's work now on exhibition at the Academy. They are masterpieces, and are worthy of the closest examination."[100]

The parity that women engravers and engraving designers experienced in the art market was directly related to the training they received from artists like Linton at the School of Design. To begin with, engraved illustration was a good career choice for women artists who commanded little capital, as the tools of the trade were cheap, accessible, and portable. All an artist needed to design an illustration, besides talent and imagination, was a pencil and paper and some knowledge of the engraving process.[101] She did not have to move near a company or set up a studio to ply this trade. Woodblock engraving was equally cheap and portable. Linton estimated that the total cost of an engraver's equipment was only 25 shillings ($3). The materials consisted of "Indian ink, wood blocks, a dozen variously shaped gravers, tint tools for cutting parallel lines, gouges, and flat chisels, an oil-stone upon which to sharpen the tools, a sandbag upon which to rest the block, a watchmaker's lens, a lamp for night work and a clear globe filled with water, partly to direct the light on to the block and partly to maintain the humidity of the room and so prevent the block from warping"[102] (Figure 17).

Whether she took up the pen or graver, every student at the School of Design was taught to draw and cut the block, so that the illustrators would understand the engraving process and vice versa. The creation of an engraving on wood involved three steps before it was printed. The design was conceived through preparatory sketches; the final version was transferred onto

Figure 17. Wood engraving students at Cooper Union, "New York City.—The Monument of a Philanthropist: The Cooper Union and Its Schools of Art," *Frank Leslie's Illustrated Newspaper* (14 April 1883): 125. Courtesy of Newark Public Library.

a block of wood measuring the size specified by the publication's editor; and the picture was gouged out with a carving tool or graver. Cooper Union students were taught to eliminate the intermediary step, thereby avoiding any need for the engraver to rethink a design or reduce or enlarge a drawing. "(we drew on wood in those days; the engravers' blocks were sent me by mail)," Mary Hallock recalled in her memoir, invoking both the difficulty of this skill, which required drawing the image backward, and the portability of the trade.[103] Otherwise woodblock illustrations were drawn on tracing paper that was turned face down onto the block to transfer the design. Either the artist or the engraver might be responsible for transferring the picture; all good woodblock illustrators knew how to design an image that an engraver could transfer exactly and all good engravers understood drawing principles well enough to transfer an artist's design exactly.

Every woodblock artist, engraver, and illustrator trained at the School of Design also was expected to express her own aesthetic sensibility. From Linton they learned that in the past the best engravers had "drawn with the graver," even when reproducing the work of another artist. True, engraving was a humble profession: "The engraver had no right to contradict the master artist." And yet, he stressed, "there is a limit to the subserviency [sic] of an engraver (stalwart or wooden)."[104] Linton promoted what he called "free hand artistry" as opposed to fidelity in copying. The ideal engraver was an artist; she had a characteristic way of cutting the block and at the same time bringing out the subtlety of the designer's style through her lines. Similarly, a good woodblock illustrator was able to draw a design that was perfect in its own right and yet lent itself to the engraver's artistic interpretation.

Engraver, poet, and polemicist, Linton derived his understanding of the equilibrium between design and execution from his experience as an artisan in industrializing England (Figure 18). During the 1840s, Linton made his name as an engraver through his work with John Orrin Smith for the *Illustrated London Times.* He also became heavily involved in radical republican causes, including Chartism, a movement in Great Britain to extend political power to working men and foster collaboration between the middle and working classes. Master engravers were more independent and more intimately associated with artists, editors, and publishers than other craftsmen, and often held in as high regard and paid as well as any other artist in England or America. But in the market economy they often became "two-legged, cheap machines for engraving,—scarcely mechanics," who mostly worked from sketches that were not their own, rarely published the resulting illustrations, and usually received payment for their work determined by the publisher.[105] In reaction to this dwindling independence (and the effects of lithography and photomechanical printing on his craft), Linton instigated a movement to reinvent the printmaking arts of engraving and etching (a metal plate and acid process).

Linton was a radical thinker, an advocate of universal adult suffrage, government-funded education, gender equality, and an end to state interference in marriage and contraception. In the 1850s he set up his first private press and produced a stream of pamphlets on English and European politics, mostly written and illustrated by himself. Walter Crane, whose rad-

Figure 18. Portrait of "William J. Linton, in 1895," *New England Magazine* 18, 2 (April 1898): 151. Courtesy of American Antiquarian Society.

ical ideas and illustrative work also influenced American illustrators, apprenticed to Linton in 1858. Forced by financial circumstances to immigrate to the United States in November 1866, Linton was introduced to Peter Cooper by Rimmer. His first employment in America was teaching engraving at the School of Design for Women.[106]

Cooper student Caroline A. Powell (b. 1852), who became a successful wood engraver in her own right, believed Linton had both strengths and weaknesses as a teacher of female pupils. "He was a man who had much personal magnetism, and I remember how enthusiastic we girls were over him. His teaching was most irregular. Sometimes he would come for an hour or an afternoon every day in the week and then we might not see him for a couple of weeks or a month. We worked away more or less in the dark in his absence, but his visits were red-letter occasions, and his talks on engraving and art generally were most interesting and illuminating." Powell insisted that the most she learned, at that time, "was from a faithful and incessant study" of the "priceless proofs" of his cuts "in the *Illustrated London News* and other publications."[107]

"Linton's distinctive merit was not a matter of tools, but of art culture," recalled John P. Davis, another former student who taught engraving and drawing on wood at the School of Design from 1880 to 1884. "He worked with his graver, using just the same kind of intelligence that he used when working with his brush. . . . Those who have learned his lesson know that the study of drawing, painting, and modeling, or whatever brings skill to the hand and quickness to the perception, is the best way to study engraving. Let art be your master."[108] Despite the infrequent appearances of their teacher, many of Linton's School of Design students excelled as engravers and illustrators. He bolstered their careers in every way he could, working with them on commissions, referring New York and Boston publishers to them, and discussing their work in print. He praised his students Bianca Bondi [Robitscher], Charlotte Cogswell, Mary Hallock [Foote], Jesse Curtis [Shepherd], Caroline Powell, Lucy Gibbons [Morse], and the Engraving School for Women at the Cooper Institute as a whole in his influential book, *The History of Wood-Engraving in America* (1882).

"Delineavit" et "Sculpsit"

The work performed for publishers by women artists at the School of Design included designing (or drawing) and engraving (or cutting) the pic-

Figure 19. N.Y. School of Design, "PEC Barrel," from Susan Warner, *Carl Krinken: his Christmas stocking* (New York, 1854), 210. Courtesy of American Antiquarian Society.

tures. Early prints produced by the school's engraving students were signed "N. Y. School of Design for Women," but as editors began to commission particular student artists, individual engravers and designers added their signatures to the plates (Figure 19). These personal signatures represented professional contacts made at the school. After working on orders in class the most experienced engravers often withdrew, "taking with them the customers they obtained." Others were "employed in the office of an engraver downtown," and a few established their own firms.[109]

Illustrators who designed pictures on paper or drew them on woodblocks sometimes distinguished their work from that of the engraver by adding the designation "del" or "delineavit" (a verb that means she or he drew this) to their signatures. Engravers also signed their work, usually with initials or a last name, and often added "sc" or "sculpsit" (a verb that means she or he sculpted this) to their signatures. Some illustrations were signed by engraving companies, which could mean the engravers designed *and* cut the image; or an engraving company might sign the title page if hired to cut the work of a number of artists in a single publication. The

Figure 20. N.Y. School of Design, del, Sarah Fuller, sc, *The Wall of Fire* (Tract Association of Friends, ca. 1852), 1. Courtesy of American Antiquarian Society.

School of Design was used as a firm name in both of these capacities during the 1850s and 1860s.

Susan E. Fuller (b. 1829) added her name and the "sc" designation to the firm name "N.Y. School of Design" (the original school) on plates in children's books and religious tracts from the early 1850s (Figure 20). In the 1860s Fuller set up her own shop at 634 Broadway, the heart of the graphic arts district, and took in apprentices.[110] Beginning her career at the New York School of Design on Broadway must have made Fuller feel comfortable working in the graphic arts district for her business card promised: "Persons having orders will be called upon by sending their address."[111] Her firm handled an assortment of jobs: "Original Drawings Made. Photographs Copied. Drawings Enlarged or Reduced. Architectural Designs, Machinery, Landscapes, Fruit, Flowers, etc. executed in the best manner upon reasonable terms." Her *Manual of Instruction in the Art of Wood Engraving* was published in two editions, 1867 and 1879.

Contacts made at the School of Design led to other contacts, as was customary in the publishing world. In 1870, an editor at the *Tribune* build-ing who hired Fuller to do "quite a large amount of wood engraving for us, mainly in cuts for Books" referred her to an associate in another depart-ment: "She is a good engraver and would like to do maps for us and it occurs to me that in cases where maps can be made substantially at leisure but *finished* at the last moment it might be well to employ her. Please con-sider it."[112] Two sisters who moved with the School of Design to the Cooper Union found a congenial place to open their business as well. Returning home to San Francisco, a young city and in need of trained artists, sister engravers Leila Curtis and Mary Curtis Richardson opened a shop, hired helpers, and filled a range of orders from "fine lettering and colored labels to great theatrical posters worked up in colors on pine boards." They also taught engraving to other women, sending them east to complete their edu-cations at the Cooper Union if they showed promise.[113]

Like Fuller, Charlotte B. Cogswell (b. 1825) began signing the blocks she cut for children's books and magazines while at the School of Design. Having apprenticed under Herrick and O'Brien, her work epitomized the white line style of wood engraving. In "The Ocean" (1860), for example, Cogswell avoids crosshatching and instead uses the proximity of the lines to distinguish between sky, sea, and land (Figure 21). The quality of her work and her abilities as a teacher impressed Linton, who suggested Cogs-well replace him as head of the engraving department in 1870 and men-tioned her in *The History of Wood-Engraving in America*.[114]

Bianca Bondi [Robitscher] first signed "Bondi sc" on a bookplate for Susan Warner's *Melbourne House* in 1864. She received her certificate in wood engraving in 1866, and graduated from the Cooper Union in 1868, at about the same time that she married. Robitscher worked as a woodcut art-ist for an array of book, magazine, and newspaper publishers. She was re-sponsible for all the illustrations in Lorenzo Niles and Orson Squire Fowler's phrenological books and many in the *American Phrenological Jour-nal*. She also worked for Randolph's Gallery, *Frank Leslie's*, the "Methodist" Book Concern, and several German language journals. Her pen and ink re-productions were exhibited at the Philadelphia Exposition in 1876, and her work received favorable comments from Worthington Whittredge, John Ehninger, and other artists.[115]

An able engraving student could draw the illustrations she cut, and often the designers and engravers of woodcuts produced at the School of Design were the same person. But as the demand for engraved illustration increased so too did the division between the two professions. Along with

THE OCEAN.

Figure 21. Charlotte B. Cogswell, sc, "The Ocean," *Merry's Book of Tales* (New York, 1860), 172. Courtesy of American Antiquarian Society.

Bondi's plate in *Melbourne House* is an illustration signed "FK sc," the engraver's initials and designation. While it was not too difficult to match those initials with Fanny [Frances] Ketchem, another Cooper Union student, it is much harder to determine how much of the picture can be attributed to her.[116] No delineator or "del" signed the work. And although Ketchem has added "sc" to her initials, that designation does not rule out the engraver as the picture's designer.

Changing of the Guard

The departure of Rimmer and Linton in 1870 from the School of Design did not destroy their allegiance to female artists, nor did it represent a change in the school's commitment to the Unity of Art ideal. Charlotte Cogswell, who took over the engraving department on Linton's recommendation, maintained Herrick's apprenticeship-like program and O'Brien's practice of allowing graduates to use the classroom as a workshop. She took it upon herself to keep the department open during the summer months, like any other business, so that students could accept and execute commissions continuously and preserve their professional identities. Cogswell also continued her predecessors' practice of teaching engraving students to design, by hiring a "first rate artist" to teach drawing on wood and establishing a special twice-a-week life-drawing session in the engraving department.[117]

Susan Carter replaced Ellen Childe as Principal of the Cooper Union School of Design for Women in 1872, the first year of another financial crisis in the nation. In Carter the tensions surrounding academic versus practical training were poised in one person. An advocate of the ideals of the aesthetic movement, Carter moved the school in the direction of the applied arts, initiating many new classes in handicraft-related fields and revamping the program to meet the demand for a workforce of designers of furniture, ceramics, metalwork, textiles, books, and other objects for household use. She also supplemented teaching pedagogy for artists with a "Normal Teachers" class. This emphasis on crafts and teaching satisfied the Advisory Council's expectations regarding industrial art education and matched similar provisions being made in public schools.[118]

But Carter never separated fine art aesthetics from industrial design practice either. Instead, she renamed the school the "Woman's Art School" and hired younger contemporary artists to teach the new classes. Among them were members of the Art Students' League and National Academy of

Design: Wyatt Eaton, J. Alden Weir, Douglas Volk, Robert Swain Gifford, Walter Shirlaw, James Carroll Beckwith, and John Twachtman. Having trained in European academies and ateliers, these young artists were eager to apply newly acquired theories and techniques to their teaching and decorative art production. In response to their ideas, Carter revitalized classes in cast and life drawing. As before, council members looked in dismay at this turn toward fine art. And like her predecessors, Carter responded that learning to draw the human form was essential to any artist's education. Besides, she declared, knowledge of fine art principles would lead to better pay, give students more professional credibility, and teach future designers to make curves.[119] Carter retained her position until 1896.

Although interest and personal ability guided women artists studying at the School of Design toward one art field or another, their teachers and directors did not advocate specialization. Instead they stressed the need to learn all the skills and principles involved in the production of an art form, as would any master artisan. O'Brien sometimes complained that the time his pupils spent in drawing class took away from the practice they needed working on their blocks, but he never suggested it was unnecessary.[120] Similarly, the school's painting teachers wanted their students to become good colorists but also to draw and design well. Learning to produce a work from start to finish impressed upon the class the link between the arts. It demonstrated the Unity of Art ideal. Such training also gave women artists entering New York City's diverse art market an array of genres and skills to sell.

Chapter 5
"Laborers in the Field of the Beautiful"

Surveying New York City's cultural landscape in 1868, the *New York Evening Post* was "surprised to learn that we possess so numerous a corps of women laborers in the field of the beautiful." In fact the "women artists of our city are already so strong in numbers as to justify the formation of a society whose object it is to assist all of their sister artists who may be in need." Many of the fifty-four artists named in the article had been pupils at Cooper Institute's School of Design for Women, where they were taught "not only how to draw and paint" but also "many branches of the mechanic arts, such as drawing on wood and stone, and in the divers processes of engraving." The reporter highlighted these various skills along with the professional nature of the artists' organization to demonstrate to the public that "their knowledge may be something more than an entertainment. These women have devoted themselves to these pursuits, not only because it administers to the love of the true and beautiful, but that it may serve as a remunerative occupation; and it is to be hoped that they will receive the sympathy and encouragement they deserve."[1]

The *Evening Post*'s description of women artists as "laborers" was more than metaphorical. Professional women artists active in America between 1860 and 1880 were both fine and industrial artists. The names of these artists are little known and their working lives far from understood today. Yet the article makes it clear that they were not amateurs or anomalies. At least the fifty or so listed were successful enough to afford studios in the city or its vicinity and to establish a professional society to help those who were struggling. Many of them were already familiar to the public, a few of them were famous, and still others, particularly those employed by the publishing industry, would become household names.[2] These artists and their association represented the Unity of Art in action.

Despite such publicity, this generation of American women artists would be forgotten for the same reason that each generation assumes it is the first to break through the barriers that have kept women out of the profession: the criteria that identifies the "Artist" changed.[3] According to the *Evening Post*, New York's women artists deserved to be taken seriously not only because they were artists in the Romantic sense—"lovers of the true and beautiful"—but because they were trying to make a living out of art. In 1868 economic ambition, not any particular genre or medium, made a woman artist a professional. That open definition would not apply to women artists twenty years later.

John Ruskin's advice to let go "of any ideas of Decorative art being a degraded or separate kind of art" was auspicious for Cooper Union's first female graduates who hit New York's city streets and village roads at the very moment industrialization was transforming American art practice. In the 1860s and 1870s, they found broad overlapping markets for their fine, decorative, and industrial arts. Fine art generally meant easel painting in oils or marble and bronze sculpture. Decorative art consisted of the design, production, or decoration of objects ranging from watercolor and pastel pictures to tiles and fabrics. And industrial art referred to designing, drawing, engraving, illuminating, illustrating, and etching all forms of black and white work, and coloring or otherwise embellishing prints. Each of these fields called for knowledge, training, and skill, attributes many women now claimed.

Steeped in the Unity of Art ideal, women artists pursued their careers in all settings, worked in all genres, and felt no qualms about crossing the various fields of art. They worked in homes and studios, shops and factories. They painted on canvas, silk, wood panels, and paper. They sketched in watercolors, pen and ink, pencil, charcoal, crayon, and pastels. They drew on wood blocks and etched on steel plates. They painted on stone, creating lithographs and chromos. They colored photographs and engraved prints. They embellished book covers and ephemera with gold leaf, feathers, and lace. They glazed tiles and plaques to be framed and exhibited or laid out as tabletops or fire backs. They decorated chinaware and founded their own potteries. They drew patterns for wallpaper and calico, invented appliquéd tapestry paintings, and established design companies with male associates. They painted murals on walls. They worked in three-dimensional media, sculpting clay and stone, making jewelry, and carving wood. They made hand-illustrated folios; painted rocks, shells, and boxes as curiosities for the parlor; and designed and decorated useful household utensils. Some made and sold frames. Women artists also taught all of these skills to other artists, and wrote and published manuals about them.

Male artists of this generation engaged in many of these activities, and until 1876 men pursued art careers in much the same way as women. Owing to the rise of design schools and new policies at art academies, men and women received essentially the same educations. They worked side by side in studios in the same buildings or neighborhoods. They exhibited together and sold their paintings and drawings to the same patrons and publishers. Women artists also joined men in artists' associations, which came together to lend mutual aid, share aesthetic ideas, encourage civic interest, and mitigate new competition.

But the experiences of most women were distinct from those of most men. The major difference between the two sexes was the economic and social position from which they negotiated the art profession. Even when both came from the middle classes, women tended to start out with fewer resources than men. They were more likely to turn to the industrial arena at some point in their working lives—to launch a career, make or supplement a living, or establish a professional identity. Although economic need was no stranger to male artists during the war years and the hard times of the 1870s, women's options were further limited by their poorer educations outside of art. These constraints gave female artists incentive to engage in art forms that promised financial security, such as the decorative arts or in publishing, rather than seek another kind of employment.

Fortunately for aspiring women artists, early industrialization democratized as well as proletarianized art production in America by creating and expanding the variety of art jobs open to women and employing skilled female artists to fill them. A number of women artists who successfully adapted to this new setting ranked among the best-paid and most-acclaimed professionals of their day. Others eked out a living in obscurity. Whatever their respective fortunes, for over twenty years many talented women artists took advantage of intersecting art arenas and labor markets to share ambitions, compete, and collaborate with their male colleagues.

An Open Field

New York and Brooklyn certainly seemed like the field of the beautiful to female artists who emerged from art school in the 1860s in search of work and studios. The Civil War brought the city both terrible poverty and fantastic wealth. Wartime prosperity, burgeoning industries, and new art markets offered artists a province for creativity. In the North at least, the war increased the number of private citizens seeking refinement through the purchase of art.[4] Despite droughts and wartime emergencies, even the farming districts surrounding New York City experienced "quickened trade" during the rebellion. "It's a mystery but a fact in my district," exclaimed one census marshal in 1865, "money was never more plentiful," while another reported with similar wonder "a tendency to extravagance in the way of dress and manner of living."[5]

Artists and art critics in the city remarked on this art boom as well. The panic of 1857 had taken its toll on artists, but things were looking up. In 1863, Clarence Cook commented that "a kind of picture mania" had taken over since the war began: "Pictures are selling daily at what would have been regarded as fabulous prices in the flush times before the Rebellion."[6] Landscape artist Worthington Whittredge also recalled that "painters sold their pictures readily and native art flourished more conspicuously" during the Civil War. "Strange to say, it had less effect upon art than upon many things of more stable foundations," he added. The National Academy's new gothic revival building at Broadway and Tenth Street was completed chiefly during the war and its opening receptions and balls were among the most prominent social events in Gotham.[7]

Women were among the artists who reaped the benefits of the city's wartime exigencies and prosperity. The Civil War stimulated a resurgence of cultural nationalism, which motivated the choices of two groups of art buyers: the growing middle classes looking for luxury items to adorn their homes and businesses, and manufacturers and merchants looking for products and designs to make and sell to those middle-class consumers. Women artists easily tapped these new markets as producers, filling vacancies left by soldiers in almost every art field and venue. Painters and sculptors found ready buyers at sales and exhibitions put on by numerous clubs and societies to assuage economic and social needs created by the war. Publishers hired female engravers, illustrators, and embellishers to decorate the books, journals, and newspapers that kept worried minds occupied. Women artists' skills were in demand, and their specialties—small paintings, decorative pieces, and cheap industrial products—became the most marketable aesthetic work in 1860s America.

The Civil War gave many artists an incentive to create artwork. In the North, young artists produced all sorts of pictures, sculptures, and decorated curiosities to sell at Sanitary Commission fairs, Army Relief bazaars, and exhibition sales (Figure 22). In 1863, *New Path* artist Thomas Lee Bulson spent all of January in Albany painting a picture for the Army Relief Bazaar to be held there in February.[8] May Alcott, who was taking art lessons

Figure 22. N.Y, Metropolitan Fair, 1864, by J. Gurney & Son. Albumen prints, stereograph. The New-York Historical Society. PR 065-0500-0041.

in Boston in 1864, also spent "nice busy happy times working steadily for the Fair" in Concord, making "about $130 worth of painted pebbles, shells, vases and a small bas-relief." These "little works of art" generated money for the soldiers and contacts for the artist: "the Fair on Monday . . . was very successful, everything of mine was sold and Mrs. Emerson bought the head that I modeled," she wrote in her dairy. She also felt "rather grand" to receive orders from Montreal and England after the fair for her "paper knives." These sales inspired Alcott to have photographs made of her colossal "head of Mercury" when it was placed on exhibition in Boston later that year, "which I expect to sell and get a percentage on each one."[9] Entrepreneurially minded women artists sold reproductions of their work as a secondary art form.

The war also provided women artists with subject matter. Writing from Penn Yan in 1864, Annie Delano informed her School of Design classmate: "Have just completed a picture I call Writing Home, representing a soldier—of course—writing on his knapsack by the campfire—a cousin, wounded and home on a furlough, was kind enough to sit for the figure." Lilly Martin Spencer was mailed daguerreotypes and specifications for portraits of beloved sons and brothers off fighting for the Union, and sold paintings of patriotic subjects and home front scenes after the conflict.[10] The "young colored sculptor" Edmonia Lewis paid her way to the marble quarries of Italy by selling reproductions of her bust of Civil War hero Robert Gould Shaw and medallion portrait of abolitionist John Brown to radical Republicans in Boston and New York.[11]

Taking a Studio

Women artists who studied at the Cooper Union during the war fit easily into New York City's cultural world. Before the war it had been considered somewhat scandalous for a lady "to hire a studio and establish herself as an artist," noted Elizabeth Dudley in the *Aldine*. But by the 1870s that course had become "so common as to excite no remark."[12] *Scribner's* agreed that "there is no other city where the woman student can pursue advanced studies in art with so few embarrassments as in New York. Here, too, studio life for women has come to be a somewhat recognized mode of existence."[13]

Only fifteen-years old in 1861, Alice Heighes Donlevy stayed on at the School of Design during the war, completing her "apprenticeship," teaching classes in illumination, and practicing her profession among the girls in the engraving shop. Donlevy was born in Manchester, England, 7 January 1846, to inventor-engraver John Intaglio Donlevy, who emigrated to the United States after his wife Alice Heighes died. She had her first art lessons in Pleasantville, New York, in watercolors. Her father married writer Harriet Farley in 1854 and two years later Horace Greeley took her to the New York School of Design for Women to be trained as an artist-engraver.[14]

Not until 1866 did the young illuminator emerge from the school to rent a studio with painter Elizabeth Clement Field. During their first year in the studio, Alice worked on commissions for engraving designs and on the plates and text for her drawing manual following the Unity of Art ideal, while Elizabeth worked toward exhibition sales on meticulously detailed paintings of plant life following the precepts of the Association for the Advancement of Truth in Art. They also met with other women from the School of Design who were now working in studio buildings and trying to found an art association.

Taking a studio was an important personal and professional move for a woman artist. A studio anywhere announced that art was the occupant's business; it signified the elevated level of her accomplishment. But to "live in N.Y. with a studio on Broadway . . . always seemed the climax of artistic happiness, and the pinicle [sic] of artistic ambition" to Annie Delano, who worked in numerous small towns in western New York and Pennsylvania in the 1860s and 1870s.[15] A New York City studio offered close proximity to a network of female associates and male advocates, artists' organizations, and industrial markets that formed a critical infrastructure for women artists. The city boasted a host of exhibition sites at the halls of civic institutes, libraries, and societies, and sale venues at the galleries of art suppliers, publishers, agents, framers, and auctioneers, such as Schaus, Lanthier, Leavitt, Loepler, Goupil, Randolph, Cottier, the American Art Galleries, and Mr. Brown, the National Academy's agent on Fifth Avenue, who all increased their gallery space and added women's art to their collections during the 1860s and 1870s. But the first contact between artists and the buying public often took place in the artist's studio, or at the seasonal receptions and open house exhibitions of studio buildings.

After the war dozens of women artists continued to keep studios in New York City, and those who could afford them rented rooms in studio buildings. The emergence of discrete studio spaces in the 1850s encouraged artists—married and single, male and female—to separate their professional and home lives. Almost every artists' studio building in New York and Brooklyn had female occupants, including Dodworth's building, Waverly House, the old New York University building, the old Art-Union building, the Sherwood building, Granite building, and Gibson building, the YMCA, and the Brooklyn Institute across the river.[16] A studio in New York University's studio building was fairly spacious with a high ceiling, a large slanted window/skylight, and a sink.

Only a few of the more established artists could afford to rent studios individually. Rooms in studio buildings usually cost between $15 and $30 a month, a hefty sum for someone just starting out. On top of that, the price

of room and board in New York City in 1861 ranged from $6 to $14 a
month, not including fuel.[17] Most women artists shared the space and expense of a studio with a friend or sister artist.[18] Painter Adelaide E. Rose
kept no. 10 in the Gibson building at 842 Broadway with illuminator Edith
W. Cook.[19] Figure painter Helena de Kay and painter/designer Maria Oakey
shared a studio/apartment in the city as single women, and continued to do
so after each had wed.[20] Henrietta and Virginia Granbery, sister painters
who migrated from Norfolk, Virginia, to attend the Cooper Union, kept a
studio together at 1267 Broadway. Sister painters Elizabeth C. and Gulielma
Field took 735 and 736 Broadway until 1867, when Elizabeth moved to a
studio at 896 Broadway with Alice Donlevy. Women artists also shared studios with husbands and brothers. Married landscape painters John and
Mary Strongitharm Pope worked in a studio together in Dodworth's building until Mary took a separate room. Mrs. Jerome Thompson painted portraits alongside her genre painter husband in the Association building. And
the painter siblings, Maria Louise and Daniel Wagner, shared a studio when
Maria visited the city from upstate New York.[21]

Women artists shared studios "for protection and companionship," as
well as to limit the expense.[22] Unattached male artists often saved money
by eating in restaurants and sleeping in their studios. Some studios were
designed with attached bedrooms for this purpose. "The studio of the
poorer class is sleeping room, and generally more or less kitchen as well,"
or one might find artists sharing a "cheap flat with a work-room in common."[23] A male artist looked for a studio that accommodated his work habits, pocketbook, and associations. A female artist needed all that and
security too. "Many cases of obscure and painful hardship" are worsened
for young female artists by the formidable expense of keeping a studio in a
"suitable" safe building with "fire-proof shutters," *Scribner's* reported. The
erection of a studio building for women artists would be, therefore, "a gen-
uine and amiable field for philanthropy"[24] (Figure 23).

Some women artists rented studios year round; others took them sea-
sonally or moved when they found a better situation. They tried to stay in
the graphic arts district. Landscape painter/etcher Eliza Greatorex kept her
studio at Dodworth's building for several years, until opening a studio and
gallery at home with her daughters. Miniaturist Mary Freeman moved her
studio three times in the 1850s, finally settling at New York University.
Helen Burt painted in no. 34, 788 Broadway in 1874, no. 55 West Twenty-
Eighth Street in 1876, and no. 4 East Twenty-Third Street in 1878. She then
moved with her sister Martha to the YMCA building on the corner of

"YOUR WASHING, MUM." (DRAWN BY S. G. McCUTCHEON.)

Figure 23. S. G. McCutcheon, "Your Washing, Mum," *Scribner's* 19 (November 1879-April 1880): 359.
Courtesy of American Antiquarian Society.

Twenty-Third Street and Fourth Avenue (across the street from the National Academy of Design), where they worked side by side in studios no. 33 and 34.[25] Landscape artists were particularly mobile, leaving the city yearly for summer residences or sketching excursions in the countryside. National Academy artist Charlotte Buell [C. B.] Coman rented studio no. 35 at 788 Broadway in 1874, moved to a new studio building in 1875 but did not like it, and moved back to studio no. 19 at 788 in 1876. She later moved to studios B and no. 13 in the Sherwood studio building at 58 West Fifty-Seventh Street.

Finances and family duty made female artists more transient than their brother artists. Women artists who were called home to nurse family members or simply to help out during the holiday season often gave up their studios.[26] During the depression of 1858, Lilly Martin Spencer closed up shop and moved both family and studio to a house in Newark, New Jersey, where they could grow vegetables to stave off starvation.[27] The family still lived in New Jersey when Spencer moved her studio back to New York City after the Civil War.[28]

A studio functioned as far more than a site of production. It was a venue for marketing and display that suggested an intimacy with the artist that might appeal to the press or bourgeois customers. Like her male colleagues, Spencer used her New York City studio to launch a new painting with a kind of assurance of its success. At 5 Waverly Place in 1867, Spencer began working on a very large (approximately 6' x 7') allegorical painting called *Truth Unveiling Falsehood* that became the focus of journalists' visits. Critics and dealers welcomed the artist back to the city and closely followed the progress of the painting in newspaper columns; some claimed the painting was certain to "achieve independence, fortune and fame for this brave woman."[29] Spencer finished *Truth Unveiling Falsehood* in 1868, but instead of selling it to an art dealer or collector she announced the painting's completion to the press and exhibited it in her studio the next season. She then circulated it to a number of other cities, all the while selling subscriptions for a large engraving of the painting, a number of which she tinted by hand.[30] Whether Spencer exploited this strategy the most effectively is not clear. What is clear is that women artists were using their studios to generate attention and compensation for their professional activities.

Women who kept studios in prominent studio buildings benefited most from studio visits, artists' receptions, and open houses. The size and locale of a studio spoke to the artist's success and prominence and advertised her abilities. Many artists with rooms in studio buildings shared the amenities they offered with their colleagues. Few young artists could afford the rents at what became New York's most famous Studio Building at West Tenth Street, which had a waiting list and mostly older, well-established residents.[31] No women artists rented studios there, although they did use the building in other ways. Landscape painter Julie [Hart] Beers who lived in Metuchen, New Jersey, kept a studio at Dodworth's in the 1860s, but used her brother William Hart's studio at 51 Tenth Street as a showroom and a pick-up and delivery depot for gallery cartmen when she was out of town. Illustrator Mary Stone, who kept studio no. 13 at 1227 Broadway, used Edwin White's New York University studio for the same purposes.[32] Occupants of studio buildings also often displayed the work of their studio-less friends and colleagues in their rooms during receptions and open hours to the public.[33]

Artist Associations

Taking a studio in New York City connected women artists to other artists interested in promoting their profession. Studio buildings were convenient ground for the cultivation of art associations: alliances of artists working in different fields of art and interested laypersons who shared a desire to promote the profession. Inspired by radical social reform movements of the 1840s and 1850s, art associations were nonhierarchical organizations, local and national in scope, founded and run by professional artists. The Brooklyn Art Association, formed in 1859 in the atelier of sculptor Henry Kirke Brown, served as a lively focal point for meetings of local artists and writers. Two years later the Association moved to rooms in the Brooklyn Institute of Music.[34]

The aim of the Brooklyn Art Association was to advance the "business" of artists by making their work known to the public, training artists in their respective fields, and promoting civic interest in art culture.[35] By administering a school of art and holding seasonal receptions, the association introduced the community of artists to the public and to prominent laymen interested in supporting local culture. It also gave artists working in distant locations or isolated studios a place to show their work, receive the press, and make professional contacts.[36]

The Brooklyn Art Association held its first seasonal reception in 1861 and hired H. R. Latimer as curator and Gordon Lester Ford as agent to assist artists in making sales and acquiring commissions. These exhibitions followed the same format as studio building receptions but with a larger pool of artists and guests invited to exhibit and attend. One month before the reception was to be held at the Brooklyn Art Association, a committee sent a letter to members soliciting pictures not shown previously in Brooklyn, and noting the days on which the cartman would call.

Male and female artists sent works to these seasonal receptions from their studios, and from private galleries, auction houses, the National Academy, and other exhibition sites.[37] They also suggested the names of fellow artists to be invited to contribute or attend. After receiving her notice for the winter exhibition, C. B. Coman asked the committee to send circulars to Julia Dillon and her sister Lily McEntee of Rondout-on-the-Hudson, New York, "cousins of [Jervis] McEntee the artist," who "desire to contribute a picture to the Academy." McEntee's painting sold at the reception that winter for $22.50. Julia McEntee Dillon (b. 1834) commenced her professional career at the Association's seasonal receptions. Having "[s]tudied in Paris," Dillon was inspired by the popularity of her peony studies to take a studio in New York City. She worked there during the winter seasons and at home in the summers, and by 1876 she stood "among the best flower painters in this country."[38]

Brooklyn Art Association receptions added to the intermingling of art and artists going on at the studio level. Exhibitors were professional artists working in any graphic medium. For example, the same reception might feature Alice Donlevy's illuminations, John G. Brown's oil paintings, Jenny Brownscombe's pen and ink sketches, John Henry Hill's watercolors, and Miss Jessie Curtis's "drawing on wood" (engraving blocks). The exhibition committee and agents recognized art as the business of every contributor. They received and returned the work of male and female artists in the same manner. They showed no gender favoritism when showing art or sending prospective buyers to artists' studios. And they charged everyone the same 10 percent commission for sale and delivery.[39]

Female painters sold pictures as readily as male painters at the Brooklyn receptions and occasionally sold more.[40] They also received equivalent prices for their art. The cost of a picture often had as much to do with its subject and size as with the reputation of the artist. Scenes with figures brought women artists the most revenue, from $150 to $1,500. Small still-life and nature scenes fetched the least, at $5 and up. Christine Chapin received $750 for a scene of a child reading a book, while John G. Brown asked $180 to $650 for similar subjects. The small landscapes of Julie Beers ranged from $45 and $200. Louisa B. Culver's flower paintings sold for as little as $25, but her landscapes and architectural subjects cost as much as $250. Similarly, Elizabeth C. Field priced her nature and flower panels at $25 to $35. But reputation and medium could affect prices. Watercolor landscapes and fruit and flower paintings by Virginia and Henrietta Granbery sold for prices ranging from $25 to $100 and oil paintings for up to $225.[41]

Both sexes negotiated the prices of their paintings through the Association's agents, and most artists appreciated their help. Only a few artists began by asking for sums higher than the norm for the size or subject of a picture. Nonetheless, both sexes commonly instructed agents to reduce prices if need be to make a sale. After viewing the exhibition for himself, marine artist J. B. Bristol asked Latimer to "make a great reduction in the price" of his painting to "see if it will be possible for you to sell it." But when Latimer secured a buyer at $150, Bristol asked him to try and persuade "the man up to $200." Bristol later became rude when the money from a sale did not promptly arrive, asking the Association if the treasurer was "so stupid as to expect" him to call for his pay.[42] Having to lower a picture's price or wait for payment was distressing for male and female artists alike, but women artists were more inclined to show only polite disappointment. When Latimer told Annie E. Sterling the price he had been offered for her "lilacs" before selling the painting, she thanked him for his "judgment in the matter." After she "saw where they were hung and under the circumstances," she "Respectfully and Gratefully" added, "the price is satisfactory."[43]

Only a tiny minority of artists had the studio space and funds necessary to undertake the enormous paintings that sold for thousands of dollars. These works were often purchased beforehand at the artist's studio and lent for exhibition by the owner, art dealer, or publisher who purchased them. All of the colossal marine and landscape paintings by Albert Bierstadt shown at the Brooklyn Art Association were already owned, except one in 1881 that was priced at $5000. Women artists rarely had the space or means to tackle such gigantic works, but a substantial number did paint landscapes following the Hudson River school or New Path ideal.[44] Most common at the Brooklyn receptions were medium-sized scenes of the countryside and seascape. Julie Hart Beers sold numerous paintings of scenes captured along the Hudson River, alongside her artist brothers James and Charles Hart and first husband Marion Beers, at Brooklyn receptions and exhibitions in New York and Philadelphia. Dozens of other women artists took their brushes outside to transfer natural views and panoramas onto paper, which they sold as independent works and engraving designs. Women artists also exhibited and sold figure scenes and portraits at the Association. But the most ubiquitous paintings and drawings exhibited by women were small still-life pictures of flowers and other nature objects.

Women oil painters often contributed art in alternative media such as watercolor, crayon, or pen and ink to Association exhibitions. These works served as inexpensive objects to sell quickly and as advertisements and studies for larger, more expensive works in progress. C. B. Coman painted watercolors that sold for $35 and up at Brooklyn receptions even though she regularly sold oil paintings for hundreds of dollars from her Broadway studio and at National Academy exhibitions. Cooper Union and National Academy graduate Jennie Augusta Brownscombe (b. 1850) sent both oil canvases and pen and ink studies to Association receptions.[45] Specializing in American scenes of city and country life, Brownscombe became one of the best-known artists of the 1870s through lithographs of her paintings and her engraved illustrations[46] (Figure 24). By exhibiting more than oil paintings, popular artists like Brownscombe educated the public and built up consumer interest in other media.

Association receptions brought potential customers in contact with a relatively new and rapidly expanding group of producers and products geared toward emergent markets. Artwork designed for reproduction brought in varying sums, as it was not yet clear what its price should be in this setting. Illustrator Mary L. Stone's watercolor sketches and paintings ranged from $20 to $100, while Fidelia Bridges asked up to $215 for hers. Engraver Charlotte B. Cogswell priced her ink and watercolor sketches at between $6 and $15. For artists working in black and white the point of exhibition was not necessarily to sell the drawing. Rather they hoped to generate work from publishers, manufacturers, or private citizens seeking designs and decorations for printed material. Alice Donlevy did not put a price on the drawings and illumination designs she exhibited, although they were for sale. Nor did Jessie Curtis price her illustrations of poems and other subjects, one of which was owned by the Aldine Press. Exhibiting art destined for publication kept the artist in the eye of the public and extended her contacts beyond those made at her design school or studio.

The Ladies' Art Association

The mixed-sex egalitarianism of the Brooklyn Art Association was typical of New York's major art institutions in the 1860s and 1870s. The National

Figure 24. Jennie Brownscombe, "A City Railroad Car," *Harper's Bazaar* 6, 19 (May 10, 1873): cover. Peter J. Eckel Collection. Princeton University.

Academy had "always been very liberal toward lady artists" and almost every design school, studio building, and exhibition site in the city accommodated them.[47] Yet, women artists still felt disadvantaged. What they lacked, they recognized, was the capital and resources that men in the business either had or could borrow or provided each other. It was rare when a woman artist "able to make her way to the metropolis" had the means to sustain herself as she pursued her initial art study or "engaged in more advanced professional labors."[48] What women artists needed was a professional organization attuned to their particular circumstances.

Like the Brooklyn Art Association, the Ladies' Art Association provided professional artists with a workspace, school, and gallery that publicized their art and connected them to patrons and publishers. It also offered a measure of financial protection and collective support. The difference was that its primary purpose was to promote the interests of women artists solely.[49]

The idea for a women's art association originated with Mary Strongitharm Pope [Mrs. John Pope] and Susan Clark Gray [Mrs. Henry Peter Gray] in the winter of 1866–67, who visited women artists in their New York studios and invited them to cooperate in the formation of the association. Nine original members met in Pope's studio at Dodworth's, where they discussed how to promote the interests of women artists. "Sketches and pictures both finished and unfinished were shown on these occasions, and subjected to criticism."[50] Pope also "offered her studio for the exhibition of their paintings."[51] From experience and observation, these women had found that female artists frequently needed aid. Thus, "a loan fund was proposed to enable members to study in Europe and to have the best advantages here, and also to be drawn from in care of illness."[52]

Mutual aid societies for the members of a trade were not new in America, nor were they foreign to the art profession; both the National Academy of Design and the Artists' Fund Society of New York began as such.[53] Like other artists' funds, the Ladies' Art Association raised money by asking each member to "contribute a picture once a year to an exhibition, which shall then be sold for the benefit of the society."[54] However, this association aspired to be much more than a mutual aid society for women artists. "The intention of the lady managers," reported the *New York Times*, "is to make the association industrial as well as philanthropical in scope. They are trying to aid women to become artists by supplying teachers, models, and materials at cost price, and propose in this way to assist them in disposing of their work."[55]

Despite its title and single-sex membership, the Ladies' Art Association was not merely an art club or ladies' benevolent society.[56] New York's women artists adopted the word "Ladies'" because a group of Philadelphia artists had taken the name "Woman's Art Association" a few weeks earlier. That association did not live beyond its first exhibition.[57] The *Times* correctly speculated that the Ladies' Art Association restricted "their charitable favors to persons of their own sex, perhaps from fear that the superior producing power of male artists would crowd out women's work, and thus defeat the object of their organization."[58] The object of an association (as opposed to a social club or benevolent society) was to help women who were laboring to gain a foothold in a profession achieve through "associate action" the success that isolated efforts did not bring.[59]

The mutual aid provided by this society focused on entrepreneurial matters. Agnes Chamberlain sent a batch of drawings and paintings to the Association "to have some person who knows the value of pictures to price all these. I know the time they take to paint but I want a competent judge to tell me their actual *value*—If they are worth a pretty fair price I will go on painting if they are not of course it will not be worth my while."[60] To reinforce the message that their business was the business of art, the Ladies' Art Association neither accepted nor distributed money as charity, and boldly printed on the edges of its circulars: "ALL CONVERSATION ON RELIGION AND POLITICS FORBIDDEN."[61] The Association was an ecumenical group, with artists from a variety of faiths making up the membership and a few prominent Quakers at the helm. Conversation on religion or partisan politics might cause strife. And strife would undermine their public-spirited work, which was to advocate for working women by quietly assisting one another.[62]

In May 1867, three of the original members, Pope, Gray, and Donlevy, formed an executive committee to invite artists outside New York City to join the Association and contribute to the loan fund. The reply sent by landscape painter C. M. Clowes of Poughkeepsie, New York, was typical: "It would give me much pleasure to contribute some work to the proposed exhibition. Hoping the Association may meet with support and success." Sculptor Lucy B. Hinton of Rhinebeck assured the committee of her "hearty sympathy and cooperation in your enterprise."[63]

The committee asked the National Academy of Design for space "to exhibit the collections of the proposed Ladies Art Association." T. Addison Richards answered on behalf of the National Academy Council that they would be "pleased to give the Society the most favorable opportunity to exhibit their productions: but are unable, at present, to provide any special space or privilege to them, over other exhibitors."[64] Although immediate assistance was denied, the letter represented recognition of the professional ambitions of the organization. Academy artists, including the husbands of Gray and Pope, understood that the point of the exhibition was to present women artists as "a class sufficiently numerous and powerful to stand by themselves and be judged among themselves" not to give them special priv-

ileges on account of their sex.[65] Thereafter, a dozen or more male academi-
cians (including several former Cooper Union teachers) served the Ladies'
Art Association as an Advisory Committee, business managers, and Honorary Members.

The first objective of the Ladies' Art Association was to found "a central point of union and reference for its members."[66] After Mrs. Pope suffered an untimely death in 1868, meetings were moved to the Women's
Bureau at 49 East Twenty-third Street (near Fourth Avenue), a handsome
residence that writer and philanthropist Elizabeth B. Phelps equipped as a
center for the intellectual, social, and professional activities of New York
women. There the Association established a permanent gallery and made
its first collection of women's work, while the Executive Committee looked
into renting rooms from the Mendelson Glee Club.[67] In 1869, it secured an
apartment of several rooms in Clinton Hall, a four-story building at Nassau
and Beekman streets used for lectures and auctions, including a studio large
enough "to accommodate twenty lady students, where they could obtain
excellent light, warmth and abundant space for their easels, at a very moderate rate, through the winter season."[68] It was "difficult to hire a studio in
those days," recalled one member, "landlords objecting to women art students as tenants." Twenty years ago, "an unknown bread winner if *a woman*
received more suspicion than courtesy." But "by officially introducing its
members" the Association altered that situation and established art as a viable profession for self-supporting women, perhaps the greatest service an
"Association for the Promotion of the Interests of Women Artists" could
offer.[69]

Clinton Hall gave the Association a headquarters in which to hold
meetings, exhibit art, offer classes, store property, and keep a studio "where
junior or other members may hire easel room at as low terms as the Association can afford."[70] Easels and easel space were offered for rent to all members at the reduced rate of $50 per annum, an option that appealed to artists
living out of town. Maria Wagner who lived and worked in upstate New
York was delighted to hear that the Association hired out "Easels and standing room for them . . . at less expense than a studio . . . we have two very
large rooms for our studio, each with north windows, and all for six dollars
per month. Yet I should almost be willing to exchange them for a garret in
New York for the winter month for the great advantage of seeing works of
art."[71] The Association also hired out the large studio at no. 4 Clinton Hall
for reasonable rates as a classroom. Association artists were given the right
of first refusal. This cheap rental was crucial to a member like Mrs. Oak-

ford, who asked the Association for her old hour back "in the autumn for a class," despite being late in paying the $28.60 rent she owed for the previous season.[72]

The structure and policies laid out in the *Constitution and By-Laws of 1871* reinforced the Association's professional aims. Like any trade association, its goal was to uphold the standards of the trade. Full members or "Fellows" had to be "professional artists or artists considered by the Executive Committee capable of being such." Art students were "Junior members." Amateurs or connoisseurs were "Associates," and honorary memberships were given to invited guests, including male artists and businesswomen, such as writer/editor Mary Mapes Dodge, who employed or otherwise supported women artists. To be accepted into the Association as a "Fellow" an artist had to be nominated by a full member who considered her "desirable for character and attainment" and voted on by ballot. She also had to submit a sample work of original design to be assessed and approved by the Executive Committee.[73]

Membership was open to women artists working in any field of art, yet always adjudicated. As in any professional organization, full membership was a privilege that had to be earned. Even a successful artist like Maria Louise Wagner, who was already known for her oil and watercolor paintings, followed the rules. "I can assure you I should have hastened to send a picture that some kind friend might have proposed me to the Art Association at this monthly meeting," she wrote the Association in 1870, "but the bye laws did not come till yesterday, too late for a picture to reach New York by the 17th. . . . I will send in the course of a few weeks pictures and money for initiation fee if that will not be presuming, before I am voted for."[74] These rules undoubtedly kept some women from applying for membership. Nevertheless, within one year thirty-five artists had joined. Incorporated in 1877, the Ladies' Art Association had headquarters in New York City and branches in Brooklyn, Paris, and London, and as many as 150 active members and hundreds of student members annually (until 1894) scattered seemingly across the United States, Canada and Europe.[75]

The organization's finances reflected the precarious economic position of most women artists. Initiation fee and annual dues were five dollars (and one artwork) for Fellows and three dollars for Juniors. During the hard times of the 1870s annual dues were reduced to two dollars for "Active Members, *i.e.*, professional Women Artists," while the dues for "Associates, *i.e.*, Women Art Students" remained at three dollars.[76] Teachers of any art specialty were invited to join for thirty cents a month, as "the bringing together of various views of information enlarges artistic expression." Any "lady or gentlemen interested in Art or Art Industry" could become a "Subscribing Member by paying the annual dues of $5.00." Several established artists, male and female, became "Life Members" by paying twenty-five dollars. Beyond these yearly dues, the Association made a little money by charging 10 percent for sales and services, small tuition fees for its classes, and reasonable rates for easel and studio rental.[77] Because even very low fees were often beyond the means of female artists, three of the members (E. C. Field, S. D. Gilbert, and Donlevy) began a bartering system that allowed students to pay for instruction with work for the Association.[78]

The Ladies' Art Association held two types of monthly meetings: "stated" meetings "for the discussion of subjects of professional importance" and social meetings for conversations and "lectures on subjects of artistic interest and the reading of essays on Art or Art-industry." The stated meetings were only open to "Fellows" and were sometimes held at a full member's residence. All members were required to bring an original work of some kind to monthly meetings for criticism. Some declined to come or sent apologies if they had nothing to bring.[79] Members who failed to comply with the rules paid 10 cents for every neglect and one dollar if they failed to exhibit an original picture within a year of joining.[80]

Social and educational meetings were open to all members and their friends, who paid one dollar a month for the privilege. The papers read at these meetings were sometimes kept as a reference for members.[81] The Association held public exhibitions, art sales, and auctions to generate public interest.[82] During the winter season in 1870 the exhibition at Clinton Hall drew increasingly larger crowds. "A select and appreciative company" attended the first reception, where pictures by Mrs. Gray, Mrs. H. J. Loop, E. H. Remmington, S. J. Gilbert, Donlevy, Cook, Griswold, Cornelia Post, and other women artists were on display. On the afternoon of the closing reception "about four hundred persons" were present.[83]

These meetings led to art classes and a plan of instruction. "Constant criticism of original drawings and paintings brought to the monthly meetings showed need of elemental education," noted an Association brochure, or as one member quipped: "the Village 'genius' generally needed foundation knowledge in drawing."[84] "What we need to do," Gray wrote Elizabeth C. Field, another founding member, is to meet the needs of those women who are not able to spend "all of their time" studying at the Cooper Institute "but who would be glad to devote a part of their time to be taught correctly."[85] In 1872 the executive officers initiated a course of classes in basic art skills and principles. The Association provided the art training that women found difficult or expensive to obtain elsewhere. At one meeting, a member told how she had "studied from the living model in her own bedroom, with locked doors, never daring to reveal the fact nor to show her sketches, even when friends expressed surprise at the 'natural genius' which enabled her to draw the human form so correctly *from imagination*."[86] And so "a life class for the use of women was started [in 1869], the fees for attendance being placed at a very low figure."[87]

Like their mentors at the Cooper Union, Association artists connected improvement in the "standard of Art Industrial education for women and children" to advance in American art generally.[88] The children of members were allowed to attend drawing classes and invited to the "children's hour," a monthly talk on "Art Industrial Subjects."[89] The Association worked to promote industrial and applied art and design education in public schools. They connected women artists' employability to the quality of their educations. To that end, the Association's executive committee extended their course offerings to include classes in "mechanical arts." In 1872, Donlevy gave free instruction in "Art appropriate to manufacture" at the Association studio, the same year a wallpaper manufacturer (prompted by Henry Peters Gray) offered a prize for the most original working design. That prize went to E. H. Remington, a figure painter who had taken advantage of Donlevy's class.[90] Technical classes in carpet designing and reproductive pen and ink drawing were officially added in 1880.

The Ladies' Art Association broadened its course list after 1876 to include decorative or household arts that promised women remunerative work. The Plan of Instruction for 1883 included figure painting, modeling, water colors, drawing on wood, fruit painting, pastel coloring, and drawing in pen and ink, as well as separate classes in painting on china, tiles, slate, silk, and panels, in decorating pottery, art needlework, designing wall paper, household art, and in principles of design.[91] An 1890 Report on the Ladies' Art Association noted there were "white and colored students in the Association." By expanding into decorative branches, the Ladies' Art Association aimed to place within the reach of all women artists art educations that would provide them with employment in their homes rather than in factories.[92]

Rented rooms in various downtown buildings served the Ladies' Art Association as classroom and studio space for fourteen years, but these locations did not eliminate the perils and expense associated with private studio buildings in the city.[93] Without the supervision provided by the staff at the Cooper Union, working and commuting in New York could prove to be quite loathsome for a single woman artist. In October 1873, Mary Cook explained her reservations in a letter declining Donlevy's proposal that she take a studio in Clinton Hall in return for teaching a class there in the winter. "Although I intend to join the classes when formed—I do not intend to take easel room, or take charge of no. 20 upon any consideration—In the first place, I promised the folks at home, that I would not, under any consideration have anything to do where that Clinton Hall Janitor was— and another reason, it is too far from home. I always had to ride, which cost me over a dollar a week, . . . I always had to crowd into a stage, stand up nearly all the way home, get the blank looks of all the people who had secure seats—and very often be the recipient of very rude remarks—I never passed a more unprofitable winter than the last—I disliked staying in the room alone—and could not work."[94]

The idea of establishing a studio building where women artists coming to New York from all parts of the country could receive both superior instruction and the protection of a home at a moderate expense originated with the Association itself.[95] But the cost of constructing such an edifice was forbidding. Not until 1881 did the Ladies' Art Association achieve its long-term goal by converting the building it occupied at 24 West Fourteenth Street (one block from Broadway) into a studio building. It hired out the large room on the first floor to be used as a classroom and let the other apartments "as studios, ten ladies being accepted as tenants." This plan was successful insofar as it made the building "public and popular" and allowed the Association to hire and fire its own janitorial staff. But the venture put the organization into debt.[96]

Throughout its numerous relocations, the Ladies' Art Association provided women artists with a central point of reference for special knowledge, help, and advice. Artists contacted the Association for all kinds of professional services, including framing and sales, art supplies, props and models, referrals, and notification about upcoming exhibitions.[97] When illustrator Juliet L. Tanner needed three blocks of wood ("7 3/4 inches by 5 7/8") to fill an order for engraving designs in Philadelphia, she wrote the Association: "as I cannot stop in New York long enough to get them I want to ask one of you to choose them for me and charge your usual commission of course."[98] A. E. Rose asked the Association to try to sell the two Orchid paintings hanging in the gallery for $60. Although if they sold "at the first price [$50 each]," she pointed out, "the commission, if the same as Schaus' or other places would be $15, I do not know though whether the Association would think that any consideration."[99] When Maria Oakey needed to find models in the city, she asked the Association. The list she received included male and female models, told whether they posed nude or clothed, and described their most aesthetic features.[100]

People interested in promoting women artists asked the Ladies' Art Association for information. The press turned to the Association for "communications on art subjects and to know what subjects are on the Easels for the coming season."[101] Helena de Kay Gilder introduced her brother-in-law T. B. Gilder to the Association so he could write "something of the art doings and prospects of the Lady Artists for the coming season."[102] People who wanted to hire teachers consulted a book of names and addresses kept by the Association.[103] Art publisher Louis Prang asked the Association to advertise and handle the details of his first cash prize contest for print designs by women artists.[104] And Howard Hinton thanked Donlevy for finding a woman to live with his family and care for his children so that his wife, sculptor Lucy Bronson Hinton, could get back to her art.[105]

Association members acted as intermediaries for women artists. When Helen Garvey of Grouton, Ohio, was hired to engrave covers for Sunday school books she wrote the Association looking for illustrations and illumination designs. Donlevy, who was already working with Garvey, sent her a drawing by Georgie Davis. Davis in return asked Donlevy for suggestions about pricing: "I really did not think it worth $10—& would have hesitated to ask even 3 . . . so on your advice took a middle course and asked 5."[106] While in Connecticut, Robert O'Brien asked Donlevy to arrange the delivery of a drawing to his engraver Sarah Demroche, which she did through another Association artist, Fanny Ketcham.[107]

Perhaps the most important function of the Ladies' Art Association was its role as a conduit between women artists and New York's industrial metropolis. After the war, hundreds of women joined the reserve of craft workers flowing through a labyrinth of large manufactories, rapidly growing firms, and small establishments, central workshops, and outworker cellars, rooms, and studios in search of ways to make or supplement their livings.[108] Through its various professional services, the Ladies' Art Association endeavored to introduce more women artists into this eclectic labor market and to maintain the elevated position of "Art appropriate to manufacture."

Industrial Meadows

In her 1863 book *The Employments of Women: A Cyclopedia of Woman's Work*, social investigator Virginia Penny listed fifty-eight distinct employments under the heading "Artists," in addition to art instruction and art criticism. These jobs ranged from illustrating picture books to gilding their covers, modeling wax figures to engraving bank notes, copying famous works of art to designing for manufacturers, and painting portraits and panoramas to coloring photographs.[109] Penny was an advocate of industrial art education for working-class women, a number of whom she sent to the Cooper Union School of Design with her reference. Intended as "a business manual for women," Penny's "cyclopedia" represented three years of research visiting "factories, workshops, offices, and stores, for the purpose of seeing women at their vocations" and obtaining impartial information by talking to people "in a casual way, they not knowing I had any object in view."[110] She sent questionnaires to 2,500 employers regarding women's work, training, and wages. What she found in almost every field was that women artists worked fewer hours for better pay than other women workers and that the ability to draw and design raised their employability and wages.

Throughout the nineteenth century, fewer well-paid jobs were available to women than to men, due to sex-based segregation and wage differentials. The general educations of middle-class girls rarely extended to the professions, which were mostly closed to women anyway. In many cases art training was the only higher education a young woman had had when she came of age. Of the employments open to her, art often held the highest status and was the best remunerated. This situation not only encouraged women to become artists, it often compelled women artists to work outside their primary field of art.

The combining of fine and industrial art occupations was a distinctive characteristic of professional life for many mid-nineteenth-century artists, male and female. In his 1867 collection of biographies, *Book of the Artists: American Artist Life*, Henry Tuckerman wrote of John Ehninger: "At one time we find him illustrating a new and popular poem, at another successfully teaching a class of ladies; now at work upon a new process of etching, by means of photography; and again engaged upon a striking conception, which needs but elaborate and patient finish to be a first class exhibition picture of its kind. . . . having the discipline of an academic education, [and] . . . the culture derived from European travel; . . . he has contributed designs to the London Illustrated Times and News; . . . and his drawings on wood, to illustrate popular books, have been numerous and skillful."[111]

Few artists of either sex enjoyed the "social privileges" (he was scion of "an old knickerbocker family") that made Ehninger's diverse occupations appear to be purely aesthetic choices. Most male painters taught art or drew illustrations for the same reasons as female painters; they had an interest and talent for the work and they needed money. "Necessity, too, obliges the artist and *litterateur* to consult the immediate," Tuckerman reminds us in his sketch of John Chapman, whom he describes as an industrial and fine artist.[112] The difference between Ehninger's combination of art occupations and that of his Cooper Union pupils was the gender-based restriction on female agency that made diversifying a more vital and ubiquitous career strategy among women.

The practice of cobbling together jobs from different specialties is easier to trace in the careers of women artists for whom paid work signified professional status. Some artists applied their skills to new areas within their primary field. Alice Donlevy illuminated type lettering for publishers, wrote and illustrated articles for magazine editors, designed prospectus covers, letterheads, and certificates for private businesses, and taught classes in mechanical art and design at the Ladies' Art Association.[113] This breadth of ability, along with her service to the Association, kept Donlevy constantly employed. She was paid as little as seventy-five cents and as much as thirty dollars for a single design. Other artists applied the skills of their field to another arena. The most common alternative pursued by oil painters was teaching. Art teaching was relatively well compensated, if the teacher had enough students to occupy her time. The price for a lesson in Northeastern cities varied from fifty cents to two dollars for one hour.[114]

Struggling female artists had no choice but to branch out within the art field, while struggling male artists had the option of seeking employment in another profession. This pattern is easily discernable in a postwar record of "professional artists" of a "worthy class" from Manchester, New Hampshire. Male portraitist J. H. Knowlton "drifted into other fields of enterprise, to neglect his native art gift," when he found art too difficult a trade, but Helen L. Squire, who had a "decided talent" as a painter of landscapes and fruit pieces in oil, "of late years made china painting her specialty" and taught "a large class of pupils in the art beautiful" because she found "a good patronage in this work." In contrast, William F. Herrick, a wood engraver employed in New York and San Francisco, left art for the insurance business and William H. Kimball, a miniature painter on ivory, became a librarian. But Miss Jane Cutter, a National Academy trained artist of "high rank," "divided her talents between water color paintings, miniature paintings, and decorated china," while conducting local art exhibitions and publishing pencil sketches and paintings in magazines.[115]

The lack of desirable alternatives made women artists more willing to accept industrial art work. For nearly every woman artist, leaving the art trade meant accepting non-professional employment or manual labor with lower wages and status. According to Penny's survey, most girls employed in shops and factories received around $3 a week for sixty hours labor, or five cents an hour. Yet even a slight art skill could double that amount. Decorating a book with gold was one of the arts of illumination.[116] Gilders in a bookbindery were paid six dollars per week "or $1 a day of ten hours, which is equal to ten cents an hour." Seamstresses sewed fifteen hours a day and earned "but thirty cents, equal to two cents an hour, without board."[117] Photo-colorists and framers worked nine hours a day and the least they made was five to seven dollars a week.[118] As a form of female labor, art work kept its value.

During the war, photo coloring replaced print coloring as a major source of revenue for women artists. "In times of excitement, when soldiers are going from their homes," one photographer told Penny, "there is much for the artists to do."[119] School of Design students recognized the benefit of learning this industrial art early on. "A number of pupils would be glad to learn to *color photographs*, which is perhaps the readiest way to turn their knowledge of art to account," Principal Field told the Cooper Union Trustees in 1862. "Miss Phillipe, one of our pupils, is quite competent to teach this, and would give lessons, at a dollar a lesson, to the whole class of twenty. A dozen or fifteen lessons would be sufficient, and many most deserving pupils would immediately find in it a means of support."[120] For full-time art students needing to pay for room and board, coloring was good employment. It offered flexible hours and relatively high wages, and it was portable. Photo-colorists worked at home, in the photographer's shop or gallery, and as itinerants.[121]

Photographers and critics alike acknowledged that only artists with special skills and knowledge produced well-colored photographs.[122] Mixing colors (especially flesh tones), creating expression, and giving the whole picture a fine finish required the same technical abilities as portraiture or landscape painting. This status kept the value of coloring work high. Two artist sisters working in New York "are busy all the time," Penny reported. "They execute different styles of painting, but have lately found it more profitable to color photographs." When busy, they each earned from $12 to $15 per week coloring photographs (two times the "normal" wage), and all their work was brought to the house. Male artists colored photographs as well, but more women artists found the work both financially and professionally viable.[123]

Easel painters who had tasted some success did not enjoy having to color prints, even if their contemporaries recognized that good coloring involved taste and skill. In the 1850s, poverty forced Spencer to do something she had said she "never would stoop to do"—color engravings, often of her own paintings.[124] After she left school, Annie Delano supplemented her painting income by teaching "coloring Photographs in watercolor." She later took on such work herself, a necessity about which she simply declared: "can't say it is a labor of love."[125] Coloring prints or painting the gold leaf on book covers may have been jobs increasingly reserved for women only, but an artist who did them could make more than ten times the wages of a seamstress who stitched a shirt. This disparity in remuneration helps explain Spencer's willingness to take on coloring work during hard times. It was simply more logical for a struggling woman artist to turn to industrial art labor, even if overqualified, than to seek out other women's work.

Art publishers were major employers of women artists, providing a market for women's original productions both as painters and designers. Boston lithographer Louis Prang (b. 1824) was particularly interested in women's artwork, and many New York women artists profited from his experimentation. Prang's initial success came from his production of small prints ("art bits"), which often were collected and kept in albums. During the 1860s, L. Prang & Company launched a novel series of chromolithographs—"admirably adapted for the decoration of dining-rooms and parlors"—with "Cherries in a Basket" and "Strawberries in a Basket" after oil paintings by Virginia Granbery.[126] They were a smash hit. "I see that Miss Granbery is succeeding admirably," Corinna B. Nye wrote Donlevy from Montreal in 1868. "I saw Prang's chromos of two of her pictures which are very good."[127] Prang also developed a market for color printed specialty items, such as Christmas cards (which he is credited with inventing). He looked to women artist for the design and production of these novel commodities (Figure 25).

The art contests Prang held to generate new designs for his company represented an encouraging source of income and employment for female painters and illustrators. In 1870, L. Prang & Company advertised its first

Figure 25. "The Fringing Room" at L. Prang & Co., from *Wide Awake*, n.p., n.d.

art contest in the women's rights journal the *Revolution* and asked the Ladies' Art Association for help. "My object in starting the project has been principally to give an impetus to female art," Prang wrote to Mrs. Gray. He asked the Association to announce the contest to its members, select and exhibit the art to be judged, name a jury, and award the prizes. Each contest was planned to benefit as many of the artists whose designs were judged as possible. Prang suggested six classes of artwork and specified sizes for the entries, so that the submissions would "conform to other pictures already upon our catalogue."[128] He offered to purchase any entries that appeared "to promise a profit by publishing," as well as to buy the winning pictures "at the artist's price, over and above the premiums that may be awarded." He also suggested that the Ladies' Art Association arrange a public exhibition of the contest entries at the National Academy of Design to generate interest in their work. Winners of the contests included Cooper Union graduates and members of the Ladies' and Brooklyn Art Associations. Rosina Emmett won first prize of one thousand dollars in Prang's 1880 Christmas card contest and fourth prize of two hundred dollars in 1881, when the contest was opened to men and Elihu Vedder won first prize.[129]

Beyond cash prizes and sales, a number of women artists won contracts to design prints, greeting cards, and other ephemera for the company.

By 1881 L. Prang & Company employed over one hundred women, including resident designer Olive E. Whitney, a dozen or so freelance artists, and a staff of finishers and embellishers. Fidelia Bridges sold a series of paintings representing the months of the year to Prang in 1875, and in 1881 he made her one of his permanent designers, a position she held until 1899. Lizzie (Lizbeth) Bullock Humphrey (b. 1841), a prolific illustrator of books and children's and general magazines in the 1870s, designed chromolithographic gift cards for Prang in the 1880s.[130] After she died in 1889, Prang produced a memorial volume of her designs[131] (Figure 26). He also endowed the Cooper Union in 1876 with up to $1,500 a year to support a teacher for the Normal Class in industrial drawing at the School of Design for Women.[132]

Designers—the artists who drew the patterns and illustrated the pictures to be engraved or lithographed—fared best of all the women artists after the war. Designers were paid according to talent and ability, some by the piece, and some by the day. First-class women designers were paid more or less the same as their male counterparts. Women artists who worked for the patent office and patent agents were paid according to "size, intricacy, finish, &c., the rate being nearly that which men receive, in some instances the same." Women artists working by the day in New York offices earned from "$1 to $2, and in two instances $2.25 and $2.50 per day," but most artists worked by the piece, earning from $1 to $60 for a single page of design for prints, carpets, wall-paper, calico, or embroidery.[133] Donlevy was paid $30 for a specimen of illumination to be engraved in 1866, and $50 for four illuminated pages in 1867. Two years later she asked $10 for a single design idea.[134]

The male engraver of a print often made more money than the woman who drew it, but the designer-illustrator was often better compensated for her time. Houghton & Company paid Mary Hallock $730 to draw eighteen designs that A. V. S. Anthony engraved for $2,066. But a highly complicated and finished drawing took far fewer hours to complete than an engraving of similar intricacy.[135] "One designer can do enough in a day to keep a man busy a week," Penny pointed out. These advantages made design-illustration an inviting field for women educated at the Cooper Union. To the people Penny interviewed, the ability to design was considered "a peculiar, and more a natural than a cultivated talent," despite the fact that good design also represented years of training. Designing required "a very different and much higher order of talent than wood engraving," they told her. That belief was reflected in the interest and respect women illustrators generated after the war.

Figure 26. Portrait of Lizbeth B. Humphrey. L. Prang & Co., Norcross Greeting Card Collection, Archives Center, National Museum of American History. Smithsonian Institution.

Publishers did not hire women designers because they were cheaper. Rates of payment for artwork varied over time and from project to project, mostly due to size and intricacy, but male and female freelance artists were paid equitably. In 1855 Boston artist Hammatt Billings (b. 1818), already well regarded as a designer, received $5 each for six book illustrations, and three years later the same publisher paid him $9 for one drawing.[136] Houghton Company paid Samuel Coleman $20 per drawing in 1867 and only $15 in 1868.[137] Around the same time, Rosina Emmett, who was still a girl, received $12 for an unsolicited drawing she sent to a magazine.[138] In 1874 *St. Nicholas Magazine* paid Donlevy prices ranging from 75 cents to $7 ($26.75 in all) for seven tiny sketches.[139] Winslow Homer, Mary Hallock Foote, Alfred Waud, Jessie Curtis, Jervis McEntee, and several other known artists illustrated *Christmastide* for Osgood & Co. in 1877, a deluxe edition of four famous American poems. Each of Homer's four drawings for "Excelsior" brought him $25. Hallock received $35 for a pair of illustrations. Waud earned $67 for his eight pictures, and Curtis was paid $100 for her sixteen drawings.[140]

Illustrators' compensation increased with their reputations. In 1857 Winslow Homer was paid a couple of dollars apiece for the five drawings he contributed to Mrs. Follen's *Twilight Stories*, but in the 1860s, he received between $25 and $50 for the large drawings he submitted to *Harper's Weekly*, $15 to $20 for ordinary book illustrations, and $25 to $40 for drawings made for deluxe editions.[141] The prices paid to women artists known only for their illustrations also rose over time. Mary Hallock Foote, known exclusively for her wood-block illustrations in magazines and books, matched Homer in earnings and reputation. In 1874, after receiving numerous rave reviews for her illustrations in a deluxe edition of Henry Wadsworth Longfellow's *The Hanging of the Crane*, Hallock was paid $500 for twenty-six drawings of various sizes made for John Greenleaf Whittier's *Mabel Martin* (approximately $20 each). In contrast, Thomas Moran received $195 for his fifteen landscapes (or $13 each) and Alfred Waud was paid $140 for his fourteen "vignettes" (or $10 each). In 1876 Hallock earned $750 (between $45 and $50 each) for seventeen drawings and one border made for Longfellow's *The Skeleton in Armor*, while Edwin Austin Abbey received $25 for his page.[142] Hallock's mastery of the human figure enhanced the value of her work. *Scribner's* praised the "refinement and power" of Hallock's drawings, calling her the "artist whose figure subjects drawn on the wood are, after Mr. La Farge's, the best that are now being made in this country."[143] Observation and imagination, mastery and intricacy set the work of an illustrator like Hallock apart, but other women artists found the field equally welcoming.

During the Civil War, technology and industrialization altered the options and prospects of women artists, creating a wide spectrum of laborers in the field of the beautiful. The most promising industrial art market was the illustrated press. Horace Greeley and other New York publishers had long championed female artists, calling for their educations and employment and following their progress in their newspapers and magazines. But after 1865, the mantle passed to a new generation of editors who encouraged female artists to create works specifically for their publications. The most successful women artists working during the immediate postwar period acted on that advice.

Chapter 6
"An Easier and Surer Path"

Returning home to Milton-on-the-Hudson after three years at "the Cooper," Mary Hallock found she could work at her drawing almost anywhere, no matter who was present (Figure 27). She took her sketchpad and pencil with her wherever she went, on summer outings to Peg's Beach and Black Pond or out-of-town holiday visits to the homes of family and friends. Eventually the back parlor of her parents' home was converted into a studio where the artist could work without interruption and where the tools she used to transpose her drawings onto woodblocks could remain undisturbed. She called this period her "hallelujah days." A host of book and magazine editors had begun commissioning her illustrations, and critics praised her talent. She was climbing to the heights of her profession through publishing, attaining the double crown of fame and good prices.[1]

If only the same could be said for her dear friend Helena de Kay Gilder! Gilder had pursued her art just as seriously, but success was so much more elusive for painters. "Easel pictures" had to be appreciated in the original, which meant Gilder had to rely on fickle Academy officials to hang her paintings well or persuade gallery owners to hold exhibitions for young artists. Even then she could only pray that reviewers from the papers would come and single out her work in their notices. To continue to paint undaunted by disappointment after disappointment was especially difficult for an artist like Gilder, whom her new husband, poet Richard Gilder, praised as a "Genius, in all the sad, mysterious, blissful meaning of the word!"[2]

After Gilder's latest "little wail" over her painting, Hallock tried yet again to convince her of her talents. "How often must I tell you that you are no longer an experiment but a most triumphant realization. The public dont know you yet but they must learn to know you, because you have your place in the Art of this age & country just as surely as John La Farge—or Richard Gilder—or—well a great deal more than Howells."[3] "I wish, dear, girl, you would have more faith in the rarest praise you win, and not be so

Figure 27. Mary Hallock, ca. 1874. Photo Archives. Huntington Library.

ready to believe in the first breath of discouragement—Someday you will be forced to believe in your self but I am impatient for you to see what every body else saw—long ago—the exceptional power and originality, the individualness* of everything you do. . . . *(I suppose one of the hardest things to realize is our own individualness)."⁴ Because her work at Daniel

Cottier's New York gallery had been favorably noticed as "something quite by itself," Hallock counseled Gilder. "You must try, now, to keep something all the time before the public—there is a great deal in familiarity with the style of a person's expression."[5]

The only difference between Gilder and her successful male contemporaries, as far as Hallock could see, was that their work was known. Why, even the notice her own work received stemmed from its having been published. What would happen if Gilder, a far superior artist, did the same? And so, in a "burst of confidence," Hallock suggested to engraver-editor A. V. S. Anthony (b. 1835), who directed the art department at James Osgood & Company, that Gilder illustrate a book with her for him. Anthony "fell in with the scheme at once" and with "unbound faith" in the two artists proposed Longfellow's Norse ballad, "The Skeleton in Armor," for the project. "How will you like Mr. Anthony's engraving your work?" Hallock queried. "He is evidently going to let us have a far field. You are to decorate and do land and sea-scapes. In short, you fill [Thomas] Moran's place, and that of the poky unknowns who have heretofore done the ornamental part—We will have a great spree talking it over when you come!"[6]

Hallock dove right into the work but Gilder, who was pregnant, waited until after the birth of her first child. Unfortunately, when Anthony received Gilder's blocks he did not think the drawings suitable for engraving and delicately asked Hallock to retouch them. Mortified by the engraver's suggestion, Hallock called off the collaboration and finished the book alone. "I was so determined to have your work published, that I would not think of anything but the success which I felt sure would follow its appearance. . . . Why didn't I mind my own business, and let you alone, instead of tormenting you into doing something which, as you say, poor child, has truly 'bored you to death.'"[7] The two artists did eventually publish together in a new gift book edition of Josiah G. Holland's *Mistress of the Manse*.[8] Reviews of the book singled out Gilder's decorative flower vignettes (engraved by Henry Marsh) as deserving the "very highest praise: in their subordinated place they are perhaps the finest adornment of the volume, and have a delicious artistic restfulness about them." But they did not direct to her painting the kind of notice Hallock had envisioned.[9]

Hallock's belief that through book illustration Gilder might gain her rightful place "in the Art of this age & country" stemmed from her Unity of Art training and work experience. By the time Hallock suggested the collaboration to Anthony, her pictures had appeared in numerous periodicals and books and been widely reviewed. Advertisements for the books featuring her illustrations always identified Hallock as the "Artist." Reviewers judged her plates based on the highest standards of criticism. When *The Skeleton in Armor* appeared in 1877, *Atlantic Monthly* editor William Dean Howells enthusiastically praised Hallock as "the artist who perhaps unites more fine qualities than any other." He pronounced one illustration "as yet quite unapproached in power by anything in American illustrative art."[10] Hallock was well aware that her art, as distinct from that of women painters, was celebrated because it was published.

Hallock's critical success depended on several developments that intersected with the Unity of Art ideal in mid-nineteenth-century America. Between 1820 and 1870 the publishing industry expanded in number and types of publications and developed a nationally based audience for American books and magazines.[11] A class of writers and artists arose who specialized in producing illustrated books and periodicals.[12] Immigrant artists and American students returning from England brought with them theories of art that supported the impulse to make illustration and engraving into fine arts. And a new engraving technique called photogravure was added to the art printing process.

Americans today take for granted the artwork that adorns their books, magazines, and newspapers. Readers rarely think about the training, ability, imagination, exploration, and even research that lies behind its production. During the mid-nineteenth century, Americans were taken with the idea of printed art as a unique form of national creative expression. Engraved art became a valued part of American culture and illustration a respected pursuit for the artist and engraver.[13] Critics assessed illustrators and engravers along the same lines as they did painters and sculptors, and many of America's finest artists turned to publishing work as a primary field. These events led to a "renaissance" in the art of woodblock illustration, temporarily making it the nation's most celebrated art form.

Women artists were at the heart of this revival. The leaders of the movement taught women to draw and engrave at the Cooper Union, publishers whose books and magazines transmitted woodblock illustration to the public commissioned their work, and reviewers singled out some of their illustrated material as the finest examples of engraved art in American publications.

Recently historians have used engraved illustration to demonstrate the constraints of convention on women artists. They argue that relegating women artists to the so-called secondary arts and domestic subject matter reinforced their subordinate position in nineteenth-century American society. And it is true that the content of women's art often reproduced the social restrictions women faced.[14] But when approached as objects that embody the social relations of production, works of art have the potential to recover the larger world women inhabited. Rather than stifling creativity, a woman's familial obligations and financial need could be powerful motivators for aesthetic innovation. Much of the explanatory power of art lies in the form and style of the images. In a context where someone other than the artist decides what the picture will portray, as was often the case in woodblock design, these characteristics can tell us more than the subject matter. Examining what an artist actually included in an image and how she drew it can give us historical insight into an illustration's meaning and effectiveness. "It is in the conception as well as the execution of her work that Miss Hallock will delight the appreciative reader," noted William Dean Howells in 1874.[15] It also was in conceiving and carrying out the design that women artists strove to make their mark.

"No one can deny that we have in this country many young women of high talent and real accomplishment as artists," observed an 1868 review. "The recent exhibitions of the National Academy of Design have contained evidences that American women can attain high positions in many of the departments of art. But the growing demand for book and magazine illustrations offers an easier and surer path to success."[16] The experiences and artwork of women illustrators over the next decade confirmed that observation. In the 1860s and early 1870s, illustration was still a budding field that attracted both men and women. Editors of the new illustrated press regularly hired women artists. Magazine and book illustration practically guaranteed financial rewards for the gifted artist. Illustration was a portable profession that married women were able to fit into domestic life. The newness of the field left it wide open for innovation and individual expression. And publishing provided the credibility and exposure that all professional artists needed. With the help of influential editors and engravers, women artists tapped into this aesthetic market early, quickly joined the professional ranks as illustrators and engravers, and became instrumental participants in the development of American illustrative art.[17]

The Renaissance of Wood Engraving

Hallock's generation of women artists entered the profession just when the mass production of graphic art in illustrated books and magazines widened artists' horizons. The number of periodicals (excluding newspapers) rose dramatically after the 1840s and then dropped slightly during the panic year of 1857. Bank failures, unemployment, difficulty in collecting subscription fees, and other problems attending the close of an easy-credit era embarrassed publishers.[18] But the popularity of magazines did not decline, and their proliferation resumed after 1863.[19] Fortuitously for women artists that upsurge coincided with the first graduating class of the Cooper Union School of Design.

With the evolution of the illustrated press emerged a recognizable group of freelance authors, illustrators, and engravers eager to supply the new weeklies and monthlies with images. Before the 1850s the publishers of illustrated periodicals were often engravers by trade. They attended to their own embellishments, or hired one or two staff artists who became associated with their publications. But as illustrated publications grew in number and size, publishers started paying for submissions. It became possible for artists to support themselves by making art for publication. Women illustrators and engravers were prominent among the artists hired by leading publishers to draw, design, illuminate, and cut the prints, pages, and covers of their magazines.

By 1868, a wide range of periodicals regularly employed women artists. These included the new art journals, such as New York's *Aldine: A Typographic Art Journal* (1868–79); the popular monthlies and weeklies, such as the *Galaxy, an Illustrated Magazine of Entertaining Reading* (1866), and *Scribner's Monthly, an Illustrated Magazine for the People* (1870); family-oriented and women's periodicals, such as *Frank Leslie's Lady's Magazine* (1863), *Riverside Magazine* (1867), and *Hearth & Home* (1868–75); and children's magazines, such as *Our Young Folks* (1865), *St. Nicholas* (1873), and *Wide Awake* (1875). Women's artwork appeared in books and pamphlets published by the Graphic Company, Hurd & Houghton, Robert Brothers, Ticknor & Fields, and others; various religious tract presses including the Catholic Publication Society; and in the catalogue offerings of lithographs, textbooks, and ephemera made by L. Prang & Company and Currier & Ives.[20]

Women artists joined the illustration profession just when wood engraving reemerged as the principal reproductive medium for printed art.[21] By 1865 most publishers had abandoned steel plates in favor of wood blocks. Electrotyping, adopted increasingly after 1850, made it possible to produce a large number of impressions, no matter what medium the original engraving was on. Some older magazines supplemented metal plates with woodcuts, but the new illustrated magazines turned to wood exclusively.[22] This change was significant for women studying art at the Cooper Union, where designing and engraving on wood was emphasized.

The most authoritative figure in the revival of wood engraving was William J. Linton, who taught at the School of Design from 1867 to 1870. Linton spent his career advancing the Unity of Art idea that engraving and illustration were fine arts.[23] Owing to his endorsements, female artists were integral to the revival of woodblock engraving. A. V. S. Anthony's "tasteful supervision" of books published by Osgood & Company from 1866 to 1889 also exerted considerable influence on the art of wood engraving, as did his choice of Hallock as primary artist for the company's gift book series.[24]

Although a single artist sometimes produced a woodcut picture from start to finish, the renaissance in wood engraving was really the joint production of illustrators, engravers, and editors. Illustrators and engravers produced the art published in books and magazines together, and editors depended on and equally valued their expertise. Designer-illustrators never took good engraving for granted, and reviewers complained when engravers did not do justice to a good illustrator's work. "Mr. Cole does not succeed with Mrs. Foote's drawings," Linton claimed. Her "*Santa Cruz Americana* . . . has lost all the manner and all the charm of the original." *Scribner's*, which called Hallock "the best of our designers on the wood," never attributed a poor engraving to her drawing. "It is well known to those who are used to seeing drawings on the wood, before the engraver has done his work that it is a most fortunate accident when the impression from the engraving gives the spirit of the original design."[25]

Reviews of illustrated books critiqued the design and engraving of illustrations separately. A positive notice of Osgood's quarto edition of "The Skeleton in Armor" discussed the artwork of both Hallock and Anthony. "The landscape in this series of pictures is almost invariably fresh and good. There are indications that the picture with verse vi. was very effective on the block; but it lacks something as engraved." Anthony's engraving, though skillfully executed, sympathized "too much with the gentler and smoother qualities of the artist's drawing; and, therefore, gives undue stress to that side of it. But these are the very qualities which it must always be the most difficult to retain in their subtlety and individuality, while translating the picture from the delicate tints of the drawing on the block to the sharp lines of engraving"[26] (Figure 28). The reviewer makes it clear that Hallock drew directly on the block yet still considered the engraving more than mechanical reproduction.

Figure 28. Mary A. Hallock, del, A.V.S. Anthony, sc, "Wild was the life we led; / Many the Souls that sped, / Many the hearts that bled, / By our stern orders," from Henry W. Longfellow, *The Skeleton in Armor* (Boston, 1877), verse VI. Personal copy.

The balanced assessment of engraving and illustration could benefit women artists. As a delineavit-sculpsit pair, Hallock was often regarded as the stronger and Anthony as the gentler artist. A review of John Greenleaf Whittier's *Mabel Martin* noted that, "on the wood" Hallock's drawings "always show a refinement and power which we have seldom seen any engraver successfully render. In this series, the grace of the drawing has sometimes degenerated into mere prettiness in the engraving, but sometimes, too, the great interest which Mr. Anthony (who stands among the very first in his profession) has evidently taken in the work under his charge, is rewarded by satisfactory and beautiful results."[27] As equal contributors to a work of art, designers and engravers could each enhance or be undone by the other.

In the 1870s wood engraving underwent a transformation with the introduction of photography into the engraving process. Photogravure was a type of engraving that did not rely on draftsmanship. Instead, the picture to be reproduced was transferred onto the block by a photographic technique, after which the engraver tried "to catch the manner of the original" with perfect exactitude through the handling of lines, dots, and crosshatching in microscopic detail. By facilitating the reproduction of the original medium (pen and ink, pencil, crayon, even the brush strokes of water colors and oils) on the block, this process led to stylistic changes in engraving.

Scribner's Monthly and its offspring *St. Nicholas*, which owed their success as much to engraved art as to any other feature, were mainly responsible for popularizing photogravure. The superintendent of the illustrative department, Alexander W. Drake kept the artwork at *Scribner's* on a high plane by promoting photography on wood as an aid to the engraver and by hiring the printer Theodore Low DeVinne, who excelled in handling wood engravings on the press. Master practitioners of photogravure, which came to be called the "New School of Wood-Engraving," worked for *Scribner's*. They included Timothy Cole, leader of the New School, and Elbridge Kingsley, who excelled in careful "white dot" reproductions. "Bold, undaunted experimenter" Frederick Juengling also worked for *Scribner's*; his engravings exemplified what "imitative care could accomplish in straight line facsimile work."[28]

Photogravure was a controversial technique. Linton, who also worked for *Scribner's*, was spokesman for what came to be known as the "Old School." He complained that the photogravure process encouraged "fogginess," or lack of definition, as engravers relied on the same "mess of meaningless dots and lines" for background, clothes, and features. Even worse, he argued, close attention to reproducing the original medium made the art mechanical, irrespective of whether the finished product was beautiful or clever. What Linton found missing from these elaborately engraved pictures was the *expression* of the line, and only the "graver-line" gave engraving artistic integrity. The "New School" did not create works in which "every line is the line of an artist, a line with meaning." The engraver now must "forget the capabilities of his own art in a vain attempt to imitate the unpleasant peculiarities of another." True, the new style could catch effects that the "old white line" could not; but the only endeavors worth noting called attention to the art of the engraver.[29]

The first generation of School of Design students had been taught to master white-line engraving. The second generation learned New School design and graver techniques as well. John Parker Davis, who had studied at the Cooper Union with Linton, taught both techniques at the School of

Design from 1881 to 1884. Davis held that the nature of wood engraving made it much more than a vehicle for the photographic reproduction of paintings. He believed in drawing directly on the block and defended the rights of the engraver to put the medium to imaginative use. Exponents of the New School contended that the original work is what gave engraving its value and that photographically reproducing the image on the block made it easier to produce an exact copy. New School engravers also claimed, with some accuracy, that photogravure gave the engraver greater flexibility in his technique. That flexibility did not matter to engravers like Linton who regarded this method as a form of deskilling. Davis agreed. But instead of rejecting the New School entirely, he joined a cohort of artists who called themselves the Original Workers on Wood. This loosely formed guild strove to keep the art of wood engraving alive by approaching it as a creative art, encouraging plein-air engraving directly from nature, and showing engraved work at exhibition halls.[30]

The best of the New School engravers *combined* new and old techniques, black dots and white lines, in a photogravure that reproduced texture and renewed expression. The most famous female wood engraver of the era was Caroline Amelia Powell (b. 1852).[31] Born in Dublin, Ireland, Powell studied white-line engraving at the School of Design during Linton's reign in the 1870s. After graduating, the young engraver approached Drake, who told her that her work was not yet the quality *Scribner's* required. Drake introduced Powell to the man he considered the magazine's best engraver, Timothy Cole, who taught her the fine points of photogravure. After studying with Cole, Powell produced hundreds of blocks for *Scribner's* and *Century* and various book publishers as a solo artist and as a partner in New York's "Photo. Engraving Company" with John Parker Davis.[32] Her engravings blended the best of Old and New School styles, relying on the line for expression and movement while creating curvature and shadows on faces and calves through dots and crosshatching (Figure 29). In the 1880s, Powell was the first woman elected to the Society of American Wood Engravers. She also exhibited work at the Columbian Exposition in 1893 and the Pan-American Exposition in 1901.[33]

The shift to photogravure opened up the field of illustration to more women artists. Lizzie Humphrey became a trendsetter for the publishing industry through her application of the new process. A native of Massachusetts, Humphrey studied drawing and painting at the Cooper Union in the 1860s.[34] With photoengraving as a catalyst, she developed an illustrative style based on the diffuse effects of charcoal sketching. She also invented

THE EIGHT COUSINS. — Page 10.

Figure 29. C. A. Powell, sc, "The Eight Cousins," ca. 1874, from Louisa May Alcott, *Eight Cousins; or, The Aunt-Hill* (Boston, 1900), 11. Personal copy.

Figure 30. Lizzie B. Humphrey, "A Christmas Tragedy: In Three Acts," *Wide Awake* 8 (1879): 24. Courtesy of American Antiquarian Society.

an early comic strip format. Humphrey combined these innovations in "A Christmas Tragedy: In Three Acts" for an 1879 issue of *Wide Awake*[35] (Figure 30). As masters of both Old and New School techniques, women illustrators played a central role in the revival of the art of wood engraving. They also helped create that "surer path"—the demand for illustrated books and magazines.

The New Illustrated Press

Between 1865 and 1889, the work of several dozen artists appeared regularly in the illustrated press, and at least one-third of those artists were women.

Men and women entering the field of illustration followed the same route to publishing. Artists submitted work on speculation to editors or engravers who then commissioned specific designs from them. Usually a new artist's work was introduced to a journal gradually, with one or two drawings published the first time around and more in subsequent issues.[36] Because illustrators were freelancers, they worked for several publishers simultaneously. As illustrated magazines and books increased in circulation, the reading public came to recognize the styles and signatures of their favorite artists and engravers.[37] Most illustrators signed their work with recognizable initials, which changed only when a woman artist married.[38] The earliest popular women woodblock designers of this "golden age" included Mary E. Edwards, who created subtly intricate designs for the *Galaxy* that emphasized the distinct qualities of wood as a medium (Figure 31), and Cooper Union alumnae Lucy Gibbons, Jessie Curtis, Addie Ledyard, Mary Hallock, and Mary L. Stone. All of these artists published in *Our Young Folks*, an octavo monthly magazine begun by Ticknor & Fields of Boston in 1865, and in *Riverside Magazine for Young People*, a juvenile monthly issued by Riverside Press of Cambridge beginning in 1867.

Women ventured into illustration at the same time that children's literature emerged as a separate genre. Since the 1820s, individual women artists had drawn and engraved graphic art for every type of book—from religious tracts to texts on science, history, biography, and drama. Art produced by women also featured among the illustrations in America's first periodicals. But not until the 1850s did women artists as a group successfully compete with men as illustrators. Their success depended partly on the emergence among the middle classes of a concept of childhood as a distinct stage of life and the development of literature and art designed specifically for young people. Some editors considered women artists more suited to this work and favored them when hiring designers and engravers, although men also specialized in art for children's publications and women artists concentrated on other literary subjects, such as travel, natural science, and the fine arts.

Those women artists most frequently hired by publishers excelled in composition, imagining and realizing a picture's content even when the editor chose the subject. Illustrators researched historical and contemporary scenes. They worried equally about background and foreground, about a figure's costume and sentiment, about creating the effects of light and of emotion, and about proportions, surfaces, and sensations. Being given a specific historical moment to depict did not necessarily limit an illustrator's

Figure 31. Mary E. Edwards, "Mr. Saul Proposes," *Galaxy* 1 (1 May–15 August 15, 1866): 85. Courtesy of American Antiquarian Society.

room to experiment with formal qualities. In her illustrations for *Mabel Martin*, Hallock captured the emotions of her historical subjects by experimenting with contemporary design techniques. After emulating the voluptuous aesthetic of the Pre-Raphaelites in her frontispiece, Hallock applies the asymmetry, diagonal composition (p. 39), and botanical framing method (p. 47) found in Japanese prints to other designs. In "The dooryard tree was whispered through," she adapts a device common to Japanese landscape prints from the Edo period of depicting a distant view through a foreground border of plant life.[39] In Hallock's more intimate scene, the barren white branches of a birch tree in winter frame the desolate figure of Mabel leaning against a farmyard door (Figure 32). Hallock's work is exceptional in its breadth of conceptual and formal qualities, yet illustration as a genre encouraged creativity in other artists as well.

Art historians have argued that images of women became the semiotic sign for the male artist's genius in late nineteenth-century painting, a signifier/signified equation that is made problematic when the artist is a woman. With that transition the domestic realm reentered the fine art arena, no longer as genre painting but as impressionism, inviting women artists back into the fold. Unfortunately, the artist's sex continues to determine the way we see depictions of women and domestic scenes.[40] Women illustrators often portrayed the world of women and children for "business" reasons, but this topic was not necessarily constraining. Some women artists approached images of female figures as an opportunity to develop new feminine ideals through design and execution. Humphrey's frontispiece for *Sally Williams, the Mountain Girl* is a case in point (Figure 33). Wind-swept, with hand on waist and staff, Humphrey's "Sally" is a snub-nosed heroine who exudes a physical self-confidence that offered midcentury girls an alternative model of femininity. The artist alters the meaning of the subject matter she is given by the way she draws it. For example, in the 1879 *Wide Awake* article, "Boston Whittling Schools," Humphrey elongates the skirts of her figures to transform girls in a carving class into self-possessed women workers.[41]

As subjects, young children offered some women artists even more liberty of expression than grown-up topics. Children were allowed a freedom of movement and emotional expression that proffered women artists an incredible diversity of surroundings, behaviors, and emotions to depict. For an artist like Addie Ledyard, a humorist at heart, children were perfect subjects and illustration an ideal medium. Small cuts of Ledyard's designs, called "equally perfect in their way" by *Scribner's*, were extremely popular.[42]

Figure 32. Mary A. Hallock, "She Leaned Against the Door" or "The Door-Yard Tree Was Whispered Through," from John G. Whittier, *Mabel Martin* (Boston, 1875), 57. Personal copy.

They appeared in virtually every illustrated magazine and dozens of novels and collections and were widely advertised in journals and the appendices of books.

Ledyard's formal style is idiosyncratic and immediately recognizable. For this Cooper Union graduate the "graver-line" tells the tale. Her scenes

Figure 33. Lisbeth B. Humphrey, del, John Andrew & Son, sc, "Sally Williams," from Edna C. Cheney, *Sally Williams, Mountain Girl* (New York, ca. 1872), frontispiece. Courtesy of American Antiquarian Society.

rely heavily on white space and thin black lines, and although the drawings seem uncomplicated and effortless the artist's ability is evident in the clever narratives these lines and spaces create. With a few strokes of the pen, the artist fashions the effect of a bridal veil or the sheer scarf of a woman in

India. Most often, she depicts characters whose large heads and big eyes create a droll effect. Some of her bookplates are more finished, with shading used to create complex surfaces lacking in her thin-lined magazine illustrations. But she does not need this complexity to create depth of field or comedy. The simplicity of her illustration does not mean it was slapdash.

A comparison of the various engravings featured in early editions of Louisa May Alcott's books sheds light on the expertise of popular illustrators like Ledyard and Hallock. Illustrations by the author's sister, May Alcott, a painter of still life in oils and watercolors who served as the model for the character of "Amy," appeared in the Roberts Bothers' 1868 edition of *Little Women*. Unfortunately, her contemporaries found fault in her drawing of the human figure. Some of Alcott's heads are too large and awkward for their bodies, others too small, and their features are indistinct. When juxtaposed to the illustrations by Hallock and John Parker Davis in the same edition, May Alcott's drawings seem unskilled and amateurish.

What Alcott lacked was the ability to create ideal figures. The people drawn and engraved by Hallock and Davis are beautifully formed and proportioned. They do not call attention to themselves as individuals. The purpose of idealization was to illuminate the commonality of feeling being communicated by the written word.[43] Good illustration did not require idealization. It required skillfulness in drawing figures and features as the artist imagined them. "I've been doing a picture of the old Witch Mother going to execution which I would like to show you because it is an effort in a new direction and I've been *obliged* to forego pretty faces for once," Hallock wrote Gilder while working on *Mabel Martin*. "I hope the engraving will keep what little expression I have struggled to get."[44] Characterization was Ledyard's goal in "Rose and her Aunts," an illustration for Alcott's *Eight Cousins; or, The Aunt-Hill*[45] (Figure 34). Here a variety of heads are drawn simply, yet distinctly, each demarcating character traits of the woman depicted. Ledyard's heads were irregular for a purpose; sadly, May Alcott's heads were just irregular.

Ledyard's images contain a playfulness that oil painting and exhibition might have stifled. After agreeing to contribute some framed pictures to an auction being held at Leavitt's, illustrator-author Mary Artemisia Lathbury (b. 1841) confided to the exhibition's organizer: "I am not sorry that I have done so once, but my work is mostly for illustration, and is much more remunerative, though from the chances of poor engraving, not always so satisfying"[46] (Figure 35). Lathbury's popular, whimsical sketches of fairies and full-page plates of children being children often illustrated her own

Figure 34. Addie Ledyard, "Rose and Her Aunts," ca. 1874, Louisa May Alcott, *Eight Cousins; or, The Aunt-Hill* (Boston, 1900), frontispiece. Personal copy.

poems and tales.[47] The illustrated press offered Lathbury a venue for employment and a channel for creativity that exhibition did not[48] (Figure 36).

Young illustrators had to weigh the sometimes contradictory pull of market forces and aesthetic goals: "my frowzy friend Mr. Roberts" of *Hearth & Home* offered me "a batter of compliments on my big blocks," Hallock wrote Gilder in 1869. "He says they are a decided success, and I am to do an unlimited number of [these] . . . stupid commonplace 'popular' subjects, while a succession of pictures keeps passing through my mind."[49] Even pictures aimed at an aesthetically unsophisticated audience were well remunerated: "you cannot imagine anything more hopelessly dreary and common place than the little book they illustrate," Hallock admitted. "But I am mercenary and these melancholy little books are a fortune to me on the Micawber plan."[50] Women illustrators sometimes felt disheartened when the business of art kept them from doing their best work. Hallock was discouraged when she could not embellish a poem she admired: "I *did*

KISS ME, KATIE!

Figure 35. Mary A. Lathbury, "Kiss Me, Katie!," *Wide Awake* 8 (1879): plate.
Courtesy of American Antiquarian Society.

WHAT did the idle fairies say
To Kitty, sewing her seam one day?

"Kitty, you are *so* tired," they said,
"Drop your needle, and hide your thread,

Figure 36. Mary A. Lathbury, "Work and Play," *Wide Awake* (1877): 204. Courtesy of American Antiquarian Society.

want to make it *nice*, but business is business! . . . I wish there was a market for things that *we* like."[51]

The connection between writing, drawing, and engraving had been impressed on women artists at the Cooper Union. In 1863 School of Design principal L. A. Cuddehy reported to the Trustees: "Our Engravers are working on designs made by Miss Curtis (an ex-pupil) to illustrate a story written by Miss McClellan, one of the present students."[52] Many women illustrators who were not given subjects to match the pictures in their heads furnished the texts themselves. Others linked up with a sibling or spouse who wrote. Addie Ledyard illustrated funny stories and books written by her sister Laura W. Ledyard (Figure 37), and Helena Gilder furnished the decorative plates for books of verse by her husband Richard[53] (Figure 38). Writing often served as a second trade for women artists since editors paid separately for written and drawn submissions.[54] Even more dear than the money that writing for herself promised was the opportunity it gave the artist to choose subjects that might better demonstrate her expressive abilities.

Art and writing had fairly equal standing in the new periodicals. Writers were as likely to be hired to "illustrate" plates with words as artists to illustrate texts with pictures.[55] In 1872 a male writer for *Hearth and Home* cunningly described "the tribulations, vexations, and patience of a sorely tried mother," as depicted in "Mother's Room" by Mary L. Stone (b. 1846), as a sacrifice comparable to that of a Civil War soldier (Figure 39). "Perhaps Miss Stone's picture is a rather strong grouping of the troubles of a mother. Perhaps these do not all come at the same instant. And yet how little anyone else knows of the trials of a mother! We men always have business at the store, shop, office, or somewhere else, when family troubles thicken, but the mother must live with these unwearied steam-engines the whole day. . . . Talk about martyrs! Talk about dead soldiers! . . . This is a life worth the living and a death worth the dying."[56]

Women artists illustrated the texts of male writers, and male writers illustrated the plates of female artists. Horace E. Scudder (b. 1838), editor of *Riverside Magazine*, wrote a "tableaux" to go with "illustrations to the little bachelor" by Lucy Gibbons [Morse] (b. 1839)[57] (Figure 40). In 1868 the *Galaxy* reported that Gibbons's illustrations "evince knowledge, culture, delicate fancy, refined sentiment, and great fertility of invention. She puts her drawings on the block with the facility and firmness of a master."[58] Morse later became an author, who oftentimes illustrated her own stories.[59] Scudder reprinted "The Little Bachelor" in his 1878 edited collection *The Bodleys* often wrong. The little birds apologized to each other, became good friends again, and agreed not to be too positive in the future.

Two Very Young Americans.

BY LAURA W. LEDYARD.

"TOM, y'oughter be ashamed er yourself!" and Daisy set her doll down very hard indeed, and folding her dimpled arms, she perked her head on one side and looked at Tom with a glance which, as she herself afterward said, "quite wizzened" him. Tom, feeling a little embarrassed under this fixed glare, began vigorously to pull his fingers one by one, and faintly murmured, "Why?"

"Tom!" (severely.)

Tom gave his middle finger a jerk which caused it to "come out" with a tremendous report.

"What yer want, Day?"

"Tom, stop dislocketing your fingers this minute!"

Tom folded his hands behind him, and, sticking out his tongue, proceeded to examine it with the most minute attention.

"Tom, you're a boy with most degusting manners. Your manners is awful, and I shall have to break off our 'gagement ef you don't stop 'em!"

"Oh!" gasped Tom, "are we 'gaged, Daisy, you an' me?"

"Yes, Tom; every young lady should orter be

"A BOY WITH DEGUSTING MANNERS."

'gaged. Sister Fan says so; and Fan's growed up and knows!"

"Oh! but, Daisy, p'raps you could find some other body bigger 'na me. I'm so little, an' my manners is dreffal bad!"

Daisy shut her great blue eyes, and waving her hand with quiet dignity, replied:

"I'se goin' to wait till you grows big!"

Tom seized this opportunity, when Daisy was not looking, and made frantic efforts to touch the end of his nose with his tongue. Daisy opened her eyes and caught him in the act.

"D-e-g-u-s-t-i-n-g performance!" she exclaimed.

"Tom" (pathetically), "what shall I do with you? My nervous cistern is so scattered, I really can't stand ut!"

Tom opened his eyes to their widest extent.

"Is ut, Daisy?"

"Yes. Fan's is, an' I s'pose mine must a caught it."

"Say, Daisy, I'm 'fraid ef you an' me is 'gaged, I'll ketch it, too; an' I'm such a lee-tle bit er boy; an' ef you could find some other body bigger an' me—— "

"Tom, you talk 'tirely too much. Now, you just sit there an' curl Ang'lina's hair, 'cause I'm goin' to eat this apple."

Tom dutifully obeyed, and for some minutes all was still. The silence was at last broken by Tom, who had been gazing pensively into Daisy's eyes.

"Daisy, your eyes is boofal, big blue ones."

After a pause: "Such round, round, wide ones!"

Daisy answered with a satisfied toss of her curly pate, and a sprightly "Round eyes is nice!"

"Yes," said Tom absently, "dey is nice; but mine is lee-tle bits er black ones—just as lee-tle!

"YOU SHOULD ORTER ER TOLD ME YOUR HAIR UD COME OFF," SAID DAISY.

Pin-eyes, mine is; an' pin-eyes an' round eyes don't go nice together. An' ef you could find some other boy bigger'an me, wiz bigger——"

"Tom, lemme see y'eyes."

Tom made his eyes as small as circumstances would allow, and looked at Daisy.

"Stop squintin'!"

Tom glared.

"Now, then, y'eyes is big and starin'; not as I pertend to say yer pritty, cause y'aint, yer hair is d-e-g-u-s-t-i-n-g! straight as pokers; straight down yer brow ter y'eyes, and straight down yer back ter yer shoulder-blanes! O Tom!"

DAISY THINKS SHE WILL CUT IT OFF.

—after thinking a moment—"you run up to the house an' get Fan's curlin'-irons, an' I'll try an' make you look 'speciable; an' bring along the little iron stove as is with 'em."

Tom departed, and soon returned triumphant. Then the curling process begun.

"O Daisy! yer pull awful!"

"Tom, be quiet."

"O Daisy! m' ear!"

"What's the matter with ut?"

"Yer fizzen it, Daisy!"

"Well, then, take ut outer the way!"

Tom looked skeptical.

"I say, Daisy" (calmly, during an interval devoted to heating the irons), "I don't think fizzen is pitty"—as Daisy continued to heat the iron, which was already red-hot—"Daisy, aint yer 'fald you'll burn yer?"

Daisy swung the iron around in the air for a while, and then, taking one of Tom's flaxen tresses, quietly wound it around them.

"What's that sizzen, Daisy?"

"Ony yer hair! it's curlin' beautiful!"

"Is ut?"

"O Tom! how degusting!" exclaimed Daisy, holding the iron before Tom's astonished gaze, "your hair came right off when I was a-frizzen ut, an' there's your beautiful frizz on th' iron."

For a few minutes they both regarded the "frizz" in speechless horror, then Daisy said solemnly:

"Tom, you should orter er told me your hair ud come off!"

"But," sobbed Tom, "it didn't never turn off—

DAISY AND TOM GO A-BEGGING.

before! Oh, dear! oh, dear! I think, Daisy, ef you could find some other body bigger an' me, wiz really curls!"

"No, Tom," said Daisy soothingly, "I'll never desert yer, Tom—never! An' besides, it don't make any matter 'bout yer hair, 'cause I'm a-goin' to cut it off, like that nice man wuz, and like yer brother Jack's, as we saw in prison!"

"Daisy!" gasped Tom, "is Jack in prison?"

"No, not Jack isn't, but the nice one is! And O Tom!" exclaimed Daisy, clapping her hands, "yer look the perfec' bundge of him now; yer ma'll be so pleased!"

This rather extraordinary announcement met with Tom's entire approval.

"Say, Tom, let's play beggars. Take off yer shoes an' stockins and I'll take off mine, and I'll wrap a shawl 'round my head, an' Fan's got a b-e-a-u-tiful basket, as was buyed at th' Injuns, an' we'll get our cold victuals in that; and oh! such fun!"

Tom assented, and so, after making their toilets and getting the basket, they set out on their journey. At the first house they came to they stopped and knocked at the lower door. The girl who answered their knock was very "quisitive" in Daisy's opinion, and Daisy told her she mustn't ask "imperdent questions." She insisted, however, upon knowing where Daisy got such a pretty dress, and was informed that "she'd always had ut." This proved entirely satisfactory, for the maid went into the kitchen and returned with several hot biscuit, which were, however, refused with scorn by Daisy and Tom. They didn't ask for hot things; they wanted "cold vittals," like beggars always had, and, highly injured, they went on their way.

"Now, Tom," said Daisy, "pritty dresses isn't

Figure 37. Addie Ledyard, illustrations for "Two Very Young Americans," written by Laura Ledyard, *Hearth & Home* 4, 38 (21 September 1872): 728. Courtesy of American Antiquarian Society.

Figure 38. Helena de Kay, plates for "Prelude," from R. W. Gilder, *The Celestial Passion* (New York, 1878), 8–9. Personal copy.

Telling Stories along with many other illustrations originally printed in *Riverside Magazine*.[60]

After the Civil War, large publishing houses backed many of the flourishing literary and family magazines. Most editors were also writers or engravers who held together the close-knit world of book and magazine publishing by wearing a variety of hats. Scudder said that although he in-

VOL. IV.—No. 38.   NEW YORK, SATURDAY, SEPTEMBER 21, 1872.   [Subscription Price per Year: 1 Copy, $3; 4 Copies, $2.75 each; 10 Copies, $2.50 each.]

Entered, according to Act of Congress, in the year 1872, by ORANGE JUDD & Co., in the office of the Librarian of Congress, at Washington.

MOTHER'S ROOM.—(See page 718.)

Figure 39. Mary L. Stone, "Mother's Room," *Hearth & Home* 4, 38 (21 September 1872): cover. Courtesy of American Antiquarian Society.

The Wife Auction.

Figure 40. Lucy Gibbons, del, Langridge, sc, "The Wife Auction," from Horace Scudder, *The Bodleys Telling Stories* (Cambridge, Mass., 1878), 94. Courtesy of American Antiquarian Society.

tended to become a writer, he soon found himself "at the desk of a literary workman."[61] Professional crossovers meant that an editor who hired an artist to illustrate a magazine story might later hire that artist to illustrate a book, perhaps even of his or her own writing. This overlapping market served the careers of women artists.

In 1868 Scudder convinced Hans Christian Andersen to allow Riverside Press to publish his new stories and fairytales in book form. In August, he wrote Andersen that he had contacted renowned German children's book illustrator Oscar Pletch "to see if we cannot manage to have him make drawings for your stories."[62] But Scudder had already commissioned Mary L. Stone to illustrate the English translations of Andersen's work to be published in *Riverside Magazine*. "There stands before me now," Scudder wrote the author in October, "an admirable drawing illustrating the former story ["The Court Cards"] by one of our young artists—a young lady, Miss Stone—who adds to her devotion to art an enthusiastic admiration of your stories. This story with the drawing will be published in the first number of the new year . . . [while] Mr. Oscar Pletsch of Berlin will probably furnish the chief designs for the proposed new volume of your stories for children."[63]

In the end, it was Stone's illustrations that adorned the first American volume of Andersen's *Stories and Tales*, accompanied by drawings of the late Vilhelm Pedersen (1820–59).[64] Energetically observed and studied, Stone's drawings combined with ease the regional specificity of folklore and dreamlike universality found in the best children's stories. "The costume of the Chicken Grethe is Swedish but I trust it is near enough to Danish not to offend those who know the difference," she told Scudder.[65] With the simplest detail—a scarf on a head, the toss of a shawl, the curve of a back—Stone gave her Andersen drawings an inventive foreignness (Figure 41).

As an editor, Scudder was responsive to anyone in whose work he found inspiration for his own writing and editing schemes. When gathering the staff for *Riverside Magazine* in 1866, he sent letters to male and female authors and illustrators asking for contributions. He also visited a number of artists in their New York studios to see if their work fit his ideas about what a children's magazine should offer.[66] His goal was to produce a magazine that would "picture the world in which children live and yet constantly enlarge the boundaries of that world to them."[67] Scudder met with landscape and figure painter John William Hennessey, whose "young girls" he pronounced "good" but portrayed with "more sentiment than we shall want." He also "[s]aw Harley the engraver and was much pleased with

GREAT-GRANDFATHER. See page 287.

Figure 41. Mary L. Stone, "Great Grandfather," from Hans Christian Andersen, *Stories and Tales* (Cambridge, Mass., 1871), plate. Courtesy of American Antiquarian Society.

him."[68] Stone pleased him as well. She turned out to be a dependable worker with "a great deal of fancy, an excellent eye for grouping and composition, and [she] is rarely at fault in drawing the human figure."[69] Despite suffering from personal and financial setbacks after leaving the School of Design, Stone was able to travel to France and Holland several times to paint and make studies from life.[70] She was "enchanted with the 'Dutch color'—not in the pictures, but in the people & houses & expressive landscape."[71] Other artists attributed Stone's accomplishments to the way she would "go to work" whether she felt like it or not: "she nearly took my breath away by the vigorous way in which she tackled the most available subject."[72]

Scudder gave Stone numerous commissions, using her drawings to illustrate a variety of texts, including his own. Stone in turn valued the aesthetic attention that working with Scudder afforded her: "If Mr. Harley [the engraver] makes any criticisms of my *lines*, I should feel obliged if you would give me the benefit of them," she wrote Scudder about a drawing made for one of his stories.[73] Scudder reprinted the Andersen woodblocks designed by Stone and engraved by Harley many times in Hurd & Houghton publications. One plate was "illustrated" in words at least two more times, as "Baby Pigs" by Alexina Black White in *Little-Folk Songs* (1871) and as "Poking Fun at Pigs" by Scudder in *The Bodleys Telling Stories* (1878). These reappearances suggest the symbiotic relationship of artists and editors working for the illustrated press.

Editorial Friends, Men o' Workers, and Spoiled Geniuses

Looking back from the 1930s, Mary Hallock remembered Horace Scudder as one of "those editorial friends of all the contributors of that period."[74] "Editorial friends" was a designation women artists reserved for that group of editors who brought them into the publishing fold after the Civil War. Born during the social and political ferment of the 1830s and 1840s, these editors were contemporaries of the first School of Design graduates. From the republican generation who came before them—the Coopers and Greeleys who set up institutions to educate women artists—they had learned to work hard while maintaining an earnest devotion to civic and individual ideals, and to value and assist others who showed the capacity for great work.

One of the editors who faithfully supported women artists was author-poet Richard W. Gilder (b. 1844). Gilder joined the newly founded *Scribner's Monthly* as assistant editor to Josiah Gilbert Holland in 1870 and became editor of its successor *The Century Illustrated Magazine* upon Holland's death in 1881. At *Scribner's* Gilder wrote a column called "The Old Cabinet," worked as managing editor, and took charge of the magazine's art features. Under his care *Scribner's Monthly* secured the work of America's most innovative male and female artists and writers and gained a wide reputation.[75]

Another editorial friend to women artists was novelist-journalist Mary Mapes Dodge (b. 1831). As a writer and the editor of *Hearth & Home* and as editor of *St. Nicholas: Scribner's Illustrated Magazine for Girls and Boys*, Dodge pioneered a new direction for the field of children's literature and envisioned a new form of art to match it.[76] "A child's periodical must be pictorially illustrated, of course, and the pictures must have the greatest variety consistent with simplicity, beauty and unity," she wrote. But they also "should be heartily conceived and well executed; and they must be suggestive, attractive and epigrammatic. . . . One of the sins of this age is editorial dribbling over inane pictures. The time to shake up a dull picture is when it is in the hands of the artist and engraver, and not when it lies, a fact accomplished, before the keen eyes of the little folk."[77]

Thanks to editors like Dodge, children's magazines became an arena in which American illustrative art distinguished itself and women artists were asked to employ their fine art skills. *St. Nicholas* was beautifully printed by the DeVinne press and copiously illustrated by the same artists working for *Scribner's Monthly* out of "the conviction that the perfect magazine for children lies folded at the heart of the ideal best magazine for grownups."[78] Prominent among those artists were women and men trained in the Unity of Art at the School of Design. Dodge also solicited work from artist members of the Ladies' Art Association and was awarded an honorary membership in return.[79]

To be sure, not every midcentury editor was the female contributor's friend. In her 1854 novel *Ruth Hall*, columnist-humorist Sara Willis Parton (b. 1811), whose pen name was "Fanny Fern," describes the "tyrannical benevolence" displayed by many of the publishing men with whom female artists and writers had to contend. The scene between Ruth and her first editor, Mr. Lescom, caricatured their preoccupation with the bottom line: "The law of supply and demand regulates prices in all cases. In literature, at present, the supply greatly exceeds the demand, consequently the prices are low. . . . You, of course, must regulate your arrangements according to *your* interests; and if anybody else will give you more than I do, you are at liberty to take it. As I said before, *business* is one thing—*friendship* is another.'"[80]

What Ruth Hall and women artists discovered was that friendship had quite a lot to do with business. Fern's characterization of Lescom was a reminder that not everyone who hired women was acting out of republican egalitarianism. She knew business had to do with more than friendship; one's work had to be good and marketable. But for a female illustrator's prospects to match her abilities she needed a friend like Ruth Hall's next editor, John Walter. Walter confessed "a warm, brotherly interest in your welfare, as well as a high admiration for your genius, and it will afford me much pleasure to aid you, whenever my services can be made profitable." Female contributors of the 1860s and 1870s encountered both "tyrannical benevolence" and "brotherly interest" in editors working for the illustrated press.[81]

Women illustrators were their own publicists, shuttling from one office to another carrying a heavy portfolio, an unnerving experience for young male and female artists alike.[82] The experience made some women artists savvy judges of the male characters they encountered in publishing. "I was introduced to Dr Holland the other day at Scribners," Hallock told Gilder. "He has a dyed moustache and a flowery impressive manner with a touch of the paternal toward me which I resented—inwardly—outwardly I was all smiles for obvious reasons—He is the great sun at Scribners."[83] Women artists became adept at negotiating with arrogant men. Artists seeking work could not risk openly expressing their opinions; but in private women artists kept one another informed about editors, writers, and artists who treated them with condescension or disrespect. Hallock's feminine charm and aesthetic talent won Holland over. In 1872 he agreed that she should illustrate his semiautobiographical serial, "Arthur Bonnicastle."[84]

Navigating the publishing world was made easier for women artists by its interconnectedness. Richard Gilder found the situation women illustrators faced so galling he preferred to act as intermediary. "Command me like a brother," he told Hallock, "tell me how many orders you would like to have, in advance, just at present, or whether you would rather your agent (R.W.G) would not crowd you during this warm weather. It is a perfect delight to me—so you needn't have the least hesitation in the matter. The idea of your taking that blessed book around am[on]g these men—makes me mad—I don't wonder you didn't want to go again to the Aldine. It made my blood run up-stream and my hair stand on end when S. looked over those sketches. He tried when you came in to talk about it—but I put a stop to that."[85] Gilder's hair probably stood on end because he recognized the sexual overtones of a situation in which a vulnerable young woman marketed her goods to powerful men, or owed her success to a man's generosity. Artists and editors found ways to skirt Victorian convention and at the same time defuse the sexual connotations surrounding a woman's indebtedness to a man. They explained their actions in the languages of brotherly protection and business interest.

Women artists understood that male advocates helped them overcome obstacles to their careers, especially the prejudice held by more conservative men. After her promoter had shown Longfellow designs for his poem *The Hanging of the Crane*, Hallock crowed that: "'Mr. Longfellow was as much pleased as he was *surprised* when he found they were made by a lady'! . . . Longfellow asked Mr. Anthony if I was 'handsome and accomplished' and how old I was. These, you see, are the important questions."[86] Although stung by the questions, the young artist felt comfortable mocking the aging poet because of the acknowledgment her work received from male editors and engravers.

The Hanging of the Crane demonstrates the way women artists used their commissions to evade gender and age stereotyping. The book's pictures follow the poem's depiction of a conjugal couple aging from marriage to parenthood to grandparenthood, delicately marking family resemblance in the faces and carriage of each generation. But Hallock exceeds Longfellow's portrayal by devising scenes that exhibit her own abilities and intelligence. In a design of a mother tending a cradle, for example, she creates a sense of interior darkness through white lines, displaying her skill in both chiaroscuro and engraving technique. While Longfellow's words inspire her views, they do not limit her invention. To illustrate his allusion to the hopes and disappointments of youth—"O sudden thrills of fire and frost! / The world is bright while ye remain, / And dark and dead when ye are lost!"—Hallock turns black and white lines into the picture that the parents of a young adventure seeker might imagine: their daring son lying dead on the banks of an unknown shore (Figure 42).

Brotherly business partners who protected their sisters also offered constructive criticism. Anthony was particularly tactful when advising Hallock. "Have you a tracing of the mother's figure?" he asked her. "She is a little *bunchy* about the neck?" Anthony phrases his comment as questions. "If you draw that from nature and are sure of your drawing, all right—but it seemed to me that if a little were taken off the top of the shoulders, . . .

Figure 42. Mary A. Hallock, "O sudden thrills of fire and frost!," from Henry Wadsworth Longfellow, *The Hanging of the Crane* (Boston, 1878), 48. Personal copy.

the figure would not look so much in a heap." After this gentle chiding, Anthony offers an endearing mollification. "Looking at it since the above was written I am rather inclined to consider the drawing correct, and so shall commence it in the morning, but I'll let the suggestion stand to keep you from getting too proud of your work." He closes with the highest complement he could give: "The little head piece is superb, but I can never keep the delicacy of the drawing, never reproduce your effect of light."[87] Their business relationship gave men and women a chance to show mutual respect and admiration openly and without fear of misunderstanding.

Women artists were pleased when editors shared their aesthetic sense. "The boy coming down the bank expressed to you just what I intended," Stone told Scudder after receiving comments on a design. She did not mind revisiting a drawing to suit his taste, so long as her "ideas" were kept intact.[88] Of course, artists and editors did not always see eye to eye: "Mr. Anthony is much pleased with the blocks," Hallock informed Gilder, "but he looks at them in *his* way, you know, which may, or may not be our way."[89] Artists were annoyed by editors' specifications, which could fluctuate between unchallenging topics and ridiculously difficult tasks.[90] "I think those young men at Scribner's have dealt hardly by me," groaned Hallock. "There must be a pic. of a man all alone in a dark lane—then a woman all alone in a dark room—then a man and a woman together anywhere out of doors in the dark. It will be a relief to get into the broad sunlight of my strawberry pic. again."[91] Despite their grumbling, illustrators like Stone and Hallock knew they were given difficult scenes to design because editors believed they excelled in creating the desired effects.

Female artists were aware that their success was often contingent on an editor's willingness to take chances. Looking back, Hallock reasoned that "large sums must have been risked on those perfectly made giftbooks, as we should regard them now."[92] Hiring young female artists to illustrate the work of male poets added to the risk.[93] These books "proved to be a business success," Hallock surmised, "largely due to the fact that the House spared no expense. I saw my homely name in print—'Miss Mary A. Hallock' had flocks of pleasant notices."[94] So too did other women artists who published in gift books. The best editors of the early 1870s never doubted that women were capable of making art that was not only worthy of publication but also of financial and personal investment. After *The Hanging of the Crane* came out, Anthony summoned Hallock to Boston, ostensibly to discuss some new work, and gave her what she called "the surprise of my life." To meet the artist, the Anthonys invited to dinner "a select audience" made up of Longfellow, Oliver Wendell Holmes, James Russell Lowell, Howells, and probably Whittier. Of Anthony's devotion to Hallock, Helena Gilder remarked: "He gave her his very best efforts, and was a firm and consistent friend of all those years." Hallock simply called him "my promoter, Mr. Anthony."[95]

Joining these brotherly editors was a phalanx of older male artists who promoted the careers of those women artists they considered worthy of notice. Serious women artists cherished masters of their field who looked upon them as individuals. "Mrs. Nye was older than Mr. Herrick," recalled Alice Donlevy. "He treated her with beautiful deference, though he criticised her drawings very severely. She had studied with good English artists, and Mr. Herrick knew she could stand more criticism than the other students who had not received her early advantages."[96] Women artists encouraged one another to take advantage of these wise critics. "Mr. Linton writes that he is to be in N.Y. the last of May and will probably call on you Sunday night . . . Show him your things—be sure you do. He may not think it polite to insist on seeing them. I think he is a dear, noble old darling—wish you could see the good, wise letters he writes about my work. I like to feel as if he had authority in his opinions."[97]

But the "noble" engravers and painters who considered it in their own interest to bolster the confidence of women artists were becoming a rare treasure. "It seems to be one thing we lack in this country—An older class of men o' workers to whom we can look up—instead of that—the men who should help us are all against us."[98] By 1875 the man considered to have "authority in his opinions" was closer in age to Hallock than to Linton. These successful and well-connected artists knew the workings of the art world and supported one another by sharing knowledge and ideas. Among them were a number of "young bloods," born in the 1840s, who cooperated easily with women artists.[99] These men joined women to found the Art Students' League in 1875, taught at the Cooper Union, tutored individual female students, and even married women artists. But chauvinism, competition, jealousy, and even sexual tension kept other male artists from working cooperatively with their female contemporaries.

Sometimes it was an artist's personality that disturbed the relationship between male and female associates. John La Farge illustrated for the same publishers and worked with the same engravers as women. He took on female pupils and mingled with them socially; his fellow artists and engravers, men and women, admired his work. But he was not the kind of man women artists looked up to. When Mary Stone met La Farge in 1873 she found him "very interesting and a lesson of patience." Hallock agreed: "Mr. La Farge's work is the result of a temperament which even his genius can hardly convert into a boon. To draw like him, one must be like him, I suppose—and one would hardly dare to wish that."[100]

Both Gilder and her studio mate Maria Oakey Dewey studied with La Farge, and he was a regular at gatherings of artists and writers at the Gilder residence. He joined the Gilders in founding the Society of American Artists and gave good accounts of Helena when he met her friends abroad. But on one visit to the Gilder home, La Farge insulted her by ignoring the portrait she was painting and only commenting on the decorative oak-leaf panels she had drawn to illustrate Richard's poems for *Scribner's*. "Why don't you women go into this sort of thing?" he asked her. Gilder knew the difference between the real criticism of a friend and the sexist kind. "L.F. and I are forever estranged," she wrote in her diary. Gilder felt betrayed by her friend as both an artist and a woman: "I cannot think he has been noble in his action."[101] Noble men did not withhold support from artists they knew personally or try to restrict the professional lives of women as a group.

Most women artists generously blamed ego rather than male arrogance for the bad treatment they received from male artists. "You say 'there is something cussed about an engraver,'" Hallock wrote Gilder. "*I* say there is something ditto about a genius—(not Richard's kind—the true kind, that is born in a man after he has become a *man*)—La Farge is great but he is also small—or narrow—or something disappointing. I am disappointed in him for not getting the better of his egotism in reference to you."[102] La Farge was what Hallock called "a genius spoiled in the making."[103] Because the spectrum of attitudes regarding women who pursued art as a profession was wide, women artists considered the individual rather than the sex when seeking or assessing a man's reaction to their work.

Husbands and Family

Competing male artists notwithstanding, American men generally accepted women's choice of art as a profession. The flexibility of illustrating made the trade particularly suited to women's social position as daughters and wives. Sketching could be done almost anywhere, indoors or out of doors, and studios were easily set up in any room with a source of light. Using family members or hired household help as her models, Hallock designed woodblocks for New York, Washington, Boston, and Philadelphia publishers while living at her parents' home on the Hudson, in a one-room cabin in California, in a remote mining village in Colorado, in a shared house outside of Boise, Idaho, and while traveling in Mexico.[104] But even with supportive families, many women who worked at home found feminine duties disruptive to their careers. Louise Bradbury wrote Donlevy that she had not "drawn a line nor painted a stroke" since she left New York City for home. "I have been chiefly employed in looking after my sick relatives," she said, "but in spite of the many favorable opportunities for administering a fatal dose, I have conscientiously refrained, remembering [your] sententious remarks about being a woman before one is an artist."[105]

On the other hand, familial duty could compel an artist to embark on a professional career, sometimes prematurely. Hallock felt that young artists sold their work "too quick and too easy" because of family obligations. "It was the pressure at home that must excuse the plucking of such unripe fruit," she said. "We women were eaten to our souls with a horror of debt."[106] Even after leaving home, women artists felt a responsibility to help their parents and families financially. Living rough in Leadville, Colorado, Hallock sent money back home after selling a block that was not quite finished. "We were then rather low in our minds about money—and the temptation was too great," she wrote her niece: "so I packed it off to Scribby [*Scribner's*]. The result was this note and a check for $150 which I enclose."[107]

Marriage rarely ended the careers of women illustrators. Many of the most popular designers married during the height of their careers and continued to publish art after changing their names. Illustrated journals increasingly carried pictures bearing the triple initials of Lucy Gibbons Morse, Mary Hallock Foote, Jessie Curtis Shepherd, Rose Mueller Sprague, Rosina Emmett Sherwood, Albertine Randall Wheelan, Fanny Eliot Gifford, and Olive Thorne Miller. Some women had no choice but to keep working after marriage. After she married, Hallock confessed to Gilder that she worked because she "must earn money." The prevalence of married women illustrators reflects the reality of conjugal life in post-Civil War America. In 1873 the American economy collapsed yet again, and until 1879 the United States suffered a severe depression. New York City workers were some of the hardest hit, but the slump was felt as far as New Almaden, California, where Hallock's husband was "ruined" by the "Sand Lots agitation" among Mexican workers and "a break in bonanza stocks," which funded his employers' company.[108] Married artists in every field, especially those who wedded other artists, felt the economic pinch. Illustration and engraving commissions that funded single women artists in the 1860s provided precious family income in the 1870s.

To be sure, ideas about women's duty to home and family forced many women—single, married, or even widowed with children—to justify their artistic ambitions. But whether a middle-class artist worked for pay had as much to do with her family's finances as with domestic ideology. After marrying, painter Agnes Chamberlain needed to know her chances of making money before deciding between artwork and housework. "Men all believe that money *saved* is better than money *made* by their wives," she told Donlevy, "– but I cannot feel but that my time is more or less wasted upon mere house hold occupations that a common servant would really do better. Of course if my pictures do not *pay* my duty would be the house hold."[109]

When Arthur De Wint Foote first came to call, Hallock was surprised to find that she could work with him in the room. "The door behind me opened with a burst of sound and closed again. A young man stood there who apologized for his entrance and asked if he might stay. As a matter of fact, I didn't believe that I could draw a stroke with him there; but I did! . . . he was of that breed I had known, yet he was different. He did not praise my work; he merely said how jolly it must be to have work that one liked and make it pay."[110] Foote never expected Hallock to stop making art when they married, as he had recognized from the start that for his wife art was both vocation and avocation. Other men who married female artists shared this insight, particularly if they too were artists or writers.

Nevertheless, women artists worried about the constraints associated with being a wife. In 1872 the writer Helen Hunt introduced the young editor Richard Gilder to Helena de Kay, then a student at the Cooper Union.[111] Inspired by his love for the young artist, Gilder wrote his first sonnets and asked her to marry him (Figure 43). Richard was supportive of Helena's career, but she still thought her artistic life might end with marriage. Helena's betrothal to Richard troubled some of her friends as well: "A letter came last week from Mary Stone," Hallock wrote her. "She seems to have felt very deeply the news of your engagement. Of course she is sorry! Says *any* woman can marry (but few are so manifestly cut out for greatness in Art) & I wouldn't tell you this, only it shows her strong affection for you and her profound faith in you as an Artist."[112]

Hallock believed marriage need not be the end of a woman's artistic life. "*If only* you, and so many other people, wouldn't take it for granted that Art is over for you, I don't believe it would be at all! The more I think

MR. AND MRS. GILDER
At the time of their marriage

Figure 43. "Mr. and Mrs. Gilder at the Time of their Marriage," from Richard
Watson Gilder, *Letters of Richard Watson Gilder*, ed. Rosamond Gilder (Boston,
1916), 60.

of it, the more it seems to me a matter of *sentiment*—this destruction of your Art. If you choose to believe yourself in bonds, you might as well be, but if you act as if nothing had happened—if you don't let your palette & brushes into the secret of your changed life, everything will go on the same, with the advantage of a new and deep experience added to those already given you to express."[113] But Helena feared that romance would undermine her aesthetic goals. "Why shouldn't you be happy I'd like to know," Hallock countered. "That is what I quarrel with you for, for not taking the good life as it comes. It would serve you right if R. should make up his mind to defer your marriage—and go abroad for two years—for the good of your mutual professions—Then you could paint and be as free as you like—It is my opinion you wouldn't like it at all."[114] The "sentiment" that marriage and "greatness in Art" do not mix, and the dearth of eligible men following the Civil War, kept many women artists from marrying.

After Helena and Richard married in June 1874, their home became the focal point for a new generation of artist-intellectuals. Every Friday evening the Gilders were "at home" to New York's rising cultural producers. Singers, actors, and musicians; writers such as Ehrman S. Nadal, George Macdonald, George Washington Cable, and Henry James; and artists such as La Farge, Elihu Vedder, Hallock, Stone, Katie Bloede, Abbott Thayer, and Winslow Homer flocked to "The Studio" at 103 East Fifteenth Street. When Hallock married she cavalierly considered it more of a problem for her publishers than for herself: "The publishers of the *Skeleton in Armor* had prepared their advertising posters of the book 'illustrated by Miss Mary A. Hallock'; they were not too pleased when she suddenly changed her name in the midst of the contract and rendered herself liable to other engagements. She might have finished the drawings just as well at New Almaden and something was said to that effect, but they made it plain that they expected them to be all in their hands before she went aboard the lugger, so to speak."[115]

More women found that it was not marriage so much as maternity and child rearing that disrupted art careers. Being a "mother faithfully" and "doing one's work as an artist also faithfully" was a difficult task. Hallock recognized the importance of family planning to a woman's career, and when the natural methods she and Arthur used to deter conception did not work she felt dismayed. Childbirth was a natural process, but she knew from Helena's experience that it involved pain and risk. Furthermore, family was too important and time-consuming to be given short shrift. Yet, even loving wives and mothers found ways to keep working. Having become pregnant shortly after moving to California, the new Mrs. Foote spoke about her worries to her sister-in-law Mary Hague. Hague revealed to her a "sure way of limiting one's family." Have your husband "purchase shields from a physician or first-class druggist," Hague counseled. Hallock later passed the information on to Gilder. Although they sounded "perfectly revolting," the shields provided a perfectly safe and sure way to prevent pregnancies.[116]

Women artists who maintained careers did not have to forgo families, however. Hallock labored incessantly as she combined marriage and maternity with hers. She supported her family emotionally and financially, especially at times when her husband was poorly paid. Whenever she could, Hallock hired a servant or took in the daughter of friends to help with the female chores. She gave birth to three children, had numerous miscarriages, and was always tending someone in the sickroom. A. J. Wiley, a young assistant engineer who was intimate with the Foote family described her habits: "The vast amount of work she produced under conditions that would have absorbed all the energies of an ordinary woman, is accounted for by the fact that she seemed not to be dependent upon propitious moods or favorable surroundings, but had the faculty of absorbing herself in artistic or literary work whenever the more pressing claims of family life relaxed."[117] Hallock's ability to make art during her child-rearing years was extraordinary, but it was ordinary for married women artists to make art for remuneration and to find profitable art work rejuvenating.

Juxtaposing Hallock's situation with that of her friend Elihu Vedder (b. 1836) shows that marriage affected male and female artists differently. Vedder and Hallock belonged to the same art circles in New York and both depended on contacts for work. When children began to add to the stress of married life, the two artists turned to different economic sources for relief. During his period of increasing responsibilities, Vedder refused to paint portraits or solicit commissions from possible patrons. Instead, he relied on good friends in England to sponsor him so that he could pursue aesthetic interests without having to paint works that would sell.[118] As Hallock's familial duties increased she too relied on friends, but as employers rather than benefactors. Hallock became more dependent on publishing as her responsibilities increased. A married woman could not receive patronage in the same fashion as a married man due to restrictions imposed by middle-class propriety. Private patrons might "subscribe liberally" to a married man's career, but a female artist's sponsors had to find ways to help her professionally without humiliating her husband. They did so by offering or finding her commissioned work and praising her art in print.[119]

Hallock pursued a new style and content at a time when her family duties were the most demanding. Entranced by her letters about life in New Almaden, the Gilders suggested Hallock turn them into an essay for publication in *Scribner's*. As she began to "write out" those things that impressed her most, Hallock decided to make sketches as well, as soon as she could "get around" after the baby's birth.[120] "A California Mining Camp," accompanied by fourteen illustrations, was published in *Scribner's* in February 1878. Ironically, marital obligations, rather than personal freedom, led Hallock to the far west and her own distinctive aesthetic territory[121] (Figure 44).

The vexed "money question"—how to support oneself and family through art—compelled women to explore new media or experiment with the formal aspects of their art. When her husband died and left her with two children, Eliza Greatorex pursued landscape painting as a profession. After gaining recognition and sales through exhibition, she turned to graphic art and popular markets. While on tour in Germany, Greatorex made pen and ink drawings of the Bavaria landscape, which she published in two books using a little known process called Albertype: "They resemble etchings, except that they are finer in details, and lighter in their aerial effects." These experimental books received the highest possible praise and convinced G. P. Putnam to send Greatorex to Colorado to record the American landscape (Figure 45). While in the West, Greatorex developed an unusually free cross-hatching style to invoke the rugged settings illustrated in *Summer Etchings in Colorado*.[122]

Greatorex had a wonderful ability to spot, develop, and exploit popular and commercial markets. In the early 1870s, the artist began making pen and ink drawings of colonial homes and other historic buildings around New York City. In 1875, suspecting that there would be a strong interest in centennial memorabilia, she circulated a prospectus announcing the publication of "a series of fifty etchings of these relics, now almost daily disappearing." Eighteen of the sketches were exhibited at the Philadelphia Centennial Exposition and published in the series *Old New York, from the Battery to Bloomingdale*, which became Greatorex's best-known work. On collected panels and woodwork from old houses and churches being demolished, she painted or sketched a historical scene or event. After her daughters decorated the edges, Greatorex sold these works of "art history" from a gallery in her home. Some of the drawings from *Old New York* were lithographed for her *Souvenir of 1876*. Greatorex's combination of artistic

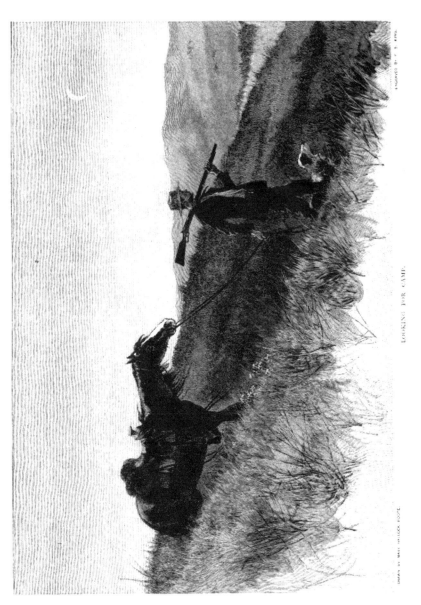

Figure 44. Mary Hallock Foote, del, F. S. King, sc, "Looking For Camp," from "Pictures of the Far West," *Century Magazine* 37, 1 (November 1888), 108.

In The Ute Pass.

Figure 45. Eliza Greatrex, "In The Ute Pass," *Summer Etchings in Colorado* (New York, 1873), plate. Personal copy.

accomplishment and entrepreneurial savvy was highly regarded; the artist was celebrated in the 1870s and 1880s in reviews, at receptions, and with honorary memberships in Sorosis, a professional women's society, and the Ladies' Art Association.

As the printed and decorative arts became more lucrative and innovative, many more artists followed Greatorex's example—experimenting, diversifying, and creating what has come to be called the Aesthetic Movement.[123] During the 1860s, Vedder struggled to find a marketable genre for his vision and style. His path was set when he created a little design called *Soul of the Sunflower* (1868), part of a set of small drawings he hoped to develop into paintings and illustrations for a story. After a successful exhibition of his oil paintings in Boston in 1879, Vedder entered *Soul of the Sunflower* in Prang's 1880 gift card contest, won first place, and turned the drawing into a painting, a glazed tile, and a fireback. In the end, however, it was not his paintings or tiles that brought Vedder fame, but his compelling illustrations of Edward Fitzgerald's translation of *The Rubáiyát of Omar Khayyám* (1884).[124] After 1876, most of America's best-known male artists became prosperous through means other than canvas painting or marble sculpting.[125]

The Power of Publishing

As quotidian as they were, the printed arts proved to be more consequential than painting for women artists at midcentury.[126] A published illustration was proof of expert approval and popular appeal. It served as a mark of an artist's professional status. Painters who marketed their work at exhibitions might be amateurs, but artists employed by publishers certainly were not. Publishing symbolized the ability to sell, which was as essential to a female artist's professional identity as her ability to create. Because it was an evolving field, both technically and professionally, illustration left the artist plenty of space for original design and imaginative execution.

Some critics worried that a great deal of Hallock's "pictorial faculty" had been "cramped" by the restriction of producing art which in subject "is a mere restatement of the text." They assumed that "paintings in watercolor and oil" exhibited more freedom. Yet the same critics acknowledged that an illustrator like Hallock might produce better work than less constrained artists. "There are not many American painters who have equal mastery of the figure and of composition, or 'picture making,' and her drawings on the wood show other artistic qualities which are as rare as these."[127] Hallock found freedom while illustrating even literary works she considered mediocre. After reading *The Skeleton in Armor* in 1875, she confided to Gilder: "It is a stupid poem—if it be not treason to say so, but very suggestive and leaves plenty of room for the artist's imagination to supply details."[128] Confronted with illustrations that defied the limitations of the medium, art critics called into question the aesthetic hierarchy that relegated illustration to a secondary status.

Illustrators understood that painting was ranked higher by the authorities who controlled the academies. Hallock often commended Gilder, the painter, for being a "true artist" unaffected by commercial concerns and vowed that when she had time she too would learn to paint. She never did. "I have made one attempt in watercolor. . . . but there is so little time for all that must be learned before I could *begin* to satisfy myself."[129] When Arthur Foote had to leave directly after their wedding, Hallock said she was "not sad at all, though at first I had to work hard at my blocks to fill a strange blankness." With the publication of *The Hanging of the Crane* imminent, she confessed to Gilder: "it's a curious fact I never had so much ambition as now."[130] So long as the standing of engraved illustration remained high, women artists embraced the art.

Illustration gave Jessie Curtis [Shepherd], who attended the Cooper Union in the late 1860s, a chance to show off her knowledge of formal principles. In "Hush up, Chloe Shine," Curtis used foreshortening to make Chloe, the poor little patient, appear to be lying with her feet toward the viewer (Figure 46). Curtis learned woodblock design from Linton, who engraved her first published illustrations and mentioned her in his *History of Wood-Engraving*. She also studied painting with Lemuel Wilmarth at the Academy of Design.[131] As a young artist, Curtis was applauded more for conception than execution.[132] Yet, dozens of Curtis's drawings were featured in books and magazines every year.[133] As she matured in the trade, Curtis took pride in her profession, showing woodblock designs at art exhibitions and continuing to work after marrying. "I have devoted myself from the first and last to telling stories in black and white pictures," she said in defense of illustration in 1889. "I think it is the grandest branch of art, on account of its wide application . . . A painting is seen by the few who come to it but a reproduction goes to the ends of the earth."[134] Through illustration the artist's egalitarian convictions were realized.

Illustration gave women artists aesthetic authority. Quick execution and emotional conception was Georgina A. Davis's forte. Hired as a staff artist by *Frank Leslie's Illustrated Weekly*, "Georgie" Davis was expert at the

"HUSH UP, CHLOE SHINE."

Figure 46. Jessie Curtis, "Hush Up, Chloe Shine," *Wide Awake* (1875): 290. Courtesy of American Antiquarian Society.

rapid, accurate sketching used for pictorial reporting. Using this method, she captured the drama of courthouse scenes, the intimacy of political parlors, the sadness of Civil War veterans' homes, and the exuberance of worship in black churches.[135] In an art piece called "The Bridge of Sighs" (1872) for the cover of the *Aldine*, Davis evokes a woman's passionate state through boldly drawn, exaggerated features and clenched fists (Figure 47). Davis also worked as artist-reporter for *The Salvation Army War Cry* in the 1880s and as staff artist for McLoughlin Brothers publishing house of New York in the 1890s. She publicized her professional position as illustrator for a major paper in an engraving for *Frank Leslie's* (3 April 1880) entitled "Illustrated Interview of Our Lady Artist with the Ute Indian Chiefs and Prisoners in Washington, D.C.—From a Sketch by Miss Georgie Davis" (Figure 48). By including herself in the picture, Davis demonstrated the confidence her success in illustration had given her.

Publishing art was mutually beneficial for illustrators and employers. It made individual women artists familiar to the public. People knew Elizabeth B. Comins, a.k.a. "Laura Caxton," because she drew the newsboys, book-

Figure 47. Georgie A. Davis, "The Bridge of Sighs," *Aldine* (1872): front cover. Courtesy of American Antiquarian Society.

ILLUSTRATED INTERVIEW OF OUR LADY ARTIST WITH THE UTE INDIAN CHIEFS AND PRISONERS IN WASHINGTON, D. C.—FROM A SKETCH BY MISS GEORGIE A. DAVIS.—SEE PAGE 71.

Figure 48. Georgina A. Davis, "Illustrated Interview of Our Lady Artist with the Ute Indian Chiefs and Prisoners in Washington, D.C.—From a Sketch by Miss Georgie Davis," *Frank Leslie's Illustrated Newspaper* (3 April 1880): 69. Courtesy of Newark Public Library.

blacks, and street musicians hawking their wares in first editions of Horatio Alger's Ragged Dick Series and other Alger books[136] (Figure 49). Comins's depictions also helped make Alger's ambitious urchins popular. Published art introduced people to American women artists as a group as well. In 1873, the *Aldine* reviewed Greatorex's prints to answer the question "Whether women cannot become artists as well as men?" in the affirmative; and then ventured to suggest that the answer to the next question, "What can the woman artist do best?" could be found in the illustrated periodicals.[137]

Women's black and white art was frequently reviewed in illustrated magazines because it had the advantage of advertising the publication in which it appeared. To see the work of expert women artists look to "THE ALDINE above all others," Greatorex's review commanded. Publicity worked both ways, bolstering women artists' careers while boosting the company's trade. *Hearth & Home* profited when attractive illustrations by Mary Stone or Mary Hallock were featured on its cover, as did Robert Brothers, publishers, who used Addie Ledyard's cunning drawings to advertise their stock. Women artists as a group benefited when *Scribner's* announced that "such well-known favorites as Moran, Bush, Magrath, Paul Dixon, Woodward, Eytinge, Bolles, Miss Ledyard, Miss Stone, [and] Miss Hallock" are always "engaged on novelties for THE MONTHLY."[138] Publishers placed women artists in lists of enticing contributors to draw the subscribers' attention to their own cultural importance, and in so doing announced the prominent position that female illustrators had achieved in America (Figure 50).

Publishing brought women artists into the professional fold. "My companions in those days were some of the most brilliant and fascinating young people of their time," recalled Hallock in her *Reminiscences*. Members of this circle, which met at "The Studio" Friday nights, "followed Helena up the Hudson for a weekend now and then, after she had discovered us on the old farm. . . . In those early days the young poets were still on trial, the essayists and artists (except Vedder) in the stage called promising. Helena, the First Friend, was the clasp in that chain of fortuitous comraderies. Reading of them later in far places where my life bestowed itself after marriage, I saw them—famous and bald and some of them fat—always as they were then; they had an immortality of youth for me."[139] In 1864, Hallock had traveled down the Hudson to join other aspiring artists assembled at the Cooper Union's School of Design, "prepared with many thrills for this wildly unexpected opportunity." Ten years later, "that oddly assorted group of girls" found themselves at the heart of America's cultural world.[140]

Figure 49. Elizabeth B. Comins, "Ragged Dick," from Horatio Alger, *Ragged Dick; or, Street Life in New York with the Boot-blacks* (Boston, ca. 1870), frontispiece. Courtesy of American Antiquarian Society.

"The Fays," from St. Nicholas, Page 496, Vol. II.

Some "St. Nicholas" Artists.

Mary Hallock Foote.
Frederick Dielman.
Walter Shirlaw.
James E. Kelly.
J. Wells Champney.
Sol Eytinge.
E. B. Bensell.
L. Hopkins.
Walter Satterlee.
Henry L. Stephens.
Frank Beard.
Granville Perkins.
R. Sayre.
Howard Pyle.

John Lafarge.
Eastman Johnson.
Fidelia Bridges.
Addie Ledyard.
H. F. Farney.
W. L. Sheppard.
F. S. Church.
M. Woolf.
H. P. Smith.
Mary A. Lathbury.
A. C. Warren.
Fred. B. Schell.
G. A. Tilden.
John A. Mitchell.

Walter Crane.
R. Swain Gifford.
E. A. Abbey.
F. O. C. Darley.
Alfred Kappes.
George Inness, jr.
Jessie Curtis.
A. H. Thayer.
George White.
Richard Gross.
F. A. Chapman.
M. L. Stone.
H. Winthrop Peirce.
August Will.

Thomas Moran.
W. D. Hennessy.
C. S. Reinhart.
R. Riordan.
Francis Lathrop.
W. H. Gibson.
James C. Beard.
G. F. Barnes.
Kate Greenaway.
F. Opper.
Walter F. Brown.
J. O. Davidson.
Mary Wyman Wallace.
E. M. S. Scannell.

[SEE NEXT PAGE.

Figure 50. List of "St. Nicholas" artists and writers, from *Scribner's* 17, 3 (January 1879): 39. Courtesy of American Antiquarian Society.

Chapter 7

"A Combination of Adverse Circumstances"

Cecelia Beaux (b. 1855) came to New York City to pursue a career as a portrait painter in the 1880s. Like her predecessors at midcentury, Beaux had chosen art as her work out of need, desire, and principle. "Although all sorts of intangibilities and uncertainties hovered about my existence," she recalled in 1930, "there was one rock-bottom reality. I must become independent."[1] To do so Beaux took advantage of the opportunities at hand. Having demonstrated a gift for drawing as a child, she was sent to study painting with an aunt who was a professional artist and then to art school in Philadelphia. In her teens, she read John Ruskin's *Modern Painters*, "and of course accepting all, was wafted to glorious heights." Without "consciously connecting" the two experiences, Beaux took "a month's lessons in china painting from a French expert, in the ignoble art of over-glaze painting," and began at once adapting it to portraiture. The results, she confessed, were "too successful," as "parents nearly wept over" her work.

Beaux describes with relish the process through which she developed this over-glaze method for portraiture, adding that youthful exuberance may have overruled her aesthetic judgment:

somehow, after four firings at a remote kiln, I managed to get upon a large china plaque a nearly life-sized head of a child (background, always different), full modelling, flesh color and all . . . Of course I used photographs, but was not content with "making up" the color. I had a solar print made, going for this to a nice old man, high up many rickety stairs in an old house at Fifth and Arch Streets. The rude copy contained nothing but measurements, but the golden-haired darling was then brought to me and placed as nearly as possible in the lighting of the photograph. I then wrote all over the solar print notes on the color—"most color," "least color," greenish, pinkish, warm, cool. This was a real study in summing up and cleavage of tones, and added greatly to the much too great vitality of the head, carrying it far from the purely decorative requisitions of the china plaque.

My reputation spread. Mothers in the Far West sent with the photograph a

Figure 51. Cecelia Beaux, *Clara Hoopes*, 1882. Oil on porcelain. Elizabeth Arthur. Courtesy of Tara Tappert.

bit of ribbon, the color of the boy's eyes, as well as a lock of hair. In such cases, of course, I never saw the child.[2]

Motivated by financial considerations, Beaux elevated china painting to a higher plane, "far from the purely decorative requisitions of the china plaque" (Figure 51). In her hands, it became a fine art.

Beaux's reminiscences reveal the ideas and material conditions that underlay American women artists' careers in the third quarter of the nineteenth century as well as new conditions and ideas that transformed their situation during the Gilded Age. In the 1860s and 1870s, industrial and decorative art were exciting new fields through which an artist could launch a career, gain an independence, or announce her professional aspirations. These burgeoning arts provided Americans with cultural products and artists with economic opportunities. Beaux's enthusiastic creativity was typical of male and female artists at midcentury, but not after 1876. Although her account radiates with pride in her invention, Beaux takes a different position at the end of her story: "Without knowing why, I am glad to say that I greatly despised these productions . . . This was the lowest depth I ever reached in commercial art, and, . . . I remember it with gloom and record it with shame."[3] As a twentieth-century fine artist, Beaux had to portray her foray into decorative art production as a fall from grace, even while admitting it had been essential to her ascent to professional independence. By 1930 the separation of art and industry, both ideologically and materially, had redefined such productions as strictly commercial endeavors with no artistic importance.[4] The skill and care with which the china children had been rendered was no less aesthetically derived than Beaux's subsequent canvas portraits, but the meaning of china painting had changed and with it the world in which women artists had flourished faded away.

America's postwar financial boom ended in panic in 1873, as the capitalist economy tumbled, carrying the nation with it. The ensuing depression lasted until 1879, and its repercussions continued into the 1880s. Out of work in 1876, and inquiring about prospects in New York City, Annie Delano listed the jobs she considered within the scope of her profession in a letter to her old friend Alice Donlevy: "I retouch negatives—work plates in albums—notes, color—ink—oil—and Crayon—paint in oils—and am successful in teaching—and with all this—from a combination of adverse circumstances—am out of employment and have so few friends or acquaintances who are in a way to put me in a way to find employment in any branch of my profession. I have thought that perhaps from your more extended life—you might hear or know of places—that might be obtained upon application." Annie's father had died four years earlier, leaving his eldest daughter responsible for her sixty-nine-year-old mother, widowed sister, and niece. She alone had a trade that might support the family, and to fulfill her duty the artist was willing to work in any branch of her profession. After reading the letter Donlevy took a pencil and jotted on it: "Anna B. Delano / Pen Yan / New York— / works in black & white."[5]

As recording secretary for the Ladies' Art Association, Donlevy received dozens of letters from women artists desperate for work between 1873 and 1879. Like Annie, they each blamed personal circumstances for their poverty. Yet these artists' inability to make a living arose from a series of adversities and betrayals that reached beyond individual biography. During the 1870s and 1880s, women artists were swept into the capitalist transformation of American society. These were decades of upheaval and transition for Americans, a time of intensive industrialization and mechanization, economic depression and occupational degradation, working-class organization and middle-class cohesion.

It was also the era of professionalization in the arts, which negated the Unity of Art ideal. Until 1876, male and female artists had negotiated the standards of artistic professionalism together. But as industrialization ate away at their status, financial depression and European imports undermined their markets, and amateurs infiltrated their ranks, American artists responded with separate professional strategies. To survive the 1870s, many female artists looked for employment and recognition in areas traditionally held by men—industrial design and applied art, and male artists tried to establish dominance in arts associated with women—minor media and decorative household art. The keystone of professionalism for all artists was training at an art academy or school of design, but since the 1850s training had been made available to almost anyone with talent in America. After the Civil War, a trip to Paris to study in a famous atelier and visit galleries, museums, and exhibitions was added as the final stage of preparation. Yet, despite the expense, thousands of American men and women still reached for professionalism.

Americans remained unusually hospitable toward aspiring female artists during the depression, prompting a *Scribner's* author to comment: "The association of the sexes on terms of perfect equality gives American art-student life one of its distinctive aspects."[6] Artists and art students were "clustered together, in the order of proficiency" rather than by gender in New York's three leading art schools: "the Art Students' League, the Academy of Design, and the Cooper Institute."[7] The training artists received in Europe differed from that at American schools in one significant way: male and female artists were not treated as potential equals. Instead, they studied with male masters in gender-segregated classes that promoted single-sex bonding.[8]

But outside of New York's art institutions the experiences of male and female artists increasingly diverged during the depression years. By 1880 the majority of the fifteen hundred or so students who attended New York art schools each year came from "the distant interior," reported *Scribner's*, and in many cases the opportunity to study was "maintained by teaching or some other form of laborious work." Although the Cooper Union charged no tuition to students who intended to use art to make a living, not everyone had families or means enough to pay for room and board while studying. "One young woman at the Cooper copies manuscript half the night, in order to draw by day. A cold boarding-house existence takes the place of pleasant homes; sometimes two young women form a partnership to share it in common; sometimes they board themselves." On the other hand, "The young men adapt themselves to circumstances more easily, and even with hilarity. In one case, three are encamped together in a large chamber where, though the total expense of living for each is kept down to three dollars a week, they entertain their friends and hold sessions of a flourishing glee-club."[9]

One of the consequences of divergent experiences was the construction of two distinct professional identities for artists, defined by activities and attributes peculiar to each sex. Looking into the studios of professional artists, the *Scribner's* author discovered men and women negotiating very different worlds. In the male artist's studio was an army of "new-comers," freshly returned from Europe, who rent expensive studios and adorn them with "tapestries and carved chests." This "congenial circle" made up entirely of young men of "the new movement" and the new "American Art Association" was rapidly replacing the elder generation, now confined to professorships at the academies, as "the most prominent element in the artist life of the city." But scattered throughout the town were also the studios of "a great obscure body, full of aspiration, recognized failures and whimsical vicissitudes of fortune, between the student class and that of established reputations."[10] Among this intermediary class the author places New York's women artists.

In the studio of "the one my lodging gives me opportunity of observing at a distance," the writer finds none other than Hawthorne's "Hilda." This woman artist is a diligent worker ("nobody is less bohemian in her own feelings than the woman artist"), navigating myriad adversities unknown to her disorderly "masculine *confrere*." Besides having to overcome the same "obscure and painful hardship," the feminine confrere must endure infesting bores and idle visitors ("because they are less afraid of her"), patronizing express-men, supercilious washerwomen, and fraternal sign painters who offer discounts "in consideration of fellowship in 'the profession,'" along with her full share of vocational trials: "Prosaic advertisers bring orders for designs for the Eugenia skirt or Centennial blacking, instead of commissions for high art. The popular taste has much increased the demand for decorated fans, lamp-shades, patterns for embroidery, and tiles for furniture. At the same time a great influx of new-comers and the enterprise of amateurs working for pocket-money, leaves less of a resource in this direction than might be imagined."[11] From the material of these hardships, many female artists crafted a professional identity.

Fellowship in the Profession

New York City was hit hard by the financial crisis of the 1870s. By the winter of 1873–74, one quarter of the city's workers had lost their jobs, and for the rest wages were declining steadily.[12] In 1874, J. C. Zachos, curator of the Cooper Union, noted the dire situation in his annual report to the Trustees: "The commercial revulsions and depressions in all departments of industry . . . have brought pecuniary distress upon many private families and individuals, have served to vindicate the value, as they have in no wise diminished the demand upon the resources of the Cooper Union." Apparently, people in every class were affected, not only the poor but "The sons and daughters of those families who in ordinary times, are well to do on salaried employments, and command comfort, leisure and general culture, are now thrown into distress and want, through the loss of position and salary of those who supported them."[13]

The School of Design section of the Annual Report recorded "a large excess of applications this year, greater than any before. . . . More than a hundred applications have been reluctantly postponed for want of room, to the next year."[14] But the next year, 355 applied for 200 places, and in 1876, 440 applied. To accommodate this demand, the Cooper enlarged its facilities and the Women's Art School stopped accepting "Amateur" students again. It increased the number of registered "Industrial" pupils to 340 in 1878, the year a record 845 women applied for admittance. The philosophy behind these actions was articulated in the 1874 report: "The Cooper Union grapples with all social and industrial problems in a very radical way, by promoting the power and the means of their solution, rather than dogmatizing upon theoretical methods. It aims to educate the industrial classes into intelligent skill, as a necessary antecedent to their prosperity and happiness."[15] Since the 1850s, the Cooper had advised American women that they might find "prosperity and happiness" if they acquired art educations. The prudence of this advice was apparent in the success of the Woman's Art School, which recorded a steady increase in "the returns of situations, employment, &c" throughout the economic crisis years, with teaching and photo crayon and color work rivaling illustrating and engraving as good moneymaking occupations for trained artists. Even during hard times, Cooper's female students were finding employment at good wages.

Outside the school, however, things seemed far bleaker. On 11 December 1874, the Workingmen's Central Council held a gathering at the Cooper Union, during which four thousand inside and thousands more outside listened as speakers analyzed the nature of the depression and suggested ways to respond to it. Leading socialists, currency reformers, and trades unionists endorsed the idea of mounting demonstrations to demand that the government guarantee work, or at least suspend evictions for nonpayment of rent and give out food dispensation to distressed families. Neighborhood meetings were held around the city to discuss the same issues.[16] Among the workers feeling the impact of the depression, packing the meetings, and discussing the extent of the disaster within their ranks were members of the Ladies' Art Association.

While women artists fell into every social class, many of them experienced the depression from the perspective of skilled artisans and workers and responded in common with them. Increased hardship stirred them into collective activity, both as laborers and professionals. Like other destitute workers, female artists became the target of a middle-class charity motivated by hard times but shaped by New York's charity reform movement. They also joined other working people in their dislike of sympathetic handouts from the better off. This discontent was aggravated by responses to their plight that undermined the status and value of their artwork.

A woman artist's feeling of fellowship with other workers stemmed from her education and experience. Outside the Cooper Union, self-supporting artists continued to identify themselves as serious and diligent workers. To compliment an artist at her firm in 1869, School of Design graduate Leila Curtis told Donlevy: "She is one of the most industrious and indefatigable workers I have had the fortune to meet."[17] For Curtis the title "worker" signified that this woman had the training and temperament necessary to become a successful artist. L. H. Reese believed that "If the want exists, and there are a few earnest workers to begin," an art school could easily be established that would become "a blessing to many a girl and woman who is now secretly longing for such an opening, to such a culture."[18] These women had learned from experience what Ruskin and Herrick maintained: that Fine Art is the operation of the hand and intelligence together, combined with *heart*, that is, earnest and aspiring endeavor.

Curtis's understanding of art and the artist surfaced in the United

States census report, which did not list artists and artisans separately until after 1870, when artists were split under the categories specified ("painters" and "sculptors") and unspecified ("artists"), and their occupations divided into "professional and personal services" ("artists") and "manufacturing, mechanical, and mining industries" ("engravers"). Women artists were listed in a separate category for the first time in the 1860 Population Census, after the establishment of institutions for women's education in the industrial arts but before the census separated artist from artisan. The new categories reflected increases in both industrialization and the division of labor in the United States.

Women artists chose the appellation "worker" while at design school, and clung to it during the decades American engravers and craft artisans fought against the degradation of their arts and labor. For the professional woman artist trained in the Unity of Art ideal, "worker" was not a metaphor; it was a recognizable type, a social position. "The strongest women are those who work quietly and thoughtfully and are hardly known but through their work," Louise A. Bradbury confided to Donlevy. "How much do we owe to the brave, true-hearted workers in our ranks—who eschewing all noise & clamour—pursue steadily the great & good objects of life— wisely making the best & fullest use of the flowers which nature has bestowed upon them."[19]

Women who called each other "worker" were distinguishing their goals, training, commitment, and aesthetic ability from those of amateur artists. This distinction was imperative for self-supporting women living in a society rapidly embracing a domestic ideology that defined middle-class females as nonworkers. In 1872, Mary Cook could not raise the hundred dollars needed to pay expenses while teaching a painting class: "The Life Class last year just paid the model," she wrote the Ladies' Art Association, "and part of that time we divided the expenses which were more than the regulation price of 20 cents each."[20] The problem was exacerbated by the attitude of the women who took the class. Cook split her income with the model, who obviously worked to make her living, but her middle-class pupils did not comprehend that art was Cook's occupation as well. "I did more than I would ever do again to get up a landscape class," she confessed. "I wrote and wrote again—and called on those who had the year before said they would be sure to join, and they all acted as if it was a personal favor, they were to do myself individually." Rather than acknowledging her professional position, Cook's prospective clients assumed that as a member of the "middle class" she shared their situation and values. They considered art an amateur endeavor for women and perceived Cook's class as a friendly alliance rather than a business transaction. From then on Cook, the artist-worker, acted on her own understanding of middle-class behavior: "I would not believe in anyone joining, until I had their money paid in advance all are so slipery on making a bargain."[21]

While elite women may have had trouble recognizing that art was a profession for some of their peers, other middle-class workers did not. One of the many worker organizations that developed during the depression years, the "Sovereigns of Industry," reached out to women artists as fellow producers. The Sovereigns of Industry was a cooperative and fraternal amalgam of workers and professionals that made trading arrangements with receptive mercantile firms to protect independent producers against the exactions and speculations of middle men in commercial relations. "This order being in direct communication with the Grange movement," Mary Byrnes wrote the Ladies' Art Association in 1874, "offers special facilities to your association for increasing your materials at lower rates. . . . women are taken into the order and can share all its offices and benefits equally with man. In fact the way is open for women to enter in upon the organization of work for women."[22] It is not clear whether any of the artists in the Association joined forces with the Sovereigns of Industry. What is clear is that the Sovereigns conflated artists and artisans. They regarded art as an occupation and female artists as a group of workers battling exploitative markets.

The dozens of trades and professions represented by the Sovereigns suggests they held no distinction between professionals and tradesmen and women. Among the members of the local chapter represented by Mary Byrnes, a housekeeper, were clerks, shoemakers, chemists, hatters, photographers, weavers, tin smiths, mail carriers, teachers, book sellers, roofers, shopkeepers, miners, opticians, sewing machine manufacturers, sewing machine operators, tailors, tea dealers, civil engineers, piano tuners, printers, saleswomen, lawyers, produce dealers, farmers, bakers, and male and female physicians.[23]

Members of the Ladies' Art Association acknowledged their responsibility to laboring women. In 1873 a fellow member commended Donlevy for supporting Emily Faithfull, a London compositor, writer, and publisher, who was visiting New York City. Faithfull employed only women to run her businesses and took to the lecture platform to encourage others to do the same. The fellow member also connected the plight of male and female producers: Faithfull "points out outwork as a base of operation for women

[for] at present there are plenty of women and men that do work, [yet they] find no employment—I do not see how she can give them that—that will enable them to enjoy all the comforts of this life."[24] In addition to Donlevy, other New York artists attended Faithfull's lecture. Jervis McEntee reported that "the English reformer and friend of the working women" was among the guests who attended Tenth Street studio building's open house. The artist residents and friends returned the favor the following night, attending a reception of the working women of New York at Steinway Hall, where Faithfull spoke.[25]

Advocates for the "producing classes" contacted members of the Ladies' Art Association because their modus operandi—democratic membership, voluntary participation, professional assistance, and education—linked them to artisan republicanism. In 1875, J. Edwards Clark, who was compiling a book on American schools to be published by the U.S. Bureau of Education, commented favorably on the producer ethic permeating the Association: "I have been greatly interested in its picture of the quiet independent manner in which women who can *do* something, have gone to work to help each other or themselves."[26] The origins of this ethic among women lay in the necessity, temperament, and principle they brought with them to New York City design schools, in the lessons they received from teachers who "knew how to cultivate a sense of public spirit among women," and in their occupational experience.[27] Like the republican artists and reformers who championed them, women artists associated "virtue" with moderation and independent "honest industry."[28]

As proud as they were industrious, women artists attempted to help each other through the depression years without accepting private charity. In this act they aligned with New York artisans and journeymen who felt betrayed by their city's response to lost jobs and low wages. As hunger and homelessness spread, New York's Mayor William Havemeyer concluded that the needs of the city's poor were being "adequately met by private donations and the various Christian and charitable institutions." Churches had set up soup kitchens and missions offered people shelter from the freezing streets. Middle-class Christians concocted schemes to induce others to help the poor. For example, the "YMCA sold 'dinner tickets' to New York businessmen to give to the unemployed." But the artisan workshop masters, craft workers, and wage laborers who abhorred dependence rejected Havemeyer's suggestion that they live off "crumbs that fall from the tables of the rich," countering that the unemployed were entitled, as a matter of right, to better than private charity. Didn't the government make sure the businesses of the wealthy kept running when they were in need, the Workingmen's Central Council asked? Why shouldn't workers be assisted in their attempts to maintain their vocations?[29]

Because working "girls do not wish to receive charity" for the same reason working men rebuffed it, members of the Ladies' Art Association rejected it as well and instead offered individually what little help they could to fellow artists and art students.[30] When the depression deepened and the situation of women artists deteriorated, the executive board formally adopted a system of labor-for-labor exchange: "This Plan, limited in public usefulness by the poverty of the Association, has been in practice for five years. It grew out of the reluctance shown by talented women in accepting any assistance in art study having the appearance of 'charity.' It is simply *long credit*. Payment is made in drawings, paintings, decorations, and work that may be used or sold at the Annual Exhibition, or in teaching drawing wherever the Ladies' Art Association has begun classes in the United States. Time being necessary to mature the student's work into a salable production (whether she becomes artist, designer, artisan, or teacher), the wisdom of waiting two or five years for payment is as self-evident as the humanity of the Labor Note System."[31]

The "Labor Note System" was an alternative to money payment, developed and brought to America by the socialist industrialist Robert Owen in 1826. Designed to enable mutually assisting companions to ply useful trades on the basis of credit and the indirect exchange of goods and services, Labor Notes were written and accepted in lieu of legal tender. Cost was the limit of price, and "each individual who gave a note, affixed his or her own price per hour for labor," explained the religious socialist John Humphrey Noyes in 1870. "Women charged as high, or nearly as high, as men; and sometimes unskillful hands overrated their services."[32] In America, the Labor Note System was touted and tested by labor reformers, utopian socialist communities, and workers' cooperatives until the market-based, corporate profit system was so entrenched that the idea of profitless equivalent exchange became unthinkable to most people. The Ladies' Art Association resorted to labor notes because the system resembled the credit businessmen offered to one another, rather than having the appearance of charity. "By this means, instruction has been paid for in writing, drawing, painting, botanical studies, teaching, care and sale of pictures, and the procuring of orders for members."[33]

Only those who were willing to live frugally attempted this kind of plan.[34] In a cost-value system prices were determined by the producer's outlay of time, energy, and materials, and for the system to work everyone had to honor everyone else's cost expenditure. No one worked for nothing, and no one refused payment (no matter how rich they were); to pay and accept payment showed respect. It was like saying: "Not pay you? That's impossible, you worked for it." Payment showed that you recognized that for everyone involved, art was business. The association carefully "honored" its members by charging 10 percent for any services it provided, and artists (no matter how poor they were) always reminded whoever provided the service to bill them. Of course, some legal tender was needed to supplement labor exchange, and so various friends of the Association including Jennings Demorest, the Society of Friends, and several Jewish donors provided funds for "Labor Note Scholarships."[35]

Gendered Class Definition

In 1875, the public spirit and business expertise of the Ladies' Art Association drew the attention of Elizabeth Duane Gillespie, director of the Women's Centennial Executive Committee. In many ways, the 1876 Centennial Exposition in Philadelphia marked an apex of cultural recognition for nineteenth-century women artists. It was the first American fair of international importance to follow the Great Exhibition that took place in London in 1851. Like European expositions, it was designed to demonstrate to the world the progress of "civilization" through fine art and industrial technology. It also was a huge, expansive celebration of national unity and independence, a chance to show how America's cultural production stood in relation to that of European countries. Exhibition officials solicited contributions of art and industry from every state, as well as foreign countries. The most popular buildings at the Centennial, which was attended by thousands of people, were the art galleries. A Women's Pavilion, which housed 600 exhibits, a library, art gallery, kindergarten annex, and the offices of the *New Century for Women*, the only regularly published newspaper at the Exposition, was a particular attraction. These exhibits stimulated an interest in fine and decorative art that benefited some artists, but they also encouraged a taste for European imports that undermined strictly American art markets and Unity of Art ideals.

The Women's Pavilion was a late addition, conceived after the original Centennial board reneged on its promise to provide room for an exhibit of women's productions in the main galleries. The project was hotly contested among women artists. Opponents thought a separate building housing women's contributions institutionalized the segregation of women's production from men's. Advocates believed it would be better for women if they occupied their own building, for then women from all over the country, working in every medium, could contribute work to the exhibit. In the end, the pavilion housed an eclectic selection that worried female professionals, who were adverse to having their art exhibited and judged along with that of amateurs.[36] A few well-known painters and sculptors refused to contribute anything to the Women's Pavilion. Others hedged their bets, sending submissions to both the art galleries and the women's building, and only exhibiting in the pavilion if rejected by the main exhibit.[37]

The Ladies' Art Association decided the benefits of a Women's Pavilion outweighed its detriments and agreed to act as Art Committee for the Business Women's Committee of the New York Women's Centennial Union. Donlevy, who by default became the committee's "highest authority," conceded that a separate exhibition gave more women an opportunity to display their art and perhaps make sales and contacts. Contributors to the Women's Pavilion were asked not to use initials, a common practice among artists of both sexes: "All signs placed over exhibits must give the FULL name, to show they are women's work."[38]

The New York committee's standards for acceptance were very high. Brooklyn artist Mary Ackerman declined the committee's invitation to submit: "I have not the vanity to suppose that my picture would pass the trying ordeal . . . and therefore am not willing to go to the trouble of sending such a large package . . . merely for the mortification of having to recall it."[39] Ellen Hardin Walworth, who was representing the committee in Saratoga Springs, wrote that she had collected "some desirable articles to forward" but many artists felt "a timidity" in sending them lest they be rejected. "So large a proportion of the artistic talent of the state is congregated in New York City that I suppose you will collect enough work there to fill the space allotted to the State, but I consider it an advantage to ladies from the country to send their work even if rejected—if nothing more is achieved the standard of excellence is elevated."[40]

As Donlevy suspected, women artists did gain exposure at the Pavilion exhibit. The first sales made were decorative art items, a "white wood frame $3.50, Tile Phantoms of the Woods $5.00, Tile Miss Gilbert $3.00." Other artists received orders based on their exhibits and one woman was asked if she would "draw designs for china" by a man with "immense potteries."[41] But when the contents of the women's building began to be dismantled

Donlevy questioned whether a separate building had benefited women artists in general. She was particularly incensed by the handling of women's art by "Mrs. Pellen," a Centennial agent who authorized an unidentified man to pack the New York exhibit as quickly as possible. "I feel no little anxiety about the 'returns,'" she wrote Gillespie, because the artwork solicited by the New York Committee has been sent from all over the state and "a stranger no matter how reliable will be puzzled by the variety of marks on the back of the pictures—Besides there is China, jewelry, and illustrations belonging to editors and publishers, of great value."[42] As representative of an association whose mission was to combat the vulnerability of women artists, Donlevy despairingly considered the significance of Pellen's action. Damaged or misdirected "returns" were evidence that Centennial directors did not respect women artists' work or understand the extent to which they depended on it for their livelihoods.

Reformers had criticized the Women's Pavilion from the beginning on similar grounds. Elizabeth Cady Stanton said the little building "was no true exhibit of woman's art" because it did not present women's actual situation. She was angry that the separate exhibition paid no attention to the products of women working in factories owned by men, or to their wages and working conditions.[43] By combining women artists on the basis of gender—professionals with amateurs—rather than on the basis of profession—fine artists with industrial art workers—the Centennial *inadvertently* endorsed the idea that women's work was naturally nonremunerative and promoted the separation of art and industry.[44] William Dean Howells questioned the segregation of female achievement and exclusion of factory workers as well. In an *Atlantic Monthly* review of the Centennial, Howells admitted he was "puzzled to know why the ladies wished to separate their work from that of the rest of the human race." "It seems not yet the moment for the better half of our species to take their stand apart from the worse upon any distinct performance in art or industry; . . . many of those pictures and pincushions were no better than if men had made them; but some paintings by women in the Art Hall, where they belonged, suffered nothing by comparison with the work of their brothers." "Woman's skill was better represented in the Machinery Hall than in her own Pavilion," Howells contended, where "she was everywhere seen in the operation and superintendence of the most complicated mechanisms, and showed herself in the character of a worker of unsurpassed intelligence."[45]

Donlevy was well aware of the important work women artists had accomplished for American industries. In March 1876, she set about trying to collect proofs of designs made by women illustrators and engravers to be placed in a scrapbook and exhibited at the Centennial.[46] Her purpose was to show that women artists had produced some of their best work for the industrial market. Publishers were happy to comply. *Wide Awake* sent an advance sheet containing three drawings by Helen Burt and the *Aldine* sent Georgie Davis's cuts "Playing Truant" and "Bridges of Life." But in some cases women's published work proved difficult to obtain. Artists who worked on wood retained very little of their work, and publishers often lost or destroyed the originals.[47] "I can recall no illustrations of lady Artists save two of Miss Hallock published in the Journal two or three years ago," *Appleton's* wrote Donlevy, "and of that we have no proof." E.P. Dutton & Co. had "no proofs of Miss Stone's drawings on glass." They suggested asking James R. Osgood & Co. but added: "It would cost you considerable for time to hunt it up, if preserved."[48]

Donlevy's scrapbook was an attempt to remedy the problems raised by a segregated Women's Pavilion and its exclusion of female operatives, both of which represented a tacit overthrow of the kind of class and gender fluidity that had characterized much of American society during the first stages of industrial development.[49] Before the Civil War, the signs of class identity were not entirely fixed for most women. Even women from culturally middle-class families entered and left the labor force without losing status. Most people recognized that the customary sexual division of labor did not serve the needs of women who lived without male support. And while some workingmen stressed the importance of keeping women's labor within the household, others allied with women workers in their own trades. Women's wage work threw open a series of possibilities for maintaining the family. However, the Centennial exhibits marked the end of what historians have called the "plasticity of gender" during early industrialization.[50] This tolerance of female self-reliance declined rapidly when industrialists began introducing women into the artisanal labor force as unskilled workers.

Hiring women did not automatically degrade art manufacture because many women had been trained in country shops, city academies, or design schools like the Cooper Union, and therefore expected fair pay and treatment. But the exploitation of women workers in other industries eventually affected the prospects of women artists. By 1845, the outwork system and garret shop had eroded all pretensions to craft apprenticeship in the clothing trades. Seamstresses in particular had endured increasingly poor working conditions, low wages, and no bargaining power. This process of proletarianization created the foundation for the exploitation of other industrial workers. With no other skill to fall back on, destitute female clothing workers became the "unskilled labor" employers sought to maximize profits. Here was a malleable workforce eager to be trained and willing to work for lower wages that employers could use to threaten or replace other craft workers.[51]

The hiring of untrained women to perform specialized tasks at lower wages hurt all workers, but was most damaging to female artisans and artists. Not only did the substitution of unskilled women in their jobs deprive trained women of work and wages, it robbed them of male support. Since industrialists hired women to deskill work and reduce wages, the presence of female workers, whether skilled or unskilled, came to imply cheap labor and an inexpensive product. This depreciation stimulated competition between men and women who previously had shared an occupational camaraderie. It also stigmatized professionals working in studios and homes outside the industrial setting through gender association, as increasingly a low-paid, inferior status was ascribed to all women's work.

To make matters worse, proletarianization had a divisive effect among women. Women artists came from a variety of backgrounds and faced different material conditions, and they disagreed about what strategies would best serve the needs of their class and profession. Despite the fact that Civil War casualties compelled thousands of culturally middle-class women to seek paid work, some of them felt uncomfortable claiming worker identity. America's growing cash economy was stimulating "essentially commercial habits of mind," but only men were associated with capitalist economic activity.[52] Allusions to "true womanhood" and sentimental domesticity undercut female self-reliance and the republican values that had motivated women to prove they could win their own competencies. By 1876 those who chose or were forced by circumstance to work outside their homes risked losing respectability.

In the 1850s Horace Greeley had bemoaned the fact that industrialization, which made wage laborers of some artisanal workers and entrepreneurs of others, was dividing Americans into discrete classes with conflicting interests. But not until after his death in 1872 did labor unrest sparked by the depression propel the majority of middle-class Americans to the side of the rich and powerful.[53] One of the distinctive features of elite society was the nonproductive role it gave women; many middle-class women felt that if they had to work their labor should be distinguishable from that of uneducated and immigrant women who supposedly made up the female workforce.

This opinion inspired a group of influential New Yorkers to found the Society of Decorative Art, which overshadowed the Ladies' Art Association after 1877. Modeled on the newly founded "Kensington School of Art Needlework" in London, which had an impressive exhibit at the 1876 Centennial in Philadelphia, the Society's expressed aim was "to benefit a class [Kensington] called 'decayed gentlewomen'" by converting "the common and inalienable heritage of feminine skill in the use of the needle into a means of art-expression and pecuniary profit."[54]

According to founding member Candace Wheeler, the "sensitive" Americans who helped her found the Society of Decorative Art rejected the phrase "decayed gentlewomen" but not what it implied.[55] Their mission was to help educated women attain a means of self-support that would not threaten their class position. It was an "unwritten law that women should not be wage-earners or salary beneficiaries," despite their having "a pathetic necessity for remunerative work," recalled Wheeler; "added to this was the fact that washing, scrubbing, and the roughest of domestic work were almost the only forms of paid labor among women." Even teaching "was out of this class," as teachers were only "grudgingly included in the fellowship of general society."[56] The founders were much taken with the way the South Kensington School had matched the labor of cultivated women with "the revival of many of the medieval arts" among "a little group of Pre-Raphaelite painters" to make embroidery "a means of artistic expression and a thing of value."[57]

Originally a member of the Ladies' Art Association, Wheeler envisioned the Society of Decorative Art (SDA) as an extension of the "idea of self-help through remunerative labor among women." Decorative art societies were founded in New York and Boston "to encourage profitable industries among women who possess artistic talent, and to furnish a standard of excellence and a market for their work."[58] These societies trained women to produce "superior" products, exhibited and sold at their salesrooms, and obtained orders for artists from manufacturers and dealers.

Other members of the SDA, who did not share Wheeler's broad vision, confined the "commercial opportunity" of "cultured" women to "the one channel of art" and then considerably narrowed that channel. "All other activities were closed to women of education and refinement under the penalty of 'losing caste,'" Wheeler recalled. "A woman who painted pictures, or even china, or who made artistic embroideries, might sell them without being absolutely shut out from the circle in which she was born and had been reared; but she must not supply things of utility—that was a Brahmanical law." Rather than encourage women to launch independent art careers or apply their skill to a variety of aesthetic fields, society members hoped "to induce each worker to thoroughly master the details of one variety of decoration, and endeavor to make for her work a reputation of commercial value."[59] Through these means women might labor in their homes, or in carefully chaperoned workshops run by the SDA, and so remain gentlewomen.

To foster women's self-support, the SDA worked to raise the status and value of traditionally "feminine" crafts, such as embroidery and lace-making, to the level of fine art. This goal seemed attainable in the 1870s, a period of extraordinarily rich activity in the decorative and domestic arts. Thousands of American amateurs were trying their hand at tile and china decoration, watercolor painting, printmaking, and other "secondary arts." Professional artists were forming associations to experiment with these media, challenge academic conventions, and revive artisan workmanship. This flurry of activity, now referred to as the "Aesthetic Movement," was a response to British products and ideas encountered at the 1876 Centennial Exposition and to a burgeoning interest in house and interior decoration.

Like British decorative art shops, the Society of Decorative Art planned to replace arts and crafts made by individual women with those designed by a few artists and produced in a factory-like setting by the rest.[60] Fortunately, Wheeler understood that the "presence of women workmen only, tends to depreciate the prices given for their work, even if it has no effect on the quality of the work itself. . . . people will enter [the sales room] with the fixed determination to pay lower prices for what they buy." But rather than mingling male and female artists to counter this "popular discrimination in price," the SDA announced that it was not "an establishment exclusively for women" and promptly entrusted its two most important aesthetic tasks to the artistic judgment of men: it asked renowned male artists to serve on its Commission of Admissions and to design its workshop made products.[61] This division of labor mirrored the separation of design and execution that was robbing male and female artisans of their labor value in other industries. Yet, ironically, the SDA realized that a clear sexual division of labor, with men as creative minds and women as skilled hands, would assure women a fairer recompense for their work.

Women had always been among the leading designer-producers of home decoration, but now male "experts" scrutinized their goods. Even worse, the new aesthetics these experts applied to decorative art rendered many artifacts originated by women valueless. Male experts warned that, "wax flowers, skeletonized leaves, and paintings on black panels would be rejected out of hand." Women painters already suffered financially due to the industrial mass-production of printed art and ephemera previously made by individual artists. Now women's ingenuity was devalued as well, as decorative products customarily invented by women were replaced by workshop-produced arts and crafts designed by men.

Wheeler recalled that male artists on the Commission of Admissions "were often amused at articles which came before them as art-work even after our most conscientious selection." Having been warned that expert artists would scrutinize their products, women continued to send objects they themselves considered art. "I recall Hopkinson Smith's delight at a glib letter from a clever Washington contributor thanking us for our criticisms of her work," Wheeler recollected, "and her remarks as to the functions of decoration, saying that she 'would rather decorate a coal-scuttle worthily than to sculpt statues for the Congressional squares.'" It is not surprising that an American who had learned to value the useful and the beautiful equally would defend the practice of decorating utilitarian things. But all the while the contributors were learning to follow the rules, Wheeler announced, and so the enterprise was a success.[62]

Women Artists in Crisis

Fine artists continued the practice of branching out into industrial and decorative art fields during the 1873 depression. Early in the 1870s, landscape painter Eliza Greatorex turned to etching to supplement her living, and later her daughters Eleanor and Kate, known for their watercolor painting and magazine and book illustration, started decorating porcelain and painting mural interiors. Ellen Thayer Fisher continued to paint pictures for exhibition and "give lessons by letter" at home in Brooklyn, but she also worked for Prang and rented a studio in New York City where she filled orders for "dinner cards and photograph mats." Sarah Denroche, whose specialty was engraving on wood, made small flower paintings on canvases and panels to sell at the Brooklyn Art Association in 1875 and the next year exhibited and sold illuminated mats at the Philadelphia Centennial.[63]

Painting in any medium was a precarious occupation during periods of prosperity, and impossible during hard times. Florence Dowe of Ithaca, New York, who painted flowers in watercolor and did "very good work in crayon," including portraits "from life," found herself "mostly finishing solar prints" in 1876. "Are water colors paying work at all?" she inquired desperately of Donlevy. "They are not here; the chromos spoil all possibility of selling them."[64] As a popular and inexpensive medium, watercolor painting had been a good field for an artist hoping to sell her work to country patrons. But during the depression clients who could not afford to pay three dollars for one of Dowe's original watercolors were happy to buy chromos for ten or twenty-five cents apiece. To make matters worse, another mechanized process, photography, was replacing Dowe's other primary field—pastel portraiture. Her most regular art job had become finishing solar prints. Painter-portraitists like Dowe and Delano felt lucky when photographers hired them to complete or color prints, as New York's upstate artists had difficulty finding enough work.

To assist women artists in disposing of their wares and to collect money for their organization during those desperate times, the Ladies' Art Association decided to hold an auction of paintings and bric-a-brac on two afternoons in March 1877 at the rooms of Leavitt Brothers, No. 817 Broadway. In the 1870s, bric-a-brac was a standard and nonpejorative term for miscellaneous small articles of antiquarian, decorative, or aesthetic interest that were collected by society persons and artists alike.[65] Fine art and bric-a-brac were commonly sold together at country bazaars and sanitary fairs and intermingled in the Woman's Pavilion at the 1876 Centennial. On the auction's first afternoon, the *New York Times* reported that, although "the paintings and water-colors were from the hands of well-known lady artists and of a high standard, the prices realized were very low." But the next day "when the collection of bric-a-brac was reached the bidding became more brisk, and the articles were more quickly disposed of."[66]

Several historians have cited the "heterogeneous mélange" of items sold at the 1877 auction and its classes in "china decoration, embroidery, photograph finishing, etc." as evidence that the Ladies' Art Association was becoming "charitable and decorative" rather than purely professional.[67] Yet, considering the financial crisis and the advent of the Aesthetic Movement, and the education of most participating artist members at the Cooper Union in the Unity of Art, it is the term "professional" rather than the professional nature of the Association that should be called into question. The 1877 auction registers the economic, cultural, and social pressures that were altering the nature of the art profession for both men and women.

Journalist D. G. Croly promised to attend the auction and have it properly noticed in the *Graphic*. But he also offered a cautionary note: "I hope the sale will be a successful one, though you of course understand that it is the worst year ever known for the sale of new works of art."[68] Prices received for paintings were so low that some artists lost money.[69] For almost thirty years, well-known miniaturist and easel painter Maria Louisa Wagner had regularly sold her work for good prices at the National Academy, American Art Union, and Brooklyn Art Association. Yet in 1877 she was compelled by economic circumstances to send several works to the auction. Wagner needed $1,000 to save her home from foreclosure. Although Wagner "should have been glad [to have] received even half or two thirds the value" of her paintings, she was thankful that Donlevy withdrew them before they were sold for next to nothing.[70] Leavitt's auction was a financial disaster for the Association. Nevertheless, the committee of arrangements was loath to rob artists of their livings and sometimes doctored accounts in a member's favor.[71]

The auction's poor results reflected the dire situation of many women artists. Some members admitted with great regret that they could not afford the Ladies' Art Association's annual dues, let alone the shipping and framing expenses if they sent a painting in lieu of money. Florence Bailey could not "be a member any longer" because she could not pay the fee. She sent a picture for the Association to sell "and thus defray any indebtedness I may have incurred." Mary Monks, a member of both the Ladies' Art Association and the Art Students' League, had intended to send something for the 1876 Christmas reception but failed to do so before returning home to help out over the holidays. "I've written the Sec. to cross my name off your books," she wrote Donlevy. "I can't pay my dues and don't care to run in debt. I'm not able to pay at the League either. I feel dreadfully poor this winter."[72] Maintaining an art career was difficult for anyone who was so poor, yet women artists understood that their independence and professional profile depended on refusing charity.

When the Society of Decorative Art announced its own bric-a-brac sale as a charitable event later that year some Ladies' Art Association members took it as the beginning of a turf war.[73] "I felt sorry to see by the Philad paper . . . that there was an 'unpleasantness' between the 'Decorative' and the Ladies Art Assoc.," Bradbury wrote in March 1877. "Does Mrs. Wheeler belong to us now at all, or has she preferred to belong only to that?" Apparently, Donlevy had written the article Bradbury drew upon. Bradbury agreed with the analysis, but she was not as troubled by the Society's work:

"The article . . . was rather severe on the Decorative Society; what a pity it has set itself in such opposition to the Association, and that it is so narrow in its ideas. I am sure the field of Art is broad enough for both to work in, the one supplementary & completing & helping the other, instead of being rivals. Theirs is perhaps the most immediately practical, . . . but ours affords more scope and range of taste and various ability. Whether either *pays*, in the common mercenary meaning of that term, is another matter."[74]

The problem was that the Society of Decorative Art's line did pay. In the same issue of the *Art Review* in which the Ladies' Art Association announced its adoption of the "Labor Note System," the Boston chapter of the SDA reported yet another year of increased prosperity: "the sales and orders amounting to over $1,000 more than those of the preceding year. . . . The total receipts have been $14,295.38; balance on hand, $3,221.26."[75] The economy was recovering, but American society had changed. During the depression, the middle classes had coalesced around the idea that it was better to support women through charity than to make them independent.

The SDA's success compelled some Ladies' Art Association members to question their own policy. Florence Bailey suggested that their organization become truly a "Ladies *Artist* aid association. . . . [R]ich members ought to keep up the association, and the poor artists (for artists are always poor) not have any expense without they reap some benefits,—and it is enough for them to pay the percentage on the sale of their pictures." Gertrude Leslie weighed the benefits of bringing it more in line with its thriving rival. "I have been thinking over the Association, & am anxious to 'see the wheels go round,'" she wrote Donlevy. "The LAA has been in existence for some years with members solely professional, [yet] it has not had the success it ought to have had." Leslie thought lay fellows should be allowed to serve on the management committees: "You see how much has been done at 4 East 20th [Society of Decorative Art], the ladies there have had the leisure & ability to push it."[76]

But "remaining professional" was the objective behind Association policy, as most members agreed this was the best way to mitigate the view that art was merely a pastime for ladies. Although poverty kept many women artists from acquiring the practical and symbolic trappings of their trade, they refused to jeopardize their reputations by allowing rich amateurs to run their association. To compete with men for employment and sales, women artists had to remain a democratic order of sister producers—artist-workers and professionals, rather than become a divided society of elite ladies and their objects of benevolence.

Cooper Union graduate and Ladies' Art Association member E. T. Graham felt that "sympathy with workers" might be enough to turn an affiliate of the Society of Decorative Art into a candidate for the Ladies' Art Association: "Miss Adams a Boston Artist (and a member of the Decorative Art of your city) has opened a school of art . . . her pupils are girls I know of as the daughters of rich men, who only work for pleasure, but she is in full sympathy with *workers* and offers every facility for such as desire to sell or take orders . . . Now what would you advise to try to have her join the L.A.A. and have Miss Ward unite with her[?]"[77] But after observing Adams's teaching Graham was not so enthusiastic: "Miss A. *is* a portrait maker and does some effective flower painting but she does not understand decorative and design I think. She has some rich girls in her class who can afford false methods or gropings but those to whom time and money are precious need the best chances."[78] Although Miss Adams had her own school, her lack of training in the principles of art clearly identified her as an amateur. So too did her unawareness that "workers" did not study as a diversion but to enhance their careers.

Wheeler had hoped that the Society of Decorative Art would benefit the Ladies' Art Association. In July 1877, she invited any member to contribute some decorative art "she can do well and which is not hackneyed" to the SDA's opening sale, and singled out a few artists with suggestions for decorated objects (chimney tiles, slate tables, mantles and firebacks), as "I am anxious the work of the L.A.A. should be first and foremost for originality and excellence."[79] And the Association did encourage its members to bring their decorative art more in line with fine art tastes and techniques, so as to raise its value.[80] But in other areas the two organizations worked against each other. Despite its aesthetic goals, the Society of Decorative Art did not have the long-term interests of professional artists in mind. By commissioning men rather than women to design its patterns the SDA may have elevated the status of decorative art, but it reinforced a gendered division of labor that eroded the value of women's work. Society promoters hurt women artists when they insisted needlework and china painting were minor arts, easily within the reach of almost every woman and requiring far less ability than painting pictures. Although these statements reassured male fine artists that female artists would not invade their territory, they undercut the position of female professionals whose livelihoods depended on the design and production of a variety of objects.[81] The Society of Decorative Art tried to ameliorate the problem of female poverty without disrupting class or gender hierarchies by revamping traditionally female arts;

the Ladies' Art Association worked to expand women's employment into newly lucrative fields, some of which were women's province but others which had been terrain held by men.

The most important difference between the Society of Decorative Art and the Ladies' Art Association lay in their mental picture of the constituencies they served. The SDA marketed its products as the work of artist-amateurs—cultured women temporarily filling a financial need through the production of art. The Ladies Art Association's raison d'etre was to counter that picture with the image of women artists—be they painters, designers, artisans, or teachers—as aspiring or working professionals. In practice, the Association offered women an alternative middle-class identity—the self-supporting artist-worker. Like the Cooper Union, it should not "be regarded merely as an eleemosynary institution but as illustrating a great idea . . . the union of productive labor, with the refinements, the training and the education that make human life worthy and happy."[82] After ten years the charitable work of the Society of Decorative Art was done and it disbanded, but the Ladies' Art Association, poor as it was, incorporated at the height of the depression and continued to represent, educate, and find work for studio and industrial artists and art teachers until 1914. The Cooper Union exists today and is still tuition free.

Professionalization and "A Great Influx of New-Comers"

The Aesthetic Movement and societies of decorative art stimulated a great interest in the so-called secondary or minor arts and inspired thousands of female amateurs to try their hand. But for professional women artists the most devastating newcomers to the field were male professionals, not female amateurs. When the market for paintings dried up in the late 1870s, male artists joined the decorative art craze, experimenting with such media as watercolor, pastel, etching, and illustration, and exploring the aesthetic possibilities of household decoration such as tile painting and interior design. In the early nineteenth century, most of these arts had been the domain of female amateurs and male artisans, but at midcentury a market for professionals was created as trained women artists took them up as alternative sources of income, exhibited them as art, and raised the quality of production. "By founding the first permanent instruction for women in painting on Pottery (Porcelain and 'China') the Association established a new industry for men in this country, vis: firing China for Amateurs," noted a Ladies' Art Association brochure. Next to this printed statement, someone has written in pen: "a complete revolution has been accomplished quietly. Men in the 'business' saw that they gained not lost by women painting on china. Attempts made before that of the Association *failed*."[83] Individual male painters had tapped into applied art markets before the Civil War, but not until popular taste rendered "decorated fans, lamp-shades, patterns for embroidery, and tiles for furniture" financially promising and aesthetically interesting did they descend on the decorative art field as a group.[84]

At first men's interest in decorative arts heightened the interaction of male and female artists. Together they formed associations to promote particular media, and set standards through membership restrictions and juried exhibitions. These maneuvers were common practice for professional societies (even the Ladies' Art Association used them) as "they helped close ranks, narrow competition from outsiders, and ensure the success of status-building efforts."[85] But as more men filled the openings in fields and markets forged by women professionals, the interaction between male and female artists began to decline. Within a decade, male artists dominated most art societies, and as elected members set standards and entry criteria for membership and exhibitions that excluded female practitioners.

To wrest the decorative arts out of the hands of women, male artists worked in concert with middle-class tastemakers, including the Society of Decorative Art and art columnists in the popular press, to transfer creative authority to themselves. Critics reviewing the first exhibition of the Society of Painters in Pastel, for instance, went to great lengths to assert the positive influence of male artists on the field: "Just as etching needed certain men of genius to raise it from the bog of amateurishness in which it floundered, so pastels required such chosen talents."[86] The declaration of male expertise in a "feminized" genre was used time and again to keep women artists with extensive exhibiting and publishing records out of the inner circles of professional organizations, until finally female members were barred altogether from some art societies in "the name of higher standards, a 'professional' membership and comfortable collegiality."[87]

This betrayal of women artists was aided by the publicity writers gave to smaller "sketch clubs" of male artists who were investigating the aesthetic possibilities and employment opportunities offered by print and decorative art media such as illustration, etching, and tile painting. Sketch clubs began as "an improving diversion" for art students outside school. On one evening or morning a week, artists gathered "at the houses of members in turn, or at some one which offers peculiar advantages," where they sketched from life either a volunteer or a paid model (pooling their resources for the "professional service") and critiqued each other's work. One of the first was "a little knot of young women [who] used to assemble in a Broadway room, which would now be far down-town, to avail themselves of the advantages of models and studio-room which co-operation made possible for them."[88] Other sketch clubs were mixed gatherings of young male and female artists interested in mutual improvement and applying "new methods."[89] But the clubs that attracted journalistic attention were single-sex affairs akin to men's social clubs, which severed the connections between male and female artists made at American art schools.

Through these clubs and their exhibitions, male artists generated a masculine public image for painters and sculptors involved with decorative art media that buttressed a separate professional identity for themselves and their art. *Scribner's* described two such clubs in January 1880. The New Art Club was a "superior group of fellows" who meet at tables in the upper room of a restaurant once a week to drink coffee, smoke cigars, and discuss "jocose" and practical matters, and proclaim "their position as pioneers in a new period of art development." The second was the Salmagundi Club, which began as a dynamic social club of friends and acquaintances (painters, sculptors, and one illustrator) who gathered at the studio of a confrere, where "Fencing and boxing went on in one corner and declaiming in another, while the fine arts pursued their way as best they could" (Figure 52). Apparently, these "boisterous early surroundings were adverse" to sincere study, and after the first year the Salmagundi Club suspended. But around 1876, after several of "the leading spirits" returned from Europe, "it was reorganized on a much more serious basis" to investigate the great "range of subject for which illustration is required by the increasing demand." Designs were "prepared on a given subject and brought down to a meeting each week for display and criticism," and the club "brought favorably into public notice by its recent 'Black and White' exhibitions."[90]

Like the Salmagundi Club, the Etching Club and Tile Club became as notable for the "masculine" antics and activities that characterized their studio meetings, dinner parties, and boat outings as for their public receptions and exhibitions, which often were also restricted to men. Women artists formed sketch clubs in the 1870s as well, and the Ladies' Art Association had always required members to bring a drawing or painting to each monthly meeting to be critiqued (or pay a small fine).[91] But the newspapers did not follow these gatherings. What made the Salmagundi, Etching, and

THE SALMAGUNDI CLUB IN EARLY TIMES. (DRAWN BY WILL H. LOW.)

Figure 52. Will H. Low, "The Salmagundi Club in Early Times," *Scribner's* 19 (November 1879–April 1880): 360. Courtesy of American Antiquarian Society.

Tile Clubs newsworthy were their artists' manly frolics and animated talk on "theory and original speculation," which emulated masculine associations of painters and sculptors in Europe. Engaging in these single-sex activities was a maneuver intended to lift male fine artists above the rest of the crowd producing decorative art and to bestow masculine traits on media traditionally associated with femininity and domesticity. In so doing, these men effectively excluded women artists from "the profession."

By the 1880s, the overwhelming view that art was an amateur endeavor for women mitigated against the recognition of women artists as a class of professionals. Sometimes only women artists themselves knew the difference between an amateur and a professional. To an outsider the Art Students' League, founded and run by male and female artists together (Cooper Institute and National Academy graduates seeking further study), seemed to include a profusion of amateurs. Yet when a *Scribner's* reporter applied that title to one woman, "whose profession in life as a married lady with pretty children and an agreeable household seemed so unmistakable that there could hardly be a doubt that painting was with her a diversion, she protested: 'But it is precisely as a married lady with pretty children and an agreeable household, and not as an artist, that I consider myself an amateur.' Social distinctions are not rigidly drawn in this little artistic world," the writer corrected himself. Instead, "A rating on the basis of individual ability generally takes the place of the ordinary gauges to consideration."[92]

Beyond the "little artistic world" of the League, middle-class notions of gender often overrode individual training and ability. Married women were presumed to be amateurs; married men were not. Before the Civil War the term amateur referred to anyone with the means to leisurely pursue art with no thought of money. Amateur artists were mostly upper-class, well-educated men who knew the difference between good and bad art. But as professional male artists adopted elite behavior, the term "amateur" declined in favor. Amateur art came to mean bad work, and the amateur artist was almost always understood to be female.[93]

In the popular press all women artists began to be lumped together. Even women artists who exhibited extensively at juried shows were not distinguished from women who took up the pen or brush for pleasure. When the china and panel painting craze intensified after 1876, female professionals had to separate their work from the "enterprise of amateurs working for pocket money." In 1885, the *New York World* wittily rehearsed widespread opinions about "woman's art" in an effort to single out Greatorex: "the swarm of hopelessly incompetent female amateurs who discover that they

Figure 53. "Mrs. Eliza Greatorex," *New York World*, 15 March 1885.

have 'a talent for painting,' and inflict the public with the blood-curdling results of this discovery, have done much to justify this aspersion of the whole sex. Nevertheless there are many women of great talent and of ability inferior to none of the other sex, who make art a source of income and at the same time do it honor."[94] According to the *World*, Greatorex deserved critical notice not simply because she was as talented as any male artist but also because as a widow she supported her family with her art (Figure 53). Honorable financial success, not simply exhibiting her works but selling them, made her a professional. Unfortunately, to differentiate between female professionals and female amateurs exhibition reviewers felt compelled to emphasize the professional's commercial ambition at the very moment male artists had begun to deny that it played any part in their production and industrial artists were being degraded by their association with it.

Original Design Versus "Art for Art's Sake"

To maintain and elevate the status and value of their work, women artists focused on original design as the quintessential skill of the professional artist. The ability to design was always the criteria for membership in the Ladies' Art Association. In an "Invitation to Contribute" sent to studio artists, the Association stipulated that only "original pictures" would be displayed at its exhibitions and sales.[95] Even finely rendered copies of oil paintings, a specialty of many women artists, were unacceptable. Martha J. Ward, an accomplished oil painter herself, questioned the practice of hanging the original work of less talented artists: Do you "admit *good* copiers in the Ladies Art Association Ex[hibition]," she asked. "[I]t would be much more attractive than any *poor originals . . . good* copies of *good* pictures are better than hundreds of originals wh[ich] find place in our Collections where copies are *excluded* and I think that is a mistake in America particularly."[96] Association members raised on Ruskin and trained by Rimmer disagreed with Ward. Good copies may have displayed good taste and exceptional skill, but they believed artists who used their inventive faculties, even poorly, were more likely to succeed in life than good copiers. "Men were not intended to work with the accuracy of tools, to be precise and perfect in all their actions," Ruskin wrote in "The Nature of Gothic." What we must do with all our laborers is "to look for the *Thoughtful* part of them, and get that out of them, whatever we lose for it, whatever faults and errors we are obliged to take with it."[97] Besides, American artists who copied European artists would never acquire creative authority.

The decision to exclude copies was consistent with new copyright laws that constructed intellectual property right as analogous to physical property right. Earlier in the century, copying was considered an art because it was assumed that only an artist could copy the work of a great master. The expression involved in making a copy turned that copy into an original work. The copy was not new, but it originated from a new author. The origin of the product, not its content, was protected, the expression not the idea. But with the rise of mechanical production and the separation of mental and manual labor, the origin of the content became the criteria for judging ownership right. Every work of art had to be planned and executed with artistry, but only the artist who *invented* the design owned its intellectual property. The labor involved in the production of a copy no longer transferred the artwork's value to the new executor. Painting, drawing, and sculpting was mere labor unless the design originated from the producer's imagination.

The Ladies' Art Association emphasized original design in an attempt to protect female artists from exploitation. It also discouraged women's entry into factory work and encouraged artists to copyright drawings and designs they intended to sell for reproduction.[98] In 1867, when artists and patrons agreed that skill and invention lay at the heart of all art work, Don-levy could demand as much as $50 for four pages of illumination.[99] But in 1878 she found herself asserting the Unity of Art ideal to fight the degrada-tion of female labor. In answer to an offer of employment from a Mr. Plummer of Hake & Co, Donlevy replied for the Association: "We know of no artists or art students who would undertake painting the cards at less than one cent each. We will furnish designs for cards,—at one dollar each but not for one cent less. . . . Your enterprise offers money only—and useful as money is, not money enough to . . . out-weigh other considerations. . . . our aim is to encourage original designs."[100] Because most women artists were so poor, Plummer took it for granted that they would gratefully accept any compensation for art-related work. But while the right price might have made coloring cards worthwhile, explains Donlevy, the need for money did not replace the need for work that enhanced an artist's professional life. Women artists wanted to work, but to retain the value of their labor they had to refuse jobs that did not unite the hand and intellect, that did not involve design.

Working women's advocates writing in 1883 declared that a woman "who has a thorough art education can to-day easily find employment" as an art teacher or designer of useful and ornamental art.[101] But their enthusi-asm was tempered by the reality of labor division in the industrial trades. "I do not think she can hope to get a permanent salaried position, at least just at present," wrote George Manson in *Work for Women*. "Men still hold the best positions, and they receive large salaries, from $1,000 to $4,000 a year. . . . hedged in as the female industrial designer is by the masculine doubt of the employer as to her ability, and the masculine jealousy of the employee whose work she seeks to do, it would be the best plan for her to do piece-work at her own home, or office."[102]

The assignment of "piece-work" and indeterminable earnings to women designers mirrored the declining wages and precarious situation of other trained female workers. Like the miniscule prices quoted by Donlevy, they indicate that by 1883 the work of women artists had already been de-graded. After all, Currier & Ives was paying women one cent a piece to color small prints in the 1850s.[103] But there was still a considerable discrepancy between the pay given women artists who invented and those who only copied, colored, or executed designs. The Ladies' Art Association expected one hundred times more for designing a card than for coloring one, while the time it took to do either might be the same. Engravers and illuminators held an intermediary yet precarious position, so much so that the illuminator E. T. Graham wondered if "75cts and $1.00 apiece" was too much to ask for "marking" in 1877, even though she got "10cts for a [single] plainly written name."[104] In 1880 Louis Tiffany and John La Farge employed four Woman's Art School graduates to copy their designs "at salaries of $10 a week," while three years later Manson claimed that eight dollars was the least one of those artists would have been paid for a single design of her own.[105] Clearly, the status of art lay in the idea, not the skill.

When Donlevy wrote "works in black & white" on Delano's letter, she was referring to the painter's ability to design—a skill both women had learned at the Cooper Union, and a woman artist's most lucrative possession in the 1870s. Yet during the depression "Black and White" work was transformed into a new art field for painters and sculptors in America.[106] At the end of the decade *Scribner's* declared that the range of art jobs that offered the artist subsistence, as he waited for his "great projects" to mature, "is widely varied. Illustration takes the first place. It is more easy of access than formerly, when drawing on wood must be done in a formal way and was a kind of trade in itself. On the other hand the standard of performance has greatly advanced, and those who are able to meet the enlightened taste of the time are already on the high road to everything desirable."[107] Working for publishers, woodblock designers like Mary Hallock Foote and engravers like William J. Linton had taken the art of "Black and White" work to its "greatly advanced" form, but to make it into a fine art it would have to be dissociated from its commercial purposes.

Shifting practices and the notions of artistry used to elevate the status of "Black and White" work damaged the careers of female professionals who relied on publishing. Through exhibition and a new ideal called Art for Art's Sake, male artists, art critics, and gallery owners invented a new role for "Black and White" work as autonomous creations. At the "Black and White" exhibitions of the Salmagundi Club, for example, artists whose primary fields were painting, sculpting, and illustrating showed only their studies and designs: "The sketches are of all shapes and sizes. Careful finish is not a requirement, the conception being the important thing. They are done in chalk and charcoal, distemper, oil, pencil, India ink, pen and ink, any and every material, but not often in color. Among the most interesting is the manner in which the ideas of the sculptor first take form."[108] The value of these sketches lay in the Romantic notion that drawing revealed the source of the artist's achievement; it was the key to his deep feeling and aesthetic awareness. Unencumbered by the technical necessities of painting or sculpture, drawing was spontaneous and free, the perfect conduit for expressing one's instinctual understanding of design. But only "Black and White" art produced for personal use or exhibition, rather than on commission or as an employment, expressed the artist's sensibility.

By using applied art media to explore the possibilities of a weekly theme, Salmagundi Club members claimed for themselves a major characteristic of the refined gentleman amateur: they made art out of a love for beauty and truth, for art's sake. This purpose made their drawings totally unlike the products of illustrators, etchers, or engravers working for publishers, who used black and white media to illustrate the words or copy the pictures of others. Their detachment from commerce elevated exhibition artists above publishing artists. "On another evening of the week the designs are placed before the Art Students' League, for a formal exposition by a professor of the principles of design exhibited in them. With all this the once happy-go-lucky Salmagundi Club may well flatter itself on having become one of the most improving agencies in the whole artistic community."[109] Art for exhibition's sake disconnected original design from illustration, separated aesthetics from economics, and distinguished fine artists from commercial artists. Creative intent took the place of training or employment as the determining feature of professional identity.

Fine artists could produce industrial or commercial art without adversely affecting their reputations while the Unity of Art ideal was dominant. Everyone did it at one time or another. But as liberalism replaced republicanism as America's dominant ideology, painters espoused a new aesthetic ideology, "Art for Art's Sake," which originated from an 1873 work by London author Walter Horatio Pater (b. 1839).[110] Rejecting John Ruskin's idea that the value of art lies in its expression of a culture's ethical principles, Pater argued that art should be evaluated only on the basis of its ability to produce pleasurable impressions in the viewer.[111] The artist is an observer, not a philosopher, storyteller, or moralist, whose job is to picture the beauties of color, form, tone, atmosphere, light. No matter the media, art should exist for its own sake, its own ideas, and be judged by its own standards of criticism.

To clarify the concept of Art for Art's Sake, John C. Van Dyke, professor of art history at Rutgers University, admonished his American audience that illustration was not art because it was subordinated to literature: "The 'average person' fails to appreciate [the] inherent pictorial beauty which of itself is the primary aim of painting. . . . the peculiar sensuous charms of color, the novelties of natural beauty, the feeling of the artist as shown in light and form and air are overlooked, and a picture is judged largely by the degree of skill with which it reveals a literary climax. . . . The popular conception of art degrades it by supposing it a means of illustrating literature."[112] Whereas the Unity of Art ideal recovered the art impulse in all creative production, the idea of Art for Art's Sake decreased the value of artwork produced for the "commercial" system. By separating art from work, this new ideology vitiated the ideals and markets that supported women artists' careers.

Male artists able to move from commercial to exhibition-oriented markets benefited most from the new venue and meaning given to "Black and White" art media. Winslow Homer, who began his career as an illustrator in the 1850s, relinquished his work for weekly periodicals in 1875 to focus on watercolor and exhibition art. At first, exhibition officials did not know Homer's first name from his last, but this changed when he began to sell his black and white drawings as independent works of art to the fashionable New York art community in and around the Century Club.[113] Eventually, Homer was able to pursue oil and watercolor painting entirely and make a living at it. We cherish the "Black and White" work of Winslow Homer today because of that shift.

The Romantic notion of drawing as aesthetic expression rubbed off on the "Black and White" work of a few female artists, at least at first. The same year Homer quit producing art for the publishing market, Hallock was surprised to receive $50 for a single sketch and expressed amusement when A. V. S. Anthony came to Milton to see and buy all her studies "to sell to anyone who believed I had a future."[114] Anthony was confident that someday Hallock's sketches and studies would be valued as clues to her artistic sensibility. But while Hallock became preeminent in her field and received commissions from Century Club members, she faded into obscurity because her art career pattern did not follow Homer's; she never left the field of illustration. Hallock is virtually unknown today because after 1880 "Black and White" work "produced" for commercial markets was not accorded as high an aesthetic value as that "created" for exhibition.

For women artists, exhibition was never a sufficient indicator of professional status. A number of female painters also did "Black and White" works for exhibition. Eliza Greatorex and several other women were counted among the leading lights of the etching movement of the 1880s.[115] But their exclusion from the inner circles of art clubs and societies kept them on the fringes of the profession. Artists who relied on popular and industrial markets or who had to dodge the "amateur" stereotype could not pretend they drew only for self-expression if they wanted to succeed financially. Imagination had to be pursued in whatever work they were given to do.

Thinking in Wide Circles Versus the Division of Labor in Art

Chafing against the limitations that middle-class philanthropy placed on women's art production, Wheeler left the Society of Decorative Art in 1878 to help found "the Woman's Exchange," an organization with the more general aim of marketing all types of well-made products by women. Then in 1879 she joined Louis C. Tiffany, who had resigned from the SDA's Committee of Admissions to go into decorative art as a profession, and together with two other former Committee members, established a collaborative American decorating firm called Associated Artists. "It is the real thing, you know; a business, not a philanthropy or an amateur educational scheme," Tiffany warned Wheeler. "We are going after the money there is in art, but the art is there all the same."[116]

Wheeler joined Tiffany because she saw the need for American designs in such industrial arts as textiles, embroideries, and wallpaper. She considered industrial art design a desirable and profitable outlet for women's artistic talents. And she hoped through textile design and weaving to fulfill her own aesthetic vision and ambitions[117] (Figure 54). While working for the Society of Decorative Art, she had observed how women and girls being taught to embroider quickly developed "characteristic American ambitions," and began voicing their own ideas about good design or the best way to work up a design.[118] Wheeler enjoyed the sight, as she believed artists who understood art principles would do better work no matter what field they intended to enter. Her partner in Associated Artists disagreed:

"Where is Miss Tounshend?" he asked.
"Gone to her lesson in water-color at the Academy," I answered; and then, seeing a rather disturbed look upon his face, I asked, "Don't you think it will be an advantage to her embroidery?"
"No," said he, positively. "I would rather have her *think* in crewels."[119]

Wheeler did not agree that thinking only within the medium in which she worked was best for the young artist, for she knew that women never made art just for money. "The girl whose mental processes [Tiffany] wished to curtail went on thinking in very wide circles," she recalled, "for she was one of those to whom *things* are secondary, and only valuable as they can

Figure 54. Candace Wheeler, "Water-lily Textile," designed for Associated Artists. Manufactured by Cheney Brothers, ca. 1885. Metropolitan Museum of Art, New York. Gift of Mrs. Boudinot Keith, 1928.

express thought."[120] John Ruskin reasoned that all workers must "desire and labor for things that lead to life," and Wheeler agreed.[121] American women chose art because it was work that promised the worker self-expression, the thinking in wide circles that gave art is real "worth." Tiffany's answer was not focused on the sex of the worker, but on the relationship between minds and hands; he articulated the thinking behind the separation of design and execution that accompanied industrialization.

Wheeler's words and subsequent activities echoed the rhetoric of the Arts and Crafts movement, an international contingent of artists interested in aesthetic reform that explicitly connected the aesthetic to class relations.[122] The movement originated in England with Ruskin and William Morris. Its leaders stressed the beauty of simplicity, craftsmanship, and functionalism and modeled production on an idealized past before working people had been dehumanized by industrial production. After Associated Artists disbanded in 1883, Wheeler lectured at the Institute of Artist Artisans and set up her own independent agency specializing in tapestries and textiles and staffed entirely by women. No strict division of labor was imposed at Wheeler's company, as all the girls and women hired "knew how to draw and had a special faculty for composition."[123]

The Cooper Union responded to the division of labor by reaffirming its commitment to the Unity of Art: "It is the purpose of the instruction in the Art departments of the Cooper Union to unite the two instumentalities in the production of Art—both designing and careful execution. Invention is specially promoted by lectures on Art which the pupils receive, the instruction in Perspective Drawing, and especially the lectures and instruction given to the Normal Class, for the preparation of teachers of Drawing in private and public schools."[124] The Cooper was also responding to another rift Wheeler had noticed: the division between design and execution that still existed at the international level, with European decorative art undercutting the market for American design. "We had no original American design in textiles, embroideries, or even in wall-papers," recalled Wheeler, "consequently, our printings and weavings were sold as imported ones. I could not see why American manufactures should be without American characteristics any more than other forms of art. Art applied to manufacture should have its roots in its own country—so I thought, at least."[125] "It is the purpose of the Trustees," J. C. Zachos stated in his 1878 report as curator of the Cooper, "to extend the instruction in the Schools of Art, more into the departments of Invention and Design, as answering a demand most truly American, where the inventive faculties are more active than in any part of the world."[126] To compete our artists need to design, announced the actions of Wheeler and Cooper, and only when we teach them to design will our nation fulfill its promise.

The problem was that the new art idea did not place "orders for designs" in the same realm as "commissions for art." The Unity of Art ideal, which fought the degradation of labor, women, and American design as one battle, lost ground in 1877 when the republican values supporting Reconstruction gave way to a liberal capitalist ethos supporting industrial development. Artists of the new generation did not think of their work as owing to their egalitarian society but to their freedom as individuals. Like other middle-class Americans, they professionalized to exclude rather than democratize their trade, and to scornfully separate art from all waged labor. Americans experienced this process as a division of artists into different social classes. The Art for Art's Sake ideal allowed self-employed artists to translate the idea of living for beauty into a commercial activity, but it did not translate commercial activity into fine art.[127] Painters, illustrators, and designers forced to develop their beautiful designs within the confines of an industrial trade rapidly lost status as artists.

When the *World* noted in 1885 that etching was Eliza Greatorex's source of income it was giving her a "masculine" identity that would rid her work of any association with amateurism. If she could not gallivant around with sketch club members, at least the female professional could work like a man. The "not art but work" stance dispelled the prevailing view that art was a pastime for middle-class women, which militated against the recognition of women artists as a class of professionals.[128] To counter that belief, some women artists adopted the republican "producer" identity. Their supporters invoked the "dignity of labor" when articulating their views on the value of women's art. An article on the aesthetics of Fidelia Bridges emphasized the artist's professional standing by calling her "an indefatigable worker."[129] Cecelia Beaux was elevated to professional status when critics who praised her "power," "originality," "skill," and "genius," also called her "an earnest untiring worker."[130] Unfortunately, the appellation "worker," like the masculine traits it implied, aligned the woman artist with an older image of the male professional, the artist-artisan, rather than with the new male professional, the art club artist. And if we take the picture offered by *Scribner's* in 1880 seriously, these "men o' workers" were "no longer an active social factor of artist life."[131]

Commercialism and Women Artists

Before the consolidation of corporate capitalism at the end of Reconstruction, artists gained cultural status if they could demonstrate the relevance of their work to industry. But the Gilded Age generation of illustrators and designers grew up in a more cutthroat environment. The mechanical production of art robbed them of jobs, the proletarianization of labor lowered their wages, and the use of art for advertising purposes stigmatized their work.[132] Painters and art critics vying for cultural influence and professional standing in this competitive environment labeled art and design produced for industrial reproduction "commercial" and inferior. Artists who found themselves dependent on industrial markets fought the "commercial" label. Some industrial artists used the new Art for Art's Sake ideal to separate their designs from those of fellow artists who worked to live. Most commercial artists, they claimed, produced "catchpenny" art, but true artists like themselves worked for love of art only—or professed to, even when practically they did not. By the 1890s, these artists described art in terms that reproduced capitalist relations. They saw themselves as the counterparts of their capitalist patrons; men of genius who stood above the artists and workers producing the goods that they had designed[133] (Figure 5).

Printing technology was key to this change. After the "half-tone" printing process solved the problem of printing text and continuous-tone pictures simultaneously, photography began to replace engraving as the means of reproducing art in periodicals. As half-tone printing began to catch on in the 1880s, fewer artists were employed to copy works of art. This technological change hurt male and female artists equally. By 1890, the familiar signatures of "Boz," Addie Ledyard, and many other illustrators and engravers had disappeared from the pages of the illustrated press. Because the quality of the screening that could be achieved by the half-tone process was considerably lower than that obtainable with flatbed (offset) or photogravure printing, a few engravers were always kept on. But new designers replaced the illustrators.

These shifts in art production created rivalries, not only between men and women but also among men. In 1901 a group of illustrators hoping to improve the status of their profession organized the Society of Illustrators "to promote generally the art of illustration." Following the lead of male artists working in decorative fields, the Society controlled its membership and held its meetings at select restaurants to promote the image of illustration as a high-class masculine endeavor and to dispel the idea that it was itself a "sort of labor union." But this "sketch club" was not able to secure long-term artistic stature for the profession among painters, elite patrons, art critics, museum and gallery directors, or even other illustrators. Instead, the Society of Illustrators struggled to enlist artists who worried that ties to

'A DAY-SY CHAIN
(To unite Art & Industry)

Figure 55. Walter Crane, "A Day-sy Chain (To unite Art & Industry)," from Lewis F. Day and Walter Crane, *Moot Points: Friendly Disputes on Art & Industry* (London, 1903), 23.

illustration would threaten their claims to expertise and independence, and by 1903 it was compelled to admit a few established women illustrators to stay alive.[134]

Some artists and illustrators refused to enhance their own standing by dissociating themselves from industrial artists. These men continued to argue that the fine and applied arts were interdependent. Illustrator Walter Crane, who studied with Linton in England and designed for American firms, articulated the position of this group in a short book called *Moot Points*.[135] Creating art in an industrial setting was not the same as making pictures that were "consciously catch-penny," he argued. "What is common is not necessarily vulgar." Commercial art was only vulgar when it lacked spirit and ability. It was not commercialism—thinking solely of profits—to make art for a living. The money question "really had nothing to do with art."[136]

Women artists' frustrations reverberated in Crane's comments: "I think most artists—worthy of the name—only want scope for their powers. But they are often narrowed and specialised by the commercial system." An artist had to be "commercially competent" to live, but the artist "does not produce for profit at all. He only asks a remuneration for his work. He only wants to live his life." Like Donlevy, Wheeler, and Linton, Crane recognized the division of labor in art as a means to divide and conquer. "Artists are not capitalists, but are really only a sort of superior-wage-earners," he reasoned. "It is quite possible they may live on the surplus values created by the manufacturer; but that does not alter their economic position of having to sell their labour or its results."[137] Designer or executant, painter, engraver, illustrator, or colorist: all artists were laborers in the field of the beautiful.

The artists, reformers, and entrepreneurs who provided women with art educations and jobs at midcentury were the most egalitarian of democrats. Like eighteenth-century republicans, their moral philosophy and political economy were inseparable. They trained middle-class women to be working artists because they knew it was the right thing to do. They believed they could remedy the ills of industrial society by applying fine art principles to industrial design, reuniting artists and workers, and sharing the knowledge and skills of their professions with women. From them, women artists learned that art made only for profit was vulgar, but so too was any work that had been stripped of thought. It was not the good pay, Wheeler reckoned, so much as the thinking in wide circles that turned art's manual labor into dignified work. What the worker must have is the opportunity for self-expression in his work, explained Ruskin, even if mechanical precision and perfection were sacrificed. As useful as money is, added Donlevy, for artists there is not time enough to let money matters outweigh aesthetic considerations. For it was not just work, Greeley had contended, but attractive industry for all women and men that created a moral society. "Commercialism *has* been chiefly answerable for the separation of designer and craftsman," Crane charged. "The actual separation of brains and hands in modern industry has brought about the death of art."[138] In America, that separation was also responsible for the demise of the fine artisan and the disappearance of women artists from historical memory.

The Unity of Art did not die a sudden death. In 1898, Beaux, Helen Sargent, and a small circle of women artists from the Art Students' League took that ideal a step further when they established the Art Workers Club for Women: "To set the professions of artist and model in a right light before each other and in the eyes of the world."[139] "In order to create beauty, the artist must study beauty. . . . the model is a necessity, and serves art as does the artist; thus the artist is responsible for the model. By the co-operation of the artist and the model, both art-workers, the highest results for art are obtained. Only the artist reaps the benefit of this mutual co-operation for art's sake. The model does not share in the reward that is her due, either as an aid to the highest results of art or as a woman."[140] To argue that the female model who came from the lowest of the working classes shared equally with the artist in the production of beauty "for art's sake" was certainly a radical move. But it was consistent with the aesthetic understanding of professional women artists whose experience demonstrated just how closely the value of their art was tied to the value of their labor.

To become a professional the woman artist had to feed, clothe, and shelter herself and those who depended on her through her art. This creative commerce is what gave her a singular identity. It also placed her at the center of the capitalist transformation of American culture. Caught by the separation between art and industry, yet convinced that manual skill contained valuable mental content, women artists held fast to the notion of the Unity of Art long after Art for Art's Sake became the dominant ideology.

Abbreviations

AHD

Alice Heighes Donlevy Papers, 1860–1911, Manuscripts Division, New York Public Library
Box 1—Letters to Donlevy as Secretary of the Ladies' Art Association,
    Folder 1—Letters 1860–69
    Folder 2—Letters 1870–1879
    Folder 3—Letters 1875–79
Box 4—Papers of the Ladies' Art Association (1867–1900)
    Folder 4—"Ladies' Art Association, N.Y., [Announcements] 1882?–1884?"

Constitution and By-Laws of the Ladies' Art Association (New York, 1871)

Microfilm copy, Ladies' Art Association, New York, Records, 1871–1914, Archives of American Art, Smithsonian Institution

CAJ

Cosmopolitan Art Journal

CU

Cooper Union Collection, Cooper Union Library

Annual Report of the Trustees

Published Annual Reports of the Trustees of the Cooper Union for the Advancement of Science and Art, Cooper Union Collection, Cooper Union Library

CUSDW Directors' Reports

Cooper Union School of Design for Women Papers, Directors' Reports, 1859–1873, Cooper Union Collection, Cooper Union Library.
        Box #1 1859–1863

CUSDW Teachers' Reports

Box 1859-, Cooper Union School of Design for Women Papers, Teachers' Reports 1859–1873, Cooper Union Collection, Cooper Union Library

CU, NYSDW Correspondence

Cooper Union, New York School of Design for Women Papers, Cooper Union Collection, Cooper Union Library
        Correspondence 1859–1873
                Box #1 1859–1860
                Box #2 1861–1862
                Box #3 1863–1869
                Box #4 1870–1873

GLF

Gordon Lester Ford Collection, Manuscripts Division, New York Public Library (Rolls N13–N17, microfilm, Archives of American Art), Smithsonian Institution, Washington, D.C.

HL

Houghton Library, Harvard University, Cambridge, Massachusetts
        Alcott Papers
        Records of the Printer H. O. Houghton & Co. of the Riverside Press
        Scudder Diaries and Correspondence

LMS

Lilly Martin Spencer Papers, 1825–1971, microfilm Reel 131, Archives of American Art, Smithsonian Institution, Washington D.C.

MHF Papers

Mary Hallock Foote Papers, Special Collections, Stanford University Libraries, Stanford, California
Transcript number

Notes

Introduction: "American Louvre"

1. Alice Donlevy, "Henry W. Herrick: The Appreciation of a Former Student," *Manchester Historic Association Collections* 4, part 3 (Manchester, N.H., 1910), 241.

2. Linda Nochlin, "Why Have There Been No Great Women Artists?" (1971), in her *Women, Art, and Power: And Other Essays* (London, 1988), 158; Joan Kelly-Gadol, "Did Women Have a Renaissance?" in Renate Bridenthal and Claudia Koonz, eds., *Becoming Visible: Women in European History* (Boston, 1977).

3. Peter Marzio, *The Democratic Art: Pictures for a 19th-Century America, Chromolithography 1840–1900* (Boston, 1979), 149, 177.

4. Neil Harris, *The Artist in American Society: The Formative Years* (Chicago, 1966), xi, 254–83. Like most histories of Western art, Harris's book maps a trajectory to modernism. Yet, as a social history, it also pays close attention to the cultural, economic, and political setting in which American artists worked.

5. Paul J. DiMaggio, "Cultural Entrepreneurship in Nineteenth-Century Boston," in his *Nonprofit Enterprise in the Arts* (New York, 1986), 44; Lawrence Levine, *Highbrow/Lowbrow: The Emergence of Cultural Hierarchy in America* (Cambridge, Mass., 1988), 86.

6. The "earnings" laws established the wife's right to "receive, use and possess her own earnings." Amy Dru Stanley argues that these acts were easily nullified or limited by the marriage contract because they did not give women the right to charge for the housework they performed for their husbands and families. Yet contemporaries considered these laws "radical in their effect" because they "presumed" that "all work and labor" performed by a married woman was done on a "separate account." Stanley, "Conjugal Bonds and Wage Labor: Rights of Contract in the Age of Emancipation," *Journal of American History* 75 (September 1988): 482. Of course, some women chose not to marry so as to retain their individuality. On this phenomenon, see Lee Virginia Chambers-Schiller, *Liberty a Better Husband, Single Women in America: The Generations of 1780–1840* (New Haven, Conn., 1984).

7. Caroline Steedman, *Landscape for a Good Woman* (London, 1986), 120.

8. Raymond Williams, *Marxism and Literature* (New York, 1977), 128–35.

Chapter 1. Democratic Proclivities

1. Joyce Appleby, *Capitalism and a New Social Order: The Republican Vision of the 1790s* (New York, 1984), 104; Alan Taylor, *Liberty Men and Great Proprietors:*

The Revolutionary Settlement on the Maine Frontier, 1760–1820 (Chapel Hill, N.C., 1990), 210.

2. James T. Kloppenberg suggests that acquisitive liberalism emerged slowly over the course of the nineteenth century. Kloppenberg, "The Virtues of Liberalism: Christianity, Republicanism, and Ethics in Early American Political Discourse," *Journal of American History* 74 (1987): 9–33.

3. Roger B. Stein, *John Ruskin and Aesthetic Thought in America, 1840–1900* (Cambridge, Mass., 1967), 10; Neil Harris, *The Artist in American Society: The Formative Years, 1790–1860* (Chicago, 1982), 91, 93; Joseph J. Ellis, *After the Revolution: Profiles of Early American Culture* (New York, 1979), 43.

4. Charles Coleman Sellers, *Charles Willson Peale*, 2 vols. (Philadelphia, 1947), 1: 80; Ellis, *After the Revolution*, 41–71.

5. Margaret B. Rennolds, *National Museum of Women in the Arts* (New York, 1987), 42; Eleanor Tufts, *American Women Artists, 1830–1930* (Washington, D.C., 1987), plates 1, 27; Robert Devlin Schwarz, *A Gallery Collects Peales* (Philadelphia, 1987), 44.

6. Philip J. Greven, *Four Generations: Population, Land, and Family in Colonial Andover, Massachusetts* (Ithaca, N.Y., 1970), 77.

7. Sellers, *Charles Willson Peale*, 2: 5.

8. Durand was apprenticed to Maverick at sixteen years old, and the next eighteen months he described as the happiest of his life. See Stephen D. Stephens, *The Mavericks, American Engravers* (New Brunswick, N.J., 1950), 48–57.

9. Because the income of wives and daughters was rarely recorded in trade or record books, women's contribution to the family income is often difficult to assess. Sources such as private letters or diaries, fictional accounts, contemporary monographs, and merchant or other purchasing records give only a vague indication of how much money women made and how it was utilized by the family.

10. The Maverick girls were not the first female engravers to sign their work in America. Mrs. James Akin of Massachusetts and Eloisa R. Payne and Miss H. V. Bracket of New York preceded them. Stephens, *Mavericks*, 58–59.

11. Thomas S. Cummings, *Historic Annals of the National Academy of Design* (Philadelphia, 1865), 29; Lillian B. Miller, *Patrons and Patriotism: The Encouragement of the Fine Arts in the United States, 1790–1860* (Chicago, 1966), 100.

12. Morse, who presided over the National Academy from 1826 to 1845, was a nativist whose cultural vision was tempered by his democratic sensibilities. Miller, *Patrons and Patriotism*, 102; Cummings, *Historic Annals*, 61; Paul J. Staiti, *Samuel F. B. Morse* (New York, 1989), 209–10.

13. American Academy exhibitions of antiques and Old Masters did not share the success of National Academy exhibitions. Miller, *Patrons and Patriotism*, 101.

14. "Sketchings. National Academy of Design. First Notice," *The Crayon* 7, 5 (May 1860): 139.

15. T. Addison Richards to "Mrs. Pope, Mrs. Gray, and Other Ladies," 7 May 1867, National Academy of Design, Box 1, Folder 1, AHD.

16. In 1848 Spencer exhibited a painting entitled *The Water Spirit*, and in 1849 her now famous *Domestic Happiness*. In subsequent years she exhibited portraits, allegories, and genre paintings. On Spencer's life and art, see Elizabeth Johns, *Amer-*

ican Genre Painting: The Politics of Everyday Life (New Haven, Conn., 1991); David M. Lubin, *Picturing a Nation: Art and Social Change in Nineteenth-Century America* (New Haven, Conn., 1994); and April F. Masten, *"Shake Hands?:* Lilly Martin Spencer and the Politics of Art," *American Quarterly* 56, 2 (June 2004): 349–94.

17. Lilly Martin Spencer to her Mother, 29 March 1850, LMS.

18. Nearly 10 percent of the approximately 1,300 exhibitors were women, and 12 percent of those exhibiting were elected members. The total number of artists listed in Groce and Wallace is between ten and eleven thousand. Of those 725 are identifiable as women (excluding any names containing initials), or about 6.6 percent of the total. In other words, the ratio of women to men exhibiting at the Academy roughly matches the numbers practicing art in the United States before 1860. *National Academy of Design Exhibition Record, 1826–1860*, 2 vols. (New York, 1943); and George C. Groce and David H. Wallace, *The New-York Historical Society's Dictionary of Artists in America, 1564–1860* (New Haven, Conn., 1957).

19. "The Women's National Art Association," *New York Times*, 12 November 1866, p. 4.

20. Daniel P. Huntington, "President's Annual Report" [13 May 1846], Minute Books of the National Academy of Design, quoted in Lois Marie Fink and Joshua C. Taylor, *Academy: The Academic Tradition in American Art* (Washington, D.C., 1975), 33.

21. Fink and Taylor, *Academy*, 32–33.

22. "The Fine Arts: The National Academy of Design," *New-York Daily Tribune*, 30 March 1854.

23. Peter C. Marzio has identified 145 popular drawing manuals published in the United States between 1820 and 1860. Usually small, thin, and inexpensive, drawing manuals ranged in price from 25 cents to one dollar. More elaborate, larger-format, thick volumes might cost between $10 and $12, although one 1844 book by an anonymous author cost only 12 1/2 cents (or one shilling). Marzio, *The Art Crusade: An Analysis of American Drawing Manuals, 1820–1860* (Washington, D.C., 1976), 3, 1, 13.

24. Some manuals offered the general public artisanal knowledge that had been highly guarded, such as Titian Ramsay Peale, "The Art of Painting in Miniature: 1 Miniature Painting with the Necessary Instructions" (unpublished manuscript, ca. 1798); W. J. Bell and M. D. Smith, *Guide to the Archives and Manuscript Collections of the American Philosophical Society* (Philadelphia, 1966), 548. Rembrandt and Titian Ramsey Peale were sons of Charles Willson Peale.

25. The system based on Sir Joshua Reynolds's aesthetic theory and Johann Heinrich Pestalozzi's pedagogy was challenged in the 1850s by John Ruskin and others, who placed shading above line in the definition of form and emphasized drawing from nature rather than from casts of classical sculpture or nudes. Marzio, *Art Crusade*, iv.

26. Rozsika Parker and Griselda Pollock, *Old Mistresses: Women, Art, and Ideology* (New York, 1981), 35.

27. Marzio, *Art Crusade*, 9; Karen J. Blair, *The Torchbearers: Women and Their Amateur Arts Associations in America, 1890–1930* (Bloomington, Ind., 1994), 18.

28. At New York art institutions, including the National Academy, the

Cooper Union, and the Art Students' League, life drawing was available to male and female students after the Civil War. Women artists studied from the nude or semi-nude model in separate life classes. [William C. Brownell], "The Art-Schools of New York," *Scribner's Monthly* 16, 6 (October 1878): 761–81.

29. Charles Willson Peale to Rembrandt Peale, in *The Selected Papers of Charles Willson Peale and His Family*, ed. Lillian B. Miller (New Haven, Conn., 1983).

30. John Gadsby Chapman, *Chapman's American Drawing Book* (New York, 1847) was first published as chapters in 1847, then in a London edition entitled *The Elements of Art* in 1848, and as a "complete copy" in 1858.

31. Chapman, *Chapman's American Drawing Book*, 9–10.

32. William Dunlap quoted in Marzio, *Art Crusade*, 1; William Dunlap to Washington Irving, 26 September 1833, New York, quoted in Harris, *Artist in American Society*, 76.

33. Henry T. Tuckerman, *Book of the Artists: American Artist Life* (New York, 1867), 218.

34. Chapman quoted in Margaret Haller, "A Backward Glance," *At Cooper Union* 12, 2 (1978): 4, Cooper Union Collection, CU.

35. A few went to Chicago, Richmond, and San Francisco. Jean Gordon, "Early American Women Artists and the Social Context in Which They Worked," *American Quarterly* 30 (Spring 1978): 56–57.

36. Harris, *Artist in American Society*, 280–81.

37. *The Crayon* 5 (January 1858): 24.

38. "City Items: Mrs. L. M. Spencer," *New-York Tribune*, 5 December 1848; Brooklyn Art Association form, "Goldbeck, Mary Freeman," Roll N14, GLF.

39. In "A Morning Among the Studios," a reporter for *Putnam's* suggested calling New York "The Artist City, or the City of Studios" in recognition of the abundance of studio spaces. Harris, *Artist in American Society*, 267–68; "The Women Artists of New York and Its Vicinity," *New York Evening Post*, 24 February 1868, 2; *Putnam's Kaleidoscope* 9 (May 1857): 555.

40. Carrie Rebora Barratt, "Mapping the Venues: New York City Art Exhibitions" in Catherine Hoover Voorsanger and John K. Howat, eds., *Art and the Empire City* (New York, 2000), 61.

41. Ibid., 64; "Art Gossip," *CAJ* 2, 1 (December 1857): 38.

42. Artists list their studios at Dodworth's Building under the addresses 806 Broadway, 896 Broadway, 204 Fifth Avenue, and 212 Fifth Avenue.

43. The *Cosmopolitan* acquiesced after the annual receptions at the Cooper Union demonstrated just how egalitarian these galas could be. *The Crayon* 5 (February 1858): 59; *CAJ* 4, 1 (March 1860): 34; Harris, *Artist in American Society*, 263–64.

44. The New York art scene derived from Harris, *Artist in American Society*, 254–82 and the LMS papers.

45. Charles E. Baker, "The American Art-Union," in Mary Bartlett Cowdrey, ed., *American Academy of Fine Arts and American Art-Union: Introduction, 1816–1852* (New York, 1953), 118, 120, 132, 108.

46. Rachel N. Klein argues that the managers of the American Art-Union sought national unity through cultural control and vied with the National Academy

for "aesthetic authority." Klein, "Art and Authority in Antebellum New York City: The Rise and Fall of the American Art-Union," *Journal of American History* 81, 4 (March 1995): 1554.

47. "Annual Report," *Transactions of the American Art-Union* (New York, 1845): 7–8.

48. Miller, *Patrons and Patriotism*, 164; Klein, "Art and Authority," 1548.

49. The Art-Union claimed portraiture was too narrow in appeal for their purposes, yet apparently bought several portraits by Mrs. Dassell, which suggests it may have purchased others. "The Late Mrs. Dassell," *CAJ* 2, 1 (December 1857): 146.

50. Baker, "The American Art-Union," 167.

51. Ralph Waldo Emerson credits this way of thinking to Emanuel Swedenborg in *The American Scholar* (Cambridge, Mass., 1837), 20–22.

52. *Life's Happy Hour* and its companion *Peace and Happiness* have never been located. Robin Bolton-Smith and William H. Truettner, *Lilly Martin Spencer: The Joys of Sentiment* (Washington, D.C., 1973), 151, 109, 99.

53. After the outlawing of the lotteries in 1851, the American Art-Union auctioned off its stock of paintings and disclosed the prices paid by the Art-Union and the auction purchaser. Prices paid by the Art-Union ranged from $9 to $1,075, which places the average price at around $105. But the mean price was less than $50 as almost three-fourths of the paintings sold for under $100 and two-thirds of those for under $50. Out of 400 paintings 8 were bought for $500 or more, 39 for between $200 and $499, 65 for between $100 and $199, 106 for between $50 and $99, 107 for between $26 and $49, and 69 for under $25. Two were listed without a price. Spencer's paintings are recorded as being purchased by the Art-Union for $196, $168, $327, and $161. The other four women listed received sums ranging from $37 to $75 per painting. Ann Byrd Schumer, "Lilly Martin Spencer: American Painter of the Nineteenth Century" (master's thesis, Ohio State University, 1959), 39; Mary Bartlett Cowdrey, ed., *American Academy of Fine Arts and American Art-Union: Exhibition Record, 1816–1852* (New York, 1953).

54. Schumer, "Lilly Martin Spencer," 39.

55. W. A. Adams to Spencer, 11 September 1851, Cincinnati, LMS.

56. Miller, *Patrons and Patriotism*, 165; Spencer to dear Parents: dear Ma and Pa, 8 December 1851, LMS.

57. Spencer to dear Parents: dear Ma and Pa, 8 December 1851; Spencer to her parents, 11 October 1850, LMS.

58. Artists rejected by the Art-Union channeled their discontent through the penny press, especially the *New York Herald*, which considered itself "the representative of a market democracy and, hence, the appropriate monitor of urban culture." The *Herald* celebrated Goupil and Vibert, art publishers who became Spencer's next patron. Klein, "Art and Authority," 1548–60.

59. Spencer to dear Parents, 8 December 1851, LMS.

60. Elliot Bostwick Davis, "The Currency of Culture: Prints of New York City" in *Art and the Empire City*, 189; Harris, *Artist in American Society*, 112; Virginia Penny, *The Employments of Women: A Cyclopedia of Woman's Work* (Boston, 1863), xvii, 59–61.

61. Homer Saint-Gaudens, "'The Man in the Street,'" in his *The American Artist and His Times* (New York, 1941), 96–97.

62. *Aldine, the Art Journal of America* (May 1869): 39.

63. Peter C. Marzio, *The Democratic Art: Pictures for A 19th-Century America: Chromolithography, 1840–1900* (Boston, 1979), 5.

64. John Rewald, *Studies in Post-Impressionism* (London, 1986), 7–8; Marzio, *The Democratic Art*, 121–22.

65. Marzio argues that reproductions were democratic departures from the elitist cult of the "original."

66. Without understanding copyright laws it was difficult for an artist to make the publishing market pay. In 1868, A. F. Tait, as Prang's agent, paid Spencer $50 for the copyright of *The Jolly Washerwoman*, a picture he had purchased from Osborn, who had bought it at an American Art-Union sale for $400. While Spencer's total remuneration for the painting and its reproduction was $450, the publisher who bought the copyright could make and sell unlimited reproductions. Lilly Martin Spencer to her mother, 10 September 1856, LMS.

67. Spencer to her parents, 29 December 1859, LMS.

68. "The Women of the Revolution" series in *Godey's* was reprinted in Elizabeth F. Ellet, *The Eminent and Heroic Women of America* (New York, 1873).

69. John Ruskin, "Techniques of Metal Engraving," *Ariadne Florentina: Six Lectures on Wood and Metal Engraving* (1872), in *The Works of John Ruskin*, ed. E. T. Cook and Alexander Wedderburn, 39 vols. (New York, 1906), 22: 369.

70. F. Weitenkampf, *American Graphic Art* (New York, 1912), 145–48; Nancy Carlson Schrock, "William James Linton and His Victorian History of American Wood Engraving," in W. J. Linton, *American Wood Engraving: A Victorian History* (Watkins Glen, N.Y., 1976), i–ii; "Engraving on Wood: Topics of the Time," *Scribner's Monthly* 18, 3 (July 1879): 456.

71. Engraver John Sartain, who was surprised and pleased to be engaged to work exclusively for *Graham's*, attributed the success of the monthly chiefly to the pictures. Frank Luther Mott, *A History of American Magazines*, 3 vols. (1938; Cambridge, Mass., 1957), 1: 547.

72. Mott, *History of American Magazines*, 1: 521.

73. Mott, *History of American Magazines*, 2: 591.

74. "The operational procedures of this enterprise were akin to those of the art unions but sufficiently altered to assure legal sanction of a lottery." Bolton-Smith and Truettner, *Joys of Sentiment*, 41.

75. In 1857 the Cosmopolitan's Directory purchased the Dusseldorf Gallery for $180,000, to form the "nucleus around which the Association's operations will center" and "to exert a benign influence upon artists and the patrons of art." The plan was to add new German artwork annually, leaving to "American talent the privilege of competing, with the Dusseldorf pictures, for popular favor." Spencer's paintings were exhibited alongside and favorably compared to the "incomparable pictures by Flemish artists" at the Dusseldorf. *CAJ* 2, 1 (December 1857): 55; Bolton-Smith and Truettner, *Joys of Sentiment*, 42.

76. "Editorial Etchings," *CAJ* 4, 3 (December 1860): 185.

77. "Editorial Etchings," *CAJ* 1, 1 (July 1856): 27.

78. Feminist historians have demonstrated how over the course of the nineteenth century the concept "genius" was gendered male. See Christine Battersby, *Gender and Genius: Towards a Feminist Aesthetics* (London, 1989); Rozsika Parker and Griselda Pollock, *Old Mistresses: Women, Art, and Ideology* (New York, 1981); and Griselda Pollock, *Vision and Difference: Femininity, Feminism and the Histories of Art* (New York, 1988).

79. Emerson, *The American Scholar*, 24, 8.

80. As an aesthetic state, "the sublime" described both the highest and noblest nature and terror and fear of death. Romantics used the word to describe artistic genius, but not until the late nineteenth century was the sublime linked to male power: to size and strength, and even sometimes explicitly to male sexuality. Ellet, *Women Artists*, 292; Frank Carnes to Mrs. Spencer, 10 December 1848, LMS; Battersby, *Gender and Genius*, 4.

81. *CAJ* 1, 5 (September 1857): 165.

82. "American Art Abroad," *CAJ* 3, 4 (September 1859): 178.

83. *CAJ* 2, 1 (December 1857): 38; *CAJ* 4, 2 (June 1860): 126; *CAJ* 3, 5 (December 1859): 214–17; *CAJ* 5, 1 (March 1861): 26–28; *CAJ* 2, 1 (December 1857): 146; *CAJ* 4, 2 (June 1860): 129; *CAJ* 3, 1 (December 1858): 47–48.

84. "The Cosmopolitan," *CAJ* 1, 2 (October 1856): 1.

85. "Art Gossip," *CAJ* 6, 2 (June 1860): 127; "Ruskin on Cheap Pictures," *CAJ* 3, 1 (December 1858): 16; "Blackwood Versus Ruskin," *CAJ* 4, 1 (March 1860): 22–24.

86. Janice Simon, "The *Crayon*, 1855–1861: The Voice of Nature in Criticism, Poetry, and the Fine Arts" (Ph.D. dissertation, University of Michigan, 1990), 338.

87. "Plea for American Art," *CAJ* 3, 5 (December 1859): 218–19.

88. "The Spirit of Competition in Art," *CAJ* 4 (March 1860): 78; "The Dollars and Cents of Art," *CAJ* 4, 1 (March 1860): 30; "Picture-craft is Now a Recognized, If Not a Legalized, Department of Trade," *CAJ* 5, 1 (March 1861): 36; "An Artist's Letter to an Artist," *CAJ* 1, 1 (July 1856): 14–15.

89. Simon, "The *Crayon*," 55–56.

90. "Sketchings: The Cosmopolitan Art-Association," *The Crayon* 4, 8 (August 1857): 252–53.

91. "The Cosmopolitan Art Association," *Cosmopolitan Art Journal Supplement* 5, 1 (March 1861): 1.

92. "Manifest Destiny: The Engraving for the Current Year," *CAJ* 2, 1 (December 1857): 45.

93. Annie Boleyn Delano to My dear Miss Donlevy, 1 January 1861 [1862], Box 1, Folder 1, AHD.

Chapter 2. *"The Unity of Art"*

1. Alice Donlevy, *Practical Hints on the Art of Illumination* (New York, 1867), 11, 12.

2. George Ward Nichols, *Art Education Applied to Industry* (New York, 1877), 2.

3. Nichols, *Art Education Applied to Industry*, 2.

4. On Ruskin's influence in America, see Roger B. Stein, *John Ruskin and Aesthetic Thought in America, 1840–1900* (Cambridge, Mass., 1967); Eileen Boris, *Art and Labor: Ruskin, Morris, and the Craftsman Ideal in America* (Philadelphia, 1986).

5. John Ruskin, "Traffic" (a lecture delivered April 21, 1864), *The Crown of Wild Olive* (1873), in *The Works of John Ruskin*, ed. E. T. Cook and Alexander Wedderburn, 39 vols. (London, 1904, 1905), 18: 433–58.

6. Ruskin quoted in "Introduction to Vol. XI," *Works*, 11: xix.

7. Ruskin, "Manufacture and Design," *The Two Paths* (1859), *Works*, 16: 320.

8. Ruskin, "The Unity of Art," *The Two Paths* (1859), *Works*, 16: 294.

9. Edwin Emery, *The Press and America: An Interpretative History of the Mass Media* (Englewood Cliffs, N.J., 1972), 179.

10. For Ruskin's "art-impulse in industry" and Thomas Carlyle's "chivalry of work," see Frederick William Roe, *The Social Philosophy of Carlyle and Ruskin* (New York, 1970), 86–127, 179–203.

11. A friend and correspondent of Ralph Waldo Emerson in the 1830s, Carlyle published his first "Article on the Working People" as *Chartism* in 1841, the same year as his influential book *On Heroes, Hero-Worship, and the Heroic in History*. Fred Kaplan, "Carlyle, Thomas," *Oxford Dictionary of National Biography* (New York, 2004), 12: 151–63.

12. Horace Greeley, *Industrial Association, an Address to the People of the United States, by the American Union of Associationists* (n.p., n.d.), 1.

13. Greeley quoted in James Parton, *The Life of Horace Greeley, Editor of "the New-York Tribune," from his birth to the present time* (Boston, 1889), 182.

14. Greeley's support for Margaret Fuller and other female writers is better known.

15. Emery, *The Press and America*, 174.

16. Daniel W. Pfaff, "Horace Greeley," *Dictionary of Literary Biography* (Detroit, 1985), 43: 258.

17. Greeley, *Industrial Association*, 2, 8.

18. Instead of offering charity, Greeley advocated what he called "beneficent Capitalism." He envisioned a day when the forces of capitalism—industry, labor, and agriculture—would complement each other in improving the common lot, a day when opportunity, work, and education would be available to all, and when "Capital would reap the benefits of a prosperous community, but would feel responsible for better living standards." He did not mind adding: if the forces of capitalism would not rise up to this moral duty the state would have to intervene. Emery, *The Press and America*, 175; Arthur M. Schlesinger, Jr., *The Age of Jackson* (Boston, 1945), 266, 364; Daniel Walker Howe, *The Political Culture of the American Whigs* (Chicago, 1979), 187; Michael Merrill, "Putting 'Capitalism' in Its Place: A Review of Recent Literature," *William and Mary Quarterly* 52, 2 (April 1995): 323; Greeley, *Industrial Association*, 7.

19. Greeley, *Industrial Association*, 3.

20. See Albert Brisbane, *Social Destiny of Man; or, Association and Reorganization of Industry* (1840); and Charles Fourier, *The Social Destiny of Man; or, Theory of the Four Movements* (1808).

21. John Humphrey Noyes, *History of American Socialisms* (Philadelphia, 1870), 10–20.

22. This process is called the "pastoralization" of housework in Jeanne Boydston, *Home & Work: Housework, Wages, and the Ideology of Labor in the Early Republic* (New York, 1990), 147–48.

23. Thomas Woody, *A History of Women's Education in the United States*, 2 vols. (New York, 1929), 2: 1; *1860 Census of the United States* XXXIII: 36, 210.

24. See, for example, M. Lagrange, "Schools of Design," *The Crayon* (1860), reprinted in the *Second Annual Report of the Trustees of the Cooper Union, for the Advancement of Science and Art*, 1 January 1861 (New York, 1861), 23–29, CU.

25. Christine Stansell, *City of Women: Sex and Class in New York, 1789–1860* (New York, 1986), 144–49.

26. Parton, *Life of Horace Greeley*, 301, 223, 224.

27. *Broadway Journal* 1 (22 February 1845): 127; *Godey's* 44 (January 1852): 93.

28. Harry T. Peters, *Currier and Ives, Printmakers to the American People* (Garden City, N.Y., 1942), 14–15.

29. The article appeared in a *New-York Daily Tribune* series called "Labor in New-York: Its Circumstances, Conditions and Rewards." The series was reprinted the following year with illustrations and some editorial changes as "Live Portraits" in *Yankee Doodle*, a humorous political magazine published in the Tribune Buildings. The series also covered book-folders, seamstresses, and patent medicine girls. "Labor in New-York: Its Circumstances, Conditions and Rewards. No. V . . . The Map-Colorers," *New-York Daily Tribune*, 25 August 1845, 2, col. 5; "Live Portraits.— No. 3. The Map-Colorer," *Yankee Doodle* (9 December 1846): 124.

30. "The Map-Colorers."

31. Horace Greeley, "The Sphere of Woman," *Union Magazine* (June 1848): 272.

32. "The Map-Colorers"; Parton, *Life of Horace Greeley*, 289–90. Illustrator Mary Hallock articulated a similar sentiment years later: "I should not wish to exhibit my books and drawings as 'woman's work', as they are not put in the market on that basis; nor should I care to contribute towards the campaign for municipal suffrage, not being strictly in sympathy with it as a means towards the progress of woman." Mary Hallock Foote to Alice B. Stockham, M.D., 15 August 1887, Boise, Idaho, MSS 223, Boise State University, Albertsons Library.

33. Horace Greeley, "Life—The Ideal and the Actual," in *Hints Toward Reforms: In Letters, Addresses, and Other Writings* (New York, 1850), 82.

34. Nichols, *Art Education Applied to Industry*, 2.

35. Ibid., 130; Frederick Rudolph, ed., *Essays on Education in the Early Republic* (Cambridge, Mass., 1965), 27–28; Rena L. Vassar, *Social History of American Education*, 2 vols. (Chicago, 1965), 1: 158.

36. Vassar, *Social History of American Education*, 1: 155.

37. Horace Greeley, "An Address at the laying of the corner-stone of the People's College, at Havana, in the State of New York, September 1, 1858," reprinted in Parton, *Life of Horace Greeley*, 527–29.

38. Jonathan A. Glickstein, *Concepts of Free Labor in Antebellum America* (New Haven, Conn., 1991), 78–80, 130.

39. Many antebellum reformers equated men's menial labor and women's domestic labor. See Theodore Dwight Weld, *First Annual Report of the Society for Promoting Manual Labor in Literary Institutions* (New York, 1833), 13; Charles A. Dana, "'Address' to Convention of American Associationists," *Phalanx* 1 (20 April 1844): 113–14; and Greeley, *Industrial Association*, 11–12.

40. "Sketchings: New-York School of Design," *The Crayon* 3 (April 1856): 123.

41. The Greeleys' "Friday evenings" were held at 63 Barclay Street in the late 1830s, in the Upper East Side in the 1840s, and at 35 E. Nineteenth Street in the 1850s.

42. Don C. Seitz, *Horace Greeley: Founder of the New York Tribune* (Indianapolis, Ind., 1926), 324; Lloyd R. Morris, *Incredible New York: High Life and Low Life of the Last Hundred Years* (New York, 1851), 77–78; "The Late Mrs. Dassell," *CAJ* 2, 1 (December 1857): 146.

43. Neil Harris, *The Artist in American Society: The Formative Years 1790–1860* (Chicago, 1982), 255.

44. Nina Walls argues that the Philadelphia School of Design achieved its goal of educating women for self-support in industrial art work *and* maintaining their middle-class status through rigid gender segregation. Nina de Angeli Walls, "Art and Industry in Philadelphia: Origins of the Philadelphia School of Design for Women, 1848–1876," *Pennsylvania Magazine of History & Biography* 117, 3 (July 199): 177–99.

45. Alice Heighes Donlevy, handwritten, undated note, Box 10, AHD, cited in Phyllis Peet, "The Emergence of American Women Printmakers in the Late Nineteenth Century" (Ph.D. dissertation, University of California at Los Angeles, 1987), 63.

46. Hamilton was known as a woman of rare and forceful intellect, possessing great executive ability. She was Vice-Regent of New York for the Ladies' Association of the Union (1858–66), for which she raised huge sums in the state of New York to save Mount Vernon. After her sister died in 1863, Hamilton married George Lee Schuyler in 1869. "New-York School of Design for Women," *New-York Daily Tribune*, 9 December 1852, 2, col. 3.

47. On the School's original board of managers were Eliza Hamilton Schuyler (Mary Hamilton's sister), who founded the Children's Aid Society, her husband George Lee Schuyler, one of the original settlers of Brook Farm, and Mrs. Abram Hewitt (Amelia Cooper), daughter of Peter Cooper. Others involved included Mrs. (Anne Charlotte Lynch) Botta, Mrs. Caroline M. Kirkland, author and editor of *Union Magazine*, Anna Shaw Curtis (active in the Children's Aid Society and Prison Reform, the Underground Railroad, and the women's rights movement along with her husband, writer and orator George William Curtis), and Mrs. Jonathan Sturgis (Anna Shaw's cousin).

48. Alice Donlevy, "Henry W. Herrick: The Appreciation of a Former Student," *Manchester Historic Association Collections* 4, part 3 (Manchester, N.H., 1910), 241–42.

49. "New-York School of Design for Women," *New-York Daily Tribune*, 9 December 1852.

50. That same year the *New York Times* ran ads for "a drawing academy by

Mr. and Miss Smith" and "Cummings' School of Design, 58 East Thirteenth St., Professional and Amateur Artist. Classes for Ladies and Gentlemen. In Oil Painting, Pastel, Water Colors, Crayon, Perspective, and Lead Pencil Drawing. Schools and Private Classes attended." *The Crayon* ran them in 1855. "New-York School of Design for Women," *New-York Daily Tribune*, 9 December 1852; *The Crayon* 1, 1 (3 January 1855): 16; *Crayon* 1, 5 (31 January 1855): 76.

51. E. P. P. [Elizabeth Palmer Peabody], "Our School of Design," *New-York Daily Tribune*, 27 November 1852, 7, cols. 1–2.

52. Ibid.

53. On Pestalozzi's influence in America, see Maurice Brown and Diana Korzenik, *Art Making and Education* (Urbana, Ill., 1993), 128–39.

54. Elizabeth Palmer Peabody, *Aesthetic Papers* (1849, reprint Gainsville, Fl., 1957), xi.

55. Elizabeth Palmer Peabody, *The Identification of the Artisan and Artist the Proper Object of American Education. Illustrated by a Lecture of Cardinal Wiseman, on the Relation of the Arts of Design with the Arts of Production. Addressed to American Workingmen and Educators, with an Essay on Froebel's Reform of Primary Education* (Boston, 1869), 34.

56. Rozsika Parker and Griselda Pollock, *Old Mistresses: Women, Art, and Ideology* (New York, 1981), 50; Robert L. Herbert, ed., *The Art Criticism of John Ruskin* (New York, 1964), 193, 194.

57. Peabody, *Identification of Artisan and Artist*, 3–4.

58. E. P. P., "Our School of Design."

59. White line engraving results from cutting out the design with the graver and leaving the plain surface of the block to print as a black ground, thus rendering the design in white line. It is a quicker and more flexible technique than the older method of using a knife to cut away those portions of the block left clear by the drawing so that the design remained in relief to be printed as black line. The variability of line in white line engraving translates textures and tones much more evocatively than the older technique.

60. Donlevy, "Henry W. Herrick," 240–76.

61. He married Clara Harlow Parkinson in 1849 and moved to Brooklyn. Diana Korzenik, *Drawn to Art: A Nineteent-Century American Dream* (Hanover, N.H., 1985), 28–31; Manchester Historic Association, *The World of Henry W. Herrick: An Exhibition of His Watercolors, 1824–1906* (Manchester, N.H., 1969–70), 27.

62. Donlevy, "Henry W. Herrick," 242.

63. Ibid., 240.

64. Ibid., 240, 243–44. 246.

65. Ibid., 244.

66. F., "Domestic Art Gossip," *The Crayon* 4, 11 (November 1857): 348.

67. Ibid.

68. Evan Cornog and Jerome Mushkat, "Peter Cooper," in Kenneth T. Jackson, ed., *The Encyclopedia of New York* (New Haven, Conn., 1995), 279–80; Edward Mack, *Peter Cooper: Citizen of New York* (New York, 1949), 124.

69. John J. Astor gave money to create public institutions only after his death, and the comparable gifts of William Corcoran, George Peabody, and Matthew Vas-

sar came after the Cooper Union was founded. Peter Cooper, Address to students in 1871, Cooper Papers, quoted in Mack, *Peter Cooper*, 250.

70. Glickstein, *Concepts of Free Labor in Antebellum America*, 41.

71. Edward Mack suggests that Peter Cooper's particular kind of philanthropy, the education of workers, was inspired by his contact with humanitarian Quakers and Unitarians. Mack, *Peter Cooper*, 129.

72. Greeley, *Industrial Association*, 2.

73. See James T. Kloppenberg, "The Virtues of Liberalism: Christianity, Republicanism, and Ethics in Early American Political Discourse," *Journal of American History* 74, 1 (1987): 9–33, 16; and Michael Merrill, "The Anticapitalist Origins of the United States," *Review* 8, 4 (Fall 1990): 465–97.

74. Mack, *Peter Cooper*, 129–32.

75. J. C. Zachos, "Report of the Curator," *Fourteenth Annual Report of the Trustees of the Cooper Union for the Advancement of Science and Art*, 1873, 6, CU.

76. Ibid., 10.

77. Susan N. Carter, "Recollections of Peter Cooper," *Century Magazine* 27, 2 (December 1883): 221.

78. Carter, "Recollections of Peter Cooper," 221.

79. Ibid.

80. Peter Cooper's institution was referred to interchangeably as the Cooper, the Cooper Institute, Cooper Union, and the Cooper Union for the Advancement of Science and Art. "Editorial Etchings—Peter Cooper," *CAJ* 2, 1 (December 1857): 49.

81. Mack, *Peter Cooper*, 244.

82. Donlevy credits Herrick with finding the School of Design a permanent home at the Cooper Union and its being legally adopted by Peter Cooper and his family. "Among the guests invited that night by Ada C. Thompson, who was one of Mr. Herrick's most irrepressible pupils and admired him very much, gladly helping in whatever he suggested, were T. D. Jones, the sculptor; Julia Dean, the actress; Joseph Kyle, the portrait painter, whose painting of himself hangs in the Metropolitan Museum; his daughter, Mary Kyle Dallas; Jacob Dallas, the artist. Rev. Henry W. Bellows was there and gave a reception afterwards to the School of Design for the same progressive purpose." Donlevy, "Henry W. Herrick," 245–46.

83. Rachel Field, *All This, and Heaven Too* (New York, 1972), 3, 505, 509–10.

84. Ibid., 514–15.

85. Humanitarian Joseph Curtis, who headed the House of Refuge for vagrants and petty criminals, was the first to interest Cooper in the plight of women and the education of African Americans. His daughter Ann Curtis taught at the School of Design until retiring on $400 a year pension. "Ann Curtis made fallen women on Blackwell's Island her particular concern, and Cooper helped her and her associates in carrying on the Woman's Home for their care. He also contributed to the Workingwomen's Protective Union, which protected women from being given starvation wages or no wages at all by their employers." Mack, *Peter Cooper*, 133–34.

Chapter 3. "Art Fever"

1. Louisa May Alcott, "Psyche's Art" (1868), in *Alternative Alcott*, ed. Elaine Showalter (New Brunswick, N.J., 1988), 207.

2. May Alcott (Nieriker) was immortalized as Amy in *Little Women*. Amy's particular case of "Art fever" is described in "Artistic Attempts." Louisa May Alcott, *Little Women* (1888; New York, 1989), 255. May's later years are documented in "An Untitled Romance," reprinted in *Alternative Alcott*, and elsewhere under the title *Diana & Persis*.

3. Mrs. L. A. Gillan to Cooper Union, 16 June 1861, Cambridgeport, Mass., Box #3, CU, NYSDW Correspondence.

4. W., "The Cooper Union—What It Has Done for Women," *Revolution* 1, 16 (23 April 1868): 247.

5. Louisa May Alcott, *Work: A Story of Experience* (Boston, 1873) in *Alternative Alcott*, 245.

6. H. S. Vrooman, 29 September 1860, Hoboken, Box #1, CU, NYSDW Correspondence; Elisha Delano obituary, T. S., *Yates County Chronicle*, 26 September 1872, Delano Family Book, Yates County Genealogical and Historical Society, Penn Yan, N.Y.; Genl Swift re. Annie Delano, 11 September 1860, Geneva, N.Y., Box #1, CU, NYSDW Correspondence; Mrs. L. A. Gillan to Cooper Union, 16 June 1861, Box #3, CU, NYSDW Correspondence.

7. Rvd. Carrigan re. Helen A. Daley, 24 September 1860, Office Irish Emigrant Society, New York; Mary M. Hamilton re. lady teacher, 6 June 1860, Dobbs Ferry, West Chester Co., Box #1, CU, NYSDW Correspondence.

8. Miss Virginia Penny to Mr. Richards, 1860, 249 Clinton Street, Brooklyn, Box #1, CU, NYSDW Correspondence.

9. Lucie A. Hale to Peter Cooper, 26 November 1860, Southold, Long Island, Box #1. CU, NYSDW Correspondence.

10. "I am a young man just starting in life and having assumed somewhat of a debt my hands are pretty much tied until it be cancelled. . . . We are a family of orphans and there are one or two younger members of the family we have to look after." J. B. Graham, 17 August 1860, Schenectady, Box #1, CU, NYSDW Correspondence.

11. Colin B. Burke, *American Collegiate Populations: A Test of the Traditional View* (New York, 1982), 14–34; Mary Kelley, "Empire of Reason: The Making of Learned Women in Nineteenth-Century America," paper delivered at the Massachusetts Historical Society, 2 November 2000, 8.

12. Thomas Woody, *A History of Women's Education in the United States*, 2 vols. (New York, 1929), 1: 337; on girls' high schools see 1: 305–6.

13. Allison Eckardt Ledes, "Female Education in the Early Republic," *Magazine Antiques* (July 1993): 28–30.

14. Karen J. Blair, *The Torchbearers: Women and Their Amateur Arts Associations in America, 1890–1930* (Bloomington, Ind., 1994), 16. Thomas Woody's survey (1749–1871) charts the number of art and music courses as equaling those in needle-

work in the early nineteenth century, with the arts gaining as the century progressed and needlework dropping to almost nil. See Woody, *Women's Education*, Table I, 1: 418.

15. Names and genres of American women artists can be found in George C. Groce and David H. Wallace, *The New-York Historical Society's Dictionary of Artists in America, 1564–1860* (New Haven, Conn., 1957); William H. Gerdts, *Women Artists of America, 1707–1964* (Newark, N.J., 1965); Charlotte Streifer Rubinstein, *American Women Artists: From Early Indian Times to the Present* (Boston, 1982); Eleanor Tufts, *American Women Artists, 1830–1930* (Washington, D.C., 1987); Margaret B. Rennolds, ed., *National Museum of Women in the Arts* (New York, 1987); Jessie J. Poesch, "'The Thirst for Self-Expression': Women in the Visual Arts in the South, 1860–1960" in Priscilla Cortelyou Little and Robert C. Vaughan, eds., *A New Perspective: Southern Women's Cultural History from the Civil War to Civil Rights* (Charlottesville, Va., 1989); Nancy G. Heller, *Women Artists: An Illustrated History* (New York, 1991); and Lisa E. Farrington, *Creating Their Own Image: The History of African-American Women Artists* (New York, 2005).

16. See entries on Carrie Swift and Sarah H. Reid in William H. Gerdts, *A Pleasant Likeness: Portraits and Landscapes of Central New Jersey, 1770–1920* (Princeton, N.J., 1989), 17, 18.

17. For example, see "Drawing Teachers," *The Crayon* 3 (February 1856): 60.

18. Helen A. Burt, 30 November 1859, Oswego, N.Y., and Miss Helen A. Burt, August 1860, Minetto, N.Y., Box #1, CU, NYSDW Correspondence.

19. Miss Frances M. Bunce to Mr. Abram S. Hewitt, 15 August 1860, Salisburg, Ill., Box #1, CU, NYSDW Correspondence.

20. Bianca Bondi Robitscher, "First Cooper Union Graduate Talks," unidentified newspaper clipping, ca.1909, Box—Robitcher, Bianca B. Bondi, CU.

21. Nathaniel Hawthorne, *The Marble Faun: or, The Romance of Monte Beni* (New York, 1990), 22–23.

22. "The Artists of America," *The Crayon* 7, 5 (May 1860), 136.

23. S. G. Hitchcock, 15 August 1860, No 61 Maiden Lane, New York; Mary M. Hamilton re Margaret Thompson, 17 September 1860, Box #1, CU, NYSDW Correspondence.

24. Virginia Penny, *The Employments of Women: A Cyclopedia of Woman's Work* (Boston, 1863), 41.

25. Ann A. Saw, October 2, 1861, Auburn, Box #2; Mary E. Terry, 8 December 1860, Ansconia, Ct., Box #1; Lizzie Dickey, 28 January 1861, Delavan, Ill., Box #2; Lucie A. Hale to Peter Cooper, 26 November 1860, Southold, Long Island, Box #1, CU, NYSDW Correspondence.

26. Lucie A. Hale to Peter Cooper, 26 November 1860, Southold, Long Island, Box #1; D. Huntington re Miss Delano, 30 August 1860, 362 Broadway, Box #1; H. S. Vrooman, 29 September 1860, Hoboken, Box #1; Mrs. L. A. Gillan to Cooper Union, 16 June 1861, Cambridgeport, Mass., Box #3, CU, NYSDW Correspondence.

27. Mrs. E. F. Ellet, *Women Artists of All Ages and Countries* (London, 1859), 292.

28. George Caleb Bingham, "The Ideal in Art" (1879), in John W. McCou-

brey, ed., *American Art, 1700–1960: Sources and Documents* (Englewood Cliffs, N.J., 1965), 148.

29. L. A. Bradbury to Alice Donlevy, 23 March 1875, Cambridge, Mass., Box 1, Folder 2, AHD.

30. McCoubrey, *American Art*, 63, 148–50.

31. Hawthorne, *The Marble Faun*, 43–46, 61, 59.

32. Mary Hallock Foote, *A Victorian Gentlewoman in the Far West: The Reminiscences of Mary Hallock Foote*, ed. Rodman W. Paul (San Marino, Calif., 1972), 65.

33. The Pre-Raphaelite Brotherhood was popularized in America through the writing of John Ruskin and an exhibition of contemporary British painting that traveled to major American cities in 1857 and 1858. Malcolm Warner, *The Victorians: British Painting 1837–1901* (New York, 1996), 22, 32.

34. Helen A. Daley to Alice Donlevy, 13 July 1869, Box 1, Folder 1, AHD.

35. Hawthorne, *The Marble Faun*, 58.

36. Ibid., 136–37

37. Annie Boleyn Delano to Miss Alice Donlevy, 3 June 1867, Penn Yan, Box 1, Folder 1, AHD.

38. Hawthorne, *The Marble Faun*, 136–37.

39. Alice Donlevy, "Henry W. Herrick: The Appreciation of a Former Student," *Manchester Historic Association Collections* 4, part 3 (Manchester, N.H., 1910), 243–44.

40. Alcott, "Psyche's Art," 208.

41. Mrs. L. A. Gillan of Cambridgeport re Miss Adaline M. Knowles, 25 June 1861, Belfast, Me, CU, NYSDW Correspondence, Box # 2 1861–62.

42. Donlevy, "Henry W. Herrick," 244.

43. Lora Romero, *Home Fronts: Domesticity and Its Critics in the Antebellum United States* (Durham, N.C., 1997), 19–21, 25; Laura R. Prieto, *At Home in the Studio: The Professionalization of Women Artists in America* (Cambridge, Mass., 2001), 41.

44. "Every year is important to me now, and I think if I could avail myself of the advantages offered by a school of design, I could become independent and gain my own livelihood. What little talent I possess seems to be in the direction of painting and if I never become a Rosa Bonheur I can imitate her example at least." Frances M. Bunce, 15 August 1860, Box #1, CU, NYSDW Correspondence.

45. Rosa Bonheur's *The Horse Fair* (1853) now hangs in New York's Metropolitan Museum of Art.

46. Hawthorne, *The Marble Faun*, 54–55.

47. Reformer Caroline Dall saw art training as the answer to the ennui of upper class women as well: "scores of times have young women of fortune asked me, 'What can you give me to do?' And to this question there is . . . no possible answer. No woman of rank can find work, if she does not happen to be philanthropic, literary, or artistic in her taste, without braving the influence of home, or, what is next dearest, the social circle, and earning for herself a position so conspicuous as to be painful to the most energetic. The woman who is prepared for all this will not ask anybody what she is to do: she will take her work into her own hands,

and do it." Caroline Dall, *The College, the Market, and the Court; or, Women's Relation to Education, Labor, and Law* (Boston, 1867), 178.

48. Louisa May Alcott, *Work: A Story of Experience* (1873), in *Alternative Alcott*, 244.

49. Miss Carrie Mayhew, 31 March 1861, South Framingham, Mass.; Miss Pauline J. Backus, 30 March 1861, Grand Rapids, Mich.; Emma Brace, 13 August 1862, Utica, N.Y., Box #2, CU, NYSDW Correspondence.

50. *Reminiscences of Mary Hallock Foote*, 52–53.

51. Louisa May Alcott, "Doctor Dorn's Revenge" (1867), in Alcott, *From Jo March's Attic: Stories of Intrigue and Suspense*, ed. Madeleine B. Stern and Daniel Shealy (Boston, 1993), 16.

52. Barbara Welter, "The Cult of True Womanhood: 1820–1860," *American Quarterly* 18, 2, part 1 (Summer, 1966): 151–74.

53. For other writers see Jane Tompkins, *Sensational Designs: The Cultural Work of American Fiction, 1790–1860* (New York, 1985).

54. Catharine E. Beecher and Harriet Beecher Stowe, *American Woman's Home* (New York, 1869), 470.

55. Lucy Larcom, *A New England Girlhood* (Boston, 1889), 157.

56. Jill Ker Conway, ed., *Written by Herself: Autobiography of American Women: An Anthology* (New York, 1972), 313.

57. Alcott, *Little Women*, 117–18.

58. Ibid., 132–34.

59. Horace Greeley, "The Sphere of Woman," *Union Magazine* (June 1848): 271–72.

60. Sculptor Harriet Hosmer described the publicly funded art patronage she received from "the citizens of St. Louis" as a form of knightly gallantry: "I have also reason to be grateful to you, because I am a woman, and, knowing what barriers must in the outset oppose all womanly efforts, I am indebted to the chivalry of the West, which has first overleaped them." H. G. Hosmer, "Sketchings: Domestic Art Gossip," *The Crayon* 7, 9 (September 1860): 264.

61. Greeley, "The Sphere of Woman," 272.

62. Julius Bing re. Miss Josephine Dewey, 1 October 1860, N. Y. Cyclopedia Office, Box #1, CU, NYSDW Correspondence.

63. Obituary clipping, "Miss Annie B. Delano, "N.p. (1915), Delano Family Book, Yates County Genealogical and Historical Society, Penn Yan, N.Y.

64. Alcott, *Little Women*, 157–58.

65. Mrs. L. A. Gillan to Cooper Union, 16 June 1861, Cambridgeport, Mass., Box #3, CU, NYSDW Correspondence.

66. Larcom, *A New England Girlhood*, 157.

67. Foote, *Reminiscences of Mary Hallock Foote*, 84.

68. Alice Kessler-Harris, *Out to Work: A History of Wage-Earning Women in the United States* (Oxford, 1982), 34.

69. Foote, *Reminiscences of Mary Hallock Foote*, 86.

70. Howard M. Feinstein, *Becoming William James* (Ithaca, N.Y., 1984), 103.

71. Diana Korzenik, *Drawn to Art: A Nineteenth-Century American Dream* (Hanover, N.H., 1985), 69, 131–32, 237.

72. Libbie to Alice Donlevy, n.d., Box 1, Folder 1, AHD.

73. Louisa May Alcott, "How I Went Out to Service" (1874), in *Alternative Alcott*, 353; *Louisa May Alcott, Her Life, Letters, and Journals*, ed. Ednah Dow Cheney (Boston, 1890), 193.

74. George Kateb, *The Inner Ocean: Individualism and Democratic Culture* (Ithaca, N.Y., 1992), ix.

75. "Worsted work" was ornamental needlework done with a fine wool yarn. Annie Boleyn Delano to My dear Miss Donlevy, 1 January 1861 [1862], Box 1, Folder 1, AHD.

Chapter 4. "Harrahed for the Union"

1. Edward Mack, *Peter Cooper: Citizen of New York* (New York, 1949), 252; Carter, "Recollections of Peter Cooper," 225.

2. Susan N. Carter, "Recollections of Peter Cooper," *Century Magazine* 27, 2 (December 1883): 219.

3. Annie Delano to "My Dear Alice Donlevy," 13 June 1861, Penn Yan, N.Y., Box 1, Folder 1, AHD.

4. Ibid.

5. The Cooper Union School of Design for Women was interchangeably called the School of Design for Females, the Female Art School, the Female Department, and the Cooper. In 1872 it was renamed the Woman's Art School, and continued under that name until 1933 when the women's and men's departments at the school were officially integrated.

6. Carter, "Recollections of Peter Cooper," 224.

7. For a description of formal aesthetic principles, see James Smith Pierce, *From Abacus to Zeus: A Handbook of Art History* (Englewood Cliffs, N.J., 1987).

8. "Sketchings. Broadway," *The Crayon* 5 (August 1858): 234; [William H. Bishop], "Young Artists' Life in New York," *Scribner's* 19 (November 1879–April 1880): 366.

9. Mary Hallock Foote, *A Victorian Gentlewoman in the Far West: The Reminiscences of Mary Hallock Foote*, ed. Rodman W. Paul (San Marino, Calif., 1972), 65–66; R.W.G. [Richard W. Gilder] to Miss Hallock, 10 August 1872, Coll. M115, Box 4, Folder 14, MHF Papers.

10. "School of Design for Females, Cooper Institute" and "School of Design for Males, Cooper Institute," *Harper's Weekly* 12, 580 (8 February 1868): 84.

11. New York City's Bishop Hughes, whose work on behalf of Catholic education troubled Cooper, praised the benefits and nonsectarian character of Cooper Union. A few African American women attended the School of Design. "A young colored girl reports with great thankfulness, that from her study here she has been considered competent to teach a public school in Williamsburgh," Carter announced in 1880, "and is preparing a teacher to take charge of the drawing in a school in Washington." Mack, *Peter Cooper*, 254; Lisa E. Farrington, *Creating Their Own Image: The History of African-American Women Artists* (New York, 2005), 52,

100; Susan Carter, "Report of the Woman's Art School," *Twenty-First Annual Report of the Trustees of the Cooper Union for the Advancement of Science and Art,* 1880, 22, CU.

12. "The Cooper Union—What It Has Done for Women," *Revolution* 1, 16 (23 April 1868): 247.

13. *Tenth Annual Report of the Trustees of the Cooper Union,* 1 July 1869, 11.

14. Ibid.

15. Annie Delano to "My Dear Alice Donlevy," 13 June 1861, Penn Yan, N.Y., Box 1, Folder 1, AHD.

16. "Sketchings. Broadway," *The Crayon* 5 (August 1858): 234.

17. Abram Hewitt to George H. Brown, 27 October 1865, Box—Hewitt, Abram Stevens, 1822–1903, CU.

18. In 1859 the Advisory Council consisted of Mrs. Jonathan Sturgis, Mrs. George (Anna Shaw) Curtis, and Miss Mary M. Hamilton.

19. In 1870 Cooper offered to bail the Academy out financially if its members agreed to combine their two art schools. Concerned about its autonomy and the problem of accepting two hundred female pupils into its program, the Academy's board declined the offer with an invitation and caveat: "But as the Academy is a Free School, it will be happy to cooperate with the Cooper Union in furthering education in Arts, by admitting to its school any or all of the pupils of the Cooper Union, who may pass the required examination." Thereafter, from twelve to sixteen Cooper graduates advanced to the National Academy school yearly. "To Messrs. Abram S. Hewitt, John E. Parsons, Committee of the Trustees of the Cooper Union," Box—Letter to the Committee of Trustees, 1870; also see Annual Reports for 1873, 1874, 1875, CU.

20. Annie B. Delano to "My Dear Miss Donlevy," 1 January 1861 [1862], Box 1, Folder 1, AHD.

21. Victor Hugo covered Desporte's trial, according to her great niece Rachel Field in *All This, and Heaven Too* (New York, 1972).

22. Foote, *Reminiscences of Mary Hallock Foote,* 65.

23. Henrietta D. Field, 3 March 1862, Box #1, CUSDW Directors' Reports.

24. Ehninger asked for $5 a day to teach one hour (and visit once later in the day), "say one hundred dollars a month." But a receipt of $20 for five weeks teaching suggests he earned less per visit or came less frequently. John Whetten Ehninger [to Abram Hewitt], 62 Lafayette Place, 25 October [1861] and "Receipt for Five Weeks Teaching," n.d., Box #2, CU, NYSDW Correspondence.

25. Robert O'Brien, handwritten "Report on the Attendance of the Engraving Class for May, 1861, Cooper Union for the Advancement of Science and Art, Female School of Design," 28 June 1861, Box 1859–, CUSDW Teachers' Reports.

26. [William J. Linton], "School of Art for Women," *Tenth Annual Report of the Trustees of the Cooper Union,* 1869, 11.

27. Worthington Whittredge (1820–1910), 4 November 1861, New York, Box #2, CU, NYSDW Correspondence.

28. Henry Tuckerman included teaching responsibilities at the School of Design in several artist profiles. Henry T. Tuckerman, *Book of the Artists: American Artist Life* (New York, 1867), 218, 464.

29. Carter, "Recollections of Peter Cooper," 219.

30. Amateurs paid ten dollars per term for drawing classes and twenty dollars for painting. They also furnished their own materials. "Cooper Institute," *The Crayon* 7, 1 (January 1859): 30–31.

31. Ibid.

32. Henrietta D. Field, October [1861], Box #1, CUSDW Directors' Reports.

33. Ibid.

34. Henrietta D. Field, 3 March 1862, Box #1, CUSDW Directors' Reports.

35. Edward K. Spann, *Gotham at War: New York City, 1860–1865* (Wilmington, Del., 2002), 152.

36. The record books of Houghton Mifflin and the Riverside Press show a few women working as compositors before the War. In September 1863, after President Lincoln instituted the draft, that number dramatically spiked, as a dozen or so "Apprentice girls" were added to the books. A few more female names appeared every year as the war progressed. Records of Payroll, Book 21, March 1856–July 1856; Book 22, July 1860–October 1863; and Book 31, 1863–64, HL.

37. In fact, the Civil War devastated women's art education entirely in some cities. The New England School of Design for Women, founded in Boston in October 1851, closed down during the war. "I visited Boston during vacation, the School of Design is extinct." Corinna B. Nye to Alice Donlevy, 26 March 1862, Montreal, Box 1, Folder 1, AHD.

38. Swedenborg's doctrine of correspondences, and possibly his father's insanity, led Rimmer to an interest in phrenology and its application to art. Truman H. Bartlett, *The Art Life of William Rimmer* (Boston, 1881), 79.

39. Rimmer to Ednah Cheney, March 28, 1864, Chelsea, quoted in Bartlett, *William Rimmer*, 42–43; Phyllis Peet, "The Emergence of American Women Printmakers in the Late Nineteenth-Century" (Ph.D. dissertation, University of California at Los Angeles, 1987), 154–55.

40. On Rimmer and phrenology, see Charles Colbert, *A Measure of Perfection: Phrenology and the Fine Arts in America* (Chapel Hill, N.C., 1997), 73–121.

41. Curriculum included classes in drawing from casts and life, design and composition, perspective and subject, painting in oil and watercolors, clay modeling, and elementary principles for teachers.

42. Shortly after Rimmer's death, Truman Bartlett asked over one hundred artists and former students for their recollections of him. Excerpts of these "curiously conflicting" opinions and critical estimates are reproduced as a "Supplement" to Bartlett's book. Bartlett, *The Art Life of William Rimmer*, 135.

43. Sartain further noted, "I am chairman of the committee on instruction of the Board of Directors of the Pennsylvania Academy of the Fine Arts, and in that capacity do all I can (as do also the other directors) to encourage female talent. We have seven or eight ladies among our students, and they *certainly* are fully equal to the males in capacity for acquiring art. Some model, others only draw. The whole of our academy studies are gratuitous." Virginia Penny, *The Employment's of Women: A Cyclopedia of Woman's Work* (Boston, 1863), 99–100.

44. Mrs. B. F. Stevenson to Mr. Hewitt, 19 October 1871, Jacksonville, Ill., Box #4, CU, NYSDW Correspondence.

45. Abram S. Hewitt to Mrs. B. F. Stevens, New York, 5 October 1871, Box—Hewitt, Abram Stevens, 1822–1903, CU.

46. T. A. Richards, 1860, Box #1, CUSDW Directors' Reports.

47. Charlotte B. Cogswell, "Report of Engraving Class for the year ending May 1st 1872," CUSDW Teachers' Reports.

48. Susan Carter, "Report of the Woman's Art School," *Fourteenth Annual Report of the Trustees of the Cooper Union*, 1873, 21.

49. "Report of School of Art for Women, principal: L.A. Cuddehy," 1 November 1863[?], Box #1, CUSDW Directors' Reports.

50. Henrietta D. Field, 3 March 1862 and (n.d., ca. 1861), Box #1, CUSDW Directors' Reports.

51. Mrs. Henry M. Field, (n.d., ca. 1861), Box #1, CUSDW Directors' Reports.

52. Robert O'Brien, handwritten report "To the Ladies of the Advisory Council," 1 November [1860], CUSDW Teachers' Reports.

53. Commissions for engraving and engraving designs ranged from $632.66 in 1859 to $2,950.34 in 1872. Between 1860 and 1875 only the engraving class (which averaged 15 pupils per term) reported annual earnings. In 1875 the photograph coloring class at the School of Design reported earning $1,724, plus one pupil who made $150 per month. Engravers that year earned $916.21. In 1876 the Woman's Art School (which fluctuated between 200 and 350 students) brought in $4,444.50 for teaching, photo-crayon, and photo-color work, while the engraving class earned $1,083.13. The year 1877 was "dull owing to hard times" and yet the School's photo class earned $2,817.50, drawing teachers $6,621, and engravers $1,475.24. In 1878 a normal class for teachers was added to the curriculum, along with "painting and teaching painting and sundries," tile painting, and pottery lessons. Together these departments brought in $10,802.06 and engraving $1,503.31. In 1879 the Woman's Art School as a whole brought in $9,525.75, while the engraving department made $1,820.59. In 1880 the School made $12,740.50 and engraving made $1,248.95. "The Cooper Union for the Advancement of Science and Art," *Harper's Weekly* 5, 222 (30 March 1861); Annual Reports, Directors' and Teachers' Reports, CU.

54. "Cooper Institute," *The Crayon* 7, 1 (January 1859): 31.

55. Robert O'Brien, handwritten report, 28 June 1861, CUSDW Teachers' Reports.

56. Robert O'Brien, handwritten report, [June 1860], CUSDW Teachers' Reports.

57. Robert O'Brien, handwritten report, 6 April 1863, CUSDW Teachers' Reports.

58. Bianca Bondi Robitscher, "First Cooper Union Graduate Talks," unidentified newspaper clipping, ca. 1909, Box—Robitcher, Bianca B. Bondi, CU.

59. Dall charged the uproar over women engravers and designers in 1860s America to a "comical form" of jealousy rather than lack of skill. Caroline Dall, *The College, the Market, and the Court; or, Woman's Relation to Education, Labor, and Law* (Boston, 1867), 184.

60. This practice stemmed from the basic trend toward mass production in manufacture, away from the production of a small number of units at a compara-

tively large profit per unit to the production of a large number of units at a smaller profit per unit.

61. Sean Wilentz calls this trend "the persistence of tradition" in *Chants Democratic: New York City & the Rise of the American Working Class, 1788–1850* (New York, 1984), 134–35.

62. Ava Baron, "Questions of Gender: Deskilling and Demasculinization in the U.S. Printing Industry, 1830–1915," *Gender & History* 1, 2 (Summer 1989): 178–99; Wilentz, *Chants Democratic*, 129–32.

63. See Jacob Abbott, "Interior of the Cliff Street Building," *The Harper Establishment; or, How the Story Books Are Made* (New York, 1855), 42.

64. "In the 1860s the International Typographical Union even established a policy of equal pay for equal work regardless of sex, though the Union only admitted those women deemed to be competent on the same terms with men." Baron, "Questions of Gender," 186.

65. Penny, *Employments of Women*, 104, 53.

66. An engraving for *Frank Leslie's Illustrated Newspaper* could be the product of an individual or as many as forty artists. In the case of a full-page engraving, twelve or so small woodblocks were fastened together and the outline of the drawing transferred on the composite wood. The block was then passed from one draftsman to another, with each artist consulting the drawing and delineating the detail of his specialty. After the drawing was complete, the supervising engraver carved out all the lines that traversed across adjacent blocks and distributed them among the engravers, according to their specific skills. Artists never signed these engravings, as the individual was subordinated to the overall process. Josh Brown, *Beyond the Lines: Pictorial Reporting, Everyday Life, and the Crisis of Gilded Age America* (Berkeley, Calif., 2002), 35–36, 39; John P. Davis in "A Symposium of Wood-Engravers," *Harper's New Monthly Magazine* 60 (1880): 442–53.

67. "Besides learning a profession, at the very time they are studying, half the pupils in the free classes wholly or partly support themselves by teaching, designing, engraving on wood, and other artistic occupations. . . . Many of the beautiful engravings in this magazine, in 'St. Nicholas,' and in the Patent Office Reports, are cut in the engraving room of the 'Woman's Art School' at the Cooper Union." Carter, "Recollections of Peter Cooper," 219.

68. Penny, *Employments of Women*, 56.

69. "Women Engravers," *Revolution* 2, 19 (Nov. 12, 1868): 299.

70. Penny, *Employments of Women*, xiii.

71. Robert O'Brien, handwritten report, June 1860, CUSDW Teachers' Reports.

72. George Caleb Bingham, "The Ideal in Art" (1879), in John W. McCoubrey, ed., *American Art 1700–1960* (Englewood Cliffs, N.J., 1965), 148.

73. Linda S. Ferber, "'Determined Realists': The American Pre-Raphaelites and the Association for the Advancement of Truth in Art," in Linda S. Ferber and William H. Gerdts, eds., *The New Path: Ruskin and the American Pre-Raphaelites* (New York, 1985), 11, 15; Gail S. Davidson, *Training the Hand and Eye: The American Drawings at the Cooper Union* (Washington, D.C., 1989), 2.

74. Malcolm Warner, *The Victorians: British Painting 1837–1901* (Washington, D.C., 1996), 20–22.

75. Mrs. Henry D. Field (letters, n.d., ca. 1861), Box #1, CUSDW Directors' Reports.

76. Thomas Charles Farrer, "To the ladies of the council and Trustees of the Cooper Union," 4 January 1862, CUSDW Teachers' Reports.

77. The original members of the Association for the Advancement of Truth in Art were Charles Farrer and his brother Henry, Clarence Cook, John Henry Hill and his father John William Hill, Charles Herbert Moore, Henry R. Newman, and William Trost Richards.

78. Ferber, "'Determined Realists,'" 20, 19, 28; and Doreen Bolger Burke, "Painters and Sculptors in a Decorative Age," in Burke, *In Pursuit of Beauty: Americans and the Aesthetic Movement* (New York, 1986), 294–339.

79. Ferber and Gerdts, *The New Path*, 240; Bulson to Mr. Farrer, Albany, 31 January 1863, "Bulson, Thomas Lee," Roll N13, GLF.

80. Hill to Miss McDonald, 26 March 1867, "Hill, John W," N14, GLF.

81. William H. Gerdts, "Through a Glass Brightly: The American Pre-Raphaelites and the Association for the Advancement of Truth in Art," in Ferber and Gerdts, *The New Path*, 61.

82. Gerdts, "Through a Glass Brightly," 43.

83. "Our Artists and Their Works. Fidelia Bridges," *Brooklyn Monthly* 2, 3 (March 1878): 69–70.

84. *Round Table* 2 (October 14, 1865): 93, quoted in Gerdts, "Through a Glass Brightly," 61–62.

85. On Cook's faith in American drawing books when placed in the right hands, see Georgia B. Barnhill, Diana Korzenik, and Caroline F. Sloat, eds., *The Cultivation of Artists in Nineteenth-Century America* (Worcester, Mass., 1997), 59, 80.

86. "Female Art Department," *Seventh Annual Report of the Trustees of the Cooper Union*, 1866, 14.

87. Bartlett, *William Rimmer*, 135.

88. William Rimmer, "Female School of Art," *Ninth Annual Report of the Trustees of the Cooper Union*, July 1, 1868, 17–18.

89. Bartlett, *William Rimmer*, 146, 135.

90. Ibid., 143–44.

91. Ibid., 141.

92. [Clarence Cook], "The Cooper Institute Schools of Design, Male and Female Departments," *New-York Daily Tribune*, 1 June 1868, p. 4, col. 6.

93. Mary Hallock to Helena DeKay, 2 June 1868, Milton, N.Y., Box 1, Folder 14, transcripts [ca. 1864]–[ca. 1869], MHF Papers.

94. *New-York Daily Tribune*, 3 July 1867, 2.

95. "School of Art for Women," *Tenth Annual Report of the Trustees of the Cooper Union*, 1869, 11.

96. Childe was to receive $1,000 of Rimmer's $4,000 pay. Rimmer to Peter Cooper, 30 September 1870, Box #4, CU, NYSDW Correspondence.

97. Petition to Abram S. Hewitt, 8 October 1870, New York, Box #4, CU, NYSDW Correspondence.

98. Mary W. McLain to the Trustees of the School of Design, 10 October 1870, Washington, D. C., Box #4, CU, NYSDW Correspondence.

99. W. J. Linton to Mrs. Botta, 16 April 1870, 25 University Building, New York, Box #4, CU, NYSDW Correspondence.

100. "The National Academy of Design. I.," *New York Times*, 24 April 1867, 4.

101. "Without some practice in drawing, nothing can be accomplished in either wood engraving or designing." Penny, *Employments of Women*, 55–56.

102. Francis Barrymore Smith, *Radical Artisan: William James Linton, 1812–97* (Manchester, 1973), 4, 6.

103. *Reminiscences of Mary Hallock Foote*, 128; Nancy Carlson Schrock, "William James Linton and His Victorian History of American Wood Engraving," Introduction to William J. Linton, *American Wood Engraving: A Victorian History* (Watkins Glen, N.Y., 1976), i.

104. William J. Linton, *The History of Wood-Engraving in America* (London, 1882), 51.

105. Linton quoted in Brown, *Beyond the Lines*, 38.

106. Smith, *Radical Artisan*, 4–8; John Murdoch, "William James Linton," *Oxford Dictionary of National Biography* 33 (2004): 944–46.

107. Quoted in George Howes Whittle, "Monographs on American Wood Engravers XV—Caroline Amelia Powell," *Printing Art* 31 (1918): 188; Peet, "American Women Printmakers," 160.

108. John P. Davis, "The New School of Engraving," *Century Magazine* 38 (August 1889): 588–89; Peet, "American Women Printmakers," 159.

109. O'Brien's reports from March 1861 and December 7, 1863.

110. In 1851 Sarah E. Fuller engraved for Nathaniel Orr & Co. Her 1864 advertisement appeared in Adams, Sampson & Co., *New York State Business Directory*. Helena E. Wright, *With Pen and Graver: Women Graphic Artists Before 1900* (Washington, D.C., February 1995–January 1996), 16; Barnhill, Korzenik, and Sloat, *Cultivation of Artists in Nineteenth-Century America*, 160.

111. Business card of Susan E. Fuller, Engraver, "Sinclair, Samuel," Roll N16, GLF.

112. Letter from Sinclair, 1870, "Sinclair, Samuel," Roll N16, GLF.

113. The Curtis sisters studied drawing and wood engraving at Cooper Union in 1858–59. In California they trained Eleanor Peters Gibbons, who later studied at Cooper Union. In 1880 Gibbons became head of the firm where she had apprenticed and authored a manual on "Drawing and Engraving on Wood." Leila Curtis to Miss Donlevy, 3 December 1869, 1117 Pine Street, San Francisco, Box 1, Folder 1, AHD; Doris Ostrander Dawdy, *Artists of the American West: A Bibliographical Dictionary* (Chicago, 1974), 1: 195; Wright, *With Pen and Graver*, 7, 16; Barnhill, Korzenik, and Sloat, *Cultivation of Artists in Nineteenth-Century America*, 160.

114. Linton counted on the regular attendance of advanced students to fill in when he was absent. In February 1870, he asked Bianca Bondi Robitscher to take charge of the class and suggested to the Trustees that she be given his salary for that month. Robitscher wrote to Hewitt in March on her own behalf, reporting on the

condition of the class and submitting a bill for her services to the school. Linton then arranged for I. W. Stewart of Brooklyn to teach the class on a trial basis. Stewart remained until June 1870, while Linton's name was "honorarily used as Director of the School." Unsatisfied with Stewart, Linton arranged for Charlotte Cogswell to head the class. She stayed until 1880.

115. Bianca Bondi Robitscher, "First Cooper Union Graduate Talks," CU.

116. Frances Ketchum is listed in the *Second Annual Report of the Trustees of the Cooper Union*, 1861, 54; and *Seventh Annual Report*, 1 July 1866, 46.

117. Charlotte B. Cogswell, "Report of the Engraving Class," November 1870 and 27 February 1871, CUSDW Teachers' Reports.

118. Thomas Woody, *A History of Women's Education in the United States*, vol. 2 (New York, 1929), 78.

119. Davidson, *Training the Hand and Eye*, 3.

120. Robert O'Brien, handwritten report, 6 April 1863, CUSDW Teachers' Reports.

Chapter 5. *"Laborers in the Field of the Beautiful"*

1. "The Women Artists of New York and Its Vicinity," *New York Evening Post*, 24 February 1868, 2.

2. Artists listed with studios in New York City and Brooklyn included figure and genre painters Mrs. Lilly Martin Spencer, the Misses Oakley, and Madame Bossie; marine subject painters Mrs. Lyman Cobb and Miss S. E. Blackwell; painter/etcher Mrs. Eliza Greatorex; still life and landscape painters Miss Mary Kollock, Miss E. H. Remington, Miss A. G. Oakes, Misses E. C. and G. Field, Miss C. Griswold, Mrs. L. B. Culver, Mrs. D. C. Van Norman, Miss S. M. Clowes, Mrs. Henshaw, Mrs. A. P. Crane, Miss M. L. Wagner, Mrs. A. G. Studley, Miss V. Ely, Miss Waters, Miss Bridges, Miss Thayer, Miss Julia Osborn, Miss De Rycke, Miss E. Fox, Miss Ione H. Perry, Miss Lizzie Hammill, Miss A. C. Lovell, Miss V. Tucker, Miss T. L. Johnson, Miss Dayton, Miss C. Deming, and Misses Virginia and Henrietta Granbery; illuminators Miss Dowling and Miss E. W. Cook; portraitist Miss M. Willets; engraver/designers Miss Lucy Gibbons, Miss T. C. Post, and Miss A. C. Fitze; and sculptors Miss Hosmer, Miss Foley, Miss Stebbins, Miss Lewis, Miss Ella Pell, and Miss Lucy B. Hinton. Also mentioned were Mrs. Julia Beers, Miss Wenzler, Mrs. H. E. Cheney (CT), and Miss Mary Cook.

3. Similar statements of surprise were made in the New York popular press every decade after 1850, as the urban population grew and more women pursued art as a career or hobby.

4. See Edward K. Spann, *Gotham at War: New York City, 1860–1865* (Wilmington, Del., 2002).

5. Roger Wunderlich, *Low Living and High Thinking at Modern Times, New York* (Syracuse, N.Y., 1992), 180–81.

6. [Clarence Cook], "Another Artists' Reception," *New-York Daily Tribune*, 14 April 1863, 2.

7. Worthington Whittredge, *The Autobiography of Worthington Whittredge* (1880), ed. John I. Baur (New York, 1969), 43; Diana Korzenik, *Drawn to Art: A Nineteenth-Century American Dream* (Hanover, N.H., 1985), 89.

8. Thomas Lee Bulson letter to Mr. [Thomas] Farrer, Albany, 31 January 1863, "Bulson, Thomas Lee," Roll N13, GLF.

9. May Alcott studied sculpture with William Rimmer and painting with William Hunt at the new Studio Building in Boston, on the corner of Tremont and Broomfield streets. May Alcott diary entries, 6 March and 12 June 1864, an unspecified date in 1865, and 1 May 1864, bMS Am1817.2 (15) and bMS Am1817 (58), Alcott Papers, HL; Neil Harris, *The Artist in American Society: The Formative Years, 1790–1860* (Chicago, 1982), 269.

10. Annie Boleyn Delano, 3 June 1864, Penn Yan, Box 1, Folder 1, AHD; Sally Bronson to Spencer, 15 March 1864, LMS.

11. According to *Harper's Weekly*, Lewis filled commissions for Civil War and other subjects while in Rome, including "a statue of Abraham Lincoln for the Central Park, one of John Brown for the Union League Club, and one of Longfellow for Yale College," as well as a Madonna for the Church of St. Francis in Baltimore, and a statue for the "Prince of Italy." *Harper's Weekly* (4 June 1870): 359 and (11 January 1873): 35; Lynda Roscoe Hartigan, *Sharing Traditions: Five Black Artists in Nineteenth-Century America* (Washington D.C., 1985), 85–98; Lisa E. Farrington, *Creating Their Own Image: The History of African-American Women Artists* (New York, 2005), 53–64.

12. Elizabeth Dudley, "The Ladies' Art Association of New York," *Aldine, the Art Journal of America* 8, 5 (1 September 1876): 151.

13. [William H. Bishop], "Young Artists' Life in New York," *Scribner's* 19 (November 1879–April 1880): 366.

14. "Donlevy, Alice Heighes" and "Donlevy, Harriet Farley," *Who Was Who in America: A Companion Volume to Who's Who in America*, vol. 1, *1897–1942* (Chicago, 1942), 331; George Rogers Taylor, "Harriet Farley," in Edward T. James, ed., *Notable American Women 1607–1950: A Bibliographical Dictionary*, 3 vols. (Cambridge, Mass., 1971), 1: 596–97.

15. Delano to Donlevy, 16 November 1875, Meadville, Pennsylvania, Box 1, Folder 2, AHD.

16. Dodworth's had studios "in Broadway" and "in Fifth Avenue." After compiling the studio addresses of women artists, I compared them with the addresses of studio buildings and neighborhoods in the Ford Collection; Donlevy Papers; "The Women Artists of New York and Its Vicinity"; Catherine Hoover Voorsanger and John K. Howat, eds., *Art and the Empire City*, (New York, 2000), 61, 66–74; *National Academy of Design Exhibition Record, 1826–1860*; *National Academy of Design Exhibition Record, 1861–1900*; Annette Blaugrund, "The Tenth Street Studio Building: A Roster, 1847–1895," *American Art Journal* 14, 2 (Spring 1982): 64–71; Neil Harris, *Artist in American Society*, 263–68; and Kenneth T. Jackson, *The Encyclopedia of New York City* (New Haven, Conn., 1995), 1163, 1284.

17. The artist returning from Europe in 1879 found the ruling rates for studios had gone up to $400 and $600 annually, or between $30 and $50 per month.

Bishop, "Young Artists' Life," 361; Virginia Penny, *The Employments of Women: A Cyclopedia of Woman's Work* (Boston, 1863), 488.

18. Louisa May Alcott describes the camaraderie found in women artists' studios in "The Sunny Side," a chapter from *An Old Fashioned Girl* (Boston, 1869).

19. A. E. Rose to Miss Donlevy, February 1869, Port Jervis, Box 1, Folder 1, AHD.

20. *In Pursuit of Beauty: Americans and the Aesthetic Movement* (New York, 1986), 418–19.

21. "The Women Artists of New York and Its Vicinity"; "Pope, John" and "Pope, Mrs. John (Mary Strongitharm)," Roll N16; "Wagner, M. L. (Miss) Maria Louise" and "Wagner, Daniel," Roll N17, GLF.

22. "Young Artists' Life," 366.

23. Ibid., 362.

24. Ibid., 355–68. Nathaniel Hawthorne's *The Marble Faun* was published in 1859.

25. "Coman, Mrs. C.B.," "Burt, Helen," and "Burt, Martha," Roll N13, GLF.

26. Mary E. Monks, 8 January 1878, Cold Spring, Box 1, Folder 3, AHD.

27. Lilly Martin Spencer to her parents, 28 June 1858 and 29 December 1959, Newark, LMS.

28. Ann Byrd Schumer, "Lilly Martin Spencer: American Painter of the Nineteenth Century" (master's thesis, Ohio State University, 1959), 78.

29. "Lily Spencer," *The Revolution* 3, 16 (22 April 1869): 252; Robin Bolton-Smith and William H. Truettner, *The Joys of Sentiment* (Washington, D.C, 1973), 63, 148.

30. Letter from C. C. Hine, 19 April 1869; Agreement letters from A.A. Childs & Co., 12, 28 May 1869, LMS.

31. Harris, *Artist in American Society*, 268; Jackson, *Encyclopedia of New York City*, 1163.

32. "Beers, Julie H," Roll N13; "Stone, Mary L," Roll N16, GLF.

33. Carrie Rebora Barratt, "Mapping the Venues: New York City Art Exhibitions," in *Art and the Empire City*, 61.

34. While Kathleen McCarthy found the alliances created in studio buildings promoting "a male subculture bound by mutual aspirations and mutual aid," I have found in them the seeds of a mixed-sex society of artists. Kathleen D. McCarthy, *Women's Culture: American Philanthropy and Art, 1830–1930* (Chicago, 1991), 8.

35. Clark S. Marlor, *A History of the Brooklyn Art Association with an Index of Exhibitions* (New York, 1970), v.

36. McCarthy, *Women's Culture*, 9.

37. Brooklyn Art Association exhibition cards or forms (filled out by the artists) specify pickup and return information that maps the movement of art works from studios to dealers to exhibitions to new owners. For an example of the letter sent to artists soliciting work, see "Wagner, M.L.," Roll N13, GLF.

38. "Coman, C. B.," letter from 14 November 1876, Roll N13; McEntee letters from 1 and 8 January 1877, "McEntee, Lilly," Roll N15; and Dillon letters from 8 January 1880, 31 December 1881, and 8 January 1883, "Dillon, Mrs. Julia," Roll N14,

GLF; "Some Lady Artists of New York," *Art Amateur: A Monthly Journal Devoted to Art in the Household* 3, 2 (July 1880): 27.

39. Marlor, *History of the Brooklyn Art Association,* v. Multiple examples of exhibition, sale, and discussion of women's art can be found in the Ford Collection.

40. "Today's Tribune reports a fair beginning and I gladly notice the Women have sold the most." Annie E. Sterling, 12 December 1880, Bridgeport, Conn., Roll N16, GLF.

41. Artist, date, title, medium, owner, and price are listed under artist's last name in the index of exhibitions in Marlor's *History of the Brooklyn Art Association.*

42. "Bristol, J. B." letters to Mr. Latimer, 12 December 1881, 19 December 1881, and to Mr. J. E. Smith, 29 December 1882, 52 East Twenty-Third Street, Roll N13, GLF.

43. Annie E. Sterling in reply to Latimer, 9 May 1879, Bridgeport, Conn., Roll N-15, GLF.

44. Sara Cole worked alongside her brother Thomas in the Catskill Mountains and exhibited with him at the National Academy.

45. Jennie Augusta Brownscombe (b. 1850), a native of Honesdale, Pennsylvania, was one of the Cooper Union students who graduated to the Antique Class at the National Academy in 1871.

46. "Coman, C[harlotte] B[uell], [A.N.A.]," and "Brownscombe, Jenny" in Marlor, *History of the Brooklyn Art Association,* 155, 137; "Coman, Mrs. C.B." and "Brownscombe, Jenny," Roll N13, GLF; "Some Lady Artists of New York," *Art Amateur; A Monthly Journal Devoted to Art in the Household* 3, 2 (July 1880): 27; *National Museum of Women in the Arts* (New York, 1987), 52–53.

47. Only the Century Club, a men's club where artists, literary men, industrialists, and philanthropists met to socialize and do business, failed to open its galleries to women artists, although women were invited to attend its receptions and exhibitions. *Galaxy: A Magazine of Entertaining Reading* 8, 4 (October 1869): 574.

48. "Leisure Moments," *Hours at Home: A Popular Monthly of Instruction and Reception* 11, 1 (May 1870): 84.

49. "Article II (Amended)," *Constitution and By-Laws of the Ladies' Art Association* (New York, 1871), 3, Box 4, Folder 10, AHD.

50. The first advisory committee consisted of Messrs. Pope, Gray, Green, and Whittredge. All the founding members of the Ladies' Art Association were artists who had been associated with the School of Design as students or advisers. "The Women Artists of New York and Its Vicinity"; "Donlevy, Alice Heighes," *Who Was Who in America,* 331.

51. Dudley, "The Ladies' Art Association of New York," 151.

52. Ellen E. Dickinson, "The New York Ladies' Art Association," *Art Amateur; A Monthly Journal Devoted to Art in the Household* 2, 2 (January 1880): 29–30. Ellen E. Pike Dickinson was a poet, journalist, novelist, and biographer, and the wife of Emily Dickinson's cousin William Hawley Dickinson.

53. The Artists' Fund, founded by male artists in 1855, set up two treasuries: one to aid Society members and one for any artists whose families might be in financial difficulties. "New York's leading painters contributed their works for the

benefit of the profession as a whole, members or non-members." Harris, *Artist in American Society*, 254–83.

54. "The Women Artists of New York and Its Vicinity."

55. "The Fine Arts. Sale for the Ladies' Art Association," *New York Times*, 28 February 1877, 5.

56. Until the 1880s, the title "Association" was reserved for organizations formed by and in the interests of particular occupational and professional groups, while "Society" and "Club" were used to designate voluntary associations of laypersons and professionals seeking to promote a benevolent, social, or cultural cause.

57. At least two women artists' associations antedated the Ladies' Art Association. In 1859 Elizabeth Ellet wrote Lilly Martin Spencer proposing a private Society of Lady Artists and in 1866 "The Women's National Art Association" held an exhibit at Wenderoth, Taylor & Brown's Art Saloon in Philadelphia. Elizabeth H. Ellet to Lilly Martin Spencer, 6 October 1859, LMS; "The Women's National art Association," *New York Times*, 12 November 1866, 4; McCarthy, *Women's Culture*, 100–101; Swinth, *Painting Professionals*, 242, note 46.

58. "The Fine Arts. Sale for the Ladies' Art Association," *New York Times*, 28 February 1877, 5.

59. *The Round Table: A Saturday Review of Politics, Finance, Literature, Society, and Art* 3, 44 (7 July 1866): 425.

60. Agnes Chamberlain, April 1876, Box 1, Folder 2, AHD.

61. Ladies' Art Association circular, n.d., Box 4, Folder 4, AHD.

62. Dickinson, "The New York Ladies' Art Association," 29.

63. C. M. Clowes, 28 May 1867, Poughkeepsie; and Lucy B. Hinton, 28 May 1867, Rhinebeck, Box 1, Folder 1, AHD.

64. T. Addison Richards to "Mrs. Pope, Mrs. Gray and other Ladies," 7 May 1867, New York, Box 1, Folder 1, AHD. Other National Academy of Design artists who advised and endorsed the Association were Joseph Hartley (President of the Salmagundi Club), John G. Brown, George Inness, Samuel Coleman, Henry Loop, William Hart, Charles Calverly, and A. H. Wyant. *Constitution and By-Laws of the Ladies' Art Association*, 13; Subscription letter, 12 April 1882, Box 4, Folder 4, AHD.

65. "The Women's National Art Association," *New York Times*, 12 November 1866, 4.

66. *Constitution and By-Laws of the Ladies' Art Association*, 3.

67. Lloyd Morris, *Incredible New York: High Life and Low Life of the Last Hundred Years* (New York, 1951), 81; Note re. Glee Club, Box 1, Folder 1, AHD.

68. Notice sent to William Humphreys of the "Evening Commonwealth" by the Ladies' Art Association, 1869, Box 1, Folder 1, AHD.

69. Written in purple ink on an article entitled "Facts Concerning the Ladies' Art Association for the Promotion of the Interests of Women Artists," pasted into "[1886–87] Ladies Art Association. A National Association founded in 1867 by women artists of New York incorporated in 1877," Box 4, AHD.

70. *Constitution and By-Laws of the Ladies' Art Association*, 13.

71. M. L. Wagner, 6 November 1870, Addison, Box 1, Folder 2, AHD.

72. Mary Oakford, 26 March 1873, Box 1, Folder 2, AHD.

73. I. Gray (re. Mrs. Fisher née Thayer), 31 July 1875, Box 1, Folder 3, AHD.

74. Wagner had been exhibiting paintings in New York since 1839 (miniatures, portraits, genre, still life, and landscapes) at the National Academy of Design and American Art Union, as well as at the Philadelphia Academy of Fine Art, Boson Athenaeum, and Brooklyn Art Association. M. L. Wagner, 13 November 1870, Box 1, Folder 2, AHD.

75. Letterhead of Ladies' Art Association stationery, Box 4, Folder 2, AHD.

76. Ibid.; *Constitution and By-Laws of the Ladies' Art Association*, 4.

77. Subscription letter, 12 April 1882, Box 4, Folder 4, AHD.

78. Jobs included "writing, drawing, painting botanical studies, teaching, care and sale of pictures and the procuring of orders for members." For more on the "Labor Note System," see chapter 7. "Tenth" in "Facts Concerning the Ladies' Art Association," Box 4, AHD.

79. H. C. Lane, 207 E Capitol St, Washington, D.C., Box 1, Folder 2, AHD.

80. Ibid.; *Constitution and By-Laws of the Ladies' Art Association*, 4.

81. "Household Art Feb. 1878 Monthly meeting after 4 p.m. Presented to the L.A.A. by a member of 77—to be kept," Box 1, Folder 2, AHD.

82. Custodian's Report for the Month of November 1869, Box 1, Folder 1; Report of the Hanging Committee written by Alice Donlevy, 14 March 1870, Box 1, Folder 2, AHD; "The Ladies' Art Association," *New York Times*, 14 March 1876, 10.

83. "Fine Arts. The Ladies' Art Association," *New York Times*, 18 December 1870, 3; *Hours at Home: A Popular Monthly of Instruction and Reception* 11, 1 (May 1870): 84.

84. The second comment is written in purple ink on "Facts Concerning the Ladies' Art Association," Box 4, AHD.

85. I. Gray to Miss Field, 16 March 1872, Florence, Box 1, Folder 2, AHD.

86. Dudley, "The Ladies' Art Association of New York," 151.

87. "Third" in "Facts Concerning the Ladies' Art Association," Box 4, AHD; "The Fine Arts. Sale for the Ladies' Art Association," *New York Times*, 28 February 1877, 5.

88. "Ladies' Art Association Classes," *New York Times*, 28 November 1888, 8.

89. "Privileges of Membership," Box 4, Folder 4, AHD; Dickinson, "The New York Ladies' Art Association," 29.

90. "Sixth" and "Seventh" in "Facts Concerning the Ladies' Art Association," Box 4, AHD.

91. According to Virginia Penny, it was uncommon to find women painting china in the 1860s. She lists "China Decorators and Burnishers" as a separate category of manufacture. Penny, *Employments of Women*, xx, 260; "The Ladies' Art Association Plan of Instruction, 1883–84," Box 4, Folder 4, AHD.

92. "Article II (Amended)," Box 4, Folder 10; "Fourteenth" and "Fifteenth" in "Facts Concerning the Ladies' Art Association," Box 4, AHD.

93. In 1877 the Ladies' Art Association rented rooms at 319 East Eighteenth Street on Broadway, within a block of *Scribner's* building. It also kept studios at 23 East Fourteenth Street and 4 West Fourteenth Street in New York, and across the river at 167 Taylor Street in Brooklyn.

94. Mary Cook to Miss Donlevy, 13 October 1873, Keene Flats, Box 1, Folder 2, AHD.

95. "The idea of a Studio Building originated with Mrs. Mary Strongitharm Pope, the first pres., as a plan for the protection of women by women." "Facts Concerning the Ladies' Art Association," Box 4, AHD.

96. In 1882, the Association initiated a subscription drive to raise a fund to secure the building's permanency. Subscription Letter, 12 April 1882, Box 4, Folder 4, AHD.

97. Ellen Fisher thanked the Association for notifying her of the "Brooklyn Fair" and "Bridgeport Exhib." Ellen B. T. Fisher, 26 October 1875 and 18 January 1877, Brooklyn, Box 1, Folder 2, AHD.

98. Juliet L. Tanner to "My dear Miss Denroche or Miss Donlevy," 27 July 1869, Philadelphia, Box 1, Folder 1, AHD.

99. A. E. Rose, 25 May 1869, Port Jervis, Box 1, Folder 1, AHD.

100. M. [Maria] R. Oakey, 7 April 1877, Box 1, Folder 2, AHD. A list of models' addresses from 1876, supplied to Miss Monks at the LAA by the School Committee for the Art Students' League, is in Box 1, Folder 3, AHD.

101. Card from William Humphreys "Evening Commonwealth," [1869], 7 Spruce Street, New York, Box 1, Folder 1, AHD.

102. Helena de Kay Gilder, 30 September 1875, Studio 103 E. Fifteenth Street, Box 1, Folder 2, AHD.

103. Dickinson, "The New York Ladies' Art Association," 29.

104. Laura Curtis Bulliard, 21 September 1870, Revolution Office, 31 Union Place, New York; L. Prang & Co, 4 October 1870, Boston, Box 1, Folder 2, AHD.

105. Howard Hinton, 18 March 1879, Home Journal Office, Box 1, Folder 3, AHD.

106. Georgie Davis, 4 June 1869, Dussey County, New Jersey, Box 1, Folder 1, AHD.

107. Mrs. B. Hubbard, 23 July 1866, Detroit; R. O'Brien to "Dear friend Alice," 29 August 1866, Waterbury, Conn., Box 1, Folder 1, AHD.

108. Sean Wilentz, *Chants Democratic: New York City and the Rise of the American Working Class, 1788–1850* (New York, 1984), 107.

109. Penny, *Employments of Women*, 41.

110. Ibid., viii. Virginia Penny was born in Kentucky in 1826 and graduated from female seminary in Ohio in 1843. She devoted her work to enlarging the industrial sphere for women and improving the condition of the working classes. Her publications include *The Employments of Women* (1863), *Five Hundred Occupations Adapted to Women* (1868), and *Think and Act* (1873).

111. Henry T. Tuckerman, *Book of the Artists. American Artist Life* (New York, 1867), 464.

112. Tuckerman, *Book of the Artists*, 217–18.

113. Correspondence regarding Donlevy's employment is sprinkled throughout her papers.

114. Penny, *Employments of Women*, 42.

115. A Staff Contributor, "Art and Artists in Manchester," *Manchester Historical Association Collections* 4, part one (Manchester, N.H., 1908), 112, 123–24, 127–28.

116. Alice Donlevy, *Practical Hints on the Art of Illumination* (New York, 1867), 17–19.

117. Penny, *Employments of Women*, xiii.

118. Penny, *Employments of Women*, 88–94.

119. Ibid., 93–94. At this same time, hundreds of women "whose husbands, fathers, and brothers [had] fallen on the battle field [made] army shirts at six cents apiece," a process that took several hours. *New York Times*, 4 September 1864.

120. Mrs. Henry M. Field, undated letter ca. 1862, Box #1, CUSDW Directors' Reports.

121. Penny notes that some colorists "have traveled through the country, stopping in various towns to carry on their business." Penny, *Employments of Women*, 91.

122. The "Women's National Art Association" accepted for its exhibition: "pictures original or copied, in oil, water-color or pastel; designs, sketches and studies of all descriptions in art; sculpture and models in plaster; wood and steel engravings. Industrial art represented in designs for prints, carpets, wall-paper, &c., and well-colored photographs." "The Women's National Art Association," *New York Times*, 12 November 1866, 4.

123. One photographer said he "prefers women for some parts of the work. Men are more powerful artists, give a better expression; women are more careful, and give a finer finish." Penny, *Employments of Women*, 88–94.

124. Bolton-Smith and Truettner, *The Joys of Sentiment*, 55.

125. Annie Delano to "My Dear Alice Donlevy," (13 June 1861?), Penn Yan, N.Y., Box 1, Folder 1, AHD.

126. Peter C. Marzio, *The Democratic Art: Pictures for a 19th-Century America: Chromolithography, 1840–1900* (Boston, 1979), 119; *Prang's Chromo* (April 1868): 4.

127. Corinna [Bouman] Nye, 29 April 1868, Montreal, Box 1, Folder 1, AHD.

128. Louis Prang to H. P. Gray, 13 October 1870, Box 1, Folder 1, AHD.

129. Rosina Emmett used her money to establish a studio with Dora Wheeler in New York City. Emmett collaborated with Wheeler, designing tapestries, curtains, wallpapers, and embroidered silk canvases for the firm Associated Artists, run by Dora's mother Candace Wheeler. She continued to design for the firm after moving to Paris, where she studied oil painting, her subsequent profession. Tara Leigh Tappert, *The Emmetts: A Generation of Gifted Women* (New York, 1993), 8; Marzio, *The Democratic Art*, 99.

130. Wright, *With Pen and Graver*, 10, 16.

131. Lizbeth Bullock Humphrey, *Child Life: A Souvenir of Lizbeth B. Humphrey* (Boston, 1890).

132. *Eighteenth Annual Report of the Trustees of the Cooper Union*, 1877, 8, CU.

133. Penny, *Employments of Women*, 59–61.

134. "The specimens of illumination that came . . . are greatly admired, and are exactly what I wanted," Detroit engraver Mrs. B. Hubbard wrote Donlevy. "The letter of Instructions will be of great service to me. I enclose draft for amt. of your bill. $30 . . . can you make a monogram of the letter H and a griffins head crest?" Letters to Donlevy from Mrs. B. Hubbard, 23 July 1866, Detroit; Anna H. Gaffray, 18 July 1867, Willow Brook; and Helen A. Garvey, 14 October 1869, Ohio, Box 1, Folder 1, AHD.

135. The book was Longfellow's *Skeleton in Armor*. Ticknor Firm Cost Books MS Am.2030.2 (21): 182 [15 December 1876], HL.

136. James R. O'Gorman, *A Billings Bookshelf* (Wellesley, Mass., 1986), 4, cited in David Tatham, *Winslow Homer and the Illustrated Book* (Syracuse, N.Y., 1992), 18.

137. Ticknor firm cost books, MS Am 1185.6 (8): 328–29, HL.

138. Tappert, *The Emmetts*, 8.

139. On the back of a note from *Scribner's Monthly/St.Nicholas*, Donlevy has written: "Indian Doll $7, Cow $4.75, Hen & Chickens $4.50, Clove Raisin $1, Sacred Bun $6, 'A hundred years ago' $3.50, Children's Choirs 75 cents." 19 June 1874, New York, Box 1, Folder 2, AHD.

140. Ticknor firm cost books, Ms. Am 1185.6 (8): 328–29, HL.

141. Tatham, *Winslow Homer*, 18–19.

142. Ticknor firm cost books, MS Am 2030.2 (21): 177 [19 October 1875]; MS Am.2030.2 (21): 182 [15 December 1876], HL.

143. "The Old Cabinet," *Scribner's Monthly Magazine* 2, 2 (December 1875): 285–86.

Chapter 6. "An Easier and Surer Path"

1. Mary Hallock [Foote] to Helena de Kay [Gilder], n.d. [winter 1873–74], transcript #69, Box 6, Folder 16, MHF Papers; Darlis A. Miller, *Mary Hallock Foote: Author-Illustrator of the American West* (Norman, Okla., 2002), 22.

2. MHF to HdKG, 8 September [1873], Milton, #40, Box 6, Folder 15, MHF Papers.

3. MHF to HdKG, February 1875, #76, Box Folder 18, MHF Papers.

4. MHF to HdKG, 12 November 1873, #48, Box 6, Folder 16, MHF Papers. The "romantic friendship" expressed by the Hallock/de Kay letters is discussed in Carroll Smith-Rosenberg, "The Female World of Love and Ritual: Relations Between Women in Nineteenth-Century America," in *Disorderly Conduct: Visions of Gender in Victorian America* (New York, 1985), 53–76.

5. MHF to HdKG, 4 May [1875], #84, Box 6, Folder 18, MHF Papers; Sally Webster, *William Morris Hunt, 1824–1879* (Cambridge, 1991), 116–17.

6. MHF to HdKG, 9 May 1875, #86; and MHF to HdKG, 19 May 1875, #85, Box 6, Folder 18, MHF Papers.

7. MHF to HdKG, 18 June [1875?], #102, Box 6, Folder 18, MHF Papers.

8. Josiah G. Holland, *Mistress of the Manse* (New York, 1877). Each also contributed a plate, engraved by John P. Davis, to Bayard Taylor's *The National Ode* (Boston, 1877).

9. "Recent Literature," *Atlantic Monthly* 39, 231 (January 1877): 114.

10. W. D. Howells, "Recent Literature," *Atlantic Monthly* 40, 206 (December 1877): 753.

11. The most thorough work on nineteenth-century periodical publishing is still Frank Luther Mott, *A History of American Magazines*, 3 vols. (Cambridge,

Mass., ca. 1938, 1957). For newer authors, see Kenneth M. Price and Susan Belasco Smith, eds., *Periodical Literature in Nineteenth-Century America* (Wilmington, Del., 1972).

12. Mott, *A History of American Magazines* 1: 37–38, 494.

13. Dale Roylance, "Graphic Arts in America, 1670–1900," in *American Graphic Arts: Three Centuries of Illustrated Books, Prints & Drawings* (Princeton, N.J., 1981), 14.

14. Barbara Balliet argues that women's illustration replicates these restrictions in "Reproducing Gender in Nineteenth-Century Illustrations," *Journal of the Rutgers University Libraries* 55 (2003): 64–94.

15. W. D. Howells, "Recent Literature," *Atlantic Monthly* 34, 206 (December 1874): 745.

16. "Women Artists," *Galaxy* 6, 4 (October 1868): 574; "Women in Art," *Revolution* 2, 15 (15 October 1868): 236.

17. Other than Felix O. Darley, Thomas Nast, and Winslow Homer, this generation of illustrators has been largely overlooked. For the next generation, see Margaret E. Wagner, *Maxfield Parrish & the Illustrators of the Golden Era* (Rohnert Park, Calif., 2000); Michelle H. Bogart, "Artistic Ideals and Commercial Practices: The Problem of Status for American Illustrators," *Prospects: An Annual of American Cultural Studies* 15 (1990): 225–81; Helen Goodman, "Women Illustrators of the Golden Age of American Illustration," *Women's Art Journal* 8 (Spring/Summer 1987): 13–22.

18. The number dropped from approximately 685 in 1850 to about 575 in 1860. The average lifespan of a periodical was about four years. The average circulation of quarterlies in 1860 was about 3,370; that of monthlies was about 12,000; weeklies, including newspapers, circulated an average of 2,400 copies. The standard magazine price was $3 a year in 1850, though some charged $5. Mott, *History of American Magazines*, 2: 7–10.

19. *Godey's Lady's Book* never mentioned the war or felt its effects, except for receiving subscription clubs from the army. Apparently, men read illustrated magazines geared toward women and children. To continue attracting male readers in the 1880s, many magazines simply dropped "Lady's" from their titles. *Godey's* 70 (March 1865): 284; Mott, *History of American Magazines*, 2: 4–5.

20. These names were gleaned from the periodical archive at the American Antiquarian Society; Linton's *History of Wood-Engraving in America*; the *Revolution*; and letters and invoices in the MHF Papers, AHD Papers, CU Collection, LMS Papers, and GLF Collection.

21. F. Weitenkampf, *American Graphic Art* (New York, 1912), 148; "Engraving on Wood. Topics of the Time," *Scribner's Monthly* 18, 3 (July 1879): 456.

22. Mott, *History of American Magazines*, 2: 186–87.

23. "Art in England in his youth was chaotic to a degree, but in book illustration it had a fire and impulse given it by the rising literary men—Ruskin, the Rosettis and the Brotherhood. . . . Mr. Linton felt this impulse, and being a man of very strong individuality, and poet and artist as well," imparted it to his pupils. Helena de Kay Gilder, "Author Illustrators II. Mary Hallock Foote," *The Bookbuyer (A Summary of American and Foreign Literature)*, Charles Scribner's Sons, New York, XI (August 1894): 7, Box 10, Folder 3, MHF Papers.

24. Anthony was engraver and art editor of fine editions for the successive Boston firms of Ticknor & Fields; Fields, Osgood & Co; and James Osgood & Company.

25. Linton, *Wood-Engraving in America*, 33, 51; "The Old Cabinet," *Scribner's* 11, 2 (December 1875): 285.

26. "Culture and Progress," *Scribner's Monthly* 13, 3 (January 1877): 424.

27. John Greenleaf Whittier, *Mabel Martin, A Harvest Idyl* (Boston, 1875); "The Old Cabinet," *Scribner's* 11, 2 (December 1875): 285.

28. Mott, *History of American Magazines* 3: 466; Weitenkampf, *American Graphic Art*, 161.

29. W. J. Linton, "Art in Engraving on Wood," *Atlantic Monthly* 43, 260 (June 1879): 705–15; Linton, *Wood-Engraving in America*, 49–51; Mott, *History of American Magazines*, 2: 188–90.

30. For the various positions taken by artist-engravers in this controversy, see George William Sheldon, "A Symposium of Wood-Engravers," *Harper's New Monthly Magazine* 60 (1880): 442–53; Joshua Brown, *Beyond the Lines: Pictorial Reporting, Everyday Life, and the Crisis of Gilded Age America* (Berkeley, Calif., 2002), 35–39.

31. Another *Scribner's* New School experimenter was Mrs. Anna Botsford Comstock, who devoted her gravure to natural history subjects.

32. See entry for *Success with Small Fruits* (New York, 1880) in Sinclair Hamilton, *Early American Book Illustrators and Wood Engravers, 1670–1870*, 2 vols. (Princeton, N.J., 1958), 2: 129.

33. George H. Whittle, "Monographs on American Wood Engravers, XV—Caroline Amelia Powell," *The Printing Art* 31 (1918); Helena E. Wright, *With Pen and Graver: Women Graphic Artists Before 1900* (Washington, D.C., February 1995–January 1996), 18; Weitenkampf, *American Graphic Art*, 161.

34. Wright, *With Pen and Graver*, 16.

35. The children's magazine *Wide Awake Pleasure Book* was published by D. Lathrop & Co of Boston until it merged with *St Nicholas* in 1881.

36. Generalizations in this section are based on an examination of 247 books published between 1800 and 1898 and available issues of ten illustrated periodicals published between 1865 and 1889 at the American Antiquarian Society, letters in the Foote and Donlevy Papers, and the diaries of Horace E. Scudder, who recorded his correspondence with writers and artists as he helped launch *Riverside Magazine*.

37. See editorial supplement (pages 6–7) advertising *St. Nicholas Magazine* at the end of *Scribner's* 7, 2 (December 1873): 258–59.

38. Between 1860 and 1880 the most prolific female illustrators of books and/or magazines were {initials used}: Lizzie B. (Lizbeth Bullock) Humphrey {LBH}; Addie Ledyard {AL}; Mary Hallock [Foote] {MAH}, {MHF}; Mary L. Stone {MLS}; Mary A. Lathbury {MAL}; Jessie Curtis [Shepherd] {JC}, {JCS}; "Miss" Scannell {EMSS}; Mary E. Edwards {MEE}; Jessie McDermott {JMcD}; Elizabeth B. Comins, a.k.a. Laura Caxton {LC}; Annette Bishop; Mary Lorimer, Anne Silvernail; Maria R. Oakey; C. W. Conant; Alice Donlevy; Georgie (Georgina) A. Davis; and Eliza Pratt Greatorex and her daughter Elizabeth Eleanor Greatorex.

Engravers are harder to identify, as many joined firms or worked anonymously. Initials, shortened names, and artistic signatures make it difficult to distinguish between the artwork of men and women, and often between illustrators and engravers. For example, the initial signature C.A.N., which frequently appears during this period, is likely Miss C. A. Northam, an illustrator listed in the 1882 index of *St. Nicholas* (for an 1880 issue), but I am not certain.

39. John La Farge was applying the principles of Japanese design to his illustrative work by the 1860s. Henry Adams, "A Fish by John La Farge," *Art Bulletin* 62 (June 1980): 269–80; Burke, "Painters and Sculptors in a Decorative Age," 316.

40. Linda Noclin, *Women, Art, and Power and Other Essays* (London, 1989), 1–36; Griselda Pollock, *Vision and Difference: Femininity, Feminism and the Histories of Art* (New York, 1988), 120–54; Rozsika Parker and Griselda Pollock, *Old Mistresses: Women, Art and Ideology* (New York, 1981), 106.

41. Edna Dow Cheney, *Sally Williams, the Mountain Girl* (Boston and New York, ca. 1872); "Boston Whittling Schools," *Wide Awake* 8 (1879): 289–97.

42. Supplement advertising *St. Nicholas* (6), *Scribner's* 7, 2 (December 1873): 258.

43. W. D. Howells, "Recent Literature," *Atlantic Monthly* 34, 206 (December 1874): 745.

44. MHF to "My dearest Helena," March 1875, #77, Box 6, Folder 13, MHF Papers.

45. Louisa May Alcott, *Eight Cousins; or The Aunt-Hill* (Boston, 1875).

46. Mary A. Lathbury, 1877, Box 1, Folder 2, AHD.

47. Born in Manchester, New York, Mary Artemisia Lathbury (1814–1913) was an artist, author, and hymn-writer. After studying at an art school in Worchester, Massachusetts, she taught drawing, painting, and French at seminaries and institutes in Vermont and New York State. In 1874, she became assistant editor for the *Picture Lessons Paper.* She wrote and illustrated juvenile stories and poems for *St. Nicholas, Harper's Young People, Wide Awake,* and various church papers and magazines. Collections of her work include *Fleda and the Voice* (1876), fairy tales; *Out of Darkness into Light* (1878), poems; *Idyls of the Months* (1885), poems; and *The Child's Story of the Bible* (1898). "Lathbury, Mary Artemisia," *National Cyclopaedia of American Biography* (New York, 1900), 10: 179–80; *Dictionary of American Biography,* VI, part 1 (New York, 1961), 13–14.

48. The same could be said about her male contemporaries, artists such as Charles Beard, who drew humorous anthropomorphic animals, and Palmer Cox, creator of the silly and immensely popular "Brownies."

49. MHF to "My dear girl," Milton, [ca. 1869], Box 6, Folder 13, MHF Papers.

50. MHF to HdKG, Milton, 23 December [1868], Box 6, Folder 14, MHF Papers.

51. MHF to HdKG, "Thanks dear Helena," [ca. 1860–64], Box 6, Folder 13, MHF Papers.

52. "Report of School of Art for Women, principal: L.A. Cuddehy," 1 November [1863?], Box #1, CUSDW Directors' Reports.

53. I have found no biographical information on Addie Ledyard, although an artist named Alice Ledyard does appear in the Cooper Union records. One clever example of the Ledyard collaboration is *Very Young Americans* (Boston, 1873).

54. Annette Bishop and Mary Lorimer illustrated their poems and stories for *Riverside Magazine*. Mrs. S. B. Herrick wrote and drew biological topics for *Scribner's*. Maria R. Oakey "paints quite as well as she writes, and our readers will agree with us that this is saying a good deal in praise of her painting." *Hearth & Home* 4, 35 (13 July 1872): 703. Mary Hallock Foote illustrated her first story, "The Picture in the Fire-Place Bedroom," for *St. Nicholas* in 1875.

55. Mott, *History of American Magazines* 1: 590–94.

56. "Mother's Room," *Hearth and Home* 4, 38 (21 September 1872): 718.

57. Horace Elisha Scudder, *The Bodleys Telling Stories* (New York and Boston, 1878), viii.

58. Hamilton, *Early American Book Illustrators*, 2: 132; "Women in Art," *Revolution* 2, 15 (15 October 1868): 236.

59. Lucy Gibbons [Morse] (1839–1936) was the daughter and granddaughter of Quaker abolitionists. She was educated in private schools and subsequently studied art at the New York and Cooper Union School of Design. She also wrote stories and engaged in philanthropic work, helping found New York City's first kindergarten for African American children and working for the Women's Prison Association of New York and the Consumers League. She joined the Unitarian Church, married James Herbert Morse, and had three children. "Morse, Lucy Gibbons, *National Cyclopaedia of American Biography*, 26: 415–16.

60. Horace E. Scudder wrote a series of illustrated compilations of stories, poems, and songs for children, with names like *The Bodleys Telling Stories* (1873), *The Bodleys Afoot* (1881), that sort of thing. Many of the artworks, by men and women, illustrating Scudder's books first appeared in *Riverside Magazine* (1867–70).

61. "Scudder, Horace Elisha," *National Cyclopaedia of American Biography*, 522–23.

62. Letter from Scudder to Andersen, 27 August 1868, Riverside, Cambridge, Mass., reproduced in *The Andersen-Scudder Letters*, ed. Jean Hersholt and Waldemar Westergaard (Berkeley, Calif., 1949), 19–21.

63. Scudder to Andersen, 22 October 1868, in Hergholt and Westergaard, *Andersen-Scudder Letters*, 166.

64. H. C. Andersen, *Stories and Tales* (New York, 1870).

65. Mary L. Stone to Horace E. Scudder, 9 September 1869, Cotuit [Port], Cape Cod, Mass., MS 801.4 (443), HL.

66. 15 June 1866 entry, Scudder, Horace Eliza Diary 16 May 1866–30 May 1868, Houghton, Ms Am2030 (252), HL.

67. The excerpt is from a letter Scudder wrote to W. Houghton, copied into his diary on 6 July 1866, Scudder, Horace Eliza Diary 16 May 1866–30 May 1868, Houghton, Ms Am2030 (252), HL.

68. 25 June 1866 entry, Scudder, Horace Eliza Diary 16 May 1866–30 May 1868, Houghton, Ms Am2030 (252), HL.

69. "She was for many years the pupil of Edwin White, and more recently of Prof. Rimmer." White (1817–77) was a National Academy member and painter of historical scenes. "Women Artists," *Galaxy* 6, 4 (October 1868): 574.

70. Mary L. Stone to Horace E. Scudder, 24 September 1870 and 9 August 1869, Audubon Park, New York City, MS 801.4 (443), HL.

71. MHF to HdKG, Fall 1873, #44, Box 6, Folder 16, MHF Papers.

72. MHF to "My dear Helena," ca.1873, #8, Box 6, Folder 14, MHF Papers.

73. Mary L. Stone to Horace E. Scudder, 8 January 1869, MS 801.4 (443), HL.

74. Hallock's letters to Scudder show intimacy even as she discusses business: "P.S. I find I have thrown myself on your comprehension in very intimate style; but I meant to do so not personally asking your sympathy for having been tired; but on the grounds of work alone; whether any good work can come out of a state of giggling weariness, when one is too tired to do anything but laugh. The question has a commercial as well as a psychological interest for me, and I only wish it might have for you as well." Mary Hallock Foote, *A Victorian Gentlewoman in the Far West: Reminiscences of Mary Hallock Foote*, ed. Rodman W. Paul (San Marino, Calif., 1972), 137–38; Mary Hallock Foote to Horace Scudder, 8 August 1891, "The Mesa Boise, Idaho," Ms Am801.4 (139), HL.

75. Gilder's father was a Methodist minister who owned and conducted a female seminary in Flushing, Long Island, where Richard secured his education as the only boy in a school for girls. He volunteered with the 1st Philadelphia Artillery during the Civil War, but after his father died in 1864 he became a journalist and editor to aid in the family support. "Gilder, Richard Watson," *National Cyclopaedia of American Biography*, 275–78; Mott, *History of American Magazines*, 3: 457–62.

76. Mary Mapes Dodge, author of *Hans Brinker and His Silver Skates*, honed her editorial skills working for *Hearth & Home*, which merged with the *Daily Graphic* in 1868 and was absorbed by Scribner & Company in December 1870. Scribner & Company chose her to edit *St. Nicholas*, which it launched in 1873 to match its general monthly. Many children's classics were first published as serials in *St. Nicholas*, including John T. Trowbridge's Jack Hazard Series, Louisa May Alcott's *Eight Cousins*, Mrs. Burnett's *Little Lord Fauntleroy*, Mark Twain's *Tom Sawyer Abroad*, and Rudyard Kipling's *Jungle Book* stories. The magazine's associate editor was the writer Frank R. Stockton. Mott, *History of American Magazines*, 3: 177, 500–505.

77. Mary Mapes Dodge, "Children's Magazines," *Scribner's Monthly* 6 (July 1873): 352–54.

78. Ibid.

79. Dodge's sister, Sophie Mapes [Tolles] was an active member of the Ladies' Art Association, serving on the Executive Committee and Council of Reference. Note from Mary Mapes Dodge accepting "Honorary Membership," 8 July 1876, Box 1, Folder 2, AHD. Honorary Members are listed on a brochure in Box 4, Folder 4, AHD.

80. Fanny Fern, *Ruth Hall and Other Writings*, ed. Joyce W. Warren (New Brunswick, N.J., 1986), 147–48.

81. Fern, *Ruth Hall*, 143, 147.

82. Michele H. Bogart, *Artists, Advertising, and the Borders of Art* (Chicago, 1995), 33.

83. MHF to HdKG, "an unfinished letter," n.d., Box 6, Folder 13, MHF Papers.

84. "Publisher's Department. To the Patrons of the 'Monthly,'" *Scribner's* 5, 1 (November 1872): 5.

85. R.W.G. to Miss Hallock, 10 October 1872, Box 4, Folder 14, MHF Papers.

86. *The Hanging of the Crane* was prepared by A. V. S. Anthony, who shared the engraving work with William J. Linton. MHF to HdKG, undated [ca. Fall 1874], #55, Box 6, Folder 16, MHF Papers.

87. A.V.S. Anthony, 18 March 1874, Boston, Box 6, Folder 2, MHF Papers.

88. Mary L. Stone to Horace E. Scudder, 8 January 1869, MS 801.4 (443), HL.

89. MHF to HdKG, January 1875, #75, Box 6, Folder 18, MHF Papers.

90. MHF to "My dearest Helena," March 1875, #77, Box 6, Folder 13, MHF Papers.

91. MHF to "My Beloved," Sunday, #11, Box 6, Folder 13, MHF Papers.

92. Foote, *Reminiscences of Mary Hallock Foote*, 112.

93. Mott, *History of American Magazines* 2: 48.

94. Foote, *Reminiscences of Mary Hallock Foote*, 102.

95. Helena deKay Gilder, "Author Illustrators II. Mary Hallock Foote," 341; *Reminiscences of Mary Hallock Foote*, 102.

96. Alice Donlevy, "Henry W. Herrick: The Appreciation of a Former Student," *Manchester Historic Association Collections* 4, part 3 (Manchester, N.H., 1910), 242–43.

97. MHF to HdKG, April 1875, #79, Box 6, Folder 18, MHF Papers.

98. Ibid.

99. "Young bloods" is Hallock's term for the artists who founded the Art Students' League in 1875. Old bloods would have been artists born before 1840, such as Elihu Vedder (b. 1836), Thomas Farrar (b. 1839), John George Brown (b. 1831), and also Fidelia Bridges (b. 1834), and Lucy Gibbons (b. 1839).

100. MHF to HdKG, Fall 1873, Box 6, Folder 16; Fall 1873, Box 6, Folder 17; and ca. 1870, Box 6, Folder 13, MHF Papers.

101. Two years later, his pupil Maria Oakey Dewing was kept from being elected a member of the Society of American Artists because, as Helena Gilder recorded, "L.F. did not second her." Gilder quoted in Kirsten Swinth, *Painting Professionals* (Chapel Hill, N.C., 2001), 68.

102. MHF to HdKG, 1875, # 91, Box 6, Folder 19, MHF Papers.

103. Landscape painter Jervis McEntee also complained of National Academy members "who are, many of them, very selfish." MHF to HdKG, n.d., # 74, Box 6, Folder 18, MHF Papers; 27 April 1873 entry, "Jervis McEntee's Diary," ed. Effie M. Morse, *Archives of American Art* 8, 3–4 (July–October 1968): 18.

104. MHF to HdKG, 23 September 1873, Milton, #42, Box 6, Folder 15, MHF Papers.

105. L. A. Bradbury, 12 April 1874, 51 Oxford St., Cambridge, Mass., Box 1, Folder 2, AHD.

106. Foote, *Reminiscences of Mary Hallock Foote*, 87.

107. From "Aunt Molly," n.d., Leadville, Colo., Box 6, Folder 7, MHF Papers.

108. Foote, *Reminiscences of Mary Hallock Foote*, 148–49.

109. Agnes Chamberlain to Alice Donlevy, April 1876, Box 1, Folder 2, AHD.

110. Foote, *Reminiscences of Mary Hallock Foote*, 80.

111. Helen Hunt [Jackson] wrote tales for *Scribner's* under the pseudonym "Saxe Holm."

112. Richard Gilder's sonnets to Helena de Kay were published in *Scribner's Monthly* in 1873. MHF to "My dear Helena," January or February 1874, #57, Box 6, Folder 16, MHF Papers.

113. Ibid.

114. MHF to HdKG, January 1874, #59, Box 6, Folder 16, MHF Papers.

115. *Reminiscences of Mary Hallock Foote*, 112.

116. Hallock conveyed this information to Gilder in 1877, after her friend had given birth to her second child, Rodman. Helena's first child Marion had died when the artist was three months pregnant with Rodman. She had three more girls, Dorothea, Francesca, and Rosamond. Mary Hallock Foote had three children: Arthur Jr., Agnes, and Elizabeth (Betty). Miller, *Mary Hallock Foote*, 50–51.

117. A. J. Wiley quoted in Foote, *Reminiscences of Mary Hallock Foote*, 32–33.

118. Vedder met his wife Elizabeth Caroline Rosekrans in Rome. Rosekrans was an art student of William Morris Hunt. Regina Soria, *Perceptions and Evocations: The Art of Elihu Vedder* (Washington, D.C., 1979), 21–22.

119. Herbert R. Smith, *Richard Watson Gilder* (New York, 1970), 13, 23.

120. Miller, *Mary Hallock Foote*, 51.

121. For Hallock's writing career, see Lee Ann Johnson, *Mary Hallock Foote* (Boston, 1980); Miller, *Mary Hallock Foote*; and Foote, *Reminiscences of Mary Hallock Foote*.

122. "Art. Eliza Greatorex," *Aldine: A Typographic Art Journal* 6, 2 (February 1873): 48; *Homes of Ober-Ammergau* (1872); *Summer Etchings in Colorado* (1873).

123. For examples, see Doreen Bolger Burke, *In Pursuit of Beauty: Americans and the Aesthetic Movement* (New York, 1986).

124. Vedder's invention was aided by a new photographic printing process that translated the subtle gradations of the drawings to the printed page. Exhibition brochure for "Elihu Vedder's Drawings for the Rubáiyát," National Museum of American Art, Smithsonian Institution (10 November 1995–9 June 1996); Soria, *Elihu Vedder*, 8, 19–22.

125. Soria, *Elihu Vedder*, 22; Doreen Bolger Burke, "Painters and Sculptors in a Decorative Age," in *In Pursuit of Beauty*, 299–305.

126. Today it is easier to find examples of Helena de Kay Gilder's illustrations than her paintings.

127. "Culture and Progress. Two Illustrated Books," *Scribner's Monthly* 15, 3 (January 1878): 438.

128. "'Maidens, within whose tender breasts, a thousand restless hopes and fears, forth reaching to the coming years, &c.' Here is certainly plenty of liberty of choice—How would *you* do it?" MHF to HdKG, Winter 1874–75, Box 6, Folder 17, MHF Papers.

129. MHF to "My dear Helena," n.d., #69, Box 6, Folder 17, MHF Papers.

130. MHF to HdKG, (Winter 1874–75), #66, Box 6, Folder 17; MHF to HdKG, (in pencil: "Jan 1874. Waiting for A.F."), #58, Box 6, Folder 16; and 26 March 1876, #110, Box 4, Folder 3, MHF Papers.

131. Jessie Curtis [Shepherd] was a native of New York City. Elizabeth Stuart Phelps [Ward], *The Gates Ajar* (Boston, 1870); Linton, *Wood Engraving in America*,

31, 33; Hamilton, *Early American Book Illustrators*, 2: 132; Weitenkampf, *American Graphic Art*, 219.

132. See "Editor's Literary Record," *Harper's New Monthly Magazine* 56, no. 332 (January 1878): 308–9; "Holiday Books," "Books of the Day," *Appleton's Journal: A Magazine of General Literature* 4, 1–2 (January–February 1878): 95.

133. Curtis's art appeared in Osgood & Company, Estes & Lauriat, and Harper's publications, *Our Young Folks, Hearth & Home, St. Nicholas, Wide Awake,* and *Aldine.* "Mrs. Jessie Curtis Shepherd," Sylvester Koehler, ed., *American Art and Art Collections* (Boston, 1889), 689.

134. Quoted in Koehler, *American Art and Art Collections*, 689.

135. For the importance of speed and accuracy in Davis's pictorial reporting, see Brown, *Beyond the Lines*, 263–64 n. 65. Numerous examples of her work can be found in 1880s editions of *Frank Leslie's Illustrated Newspaper.*

136. Horatio Alger, Jr., *Ragged Dick; or, Street Life in New York with Bootblacks* (Boston, ca. 1868), frontispiece.

137. "Art. Eliza Greatorex." *Aldine, A Typographic Art Journal* 6, 2 (February 1873): 48.

138. "Our Contributors," *Scribner's* 1, 6 (April 1871): supplement "Publishers Department. A Talk with Our Readers"; "Some 'St. Nicholas' Artists," *Scribner's* 17, 3 (January 1879): 39.

139. Foote, *Reminiscences of Mary Hallock Foote*, 100–103.

140. Ibid., 65, 76.

Chapter 7. *"A Combination of Adverse Circumstances"*

1. Cecelia Beaux, *Background with Figures: Autobiography* (Cambridge, Mass., 1930), 84.

2. Beaux, *Background with Figures*, 84–85; Tara Leigh Tappert, *Cecelia Beaux and the Art of Portraiture* (Washington, D.C., 1995), vii.

3. Beaux, *Background with Figures*, 85.

4. The term "commercial art" dates back only to the turn of the twentieth century. Michele H. Bogart, *Advertising, Artists, and the Borders of Art* (Chicago, 1995), 6.

5. Delano to Alice Donlevy, 26 August 1876, Penn Yan, N.Y., Box 1, Folder 3, AHD; Elisha Delano obituary, *Yates County Chronicle*, 26 September 1872, Delano Family Book, Yates County Genealogical and Historical Society, Penn Yan, N.Y.

6. [William H. Bishop], "Young Artists' Life in New York," *Scribner's* 19 (January 1880): 355.

7. Students in New York art schools were segregated by gender only when a nude model was present.

8. Kirsten Swinth, *Painting Professionals: Women Artists & the Development of Modern American Art, 1870–1930* (Chapel Hill, N.C., 2001), 37–40.

9. Bishop, "Young Artists' Life," 355.

10. Ibid., 360.

11. Ibid., 367.

12. Edwin G. Burrows and Mike Wallace, *Gotham: A History of New York City to 1898* (New York, 1999), 1022–23.

13. J. C. Zachos, "Report of the Curator," *Fifteenth Annual Report of the Trustees of the Cooper Union for the Advancement of Science and Art*, 1874, 5–6, CU.

14. J. C. Zachos, "The School of Art for Women," *Fifteenth Annual Report*, 9.

15. Zachos, "Report of the Curator," *Fifteenth Annual Report*, 5–6.

16. Burrows and Wallace, *Gotham*, 1024.

17. Leila Curtis letter, 3 December 1869, San Francisco, Box 1, Folder 1, AHD.

18. L. H. Reese, 11 December 1877, 345 Madison Ave., Box 1, Folder 3, AHD.

19. [L. A. Bradbury] to "My dear little petticoated Quixote," 18 June 1878, Isle of Man, Box 1, Folder 3, AHD.

20. Female models cost forty cents an hour. [William C. Brownell], "The Art-Schools of New York," *Scribner's Monthly* 16, 6 (October 1878): 777.

21. The death of Mary Cook was announced in the *Graphic*, January 1878. Mary Cook to Alice Donlevy, 13 October 1873, Keene Flats, N.Y., Box 1, Folder 2; L. A. Bradbury to Dear Alice, 23 January 1878, Winchester, Mass., Box 1, Folder 3, AHD.

22. Mary Byrnes to Miss Alice Donlevy, "President-pro-tem of 'Ladies Art-Association,'" 27 November 1874, Pioneer Council No. 1, Sovereigns of Industry, Philadelphia, Box 1, Folder 2, AHD; Steven Hahn, *The Roots of Southern Populism: Yeoman Farmers and the Transformation of the Georgia Upcountry, 1850–1890* (New York, 1983), 222.

23. "Charter Members" and "New Members," Sovereigns of Industry, Philadelphia Pioneer Council, 1874–79, Reel 11, Manuscript Collections on Early American Labor Movement, 1862–1908, American Bureau of Industrial Research.

24. Letter to "Dear Alice," 30 January 1873, Philadelphia, Box 1, Folder 2, AHD; "Faithfull, Emily," Albert Johannsen, *The House of Beadle and Adams and Its Dime and Nickel Novels* (Norman, Okla. ca. 1950).

25. Henrietta Desporte Field introduced Faithfull, "who addressed the meeting in a most interesting manner." Entries for 25 and 27 January 1873, "Jervis McEntee's Diary," ed. Effie M. Morse, *Archives of American Art* 8, 3 and 4 (July–October 1968): 14.

26. J. Edwards Clark, Department of the Interior/Bureau of Education, 9 June 1875, Washington D.C., Box 1, Folder 3, AHD.

27. Donlevy, "Henry W. Herrick," 242–43.

28. David Montgomery, *Beyond Equality: Labor and the Radical Republicans, 1862–1872* (Urbana, Ill., 1981), 410–11.

29. On Havemeyer's response to the Workingmen's Central Council, see Burrows and Wallace, *Gotham*, 1023–25.

30. Caroline Dall, *The College, The Market, and The Court; or Woman's Relation to Education, Labor, and Law* (Boston, 1867), 464; Burrows and Wallace, *Gotham*, 1023.

31. "The Ladies Art Association, New York," *American Art Review* 2, part 2 (Boston, 1881): 40.

32. John Humphrey Noyes, "Connecting Links," *History of American Social-isms* (1870; reprint New York, 1961), 97.

33. "Facts Concerning the Ladies' Art Association," Box 4, AHD.

34. Roger Wunderlich, *Low Living and High Thinking at Modern Times, New York* (Syracuse, N.Y., 1992), 44.

35. "Labor Note Scholarships," Letter from the Committee on Ways and Means, 12 April 1882, New York, Box 4, Folder 4, AHD. In 1887 the Association petitioned New York State's Congress for aid to extend the system and in 1889 was granted $18,000 to provide free art education to women and children, white and colored. "Facts Concerning the Ladies' Art Association for the Promotion of the Interests of Women Artists"; "Petition" of 17 January 1888; and "The People of the State of New York, represented in Senate and Assembly do enact as follows," 1 February 1889, Box 4, AHD.

36. On the controversy surrounding the Women's Building, see Wanda M. Corn, "Women Building History" in Eleanor Tufts, ed., *American Women Artists, 1830 to 1930* (Washington, D.C., 1987), 26–34; Jeanne Madeline Weimann, *The Fair Women: The Story of the Woman's Building, World's Columbian Exposition, Chicago 1893* (Chicago, 1981), 1–6; and Whitney Chadwick, *Women, Art, and Society* (New York, 1990), 210–11.

37. "There is no room in this Building that can be appropriated for the works of women artists, but I am instructed to say that . . . in the reception of these Paintings the commission will make no distinction." M. McElrath, Secretary, International Exhibition, 21 March 1876, Box 1, Folder 2; letters about and from Lilly Martin Spencer, 28 March 1876 and 7 April 1876, Box 1, Folder 3, AHD.

38. Printed slip of paper inserted into "International Exhibition, Women's Dept. Permit For Space," Box 1, Folder 2, AHD.

39. Mary Ackerman to Alice Donlevy, 2 April 1876, 236 Warrent St., Brooklyn, N.Y., Box 1, Folder 3, AHD.

40. Ellen Hardin Walworth, 10 April 1876, Saratoga Springs, Box 1, Folder 3, AHD.

41. Letters from Esther A. Caldwell, 20 November and 22 June 1876, International Exhibition, Women's Dept., Philadelphia, Box 1, Folder 2, AHD.

42. Letter to Mrs. Gillespie, [c. 1877], Box 1, Folder 2, AHD.

43. Chadwick, *Women, Art, and Society*, 210–11.

44. Having a surplus left in 1878, the Woman's Centennial Committee appropriated $1,500 to the Woman's Art School at the Cooper Union, "as a part of the permanent endowments" to help "such indigent students as could not support all their expenses of living, while in attendance in the Art School," *Nineteenth Annual Report of the Trustees of the Cooper Union for the Advancement of Science and Art*, 1878, 11.

45. William Dean Howells, "A Sennight of the Centennial," *Atlantic Monthly* 38 (July 1876): 101; Roger B. Stein, "Artifact as Ideology: The Aesthetic Movement in Its American Cultural Context," in Doreen Bolger Burke, *In Pursuit of Beauty: Americans and the Aesthetic Movement* (New York, 1986), 28.

46. Letter regarding dimensions of the glass case to hold the Association's exhibit, International Exhibition Co., 11 June 1877, Philadelphia, Box 1, Folder 3, AHD.

47. Mary A. Lathbury, 18 March 1877, Orange, N.J., Box 1, Folder 3, AHD.

48. C. S. Pratt, *Wide Awake*, D. Lathrop & Co., 10 May 1876, Boston; Isaac Newburgh, Office of the *Aldine*, 15 April 1876, Box 1, Folder 2; O. B. Bruce, *Appleton's Journal*—Editorial Rooms, 14 April 1876; Hurd & Houghton, 2 May 1876, New York; and E.P. Dutton & Co, 18 April 1876, Box 1, Folder 3, AHD.

49. Thanks to Donlevy female engravers were probably better represented than male engravers who, "were it not for examples by Philadelphia's Frederick Fass, official engraver of the Centennial Exhibition catalogue," would not have been exhibited at the fair at all. Diana Korzenik, *Drawn to Art: A Nineteenth-Century American Dream* (Hanover, N.H., 1985), 216.

50. Christine Stansell, *City of Women: Sex and Class in New York, 1789–1860* (Urbana, Ill., 1987), 141–44; Barbara Taylor, "'The Men Are as Bad as Their Masters': Socialism, Feminism, and Sexual Antagonism in the London Tailoring Trade in the Early 1830s," *Feminist Studies* 5 (Spring 1979): 30.

51. Ava Baron "Women and the Making of the American Working Class: A Study of the Proletarinaization of Printers," *Review of Radical Political Economics* 14, 3 (Fall 1982): 23–42.

52. Jeanne Boydston, *Home and Work: Housework, Wages, and the Ideology of Labor in the Early Republic* (New York, 1990), 20–21; Stansell, *City of Women*, 148–49.

53. Burrows and Wallace, *Gotham*, 1026; Horace Greeley, *Recollections of a Busy Life* (New York, 1868), 503–4; Montgomery, *Beyond Equality*, 414, 388, 411.

54. Candace Wheeler, *Yesterdays In a Busy Life* (New York, 1918), 210–13; Amelia Peck and Carol Irish, *Candace Wheeler: The Art and Enterprise of American Design, 1876–1900* (New York, 2001), 20–27.

55. Working for the Sanitary Commission during the Civil War, Wheeler became acquainted with Mrs. J. J. Astor, Mrs. David Lane, Mr. August Belmont, Miss Cooper, and Mr. Wm. C. Bryant, who helped her found the SDA. Wheeler, *Yesterdays*, 216.

56. Wheeler, *Yesterdays*, 210.

57. Ibid., 211.

58. Ibid., 226, 216.

59. Ibid., 226–227, 217.

60. Anthea Callen, *Women Artists of the Arts and Crafts Movement, 1870–1914* (New York, 1979) and Callen, "Sexual Division of Labor in the Arts and Crafts Movement," *Women's Art Journal* 5 (Fall/Winter 1984–85): 1–7; Kathleen D. McCarthy, *Women's Culture: American Philanthropy and Art, 1830–1930* (Chicago, 1991), 50–52; Stein, "Artifact as Ideology," 23–51; and Swinth, *Painting Professionals*, 37–62.

61. "The New Society of Decorative Art," *New York Times*, 16 June 1877, 4.

62. Wheeler, *Yesterdays*, 219–20.

63. April F. Masten, "Eliza Pratt Greatorex" and "Eleanor Elizabeth Greatorex," in John A. Garraty and Mark C. Carnes, eds., *American National Biography*, vol. 9 (Cary, N.C., 1999); Ellen Thayer Fisher, 26 October 1878, 358 Adelphi St., Box 1, Folder 2, and 23 January 1878, Box 1, Folder 3, AHD; "Denroche, S.B.," in Clark S. Marlor, ed., *A History of the Brooklyn Art Association with an Index of Exhibitions*

(New York, 1970); and E. A. Caldwell, International Exhibition, Women's Dept., 14 June 1876, Philadelphia, Box 1, Folder 2, AHD.

64. Florence Dowe, 24 March 1876, Ithaca, N.Y., Box 1, Folder 3, AHD.

65. Not until the twentieth century discarded nineteenth-century collections of stuff did bric-a-brac acquire its negative connotation and come to mean random junk not deserving of individual notice. M. H. Dunlop, *Gilded City: Scandal and Sensation in Turn-of-the-Century New York* (New York, 2000), 106–7.

66. "Bric-a-Brac Sale by Leavitt," *New York Times*, 4 March 1877, 2.

67. "The Ladies' Art Association," *American Art Review* 1 (Boston, 1880): 43; Swinth, *Painting Professionals*, 117–18; McCarthy, *Women's Culture*, 101–2; and Laura R. Prieto, *At Home in the Studio: The Professionalization of Women Artists in America* (Cambridge, 2001), 45.

68. D. G. Croly, The Graphic Company, 23 February 1877, New York, Box 1, Folder 3, AHD.

69. L. A. Bradbury, 3 December 1876, Winchester, Mass., Box 1, Folder 3, AHD.

70. M. L. Wagner, 13 March 1877, Rochester, N.Y., Box 1, Folder 3, AHD.

71. L. A. Bradbury, 19 April 1877, Winchester, Mass., Box 1, Folder 3, AHD.

72. Florence Bailey, 10 February 1879, Mount Washington, Md., Box 1, Folder 2; Mary E. Monks, 8 January 1878, Cold Spring, Md., Box 1, Folder 3, AHD.

73. "The Right Chord Struck," *New York Times*, 25 November 1877; and "New Loan Exhibition," *New York Times*, 4 December 1877.

74. L. A. Bradbury, 13 March and 23 January 1878, Rangeley Place, Winchester, Mass., Box 1, Folder 3, AHD; Peck and Irish, *Candace Wheeler*, 28–29.

75. "Society of Decorative Art, Boston," *American Art Review* 2, part 2 (Boston, 1881).

76. Florence Bailey, 10 February 1879, Mount Washington, Md., Box 1, Folder 2; Gertrude Leslie, 19 March 1878, Box 1, Folder 3, AHD.

77. E. T. Graham, 14 October 1877, Hillside, Box 1, Folder 2, AHD.

78. E. T. Graham, 30 November 1877, Box 1, Folder 3, AHD.

79. C. Wheeler, 5 July 1877, 67 Madison Ave., Box 1, Folder 3, AHD.

80. "Household Art, presented to the L.A.A. by a member of 77," February 1878, Box 1, Folder 2, AHD.

81. McCarthy, *Women's Culture*, 46.

82. "Eleemosynary" is an adjective that means "relating to charity or almsgiving." Zachos, "Report of the Curator," *Fifteenth Annual Report*, 6.

83. "Facts Concerning the Ladies' Art Association," Box 4, AHD.

84. Bishop, "Young Artists' Life," 367.

85. Swinth, *Painting Professionals*, 65.

86. "The Painters in Pastel," *New York Times*, 17 March 1884, 5, as quoted in Swinth, *Painting Professionals*, 74.

87. Swinth, *Painting Professionals*, 68.

88. Brownell, "The Art-Schools of New York," 770.

89. Bishop, "Young Artists' Life," 357–58.

90. Ibid., 367–68.

91. For invitations and regrets for sketch club meetings, see Box 1, Folder 3,

AHD. On Ladies' Art Association meetings, see "Facts Concerning the Ladies' Art Association," Box 4, AHD.

92. Bishop, "Young Artists' Life," 357.

93. Swinth, *Painting Professionals*, 27.

94. "Our Female Artists. Fair Hands Under Whose Touch the Canvas Glows and Lives." *New York World*, 15 March 1885, in "Greatorex, Eliza," Roll N14, GLF.

95. "Invitation to Contribute," Studio, Ladies' Art Association, August 1876, 896 Broadway, Box 1, Folder 2, AHD.

96. After traveling to Europe or visiting the Centennial, many American "connoisseurs" looked askance at the products of indigenous artists. Martha J. Ward, 13 November 1876, Pittsfield, Vt., Box 1, Folder 3, AHD.

97. John Ruskin, "Nature of the Gothic," *Stones of Venice* (1851–53) in *The Works of John Ruskin*, ed. E. T. Cook and Alexander Wedderburn, 39 vols. (London, 1904, 1905), 10: 192–96.

98. Written in purple ink next to "Fourteenth" is "The Association does not approve of the introduction of women in factories." "Facts Concerning the Ladies' Art Association for the Promotion of the Interests of Women Artists," Box 4; Agnes Chamberlain to the Ladies' Art Association, ca. 1876, Box 1, Folder 2, AHD.

99. Anna Graffray[?], 18 July 1867, Box 1, Folder 1, AHD.

100. Reply to Mr. C. S. Plummer of Ph. Hake & Co., 29 March 1878, Box 1, Folder 2, AHD.

101. Mary Livermore, *What Shall We Do with Our Daughters?* (Boston, 1883), 100.

102. George Manson, *Work for Women* (New York, 1883), 8–9.

103. Harry T. Peters, *Currier and Ives, Printmakers to the American People* (Garden City, N.Y., 1942), 14–15.

104. E. T. Graham, 31 October 1877, Hillside, Box 1, Folder 3, AHD.

105. J. C. Zachos, *Twenty-First Annual Report of the Trustees of the Cooper Union for the Advancement of Science and Art*, 1880, 21.

106. Paul Raymond Provost, "Winslow Homer's Drawings In 'Black-and-White,' c. 1875–1885," 2 vols. (dissertation, Princeton University, 1994), 1: 16.

107. Bishop, "Young Artists' Life," 364.

108. Ibid., 368.

109. Ibid.

110. Walter Horatio Pater, *Studies in the History of the Renaissance* (London, 1873).

111. Ruskin, "Traffic" (lecture delivered 21 April 1864), *Works*, 18: 433–58.

112. John C. Van Dyke, *Art for Art's Sake: Seven University Lectures on the Technical Beauties of Painting* (New York, 1893), 6.

113. Note to Brooklyn Art Association regarding name, n.d., "Homer, Winslow," Roll N14, GLF; Provost, "Winslow Homer's Drawings," 1: 124, 16. On the development of black and white work into a fine art, see Maureen C. O'Brien and Patricia F. Mandel, *The Painter-Etcher Movement* (Southampton, N.Y., 1984), 8–17.

114. Letter from Mary Hallock to Helena de Kay quoted in Mary Hallock Foote, *A Victorian Gentlewoman in the Far West: The Reminiscences of Mary Hallock Foote*, ed. Rodman W. Paul (San Marino, Calif., 1972), 102.

115. See Sylvester Rosa Koehler, *Etching: An Outline of Its Technical Processes and Its History, with Some Remarks on Collectors and Collecting* (New York, 1885) and Phyllis Peet, *American Women of the Etching Revival* (Atlanta, 1988).

116. Wheeler, *Yesterdays*, 232.

117. Mary Blanchard, "Embroidery, Expertise, and the Modernist Vision in Gilded Age America," *American Quarterly* 54, 4 (December 2002): 661–79.

118. Wheeler, *Yesterdays*, 221.

119. Crewels are fine worsted yarns used for embroidery and tapestry.

120. Wheeler, *Yesterdays*, 235.

121. John Ruskin, *Works*, 7: 257.

122. For example, see William Morris, "How We Live and How We Might Live" (lecture delivered 30 November 1884).

123. Wheeler, *Yesterdays*, 227, 231–32, 237–39.

124. *Eighteenth Annual Report of the Trustees of the Cooper Union for the Advancement of Science and Art*, 1877, 7.

125. Wheeler, *Yesterdays*, 236.

126. J. C. Zachos, "The Art School for Women," *Nineteenth Annual Report*, 10.

127. This idea is developed in Mary W. Blanchard, *Oscar Wilde's America: Counterculture in the Gilded Age* (New Haven, Conn., 1998).

128. Leo Steinberg, *Other Criteria: Confrontations with Twentieth-Century Art* (New York, 1972), 57–61.

129. "Our Artists and Their Works. Fidelia Bridges," *Brooklyn Monthly* 2, 3 (March 1878): 70.

130. Here my argument may seem to run counter to Sarah Burns's perceptive analysis of the way art criticism has "read" signs of the artist's femaleness or maleness into portraits painted by Cecelia Beaux and John Singer Sargent. Burns maintains that phrases like "earnest untiring worker," which "occupied the crevices of the discourse" on Beaux, were part of a "language of difference that constructed a hierarchy of value" meant to "maintain masculine-determined social order in a world where emergent feminism threatened established gender boundaries." True. But I would add that the history leading up to that art criticism suggests reviewers who used such phrases may have been following the lead of women artists themselves. Sarah Burns, "The 'Earnest, Untiring Worker' and the Magician of the Brush: Gender Politics in the Criticism of Cecelia Beaux and John Singer Sargent," *Oxford Art Journal* 15, 1 (1992): 37, 45.

131. MHF to HdKG, April 1875, #79, Box 6, Folder 18, MHF Papers; Bishop, "Young Artists' Life," 367, 360.

132. Michele Bogart, "Artistic Ideals and Commercial Practices: The Problem of Status for American Illustrators," *Prospects: An Annual of American Cultural Studies* 15 (1990): 245–53; Bogart, *Artists, Advertising and the Borders of Art*, 5–6.

133. Lewis F. Day and Walter Crane, *Moot Points: Friendly Disputes on Art & Industry* (London, 1903), 9.

134. Bogart, "Artistic Ideals and Commercial Practices," 236.

135. Day and Crane, *Moot Points*, 21.

136. Ibid., 2–8.

137. Ibid., 8–10.

138. Ibid., 16, 19.

139. David Slater, "The Font of Inspiration: Minnie Clark, the Art Workers' Club for Women, and Performances of American Girlhood," *Winterthur Portfolio* 39, 4 (2004): 247.

140. "Art Workers Club for Women," *Constitution and By-Laws*, 1889, reproduced in Julie Graham, "American Women Artists' Groups: 1867–1930," *Women's Art Journal* (Spring/Summer 1980): 7–12.

Index

Acknowledgments

Writing is rewriting. It involves getting something down, talking, reading, laughing over tea, thinking, eating, and writing it again. Many people helped me write this book.

For reading and commenting on drafts of chapters, thank you so much Vincent DiGirolamo, Donna Rilling, Bob Lockhart, Casey Blake, Brooke Larson, Jackson Lears, Jan Lewis, Alice Kessler-Harris, Michele Bogart, Tammy Proctor, Scott Sandage, Dee Garrison, Leonore Davidoff, Victoria DiGrazia, Carol Williams, Lauren Lepow, Robin Schore, Jonathan Earle, Beatrix Hoffman, Colleen O'Neill, Henry Yu, Laura Coyle, Amy Ogata, Sally Mills, Gennifer Weisenfeld, Melissa Homestead, Nina DiAngeli Walls, Kirsten Swinth, Carol Turbin, Jane Censer, Kimberly Latta, Patricia O'Neal, Lucy Maddox, Melissa Dabakis, and several generous anonymous readers.

For talking over ideas, special thanks to Cara Masten DiGirolamo, Gail Day, Julie Hammer, Molly Williams, David Goldschmidt, Carol Mavor, Sarah Gardener, Grazia Lolla, Owen Greenan, Ned Landsman, Walter Johnson, Padma Kaimal, Harry Berger, and Judy Flanagan.

For passing valuable information, references, or images my way, thank you Bert Hansen, Helena Wright, Josh Brown, Louis Masur, Janet Greene, Eunice Lipton, John Williams, Sally Mills, Mary Blanchard, Chris Rasmussen, Catherine Rivard, Barbara Balliet, Griselda Pollock, Elaine Showalter, Fred Orton, Gigi Barnhill, Caroline Sloat, Ulla Volk, Caroline Langan, and numerous unnamed librarians and archivists.

For financial assistance, I am grateful to Rutgers University for the Marion Johnson Fellowship, American Association of University Women for travel grants, American Antiquarian Society and Diana Korzenik for the "Drawn to Art" Fellowship, and Stony Brook University.

Heartfelt thanks for inspiration and personal support to my father Ric Masten, my sisters Ellen Masten and Jerri Hansen, Cherie Campbell, Gill Redfearn, Cynthia Williams, Sally and Joe Foster, Diane DiGirolamo, Melissa Brownlow, Laura Flanagan, Christian Hansen, Thomas Hunt, and Tom Davies.

You lived this creation with me, Vince and Cara, and made it a pleasure. I owe you.